Praise for *HOAX*

"A thorough and damning exploration of the incestuous relationship between Trump and his favorite channel."

—The New York Times

"Stelter's critique goes beyond salacious tidbits about extramarital affairs (though there are plenty of those) to expose a collusion that threatens the pillars of our democracy."

—The Washington Post

"A Rosetta Stone for stuff about this presidency that doesn't otherwise make sense to normal humans."

—Rachel Maddow, author of #1 *New York Times* bestseller *Blowout* and host of MSNBC's *The Rachel Maddow Show*

"Stelter's account gives a sense that ... there's no one really in control—that Hannity, Carlson, Ingraham and the *Fox & Friends* morning team can essentially do what they want."

—Associated Press

"[Stelter] chronicles the symbiotic relationship between [Trump] and Rupert Murdoch's most famous product.... *Hoax* is amply documented."

—The Guardian

"A deep, dispiriting dive into the nefarious intersection of politics, conspiracy, lies, and money as served up by Donald Trump and Fox News."

—Kirkus Reviews (starred review)

HOAX

DONALD TRUMP, FOX NEWS, AND THE DANGEROUS DISTORTION OF TRUTH

BRIAN STELTER

ONE SIGNAL
PUBLISHERS

ATRIA

New York | London | Toronto | Sydney | New Delhi

An Imprint of Simon & Schuster, Inc.
1230 Avenue of the Americas
New York, NY 10020

First One Signal Publishers/Atria Paperback edition June 2021

ONE SIGNAL PUBLISHERS / ATRIA BOOKS and colophon are trademarks of Simon & Schuster, Inc.

For information about special discounts for bulk purchases, please contact Simon & Schuster Special Sales at 1-866-506-1949 or business@simonandschuster.com.

The Simon & Schuster Speakers Bureau can bring authors to your live event. For more information, or to book an event, contact the Simon & Schuster Speakers Bureau at 1-866-248-3049 or visit our website at www.simonspeakers.com.

Interior design by Renato Stanisic

Manufactured in the United States of America

10 9 8 7 6 5 4 3 2 1

Library of Congress Cataloging-in-Publication Data has been applied for.

ISBN 978-1-9821-4244-5
ISBN 978-1-9821-4245-2 (pbk)
ISBN 978-1-9821-4246-9 (ebook)

For Sunny and Story

CONTENTS

It will go away. Just stay calm. It will go away.
—DONALD TRUMP, MARCH 10, 2020

In serious situations, truth matters.
—SEAN HANNITY, MARCH 11, 2020

HOAX

PROLOGUE

On Wednesday, January 6, 2021, when thousands of President Trump's deluded supporters stormed the U.S. Capitol, House Republican leader Kevin McCarthy sheltered in place with his security detail and racked his brain about what to do. McCarthy had promoted Trump's anti-democratic crusade to stay in power despite losing to Joe Biden. But now everything was at risk—the lives of his fellow lawmakers, the future of his party, the entire American experiment. Medieval battle scenes were playing out in the people's house. The police were overwhelmed. McCarthy needed Trump to call off the mob.

So he placed a call to the most influential body in the president's life: the Fox News Channel.

"People are getting hurt," McCarthy told anchorman Bill Hemmer. "Anyone involved in this, if you're hearing me, hear me very loud and clear: This is not the American way. This is not protected by the First Amendment. This must stop now."

The live shots on Fox were mostly from a distance, showing people waving flags and hanging out on the Capitol steps, more like a concert than a coup attempt. Viewers couldn't see the armed standoff at the doors to the House floor, or the marauders who were roaming the hallowed halls of the Senate. Like a mad scientist suddenly fearful of the monster he'd helped create, McCarthy tried to explain that the armed occupation was so much worse than it looked on live TV.

"I watched barriers being broken. I watched people breaking windows," he told Hemmer. "I watched people running into a building." He said the violence was un-American.

McCarthy hoped the president was watching. And he had every reason to believe he was, because the president was almost always watching. Fox was Trump's viewfinder—his primary way of seeing the world around him. He took directions from Fox. And the network's anchors took full advantage of this power.

Hemmer asked: "Would you personally reach out to the president for more support?"

"I've already talked to the president," McCarthy said. "I called him. I think we need to make a statement, make sure that we can calm individuals down."

McCarthy was alluding to the problem: His initial phone call to the president, around 2:30 p.m. Eastern, had been a failure. The president seemed intoxicated by the live pictures of the attack. He only half-listened to McCarthy's plea for help. At 2:38, Trump posted a generic tweet, telling his fans to "stay peaceful," even though the peace had been shattered more than an hour earlier. McCarthy needed more from Trump—a much more forceful message to stop the insurrection. Shortly after 2:50, he heard an officer say "shots fired" over the police radio. Then he heard that the crowd was swelling outside. Since appealing to Trump directly didn't work, McCarthy had gone the Fox route.

Hemmer was anchoring that day from Atlanta, where millions of Georgians had just voted in the runoff elections that tipped control of the Senate to the Democrats. Years of history were being made in mere hours. Hemmer's view of the insurrection at the DC Capitol was limited—he only knew what he saw on the TV monitor in front of him—but he could hear the alarm in McCarthy's voice. From 3:06 until 3:12 p.m., Hemmer kept bringing the conversation back around to Trump, gingerly of course, since virtually the entire Fox audience loved the president and hated hearing criticism of him. But criticism was necessary in this moment: The Capitol was being ransacked by domestic terrorists, and the president was just sitting back and watching TV. "His initial reaction was not horror, which was almost everybody else's reaction," Maggie Haberman of *The New York Times* reported. "His initial reaction was to watch the show."

Hemmer asked McCarthy if Trump needed to say and do more, and then the anchorman made a very off-brand quip about "the law-and-order president," shortly before McCarthy's cell phone signal faded out. One minute after the interview ended, at 3:13, Trump tweeted a more effective condemnation of the attack, and even echoed Hemmer's words: "I am asking for everyone at the U.S. Capitol to remain peaceful. No violence! Remember, WE are the Party of Law & Order."

Once more, Fox News had steered the president back on script.

But without Fox, there never would have been a President Trump, nor would his war on truth have been so scarily effective, nor would his Big Lie about the election have poisoned the minds of so many people.

McCarthy personified how both the GOP and its media organs had been radicalized by the Trump years. Two months before the riot, he had wormed his way into a closet-size television studio and slid a microphone onto his lapel. The election was over and the vote was decisive: Biden was the winner. But the vote count was still underway in Georgia and several other key states, so none of the major networks were ready to project Biden quite yet. Trump and his TV cheerleaders were determined to fill the info vacuum with fraudulent claims about voter fraud. And McCarthy was there to help. He pitched Fox's Laura Ingraham a conspiracy theory: "Why is it that in these major states, that the big cities stop counting till all the rural votes come in, so they know how many more they need?" He prattled on, finally delivering the most memorable sound bite: "President Trump won this election, so everyone who's listening, do not be quiet," he said. "Do not be silent about this. We cannot allow this to happen before our very eyes. We need to unite together."

Ingraham was visibly pleased. "Congressman, thank you so much for being out there and being vocal," she said. "I hope we see others."

Sure enough, other lawmakers followed his and Trump's lead. "Trump was probably watching the interview, and seeing this likely encouraged him to keep up his efforts to slander our democracy," MSNBC's Steve Benen pointed out the next morning. "For another, McCarthy is the leader of roughly two hundred House Republicans, each of whom just received a signal to question the legitimacy of the 2020 presidential election and its outcome."

Back at the Capitol, at a quarter past three in the afternoon on January 6, McCarthy reestablished his cell phone connection, and he called in to the CBS and ABC broadcast networks. Every major network was running special live coverage of the Capitol siege. In the TV business, this is known as "rolling" coverage—no commercial breaks, no clear plan, just rolling with the news event and seeing what happens next.

In an earlier era, the House minority leader would have prioritized the broadcast networks, believing they had the biggest audience. But by 2021 everyone in politics knew that cable, not broadcast, was paramount. Plus, everyone knew that Trump was glued to Fox. So it's no wonder why McCarthy called there first.

He was far from the only Dr. Frankenstein feeling threatened by his monster on January 6. At 3:39 p.m. Fox correspondent Griff Jenkins was walking along Pennsylvania Avenue when a band of Trump diehards turned on him. "Liar!" one man chanted. "Fake news? Yeah, fake news," another exclaimed, right into the microphone. Jenkins sounded surprised by the heckling—Trump fans usually targeted CNN and NBC, not Fox! But Biden's victory was the beginning of an unprecedented backlash against Fox. A portion of the political base shared by Fox and Trump had been radicalized, over a period of years, and the result was a bloodstained riot. There were Confederate flags, nooses, and actual pitchforks. There were pipe bombs at the Democratic and Republican Party offices. There were gruesome acts of violence against police officers committed by men who had claimed, in their previous lives, to "back the blue." Rioters dragged officers down flights of stairs, beat them with American flags, and stole tactical gear. Others in the mob were trampled and assaulted. America's government was under attack from the inside.

And it was hard to imagine that any of this could have happened without Rupert Murdoch's propaganda machine of a network. Fox News was a radicalization engine. And some employees knew it. They felt it in their bones. When I was trying to fall asleep early in the morning of January 7, trying to forget the terror of the long day, my phone lit up with a text from a guilt-stricken Fox News veteran. The four words were like something out of a nightmare:

"What have we done?"

"Fox News brain"

Fox News enabled Donald Trump in ways that changed the country forever. Trump was afflicted by "Fox News brain," a diagnosis that was ID'd by a White House aide. It was fun for a while, at least for Fox stars like Sean Hannity, to treat the most powerful man in the world like a marionette. But in 2020 and 2021 the Trump-Fox feedback loop had life-and-death consequences. And there has to be a reckoning.

Trump's vow to end "American carnage," which was rooted in the fearmongering that Fox aired during Barack Obama's eight years in office, ended in actual carnage at the Capitol. America came shockingly close to a massacre of congressional leaders. It was a riot of lies, led by people who internalized right-wing media's 24/7 talk of "taking our country back" and actually tried to do it. One of the men arrested in connection with the assault at the Capitol was a frequent Fox News guest.

The riot was certainly not the first time that televised lies had provoked physical pain. Precisely one year earlier, in January 2020, the president's Fox obsession combined with the network's obsequiousness did real damage when the world learned of the novel coronavirus. While the virus was silently spreading across the United States, some of Fox's biggest stars denied and downplayed the threat it posed; Trump echoed them; and they echoed back. "The thing that's going to end this is the warmer weather," Fox jester Greg Gutfeld said on February 24, 2020. "Thank God for global warming," cohost Jesse Watters wisecracked. "It's going to disappear," Trump said on February 27. "One day—it's like a miracle—it will disappear."

By the fourth and final year of Trump's presidency, most Americans knew that he was untrustworthy, but the Fox base still trusted him. They also trusted Hannity, who dismissed "coronavirus hysteria," and Ingraham, who called Democrats the "panDEMic party," and Watters, who said, "I'm not afraid of the coronavirus and no one else should be that afraid either." Fox's longest-tenured medical analyst, Dr. Marc Siegel, told Hannity on March 6, "at worst, at worst, worst case scenario, it could be the flu."

This was shockingly irresponsible stuff—and Fox executives knew it, because by the beginning of March, they were taking precautions that belied Siegel's just-the-flu statement. The network canceled a big event for hundreds of advertisers, instituted deep cleanings of the office, and began to put a work-from-home plan in place. Yet Fox's stars kept sending mixed messages to millions of viewers. This went on and on until March 13, when *Fox & Friends* cohost Ainsley Earhardt claimed it's "actually the safest time to fly" and guest Jerry Falwell Jr. said people were "overreacting" to the virus. Fox News CEO Suzanne Scott finally asserted herself and hauled the show's producers into her office. No more denialism, she said. But she was two or three weeks too late, just like Trump was. The virus had been unleashed.

There were dozens of reasons why the United States lagged so far behind other countries in preparations for the pandemic. Some were cultural, some were economic, some were political. But one of the undeniable reasons was televisual. Fox failed its viewers—including the commander in chief—at key moments during the pandemic. Four out of five Fox viewers were over the age of fifty-five, in the demographic most at risk. Plus, the network was favored by men, with 54 percent male viewership, and Covid-19 was much deadlier among men. As ICU admissions surged and the death toll rose, Fox's most vociferous critics said the network had blood on its hands.

No one will ever be able to say, with absolute certainty, how many Fox News devotees died from the virus. And it is impossible to know how much an individual's choices are influenced by the TV hosts they trust. But just as doctors are taught to do no harm, journalists are trained to "minimize harm," in the words of the Society of Professional Journalists' ethical code. Some Fox staffers privately admitted that the don't-worry tone of the talking heads was harmful. They used words like "dangerous," "unforgivable," and "hazardous to our viewers" to describe the network's early coverage of the pandemic.

Fox's conduct had spillover effects because of the network's influence in the Trump White House and throughout the federal government. It is impossible to know how many Americans who died as a result of Covid-19 would have survived if the government had acted more swiftly in February and March. But it is obvious that Fox's fingerprints were all over the government's response. As the months stretched on, Fox booked guests who minimized the death toll and mocked mask-wearing. The tone was set early, from the top, when Trump rallied the ideologically faithful in South Carolina on February 28. "The Democrats are politicizing the coronavirus. You know that, right? Coronavirus. They're politicizing it," he said. He likened the Democrats' conduct to "the impeachment hoax" and said, "this is their new hoax."

It was his new favorite word, on the trail and on Twitter: HOAX. He used it almost every day, and so did his friends. Hannity used the same frame as Trump on March 9, when he bashed Democrats and members of the media for exaggerating the threat of the virus. "They're scaring the living hell out of people and I see it again as like, 'Oh, let's bludgeon Trump with this new hoax,' " he said.

The word "hoax" was one of Trumpworld's weapons. "Hoax is a potent word, in being an angry and mean one," linguist John McWhorter told me. "It's the quintessence of Trumpian self-expression."

Before running for president, Trump used the word to dismiss global warming. It is "a total, and very expensive, hoax!" he tweeted in 2013. He continued to shout about "global warming hoaxsters" in 2014, then dropped it for a while. "Fake news" became his mantra after the 2016 election. When its effects started to wear off, he shifted to hoax.

"Hoax" carries something that "fake" doesn't, McWhorter said: "Hoax carries an air of accusation, of transgression. The hoaxer is being accused of deliberately hoodwinking the public, of being a Barnum. FAKE is more flexible—the news could end up 'fake' on the basis of assorted factors, such as blinkered ideology, mission creep, there being multiple perspectives, etc. But to say HOAX clears away all of that nuance and just calls people out as malevolent."

It was a logical leap for a pathological president who indulged illogical conspiracy theories and led a war on truth.

Trump mostly employed the word in connection with impeachment and Russia. He used it just once in the context of the pandemic, but it was still unconscionable. Amanda Carpenter, the Ted Cruz communications director turned CNN commentator who wrote a book about Trump's make-you-question-your-reality techniques, known as gaslighting, said she thought the "nonsense about calling it a 'hoax' initially but then saying he was only referring to the Democrats' 'overreaction' was really strong gaslighting. He clearly wanted the idea of a 'hoax' associated with the virus." And it wasn't just Trump, Carpenter said; it was parrots like Hannity too: "They were downplaying the threat and acting like anyone who was worried about it wasn't sincere and this was all a scam to get Trump. That's something that stuck and did tremendous damage."

By autumn, when the Covid-19 death toll surpassed two hundred thousand souls, Fox executives were candid with me: Their audience did not want to hear about the coronavirus anymore. Period. End of story. But the audience *needed* to hear it, because the story was growing and getting worse as Americans headed indoors for the winter months. Trump, the Fox viewer in chief, personified the network's disregard for the crisis. Everything about his demeanor, even his body language, screamed, *I'm over it*. When he came down with the virus himself, he became severely ill and his team hid that fact from the public; then they tried to turn his hospital stay into a triumphant superhero tale, complete with a dramatic flight home to the White House at sunset. There, he went back to ignoring Covid-19.

All Trump wanted was to stay in office, even though he showed pathetically little interest in doing the job. At nearly every campaign rally, he threw around the word "hoax" and planted seeds of doubt in the minds of his voters and viewers. On October 25 in Manchester, New Hampshire, he ranted about mail-in balloting and said "The Democrats know it's a hoax, and they know—and it's going to cause problems." On October 26 in Lititz, Pennsylvania, he said, "You don't want the ballot hoax, because wait and you'll see, they'll have so many problems." On October 27 in Omaha, Nebraska, he denounced "the whole ballot hoax" and said "there's so many bad things happening." The lies were as egregious as they were voluminous: "You know, they throw away ballots if it has the name Trump on it, boom." And the conspiracy theories were as sweeping as they were stupefying: "It's a big tech hoax," he said, claiming that social media platforms forced negative news about Trump to "trend."

Every lie about the integrity of the election was a deposit. And on November 3 he started to make withdrawals. He tried out new slogans: "Mail-in ballot hoax," "Rigged election hoax." Eventually he just started to call it the "Election Hoax" and expected his fans to know exactly what he was talking about. Most of them did. This is really what it meant to have "Fox News brain." First the network's shows obsessed over so-called "irregularities" and fears of voter fraud. Then, once the lies and distortions had sunk in, the shows obsessed over the polls that revealed how many GOP voters fell for the lies. I felt like I was watching the TV upside-down. Nothing made sense anymore.

Trump despised the news anchors on Fox News. They had a tendency to be "nasty," he told aides, and some of them belonged on CNN or MSNBC, not on the network he promoted to his tens of millions of followers. So he avoided the newscasts and relied on propagandists like Hannity and Maria Bartiromo to tell him what he wanted to hear. He depended on them to keep the walls of his alternative reality intact. And they abused their access to him.

On November 27, Fox announced that Trump's first TV interview since losing the election would be a phone call to Bartiromo on her show *Sunday Morning Futures*. Of course, Fox didn't bill it as his first interview "since losing." Bartiromo was on his side and wanted him to prove his case. But first she wanted to say her piece, so she kept Trump waiting while she read a mind-numbing introduction and interviewed a senator about "radical" Democrats.

The power imbalance was something to behold: The president had the joint chiefs and the cabinet and any number of world leaders at his beck and call, but when it came time for an interview on Fox News, he was just another caller who needed to be patched into the control room switchboard.

When Bartiromo finally welcomed Trump to the show, he basically read his Twitter feed out loud. He threw in a couple "hoax" references for good measure. "This election was a fraud," he said. "It was a rigged election." Bartiromo's response showed that she agreed: "This is *disgusting*," she said. "And we cannot allow America's election to be corrupted."

The election was over, everywhere except in this radicalized prison of propaganda, where it would never be over. Bartiromo thought she was doing Trump a service; she was so proud that she had been able to book the president, so proud to provide a platform for his claims. But she was really doing Trump a grave disservice. She was exposing just how delusional he was. Time and time again, the Fox stars who ostensibly wanted to help Trump actually hurt him.

I wasn't alone in noticing that the same people who doubted the lethality of the pandemic were now disputing the results of the election too. It made for a particularly pernicious combination of denialism, something that one of Fox's liberal commentators, Marie Harf, identified early on. Republicans were pushing two stories, she said on the talk show *Outnumbered* on November 20: They were rejecting Covid-19 safety measures and they were "pushing to reject the election results."

"Both are broader trends that are really disturbing," she said. "Both are a rejection of math, of expertise, of science, and both are really dangerous to the American people and to our democracy."

Harf was right. The GOP's state of denial was all-consuming. Fox management claimed that they didn't mind someone like Harf saying so; they wanted to be able to say that the network was home to all points of view. But they also knew that the Fox base hated hearing progressives' provocations. And they knew that Harf's truth-telling at lunchtime was seen by a fraction of the audience that Hannity had at night. Prime time had the real power. And management had no control over prime time.

"Batshit crazy"

Until 2020, Sean Hannity was the most powerful person at Fox in the Trump age. When people asked him who was in charge of the channel, he said, "Me." And most people at the channel agreed with him.

There was a power shift during the pandemic, however, as Tucker Carlson emerged as the highest-rated host on Fox. His 8 p.m. show topped Hannity's 9 p.m. show most days of the week. Carlson spoke "MAGA" even more fluently than Hannity and exemplified Fox's increasingly extremist bent. Every hour of *Tucker Carlson Tonight* said the same thing: that the corrupt elites in both parties deserved to be overthrown. I always thought it sounded a little odd coming from Tucker Swanson McNear Carlson, whose bow tie was one of his defining attributes even for years after he stopped wearing one, and whose personal wealth was a testament to TV excess. But odd or not, he formed incredibly strong bonds with millions of conservatives who resented the cultural diversification of America. He was willing to sit behind a camera and say, with faux courage, "How, precisely, is diversity our strength?" And his super-fans were able to spend all day behind a computer screen sharing his screeds.

By the beginning of 2021, Fox was running "TUCKER ON TOP" ad spots that promoted his No. 1 status in the ratings, with the subtext being that he was bigger than Hannity. Carlson believed that his ratings would be even higher, were it not for the weak 7 p.m. show before his, *The Story with Martha MacCallum*.

Television hosts are prone to spend way too much time thinking about their "lead-in," an insider term for the show that airs right beforehand. Sane TV stars recognize that they are just runners in a relay race, grabbing the baton from their lead-in and handing it off to the next host. But television is not an industry that nurtures or rewards sanity. Plus, her handoff really was disappointing by Fox's high-rated standards. If, let's say, MacCallum ended her hour with 2 million viewers, and Carlson was such a ratings magnet that he ended his hour with 3.5 million, then imagine how much more popular he could be if his lead-in was 3 million plus!

This lead-in tension became an overflowing fount of gossip in and around Fox. "Tucker is jealous of the later hours," one source said. He got his wish a few days before Biden's inauguration, when Fox demoted MacCallum to 3 in the afternoon and launched a new bomb-throwing opinion hour at 7 in the evening. What was polarizing for the public—additional hours of right-wing barking—was more profitable for the company and more pleasurable for Carlson. It was a win-win, except America lost.

Carlson and Hannity were the twin poles that defined Fox in the Trump era. Both men could do practically whatever they wanted, and from wherever. Carlson sometimes hosted his hour from the middle of a forest in Maine, where he had a summer home on an island in the middle of Bryant Pond, ninety minutes north of Portland. He took a boat from "Carlson Island" to the mainland to host *Tucker Carlson Tonight*, where he decried so-called "elites" who wall themselves off from the rest of the world. Instead of a wall, he had a moat.

The rest of the year, he used a studio near his beach retreat on a barrier island on Florida's Gulf Coast. He told friends that TV life took a tremendous toll on his family—death threats, invasions of privacy, all the rest. The threats were despicable. But people looking at Carlson from the outside in thought he was living a dream come true. His pulpit was so powerful that he didn't even need Trump. And he was working from home before the pandemic made it the norm.

Hannity also worked from home most days, thirty-eight long miles from Manhattan, in a $10.5 million mansion on the North Shore of Long Island. He loved it out there. There was only one way in and one way out of his village, and a police station that kept track of every car that drove by. Billy Joel lived half a mile down the road. Hannity was close to his favorite fishing spots and the airstrip where he kept his private jet. He had a pool and a boat dock in the backyard, and a tennis court nestled in the woods nearby. One of his favorite toys? His helicopter.

Unlike Carlson, who started out as a fact-checker and writer, Hannity originally wanted to be a radio star. In the early nineties Hannity was a Rush-Limbaugh-in-training—a right-wing radio host who hoped to be a tenth as rich as Rush someday. A Long Island native with a blue-collar New York accent, he learned the medium at UC Santa Barbara, where he landed a weekly show on the campus radio station. If you scour the university's website now, you'll find no mention of this famous ex-student, one of the most influential men to ever walk the quad. That's because he never graduated from Santa Barbara, or any other college. In 1989 his radio show was halted when he made anti-gay remarks and claimed "the media" was covering up the truth about AIDS. When this controversy resurfaced in 2017, he expressed regret for "ignorant" remarks in the past. But at the time he used the episode as a launchpad. Hannity billed himself as "the most talked-about college radio host in America" and scored a hosting gig at a right-wing station in Huntsville, Alabama. That's where he met his wife, Jill. After two years he moved to a bigger market, Atlanta, where he shouted into a mic about Bill Clinton every day and snagged the ear of the second most important person in his life: Roger Ailes. Fox News was in need of a young Limbaugh. Ailes shipped him up to New York for a tryout. "He saw something that I didn't even think I knew I had," Hannity told me in a 2011 interview.

Hannity's Long Island mansion and his oceanfront Naples, Florida, penthouse were two über-expensive symbols of how Ailes changed his life. Hannity was a living connection to Fox's past— the only prime time host at Fox News who was there on launch day and was still there nearly twenty-five years later. His tenure and ratings gave him tremendous power. He could get almost anything he wanted. In a mid-2010s contract negotiation, he won the right to work from home: Fox installed a state-of-the-art studio so that he could helm his nightly TV show from his mansion, the same way he already did his afternoon radio show. Radio kept him tethered to Republican voters—and TV kept him tethered to Trump. But that wasn't a good thing.

Hannity's friends told me that he was burnt out for long stretches of the Trump presidency. Being the president's "shadow" chief of staff, as he was known around the White House, could be a thrill, but it was also a serious burden. He counseled Trump at all hours of the day: One of Hannity's confidants said the president treated him like Melania, like a wife in a sexless marriage. Arguably he treated Hannity better than he did the first lady. Hannity's producers marveled at his influence and access. "It's a powerful thing to be someone's consigliere," one producer said. "I hear Trump talk at rallies, and I hear Sean," a family friend commented.

Hannity chose this life, so no one felt sorry for him, but the stress took its toll. "Hannity would tell you, off off off the record, that Trump is a batshit crazy person," one of his associates said in 2019. Another colleague concurred in 2020: "Hannity has said to me, more than once, 'he's crazy.'"

But Hannity's commitment to GOP priorities and commitment to his own business model meant that he could never say so publicly. And if one of his friends went on the record and quoted Hannity questioning Trump's mental fitness, Hannity would end that friendship.

Early on in the Trump age, Hannity gained weight and vaped incessantly, both of which some members of his inner circle blamed on Trump-related pressure. "If you were hearing what I'm hearing, you'd be vaping too," Hannity commented to a colleague. He was very sensitive to trolls' comments about the added pounds, especially from his chest up, since that's all viewers saw of him most nights, when he was live from his palace. (For the record, I can relate to stress eating.)

Hannity's calls with POTUS were a never-ending stream of grievance and gossip. Trump was a run-on sentence, so prone to rambling that "I barely get a word in," Hannity told one of his allies. He sometimes spoke with the president before the show and again afterward, usually in the 10 p.m. hour, when Trump would rate his guests and recommend talking points and themes for the following day. Trump wanted more of Gregg Jarrett, more of Dan Bongino, more of Newt Gingrich—in other words, the toadiest toads. The president legitimately deserved a producer credit on Hannity's show.

Hannity also stayed in constant touch with Trump's son Don Jr., son-in-law Jared Kushner, Trump 2020 campaign manager Bill Stepien, and Republican Party chair Ronna McDaniel. According to *The Washington Post*, Hannity sent suggestions to the campaign apparatus and fretted about strategy.

But the talk show host swore that no one knew the truth about his relationship with Trump and sneered at reporters, such as yours truly, who described his essential role. He certainly didn't disclose his role in Trumpworld the way a media ethicist would recommend.

Once in a while, I noticed, the curtain slipped, and his own colleagues pointed out the extraordinary position he held. As the coronavirus crisis deepened in March 2020, Geraldo Rivera said to Hannity on the air, "I want you to tell the president, when you talk to him tonight, that Geraldo said 'Mr. President, for the good of the nation, stop shaking hands.' It's a bad example. We don't need it."

Geraldo was right. But Trump didn't want to hear it. And Hannity didn't make a point of emphasizing it. Instead, he used his perch to defend Trump's mismanagement of the pandemic and every other failure of the Trump presidency. And in this way, I concluded, Hannity helped doom Trump's reelection chances.

Trump called Fox "my network," but the network led him astray by feeding his ego with fantasies and fictions. The prime time shows were the worst offenders: Trump programmed Hannity's show and Hannity produced Trump's presidency. Hannity fed misinformation to Trump and Trump fed it right back to Hannity. Both men thought they were benefiting, but they both suffered.

The calls and counseling continued right up until Election Day—when the relationship between the two men began to break down. Hannity, according to one source, was "disgusted" by some of Trump's election denialism. I was skeptical of this claim, however, since Hannity devoted so much time to the Big Lie throughout the month of November and well into December. At least Carlson was wise enough to focus on other Fox-friendly subjects. Hannity kept inviting Kayleigh McEnany to hold up packets of paper and swear that the legal path to a second term was right around the corner, even though Trump's suits were laughed out of court left and right. McEnany and other Hannity guests filled the Fox audience with false hope night after night and never, ever delivered. The excuse I heard internally was that Hannity was a people-pleaser. If last night's ratings indicated that the viewers wanted to hear about voter fraud fantasies, then, by golly, give them more fraud. An hour full of fraud. Hannity was never going to risk alienating the audience. "Sean knows the audience better than anyone," a coworker said. So if Hannity really was "disgusted" by Trump's unreality toward the end of 2020, well, he was bathed in the very same disgusting stench.

Inside Fox, even though staffers rarely saw him, Hannity had a reputation as a nice, generous guy. He paid bonuses to his staff out of his own deep pockets. He ordered meals and care packages to the homes of colleagues who'd lost loved ones. He even offered to hire a private investigator when an acquaintance died in a mysterious car crash. When the network descended on New Hampshire for primary election coverage, Hannity footed the bill for the open bar. A member of Hannity's production crew, a Democrat, quipped to me, "I want to fucking hate him so bad. But he's so nice to me."

So that was Hannity: a warrior on the air, a pacifist off the air.

Carlson was more persnickety, more demanding of his staff, more protective of his privacy. But by mid-2020 everyone could tell that he was ascendant. Hannity's show was stale on its best night. Carlson's show was piping hot. The old 8 p.m. host Bill O'Reilly asked, "Who's looking out for you?" while Carlson claimed to know the answer: "No one's looking out for you." Executives at Fox felt like Carlson had taken the O'Reilly mantle, so to speak, and they were much more interested in his ratings than his rhetoric. One manager paid him the highest compliment in Fox-speak by saying "Tucker is never, ever, ever predictable." I disagreed, arguing that Carlson quite predictably steered clear of Trump controversies, and fronted the American whitelash instead, but the point held.

"Profit machine"

Carlson and Hannity were the public faces of the brand, but credit and blame for Fox News began several income brackets higher, with Rupert and Lachlan Murdoch.

Rupert, or KRM as he's known around the company (his given first name is Keith), was the octogenarian patriarch. Lachlan was the favorite son and CEO of Fox Corp, which had a market cap of $22 billion at the beginning of 2021. The sprawling Fox News operation was like the family's ATM. Before the pandemic upended everything, the network was on a path to $2 billion in profits, according to sources I interviewed.

Now let me tell you something: You probably chip in for Fox News, even if you despise it. Fox's foundation is a fantastic combination of advertising revenue and subscriber fees. Almost every cable and satellite subscriber in the country pays two bucks each month for Fox News and Fox Business. No cable operator has ever seriously flirted with dropping Fox to save money because, among other reasons, they believe the right-wing backlash would cripple their business. In the fiscal year that ended in June 2020, Rupert banked $34 million from Fox. Lachlan made $29 million. Father and son ran broadcast and local TV divisions and invested in new streaming ventures, but their cash flow largely came from Fox News. The news channel's success kept the private planes fueled up. It kept the hedges trimmed at Lachlan's newly acquired $150 million Bel-Air mansion.

Some of Trump's most powerful confidants, or, as I call them, wingmen, made even more than the execs. Hannity cleared $30 million a year from Fox—on top of the money he made for his daily radio show. Bret Baier made $12 million a year. Laura Ingraham, who hadn't been there as long, netted closer to $10 million. Some of Fox's most popular talking heads made more than half a million each. They were called contributors and they were paid to be reliable (to say yes when bookers call) and monogamous (to say no to every other network). Many hosts and contributors leveraged their Fox platforms for book contracts and speaking tours that could pay millions.

With an endless stream of cash came endless ways to keep the wingmen happy. But the money also came with constraints. Fox staffers lived in constant fear of alienating the audience. Producers knew that the "base" couldn't stand to see bad Trump news in the banner and couldn't bear to hear too many liberals speak for too long. That may be the single most important thing to understand about Fox: Everyone there was profoundly afraid of losing the audience and the resulting piles of cash.

"They're making too much money to change," said one veteran producer who resigned in disgust.

"Fox News is not a 'news network.' Don't think of it as a network at all," said a veteran host. "It's a profit machine."

Sometimes money was a silencer. During the first Trump impeachment, Fox's senior judicial analyst Judge Andrew Napolitano said Trump had confessed to criminal behavior and should be impeached. This was the "wrong" opinion at Fox, and he was punished by not being booked on shows. Napolitano complained and the execs blew him off. "He should go home and count his money," one manager said to me snidely. Shut up, and take your check.

Sometimes the money was a balm. In 2013 Ailes agreed to pay Shep Smith around $15 million a year in part to appease Smith because he was demoted to make room for Megyn Kelly. "They bought people off, it's as simple as that," the head of a rival network said.

But money didn't solve every problem. After Ailes was ousted and Trump was elected, Lachlan Murdoch was willing to pay upward of $25 million each year for four years to keep Kelly. She left money on the table—about $30 million—by fleeing to NBC for a three-year, $23 million-a-year deal. And when Shep hit his breaking point, he walked away from his contract with a year and a half still to go, apparently giving up more than $15 million. He joined CNBC one year later in a much less visible role. Both anchors challenged the prevailing Fox belief that money cures all.

One member of the Murdoch family also hit a breaking point. Lachlan's brother, James, just fifteen months apart in age, was a world apart in his political views. In the Trump age, his disgust with Fox News was a big factor in his departure from the family business. Trump split up families—even billionaire families. One week after the January 6 attack on Capitol Hill, James and his wife Kathryn issued a statement that excoriated the family name without technically saying so. "Spreading disinformation—whether about the election, public health, or climate change—has real-world consequences," the outcast couple said. "Many media property owners have as much responsibility for this as the elected officials who know the truth but choose instead to propagate lies. We hope the awful scenes we have all been seeing will finally convince those enablers to repudiate the toxic politics they have promoted once and forever."

Disinformation. Lies. Toxic politics. James was trashing his father's contributions to society. He had a long-term vision for how to intercede, but in the Trump years Rupert and Lachlan were in charge, and they were responsible for an unprecedented entanglement between a network and a narcissistic president.

Never before had a TV network effectively produced the president's intelligence briefing and staffed the federal bureaucracy. Never before had a president promoted a single TV channel, asked the hosts for advice behind closed doors, *and* demanded that they be fired when they stepped out of line. Until 2017, we would have dismissed this as a way-too-farcical drama: a dysfunctional White House, a delusional president, and a drama-filled network that misinformed him from morning through night.

"It's hard to think of a similarly close relationship between a president and a single outlet," historian Jon Meacham told me in the first weeks of the Trump presidency. "Politicians have always had favored reporters to whom they leaked, but I really think you would have to go all the way back to the overtly partisan press of the nineteenth century to find a parallel."

Hannity and Carlson were two members of a crazy, jam-packed

cable news cabinet. While Hannity deserved credit for getting long-time Fox News commentator John Bolton hired as national security advisor, Carlson got the credit when Bolton eventually fell out of favor with Trump. The sacking of Jeff Sessions? Jeanine Pirro was in Trump's ear for that one. The resignation of Kirstjen Nielsen? Lou Dobbs was central in it. Pat Cipollone leading the president's legal team? Laura Ingraham was instrumental.

The network gave the Trump administration a huge boost, but also created enormous tension within the White House. Trump's obsession with the opinion shows caused chaos when he latched on to impossible and downright illegal policy ideas. Aides begrudged the fact that Hannity was oftentimes more powerful than they were. But they watched Fox too, because they needed to know what the boss was hearing and what mood he was going to be in. They tried to get certain officials booked on certain shows with the knowledge that Trump was easily manipulated by what he saw on the air.

During the Trump presidency, I felt that the average news consumer did not understand just how wedded Fox and Trump were. The average voter didn't know just how many of Trump's actions and inactions were dictated by the network. Frankly the average political journalist didn't watch Fox often enough to really get it either. I frequently read stories by White House correspondents that described unvetted White House hires and unhinged policy decisions and unglued tweets but left out the cause: Fox's influence.

The only outlet that dedicated itself to keeping track was Media Matters for America, a progressive group founded by David Brock to monitor and confront conservative media. In 2019 the group's senior fellow Matt Gertz counted every single time Trump tweeted in direct response to a Fox News or Fox Business program and found at least 657 instances in a single year. Fox hated Media Matters, but Gertz's data checked out. He said he kept count because so much of "what they are saying is impacting the President of the United States and, through him, our daily lives."

Trump's TV-watching time was coded in his internal schedules as "Executive Time." He watched, he tweeted, he called Hannity, and he watched some more. The decisions that most seriously damaged his presidency could be traced straight back to his TV habits. For example, Gertz said, "Trump's hatred for Ukraine seems to have originated with Sean Hannity's show telling him that Clinton had colluded with that country in 2016." The end result: impeachment number one.

Fox's influence was constant. When he threatened North Korea and said he had a bigger "button" than Kim Jong Un, it was because of a Fox segment about Kim's "nuclear button." When he told Iran to "never threaten the United States again!" it was because of a Fox segment about Iran's saber-rattling.

Trump granted pardons because of Fox. He attacked Google because of Fox. He raged against migrant "caravans" because of Fox. He accused public servants of treason because of Fox. And he got the facts wrong again and again because of mistakes and misreporting by the network. When Kobe Bryant died in a helicopter crash, Trump sent condolences but got the death toll wrong, because of Fox. Trump was a teetotaler, but he behaved like an addict. In that analogy, the Murdochs were the dealers.

It must be said that Fox News wasn't always like this. For twenty years, the network was conservative without being conspiratorial, at least most of the time. It was patriotic without being propagandistic. But it evolved over the years, or devolved, to become a chest-thumping house ad for the MAGA agenda. Trump propped up the network and the network propped up Trump. Anchors and guests who pointed out Trump's lies were marginalized. Commentators who covered up his failings and foibles were promoted. This was the Fox News presidency in action.

From the day Trump entered the presidential race to the day he flew off to Mar-a-Lago to avoid Biden's inauguration ceremony, I had a front-row seat to the Trumpification of Fox and the Foxification of America. I watched as the president received fucked-up medical advice and misinformation from unqualified talking heads on Fox and shared even worse advice with millions of viewers. I didn't think he could sink any lower—until he mused about injecting disinfectants into the body, and health officials across the country had to warn people not to listen to him. His conduct only deteriorated in his closing months, when he ignored the coronavirus and concocted new conspiracy theories and incited an insurrection.

Like so many Americans, I'm shocked and angry. So what you'll get in these pages is not the Stelter in a navy blue blazer that you see on CNN. I'm writing this book as a citizen, as an advocate for factual journalism, and as a new dad who thinks about what kind of world my children are going to inherit. This story is about a rot at the core of our politics. It's about an ongoing attack on the very idea of a free and fair press. It's about the difference between news and propaganda. It's about the difference between state media and the fourth estate. So excuse me if I swear a little—but I am alarmed, and you should be too.

"We surrendered"

Before going any further, let me share where I'm coming from. I'm obsessed with news. Always have been. In 1995, when I turned ten, I logged on to the World Wide Web using dial-up AOL and a computer set up by my grandpa. My first stabs at journalism were homemade websites about *Goosebumps* books and Nintendo video games. From my basement in Maryland, I would tie up the home phone line calling companies for video game gossip. I would send instant messages to people with the last name Stine trying to meet family members of author R. L. Stine. I eventually found R.L. and his son Matt. They were two of my first "sources."

My dad, Mark, was an appliance repairman. He drove an hour south to Washington every day and replaced stoves and dishwashers in upper-middle-class neighborhoods. In 2001, after ample lobbying on my part, he took me to George W. Bush's inauguration. I treasure the memory because his heart gave out a week later while coaching my youngest brother's basketball team. He slipped into a coma and died. My mom somehow got me and my brothers through it. And she supported my journalism fixation in every way she could, even when I ran up expensive phone bills with all-night dial-up modem calls.

Through high school, through college, my drug of choice was news. I slept on the couch with the TV on when Iraq was bombed. I sat in the studio audience for *Crossfire*. And I created a website dedicated to cable news. I launched the blog on New Year's Day 2004, cloaked in the name *CableNewser* because I figured nobody would take me seriously if they knew I was an eighteen-year-old college freshman at Towson University in Maryland! The blog took off. Fox's PR people saw it as an opportunity—they started to send me overnight ratings data showing how Fox was trouncing CNN and MSNBC. I called this data The Scoreboard. I launched the blog for fun, not profit, but I did make a few quick bucks using a donation system that was in vogue at the time. The most generous donation came from Tucker Carlson, who sent $100. I can't remember if I thanked him. So: thank you, Tucker.

Within six months I had revealed my real name, renamed the

blog *TVNewser*, and visited the cable networks in person, making connections that have helped me to this day. I became friendly with Sean Hannity, for example, and learned some important lessons about broadcasting from him. When I left my blogging days behind and joined *The New York Times* in 2007, he sent me a congrats note: "Your hard work and dedication has really paid off, and you should be very proud. Also the fact that you did all of this while going to school makes this even more incredible." There were other notes like that too, but we labeled some of our emails "off the record," so I can't share them.

Other cable news stars reached out too. In 2006 Carlson booked me on his MSNBC talk show and dubbed me "the most powerful person in television news." That was never true about me, but it is true about Carlson now, at least in right-wing TV.

Back while I was blogging for beer money in the mid-2000s, cable news became an incredibly profitable business. Fox locked down the conservative audience and provided cover for Bush while MSNBC began to find its liberal voice. I continued to chronicle this at the *Times*, and then I lived it at CNN starting in 2013. When I joined the network to anchor the Sunday morning program *Reliable Sources*, I immediately realized how little I actually knew about TV. One month in, I bumped into Fox News chairman and CEO Roger Ailes at a party and told him I was struggling with the teleprompter. He told me to stop squinting and "move the fucking camera closer!"

"You don't work for the equipment," he said, "the equipment works for you. You're talent now."

"Talent" is a discomfiting term for anchors who just want to report the news, but it's de rigueur in the TV business. I quickly learned the other lingo: A video clip is a "soundbite," or "SOT," short for "sound on tape." A live interview segment is a "hit." A great guest is a "good talker." A waiting area for the guest is a "green room." A "good talker" waits in the "green room" to "do a hit," unless they get canceled, or "killed." Sometimes, when I can tell my segment is going to be bumped due to breaking news, I'll ask, "Am I dead yet?"

Aside from having to wear makeup and having to deal with death threats (more on that later), I love TV. At CNN, I cover the wide world of media, including Fox, just like I did at *TVNewser* and the *Times*, which means that I keep in touch with scores of sources. And that's ultimately why I'm here writing this book. I felt compelled to write it because of what I heard from inside Fox—from anchors and producers and reporters who were appalled by Trump's gradual takeover of the network. They said management encouraged pro-Trump propaganda and discouraged real reporting, and they said many staffers went right along with it.

"They are lying about things we're seeing with our own eyes," one well-known Fox commentator said, embarrassed about their colleagues' conduct.

"We surrendered to Trump," one anchor said to me with remorse in his voice. "We just surrendered."

"What does Trump have on Fox?" another anchor asked, convinced there was a conspiracy in play. Dirty pictures of Rupert?

In the course of my reporting over the last four years, I didn't find any dirty pictures. But I did find a lot of people who felt dirty. Some were desperate to talk. Others were terrified. Ailes made people paranoid and punished those he suspected of leaking. That same fear of retribution was still very real even in the post-Ailes years. Employees suspected their work phones were tapped and assumed their emails were monitored by management. I cannot overstate the level of paranoia among Fox employees.

And yet many people—from anchors to assistants—still spoke

with me because they wanted the truth to come out. One day I schmoozed with Lachlan Murdoch at a cocktail party; the next day I heard from a production assistant who said she couldn't "take it anymore." Once the pandemic cut off the party circuit, I Zoomed with sources and traded messages via the Signal app. I initially spoke with more than 140 staffers at Fox, plus 180 former staffers and others with direct ties to the network. After the publication of the hardcover edition of this book, upward of a dozen new sources reached out, and I was able to learn even more about the inner workings of Fox. The frustration on the part of many sources was palpable. Staffers described a TV network that was off the rails. Some even said the place where they worked, that they cashed paychecks from, was dangerous to democracy.

See, anyone who views Fox News as a mere cable channel, no different than AMC or TBS, is missing what it really is. Fox is an addictive substance. For its biggest fans, Fox is an identity. Almost a way of life. Hardcore viewers rarely change the channel or seek out a balanced media diet. They compare the network to a church, to a senior center, to a city hall. They flock to it for reinforcement, for inspiration, for comfort food. "To some, Fox is family," sociologist Arlie Russell Hochschild wrote in her study of Tea Party supporters in Louisiana. She found that the channel "stands next to industry, state government, church, and the regular media as an extra pillar of political culture all its own." That's a lot of responsibility, and in the Trump era the producers regularly failed to live up to it.

Anchors and commentators felt excruciating pressure to please the Fox base—and avoid their wrath. There's no pleasant way to say this: Many of the viewers became radicalized over time. What many Americans recognized as mendacity, the Fox base registered as honesty. The achievements of a multicultural America, the progress toward a more equal society, were perceived as loss. The truths told by Trump critics were dismissed as lies. A 2019 PRRI survey found significant differences between "Fox News Republicans" and other Republicans who said Fox was not their primary news source. "Fox News Republicans" were much more closely wedded to Trump, with 55 percent saying there was nothing Trump could do to lose their approval. This was "I could stand in the middle of Fifth Avenue and shoot somebody" level of support. Of the Republicans who relied on other sources of information, only 29 percent made such an extreme statement.

Fox News was always on one level a political project, but the staffers who confided in me were disturbed by how thoroughly Fox and the GOP were merged by Trump, Hannity, and a handful of other power players. Many of the staffers said America deserved a much more responsible version of a conservative news network. They said Fox should have a traditional standards and practices department and a commitment to fact-checking and a leadership team that accounted for its mistakes. I agreed with them. But would anyone have watched that network?

Most of the sources for this book only spoke on condition of anonymity. I don't take confidential sourcing lightly, but it was necessary in these situations, because people wouldn't speak at all otherwise. I laughed several times when I heard folks on Fox bemoaning the use of anonymous sources, knowing those very same people were confidential informants for me. That's how this hypocritical business works.

Now let me tell you what I learned.

THE CREATION

"Everybody can be bought"

In 1996, while Donald Trump was buying up buildings and beauty pageants, Rupert Murdoch bought Roger Ailes. Murdoch hired the GOP political operative and gave him a pile of money to build a news channel from scratch in the basement of the News Corp building in New York City. It was one of the most fateful decisions in modern American history.

Ailes had both political and personal motivations for partnering with Murdoch. He wanted the Republican Party to win on television the way Rush Limbaugh was winning on radio. And he wanted to stick it to his old bosses at NBC, who'd ripped the America's Talking cable channel out of his hands to create MSNBC.

At the time, TV experts thought MSNBC, not Fox News, would be the most formidable challenger to CNN. ABC was talking about launching a news channel too. Fox was seen as least likely to succeed. Both NBC and ABC had established news divisions to draw from, while Fox hardly had any news infrastructure at all. Ted Turner delighted in saying that he was going to "squish Rupert like a bug." But Murdoch and Ailes converted the jeers into fuel. At a pre-launch press conference, Ailes vowed that Fox News would be No. 1.

Many of Ailes's former lieutenants believed in him and left NBC for the new channel. Ailes claimed that a total of eighty-two staffers followed him to Fox (it was more like fifty, I was told). Whatever the actual number, the brain drain was enough to prompt NBC boss Bob Wright to call Ailes and complain.

"You've been poaching my people," Wright said.

"You guys ought to know the difference between recruitment and a fucking jailbreak," Ailes responded. "They're coming down the bedsheets over there, and you better try to stop them."

Like Trump, Ailes saw himself as "a counterpuncher." He famously told his executives, "Don't pick a fight with someone who likes to fight," a line he learned from his father. With this new channel, Ailes was fighting the entire media establishment. His former boss Richard Nixon would have been proud. In the early seventies Nixon and VP Spiro Agnew believed they were at war with a liberal cabal of television networks, run by, as Agnew once said, a "small and unelected elite." Terms like "media bias" entered the lexicon, and by the early nineties, there was a well-funded right-wing machine that raged against liberal media bias. So when Ailes said his channel would be "fair and balanced," on the premise that the rest of TV news leaned left, millions of conservatives knew what the slogan meant.

Ailes showed up to the Television Critics Association's press tour in July 1996 and officially announced the name of his new channel. Before he took the stage, reporters received a handout portraying poor public opinions of the press. It was a "fake news" manifesto twenty years before Trump turned "fake news" into a mantra. The handout cited one poll where only 14 percent of respondents gave journalists positive marks and another where 67 percent said TV news was biased. Ailes said Fox News was the solution: He swore he wanted Fox reporters to "just give the viewers the facts and the information." He knew exactly what he was really doing, but he insisted, "I'm just announcing balanced and unbiased coverage. If that's traumatizing some people, so what?"

Ailes's bombastic bromides were irresistible to television critics. He was practically writing their columns for them. "He says rude, obnoxious things that make for more interesting newspaper stories," one writer admitted after the press tour appearance.

Remind you of anyone?

Ailes and Trump ran in the same New York media circles for decades. To hear Ailes tell it, "Donald and I were really quite good friends for more than twenty-five years." And to hear Trump tell it, "Roger owed me."

The two men had a lot in common: Similar fears of crime. Similarly racist views about immigration. The same generational references, since Ailes was just six years older than Trump. Both men were tail-chasers and wife-cheaters. Both had a taste for conspiracy theories. Both had paranoid streaks. And both ran their businesses as fiefdoms. With Ailes, Fox hosts were reminded to lavish him with credit whenever writing a book or giving a speech. With Trump, lieutenants were reminded that his mind wandered whenever conversations weren't about Trump.

Both men also appreciated the power of public relations— whether they were building up their own brands through puffy magazine profiles or knifing a rival in the back through a well-placed hit piece.

Trump never saw any distinction between the press and PR. Whenever he could, he used the press to score points and further his own interests. The late columnist Jimmy Breslin wrote that Trump took over news reporters in New York City "with the art of the return phone call." All it took to control the city's news media, Breslin wrote, was "two minutes of purring over the phone."

Whether Trump was talking about some personal feud or business scheme, he was always a reliable source of copy for gossip columnists who had inches to fill. And all this coverage, in turn, impressed the bankers who kept Trump afloat. Breslin said Trump was living by rules instilled by his pop: "Never use your own money. Steal a good idea and say it's your own. Do anything to get publicity. Remember that everybody can be bought."

Bought—or conned. Reporters in search of a tantalizing story sometimes took dictation from a man by the name of "John Barron," who was actually Donald Trump posing as a flack for Donald Trump. He used the alter ego to lie his way onto the *Forbes* 400 list and defend himself in the pages of *The New York Times*. The creation of "John Barron," sometimes spelled as "John Baron" with one r, was inspired by Trump's father, Fred, who used the same tactic in his own business, according to Trump biographer Michael D'Antonio.

Once Trump had first-name status in the press, Donald ditched the disguise and dished out tips to writers who gave him anonymity. Sometimes they'd describe Trump as a "source close to Trump," a technique he continued to employ while in the White House. Hannity was the foremost beneficiary.

"When he says sources, he usually means the president," a member of Hannity's inner circle told me (anonymously of course).

Hannity didn't have to tell his bosses or get approval before citing his West Wing sources. He could say whatever he wanted. On January 2, 2020, Trump briefed Hannity on the Baghdad airstrike that killed Iranian General Qassem Soleimani minutes before airtime. Hannity was on vacation, so he called in to his own show to recite what Trump had told him. Everything was attributed to "sources."

The president laundered whatever he wanted through Hannity, and the host dutifully attributed the info to unnamed "sources." In other words, Hannity borrowed from the language of journalism—by saying he had "sources" and access to special knowledge—while deriding journalism every chance he got.

Trump was equally hypocritical. He routinely implored Americans not to trust anonymously sourced reporting and claimed that members of the media maliciously made up info and attributed it to sources—at the same time he was Hannity's No. 1 anonymous source.

Lying on that level was downright pathological. But Trump had a good thing going. He had an entire galaxy of pro-Trump media operators by his side. He didn't need to play "John Barron" anymore—because he had thousands of them.

Let's rewind a little bit. Back when Trump was divorcing Marla Maples and buying the Miss Universe Organization, Ailes was building his network into a juggernaut. Launch day was October 7, 1996, complete with *Hannity & Colmes* at 9 p.m., the time slot Hannity still occupies today. Ailes poached Hannity from radioland and cast a mild-mannered liberal, Alan Colmes, as Hannity's sparring partner. Colmes also grew up on Long Island and also came out of talk radio, but that's where the similarities stopped. Hannity was the handsome patriot and Colmes was the nerd. Colmes was allowed his say . . . so long as strongman Sean was there to push back.

Fox wasn't hard-right-wing back then. The network aired news programs about health and travel and medicine and religion. You could call in to the weekend show *Pet News* and ask questions about your sick puppy. And that "sick puppy" was not slang for Bill Clinton. "We had a bit of an agenda, but we weren't crazy right wingers," former Fox host Juliet Huddy said. Hosts like Hannity were certainly tough on President Clinton during the impeachment process, and a conservative perspective was suffused throughout many of its talk shows, but it wasn't overpowering. "The other networks leaned left, and we needed to provide the other side," Huddy said.

Louis Aguirre cohosted the first show on the first day—*Fox X-press*—which went on to become *Fox & Friends*. Aguirre was twenty-nine, and it was his first time hosting a national show. He told me he was "completely oblivious that it would become what it is now."

"I was not very political at all," Aguirre said, "but neither was the show back then." It was lighthearted—"much more pop culture sprinkled with the day's news." Looking back, though, he can see how the channel's DNA was apparent on premiere day. New York City mayor Rudy Giuliani, a friend and political ally of Ailes, was the very first in-studio guest, Aguirre recalled: "I remember the entire interview was scripted, which I found strange at the time."

The September 11, 2001, terrorist attacks were a turning point for Fox. After 9/11, the network started to crush CNN in the ratings race. The Ailes-Hannity brand of macho talk and in-your-face patriotism paid off. The entire history of Fox is a series of turns to the right, and the 2003 invasion of Iraq was another one of the turns.

Ailes ruled through brute force. He wanted people to believe that he had eyes and ears everywhere, and to a frightening degree, he did. Along with a network of sycophants and informants who rose up to rat out colleagues for their own selfish reasons, Ailes had surveillance cameras all over the News Corporation building and had discreet ways to listen in on phone calls. Like Trump, he saw fear as a power source. As Trump famously told Bob Woodward, "Real power is—I don't even want to use the word—fear."

With Ailes, I saw it up close. My first time at Fox News HQ, in 2004, I was seated in a conference room with some execs, talking about my *TVNewser* blog, when Ailes charged in. He hated the way the FoxNews.com homepage was covering some long-since-forgotten scandal. "Fix the godforsaken headline!" he roared.

Ailes never understood the web, but he understood how to make a first impression. The man ruled Fox through a mixture of fear, charm, loyalty, and money. Many staffers likened the Ailes-era Fox to a cult—even the folks who liked working there.

I heard from them through the anonymous tip box at the top of my *TVNewser* website. Junior staffers sometimes sent in tips in order to get workplace problems solved, as when Fox had a serious bug infestation in the basement newsroom. When I shared their complaints on the blog, Fox brought environmental specialists into the building, and then things got even worse. Rumors ran rampant about the insecticide that they used. A technician thought it made him sick. So many employees came to me with concerns that Ailes had to come downstairs and address the newsroom. If you have a problem, he roared, take it to HR, not *TVNewser*. (Disconcerting advice, given what we know now about his abuse of women.) Ailes called me a wannabe journalist and criticized the "anonymous crap" that, he claimed, was "meant to damage us." He may as well have called it a "hoax."

Ailes's visit was a warning to stop leaking. And staffers did stop for a little while. But eventually the tips resumed, as did Ailes's preoccupation with my blog. At one point the Fox News PR department dispatched an intern to strike up a relationship with me. We went out a couple of times in New York City—we went to the late great Coffee Shop restaurant in Union Square, we rode the subway uptown, we even spent a late evening on her rooftop. There were moments when I thought these were dates—but her flirtatiousness was all part of the ruse. Years later I found out the intern was assigned to take copious notes and feed information back to her bosses. One email I viewed, dated Tuesday, September 6, 2005, was delivered at 11:30 p.m. and listed what I told her during our faux-date; who called me during dinner (a PR person from a rival network); and what I said on the phone. Early the next morning the young woman was hauled into Ailes's office because he wanted a full debrief. She was also tasked with friending me on Facebook and scouring my page for any evidence of anti-Fox bias or other material that could be used against me. All she found was funny photos of college revelry. A photo of beer spilled down my pants showed up on a rival website with the caption "TVBOOZER."

All things considered, these were sophomoric operations; more sophisticated surveillance ops and social media armies came along later. But Ailes's tactics against me showed how paranoid he was, and how much control he wanted. PR staffers were told to act like covert ops agents and engage in profoundly unethical behavior. And they did, because they were caught up in the thrill of the job, the us-against-the-world spirit of the place.

Ailes had the swagger of a man who said that he had elected three presidents. And he had standing to say it: His media strategies lifted up Nixon and Ronald Reagan and George H. W. Bush. He had tremendous power. At the same time, he waved away flatterers and critics who claimed he controlled the Republican Party. He cared about politics, but he cared most about profits. During the Obama years, Ailes quipped, "If I were running the GOP, we'd be winning."

"An invisible hand"

Fox's biggest right turn of all, triggered by the 2008 election of Barack Obama, erased Hannity's cohost Alan Colmes from the picture. One of Sean's friends put it this way: "Alan was no longer needed."

Colmes was sent off to the Siberia of Fox News Radio in the weeks after Obama's victory. Hannity was now the solo host. The pretense was going, going, gone: *Hannity & Colmes* had never been a fair fight, but at least it was a fight. Not anymore. The ascendance of a black president radicalized the network and ushered in an era with fewer left-right debates and more lectures. Hannity the star began to transform *Hannity* the show into what it is today—a nightly anti–Democratic Party attack ad for people who distrusted the nightly news.

Hannity was still second banana to Fox's other consistent prime time player, Bill O'Reilly. *The O'Reilly Factor* was the ratings leader, thanks in part to O'Reilly's bravado and in part to a simple formula that worked incredibly well: a "Talking Points Memo" monologue at the very top of the show; culture war segments with catchy names; recurring segments with curmudgeonly older men and attractive younger women; viewer emails and book recommendations at the end of the hour. We don't have to lead with the news, O'Reilly told staffers, "we lead with themes"—themes like the War on Christmas, which he introduced, which preyed on white Christian America's anxieties about multiculturalism. If viewers turned on O'Reilly's show at 8:05, or 8:40, they basically knew what they'd get, kind of like an episode of *Law & Order* or *CSI*. They could doze off for a few minutes and not be disoriented when they woke back up. Viewers liked that. They liked O'Reilly more than anyone else on Fox's air. And this fostered some serious tension between O'Reilly and Hannity. Each man bad-mouthed the other behind his back, with O'Reilly ridiculing Hannity's GOP ass-kissing and Hannity delighting in O'Reilly's failed attempt at a radio show. They almost never spoke. They hardly ever saw each other. They definitely didn't watch each other's show. But they studied each other's ratings almost as obsessively as their own. Hannity was never content with being No. 2, but there wasn't a path to No. 1 as long as O'Reilly was in the way.

Here's the most important thing to understand about TV ratings: They're one of the most addictive substances in the world. They're controlled by Nielsen, which monitors TV sets in tens of thousands of homes across the country and extrapolates total viewership from there. The Nielsen numbers are specific enough to be habit-forming but vague enough to be maddening.

Other networks are awed by Fox's ratings power. Fox News wakes up at the television equivalent of third base while its rivals are still swinging at the ball. Non-news cable channels might as well show color bars overnight. Fox's little sister channel, Fox Business, only has ten thousand viewers watching in the middle of the night. But at 4 a.m. Eastern, when daybreak still feels so far away, Fox News already has five hundred thousand people watching. And this is the low point of Fox's day. The network has a built-in base that's unlike anything else on cable. As more folks wake up and turn on the TV, the Fox News audience climbs into the millions. Plotted onto a line graph, the ratings look like a rocket taking off into orbit during the *Fox & Friends* hours. These three yardsticks tell the network's story:

1. *Total viewership at any given time.* This is a popularity and
loyalty contest. While other news viewers channel-surf
a lot or flip between CNN and MSNBC, Fox viewers are
extraordinarily loyal, to the point of falling asleep with the TV.
Fox has been No. 1 in total viewership since George W. Bush's
first full year in office. During the height of the pandemic in
March 2020, 2.2 million people watched Fox at any given
time.

2. *Cumulative viewership.* This is a channel's total reach each month. CNN has more grazers (people who watch for short periods of time) while Fox has more gorgers. In a typical month, at least 68 million people watch CNN and 63 million watch Fox for a few minutes or more. The takeaway: Cable news networks have a huge amount of power to shape the national discourse.

3. *Viewership in the twenty-five- to fifty-four-year-old demographic.* This is where the money is made. Most ad sales deals are pegged to the "demo" because advertisers want to reach moms more than grandmas. Ailes once joked that he "created a TV network for people 55 to dead," and Fox's median viewer is about sixty-seven years old. But the cable news wars are fought among the twenty-five- to fifty-four-year-olds.

Hosts like Hannity get multiple emails every day with the previous day's ratings, broken down by hourly and every-fifteen-minute increments. Sometimes they can also access minute-by-minute ratings. Many hosts stare at the ratings until the numbers start to make sense. (As a noted economist once observed, "If you torture the data enough, it will confess.") News ratings rise and fall based on the news cycle, the time of year, the weather, and what else is on TV, kind of like a giant glacier melting and refreezing. Still, hosts drive themselves crazy overanalyzing the charts.

On this point, about the obsession with ratings, your typical cable newser has an awful lot in common with the president. Trump spun the *Apprentice* ratings to tell a persuasive story about his popularity even when his audience was slipping away. I wish I hadn't thrown away the angry note that he sent me, scrawled in black Sharpie, when he accused me of shortchanging *The Apprentice* in a *New York Times* story about reality TV. I should have framed it. Trump could twist the ratings to make them say almost anything, and when that failed, he flat-out lied about them. Billy Bush recalled a day when he got fed up and called out Trump on his fabrications: "I said, 'Wait a minute, Donald, you haven't been No. 1 in five or four years, not in any category, not in any demo.' He goes, 'Well, did you see last Thursday? Last Thursday, 18–49, last five minutes!' 'Nope, still not true.' " After the cameras stopped rolling, Bush says Trump remarked "Billy, look, you just tell them and they believe it. That's it. They just do."

Inside Fox News, the ratings obsession was inescapable. It came up in almost every single one of my conversations with sources. Think about it: When a network has been winning for eighteen years, there's tremendous pressure to keep the winning streak alive no matter what. Getting tired of winning, if I may borrow a phrase from Trump, is never an option. Some shows held daily staff meetings to study the numbers. "Ratings are the only thing that matters," a Fox veteran said matter-of-factly. The Nielsens are like "an invisible hand," pushing everyone in a rightward direction, another said.

On October 6, 2011, I tagged along when Hannity went on the road for a special show in Atlanta, where Fox installed a temporary stage in Centennial Park for hundreds of his biggest fans. He was there to celebrate Fox's fifteenth anniversary and its victories over the competition. Hannity welcomed the crowd by gesturing over to the CNN world HQ building across the street and asking, "Do you think it's any coincidence that the CNN logo is in the background?" His fans cheered.

Fox was chugging along at the time. Obama was president and Fox was the network of choice for Obama haters. Ailes was the prototypical viewer—an aging white male pissed off about progressives trying to change the aging-white-male-dominated country he cherished. He told everybody who would listen that he was trying to protect and defend America. Fox News and Fox Business were his weapons.

"For Roger, journalism was . . . It was a means to an end," his onetime protégé JP Lindsley said.

In 2009 Lindsley went from an assistant job at *The Weekly Standard* magazine to editing the Ailes family's local newspapers in the Hudson Valley. Ailes treated Lindsley like an adult son (perhaps because his actual son, Zac, was still just in middle school) and let Lindsley live in the family's guest home—until "Ailes Jr." had a falling out with the family and resigned in dramatic fashion in 2011.

Ailes "loved to be the puppet master," Lindsley said. "He saw himself as a chieftain of the Republicans, like it was his job to determine the best candidates."

Lindsley insisted that Ailes appreciated journalism, and understood the standards and ethics that get drilled into J-School 101 students, "but he would override those concerns by saying 'this is for the good of the Republic.' That's how he would justify excursions outside journalistic boundaries." Take Fox's relentless campaign against Obama. "He really, truly thought President Obama was a really sinister, bad guy," Lindsley said. "He really did believe that the president was not born in the United States." But, interestingly, these beliefs only came out in private conversations. Ailes never ordered the network to go full birther. On the contrary, he would tell his hosts to knock it off. I can attest to that firsthand. In 2009 I had the unenviable task of writing the first story in *The New York Times* about "birtherism." I pointed out that Lou Dobbs, then a CNN host, was raising the citizenship issue, and several MSNBC shows were mocking it, while Fox hardly addressed it at all. The point was that Ailes was capable of restraint when he thought it served his network's interests. In this case, he didn't want Fox to be lumped in with Dobbs and the right-wing fever swamps of the internet. Fox was more powerful, he knew, when it was grouped with NBC and CBS. Besides, Fox's base already suspected Obama was a foreigner. There was no need to say the obvious and racist part out loud. (Years later, though, he hired Dobbs to juice the ratings for Fox Business.)

The Tea Party was an early test of Fox's political mobilizing power. Democrats took power; a black man moved into the Oval Office; a woman became the House Speaker; and Fox's biggest stars suddenly stood up and said *stop spending our money.* Of course, the organizers swore that the movement was all about reining in spending and reducing government, regardless of color or gender. Hannity and Glenn Beck promoted Tea Party events across the country and pushed ahead to a special day of live coverage on Tax Day. "Anybody can come," Hannity said. "Celebrate with Fox News," Beck said. The rallies drew large crowds and mirrored Fox's older, almost-all-white audience. Harvard researchers said Fox served as a "social movement orchestrator," spreading the word and cheering the Tea Party on. It was a perfect with-us-or-against-us emblem. After a follow-up rally in DC in September, Ailes bought a full-page ad in *The Washington Post* asking, "How did ABC, CBS, NBC, MSNBC and CNN miss this story?" That was a lie, of course; the rally was widely covered by all the networks. But Fox needed to present itself as the One Real True Source. Murdoch denied reality when he said, years later, "We don't promote the Tea Party. That's bullshit." He claimed Fox merely "recognized their existence." But the coverage went much further than that. The posturing, the appeals to white identity politics, the screams about media bias—all of it was a foreshock to the Trump quake. I couldn't help but notice that ten years after the first "party," when Trump's tax cuts and policies caused the deficit to balloon to historic levels, there wasn't any heartland uprising or "Hannity" tea-bagging.

At the height of the Tea Party's perceived power, I interviewed Paul Rittenberg, the head of ad sales at Fox, who articulated his pitch to advertisers. "People who watch Fox News believe it's the home team," he said. He wasn't labeling the network as "conservative" or calling Fox the voice of the opposition, the way pissed-off Obama aides were, he was just reflecting the point of view of the audience. "Home team." It was powerful, and pure tribalism.

Conventional wisdom at Fox was that it was more fun and more profitable to be on offense, against Democrats, than on defense with Republicans. It's easier to be "against" than "for" something. Negative partisanship was the winning potion. Every year, I wrote another story for the *Times* about CNN floundering in this newly competitive landscape, with Fox winning on the right and MSNBC on the left. The big on-air rivalry of the era was between O'Reilly and MSNBC's Keith Olbermann. But the stakes weren't really that high—it wasn't like Obama was getting policy ideas from Olbermann. The country wasn't being run by a shadow cable news government. How quaint.

Looking back, though, I can see that the Trump seeds were being planted in Fox.

"In Fox's early days," a former anchor said, "it was like professional wrestling. It was all predetermined. 'I'll say this, and then you say that.'" But the anchor noticed a change in the green-room pre-gaming: "Once Obama took office, guests of different political stripes were less genial off-camera. Segments became less choreographed, with the conservative invariably taking an extreme line of attack that went beyond the established norms of political punditry."

The barbs were so much more personal. After one heated exchange on Obamacare, the anchor sighed, feeling like he had failed to keep the discussion civil. He stepped outside to get some fresh air, and bumped into the conservative guest that he'd just been trying to corral ten minutes earlier.

"That worked well," the guest said. "Did you like that?"

"Yeah, I guess," the anchor responded. "It just feels sometimes like instead of informing people, cable news is inciting them."

Millions of people shared his concerns about the damage caused by cable news food fights. Jon Stewart once called cable TV a "24-hour political-pundit, perpetual-panic conflictinator." Cable did not cause our problems, Stewart said, "but its existence makes solving them that much harder."

That's how this anchor was feeling, but his chipper guest walked away, just happy to have had a few precious minutes of airtime. Less than an hour later, the anchor's agent called, sounding distressed. He got right to the point.

"Are you unhappy to be working at Fox?"

"No."

"Then why the fuck are you complaining about it?"

"I'm not," the anchor insisted. "What are you talking about?"

"Roger called and screamed at me that you're bad-mouthing Fox."

"Shit," the anchor said. He instantly remembered what he'd said outside. The guest must have turned around and called Ailes. The anchor and agent came up with a solution: a mushy, gushy handwritten note to Ailes, telling him how grateful the anchor was to be working for him at Fox.

"I'm convinced it saved my job," he told me. "And I never again opened my mouth to anyone in the office unless it was to talk about my children, sports, or the weather."

• • •

For Juliet Huddy, the Obama years were a wake-up call about Fox and Ailes's true agenda. "It became just a constant barrage of anti-Obama—criticizing Obama just nonstop," she recalled. "There was no room for objectivity."

During her time on Fox's morning show, Huddy felt like the hosts were expected to perform like puppets, and it infuriated her. The segments and angles and guests were all generally chosen by the producers, not the anchors. Hosts could go off-script, but that pissed off the producers, who had already set the show's broader narrative. The lack of control "was always really difficult and frustrating for me," Huddy said.

The prime time shows were much more talent-driven, with hosts like Hannity calling the shots. But the morning and daytime shows were largely producer-driven, to the chagrin of men and women like Huddy, who felt like she had to edit the pre-written questions and teases on the fly. A dozen different Fox hosts and commentators told similar stories about how boxed in they felt.

"Endless amounts of airtime were really dangerous," one said, which was striking to hear because most people in the TV biz want more, more, more airtime. But this person walked away from *Fox & Friends* wanting less. "We had no time to read what was next in the prompter," they said.

And this is the hyperpartisan television factory that, in the Trump age, wound up producing the president's daily intelligence briefing.

"Mayor of Crazytown"

Here's what everyone should understand about Fox's relationship with Trump, a former *Fox & Friends* producer said: "People think he's calling up *Fox & Friends* and telling us what to say. Hell no. It's the opposite. We tell *him* what to say."

Fox & Friends was the three-hour us-versus-them bitch session that embodied everything that Fox fans loved and critics lamented about the network. Ever since the show's launch day in 1998, the *F&F* set has looked largely the same: Steve Doocy has sat on one side of the curvy couch, and Brian Kilmeade has sat on the other side, with a beautiful woman in between. The woman has changed four times: First E. D. Hill, then Miss America 1989 Gretchen Carlson, then *Survivor* contestant and former *The View* cohost Elisabeth Hasselbeck, and now Ainsley Earhardt. So in other words, the woman comes and goes while the men stay the same.

The show's dynamic is plain to see: Kilmeade is the everyman. Doocy is the comic. Earhardt is the Southern belle. The trio is paid at least $2 million a year, each, to entertain Trump and 2 million other viewers. Given that *F&F* makes well north of $100 million a year in advertising, and how much influence the show wields, the hosts probably deserve more money. Because as *F&F* goes, so goes the Fox audience, and so goes the GOP. Scandals are conceived on this couch. Conspiracy theories are floated and then amplified. The talking points that start here end up in Trump's mouth and in newspaper columns and fundraising emails and the Facebook feeds of countless Fox addicts.

Morning TV is about companionship. That's what Dave Garroway understood when he launched the *Today* show in 1952. It's what Bryant Gumbel and Katie Couric and Charlie Gibson and Diane Sawyer all understood. And it's what Ailes grasped when he cast the "Friends." Viewers are at their most vulnerable in the morning—half-awake, half-dressed, sometimes half-sober and half-alive. Unlike other programs, these shows have to be consistent and comforting. *F&F* delivers that, complete with cooking segments and playful competitions out on the plaza, nicknamed Fox Square. When fans are watching, they want to be a part of the show. They want to be there. And one lucky viewer—Trump—got to be. Because Ailes turned Trump into a political pundit in March of 2011.

At the time, Trump was pushing his racist birther lie while testing the waters for a 2012 presidential run. Ailes tested something too: a Trump call-in segment on *Fox & Friends*. On March 28, the hosts teed up Trump to irresponsibly fearmonger about Obama's birthplace. Gretchen Carlson looked skeptical, but the men went right along with Trump's lies. Doocy even took a shot at the news media, telling Trump, "They're trying to paint you as the mayor of Crazytown for bringing this up."

More like president of Crazytown, but okay.

Fox hosts were still forbidden from going full birther themselves, but they were free to interview Trump about it. Kilmeade wrapped the interview nonsensically: "Donald Trump, who we all know was born in this country, all you have to do is read the side of his building." Huh? Doocy, seizing a chance to suck up some more, said, "Which one!" These two were falling over each other to be Trump's wingmen. Carlson didn't play along, but she didn't loudly protest either. She stayed at the network for another four years.

This, it turned out, was the first episode of "Monday Mornings with Trump," a weekly segment that changed the course of American politics. Ailes even ordered up TV promos for the segment. "Bold, brash, and never bashful, the Donald now makes his voice loud and clear every Monday on Fox," the announcer said. Trump loved it. He was ticked off that people weren't taking his political gambits seriously, and the segment helped him change that by giving him a direct connection with the conservative base. Through the weekly calls, he got to know Ailes's priorities. He got to know

Fox's priorities. He got to know the people who became his voters. And they got to know him.

For all the justified scrutiny of *The Apprentice* as a platform for Trump's eventual presidential run, *Fox & Friends* was even more powerful. Trump alluded to this, years later, in an interview for a documentary: "I'm not sure that I ever would have been standing at this very powerful, important, even sacred spot—the Rose Garden in front of the Oval Office at the White House—if it wasn't for Roger."

Looking back at Trump's tweets, a campaign foundation was being laid. "I will be doing *Fox & Friends* in 10 minutes at 7.00. Many things to talk about! ENJOY," he tweeted one day in 2014 to his 2.6 million followers. A tweeter replied, "The fact that Fox likes Trump so much is clear indication he should never be President." But dozens of fans also replied and urged Trump to run. This happened every week. Some of his Twitter cheerleaders were sock puppet accounts, designed to make it look like he had more support than he did. But some of the cheering *was* authentic, including from the hosts on the *Fox & Friends* couch. Through the topics chosen by producers, through the coaching of the hosts, and through the feedback on Twitter, Trump learned how to be the Fox News president.

Most Monday mornings, Trump was just half a mile away from Fox's studio, in Trump Tower, but he usually called in rather than joining in person, like every other guest was expected to do. Ailes didn't really mind. Trump's voice was enough to keep people watching. And for Trump, calling in made him seem hard to get, busy, and important.

"Ailes was always trying to test people," Lindsley said, "to see who might be good." He wondered if that's what the Trump call-in segments were about. Trump's willingness to throw bombs and stoke hatred of Obama sure kept people watching. The birther smear helped cement the impression of Obama as a foreigner in the minds of millions of viewers, wedded Trump to the Fox base, and foreshadowed Trump and Fox's full-throated embrace of white identity politics. It was pivotal. But he dropped the crusade when NBC advised him that *Apprentice* ratings could suffer if he kept it up. Years later, when I interviewed Trump on the phone during the campaign in June 2016, he tried to wave away my questions about his birther beliefs.

"I don't ever talk about it," Trump said. "You know why I don't talk about it? Because once I talk about it, that's all they want to write about."

Blaming the media for scrutinizing *his* racist smear! Now that's a twist.

"People don't care if it's right"

"Monday Mornings with Trump" often made news, of the did-he-really-just-say-that variety, but *Fox & Friends* was never much of an attention magnet before the 2016 election.

"We were like a backwater, even within Fox," a former *F&F* producer said. "Other shows didn't respect us," another staffer affirmed. *F&F* was perpetually understaffed and underappreciated. News anchors like Shep Smith rolled their eyes at the a.m. shenanigans. Still, staffers knew that management cared a lot about the show, because Ailes called the control room incessantly. The show reflected Ailes's hatred of Obama, fear of Muslims, and comfort with white male dominance. Ailes wouldn't explicitly tell the hosts what to say, but he made sure they knew what he thought, and that was enough. "The three chatterboxes," as the former producer dubbed the hosts, knew how to frame stories that Ailes wanted to promote and knew how to ignore inconvenient stories altogether.

This former producer had a lot of bruises from his time working on the show, and a lot of regrets. He said he felt himself being brainwashed while watching and creating the show simultaneously. "All I did was read conservative outlets and right-wing media," he said. "For *years*." He voted for Obama, but once "they did such a good job destroying Hillary Clinton, I decided I wouldn't vote for her," he admitted. He cited the obsession with the so-called "Clinton email server scandal" as a prime example.

He wondered what would happen if Fox's biggest fans went through the same sort of process he did—quitting Fox and turning off the network and all of its like-minded sources. "People don't care if it's right, they just want their side to win. That's who this show is for," he said. "It's sad."

Producers and writers at *F&F* viewed the morning show as the inverse of a newspaper's front section—the editorial page in the back of the paper was the front page of *Fox & Friends*, consuming most of the show. News headlines were tucked away and usually delegated to a newscaster. But even those headlines were written in such a way so as to appeal to the audience. One day, a staffer who wrote a few simple lines of copy about White Castle introducing vegan burgers was castigated by her superior. What did she do wrong? She positioned the new meat-free option as a positive thing, an improvement to the menu.

"No," the head writer told her, "we hate this."

Vegan burgers? They're part of the "war on meat," which, I swear, is an actual phrase that's been uttered on Fox more than once.

"You need to say this is ridiculous," the boss added.

When unexplainable idiocy came out of the mouths of *F&F* hosts, this was part of the reason why. The straight-out-of-school writers had to unlearn journalism skills and reflect a right-wing world view that didn't always come naturally.

I peeked at the research packets that were prepared for the hosts. Some of the show's sources of information were predictable—Fox's website, ABC, *The Hill*, *Politico*—but the *F&F* packets also contained lots of sensational links to *TMZ* and the *Daily Mail* and plenty of stories from hard-right sites like *Breitbart*. What tended to get *F&F* in trouble, the producer said, was the *Breitbart*-type stuff that Ailes wanted—the stuff that seemed too outrageous to be true. Then came the lectures from senior producers: "What the hell? You have to get confirmation on these things."

"When they say 'we can't keep messing things up,' what they really mean is 'we can't keep getting caught,' " the former producer said.

Multiple staffers lamented the existence of a Twitter account called @BadFoxGraphics, which existed to catch the show's typos and other screwups. A famous example was the banner that said "TRUMP CUTS AID TO 3 MEXICAN COUNTRIES," when the news was about three Central American countries. Staffers feared the ire of @BadFoxGraphics. It was a rare bit of accountability for a network that acted untouchable.

The former producer came up with ways to block out his embarrassment about the programming—like looking at the balance in his bank account. "We provide entertainment to a certain group of people who like a certain kind of thing," he told himself to justify the unsubstantiated takes. It always came back around to the audience. "We were deathly afraid of our audience leaving, deathly afraid of pissing them off," he said. "But we also laughed at them. We disrespected them. We weren't practicing what we preached."

This "do as I say, not as I do" attitude was one of the first things the producer noticed when he started working for *F&F*. Anti-marijuana segments were a layup on the show. Then he headed to a house party with colleagues for the first time and saw half the staff out on the balcony getting high. "Okay," he said to himself, "so we don't really believe all this stuff. We just tell other people to believe it."

"You know what we need," a senior producer of *Fox & Friends* told her staff during a rare dip in the ratings. "We need outrage."

That's really what *F&F* was about. Certain segments were designed to instill fear; others, to stoke hate; others, less often, to spark love. And the hosts were encouraged to ask viewers for feedback to confirm that the segments were having the intended effect. Gavin Hadden, the executive producer, sometimes had the foxfriends@foxnews.com inbox up in a window on his computer in the control room to monitor responses as the seconds rolled by. Had the viewers had enough of Geraldo yet? If so, wrap him! It was the closest thing to Choose Your Own Adventure on TV.

Hadden was one of the most important people at Fox that no one outside Fox ever heard about. He joined *F&F* in 2006, when Gretchen Carlson was the female cohost, and worked his way up to the top spot by proving he knew "what works" and what doesn't. What works:

- Stories about undocumented immigrants killing Americans
- Stories about citizens standing up to the government bureaucracy
- Stories about college students disrespecting the flag
- Stories about hate crime hoaxes
- Stories about liberal media outlets suppressing the truth
- And, whenever possible, stories involving attractive women (They could be the hero or the villain, it didn't matter, but they had to be attractive.)

"Job one is to titillate the audience," the former producer said. "For celebrity stories, I had to pick the sexiest photos. And then I'd still hear, 'Can you find hotter photos of her?' Sigh. Okay, we'll spend another thousand bucks on three photos from Getty." It got to the point where the producer knew, without being told, which specific photos of Angelina Jolie the execs would expect to see. This sexualized approach spilled over to other parts of the show. If it was a quiet news day and the producers needed to fill a spare block, "we would look and see, what are the locals doing?" Fox tapped into its network of stations in big cities all across the country. "Then we would Google around to find the hottest reporter." Workers striking in Detroit or rush hour flooding in Houston? Sometimes that's how the editorial call was made.

"You have to understand how completely sexualized Fox is," a former star said. What was visible to viewers on the air also affected the culture off the air.

Sex is what Ailes wanted, and sex is what he got. He used his power to enforce the short skirts and "leg cams" and exploitative segments that kept men watching. He also abused his power by preying on dozens of women, including Gretchen Carlson, who hatched a plan to hold him accountable. Ailes's downfall would coincide with Trump's takeover of the American right.

"Planet Trump"

Until the moment the twice-divorced reality TV star, pageant owner, former casino operator, real estate developer announced his candidacy, the political class doubted he'd actually run for president. Whenever he threatened to jump into the race, it was dismissed as a stunt designed to juice the ratings for *The Apprentice*.

But close watchers of Fox News could tell that Trump was serious in June of 2015. Trump's media handler Hope Hicks arranged a series of pre-launch interviews with Fox to put the words "Trump" and "president" in close proximity over and over again, leading up to the big day, June 16.

We all know the story by now: the golden escalator, the unexpected announcement, the rambling address, the bystanders who were paid to stand there and cheer. Trump's presidential launch speech was a TV show, just like the rest of his campaign. When I step back and look at it five years later, I see striking similarities to the start of Fox News. Both launches were mocked by insiders and embraced by outsiders. Both were backed by deep-pocketed men and driven by an underdog sensibility. Both Trump and Ailes were right-wingers in the blue heart of midtown Manhattan. Trump positioned himself to fill the same sort of void in politics that Fox filled on TV.

Some of Fox's stars caught on to this symmetry early. For all the ridicule of the newfound campaign, even on Fox's airwaves, Trump's run was embraced by a subset of Republicans who believed he was selling something special. While others heard a rambling and racist campaign speech, 5 p.m. cohost Kimberly Guilfoyle heard a rousing call to arms. "It was like *The LEGO Movie*, the theme song 'Everything Is Awesome.' It really got me excited. I felt richer just listening to him!" Guilfoyle exclaimed while the control room re-racked the tape of Trump gliding down the escalator for the umpteenth time.

Guilfoyle, who was once the first lady of San Francisco through her marriage to the city's mayor, Democrat Gavin Newsom, was tapped by Ailes in 2006 to be a weekend host and legal analyst. Guilfoyle was mighty hungry for airtime. "Kimberly's an avatar," a Fox insider said. "If MSNBC offered her a better gig with more money, she'd be a raging liberal."

Guilfoyle maintained that she'd always been a registered Republican. She occupied what was known as the "leg chair" on the set of *The Five*, and it was a prime perch from which to be noticed by Trump. "Let's see" what happens, she said on launch day, already sounding like Trump. "I don't know. I think it will be fun!"

"I get it, that he's entertaining," cohost Dana Perino said, piping in with the GOP establishment position. Perino, the former Bush 43 press secretary, scoffed at Trump and wondered how long his stunt would last. Come on, she said, prodding her cohosts, "you're gonna build a wall and you're gonna make Mexico pay for it?" She pushed the show's satirist Greg Gutfeld: "On what planet could that actually happen?"

"Planet Trump," Gutfeld replied.

Gutfeld looked at Trump very skeptically, but noticed something Fox-y about the topics Trump hit in his speech. "He did ISIS, Obamacare, immigration, Bowe Bergdahl," Gutfeld said. "He did the *Five* rundown!"

Yes he did. The merger was officially underway. But Fox was not the Trump Channel right away—in fact, the newfound candidate was a source of tension inside the network. Trump's weekly segment on *Fox & Friends* was tabled the day he entered the presidential race. Ailes told him he couldn't appear to be playing favorites among declared candidates. Ailes was a Bush guy at heart, having worked so closely with H.W. decades earlier. According to Ailes's confidants, he favored Jeb Bush early on in the primary season. He also told his New Jersey neighbors that he was pulling for Chris Christie.

The kingmaker didn't want to make or break anyone this early on. He wanted to watch the race unfold on his own network. Trump tweeted out a thank-you to the "Friends" for the "long and successful run we had together," showing his respect for the platform and his belief that he'd helped the show's ratings. He still called in, but now for campaign interviews, which were effectively the same thing. He bashed his rivals, bragged about his polls, and live-tweeted along with the show. *F&F* was the closest Trump could come to crawling inside the TV set and living *on* television. He said whatever he wanted to say, no matter how unhinged, and only received the gentlest responses.

But he wanted even more. He began to badger the Fox refs by tweeting his complaints about commentators who weren't Trumpy enough, from Juan Williams on the left to Karl Rove on the right, and by retweeting fans who warned Fox to fall in line. He felt that powerful forces were aligned against him—and he wasn't entirely wrong about that. When his campaign began, Rupert Murdoch claimed to detest him. Murdoch was always more of a Paul Ryan or Jeb Bush kind of Republican. He wanted comprehensive immigration reform and tax cuts and relaxed regulations, not "Mexicans are rapists" rhetoric. In mid-July, Murdoch tweeted, "When is Donald Trump going to stop embarrassing his friends, let alone the whole country?" Behind the scenes, Murdoch tried to prop up contenders like Ben Carson, who prepped for his 2016 run by being a paid pundit on Fox. And Murdoch urged others, like Michael Bloomberg, to step into the ring and challenge Trump as well. So much for that.

But the aging mogul also respected the reasons why Trump's rants resonated. Trump almost immediately polled at the front of the crowded pack, which meant he was important to Murdoch and Fox. And Trump was preoccupied by Fox's coverage of his campaign, which meant he was frequently on the phone with Ailes, complaining. Most of his gripes were about Megyn Kelly.

The host of *The Kelly File* was Fox's No. 1 rising star. Kelly branded herself as a free-thinker in contrast to O'Reilly's faux folksiness and Hannity's blind partisanship. She knew to stand on the side of Fox's viewers, yes, which meant insisting Santa is white amid heaps of social media mockery, but she was also willing to buck the system. She wanted to be unpredictable. Uncontrollable. And she was succeeding like no one at Fox ever had. Over the course of a decade, she transformed from an unhappy lawyer to a bona fide television star. Her career trajectory was the stuff of TV news dreams: from bottom-of-the-ladder general assignment reporter to Supreme Court correspondent to mid-morning co-anchor to host of her very own two-hour afternoon show. Kelly was everywhere: She was a regular on *The O'Reilly Factor*. She anchored election night. And in 2013, Ailes moved her to prime time.

Almost immediately, *The Kelly File* at 9 p.m. was one of the hottest shows on cable. The talk show tilted right but got good press for Kelly's surprising "independent" moments. It was a win all around: for Kelly, for Ailes, for the Fox ad sales execs. The only loser was O'Reilly, who hated seeing Kelly challenge him in the 25–54 demo.

O'Reilly publicly claimed to stand up for Kelly, and she said she respected him too, but they sniped at each other's shows at every turn. O'Reilly resented her good press and her relationships with Rupert and Lachlan. Kelly mocked O'Reilly's "looking out for you" shtick and his lackadaisical approach. (He taped his show several hours ahead of time, while she was live.) Execs dreaded the end of the month because O'Reilly would argue over the ratings results. If Kelly was No. 1 in the demo, he would come up with a reason to say it shouldn't count. The way O'Reilly saw things, he had made Kelly a star by giving her airtime on his show. "*The Kelly File* was formed from me!" he groused. Ailes laughed away O'Reilly's bellyaching: "He thinks he made her a star? No, I made her a fucking star."

"I thought you were my friend"

"What did you do to piss off Trump?"

Ailes was on the phone with Kelly. He knew the answer to his question, but he wanted to hear Kelly's side of the story. It was July 29, 2015, and the night before Kelly had led with a segment about Trump's 1991 contentious divorce from Ivana. Kelly confronted a *Daily Beast* reporter who had just written a story about the time Ivana testified under oath that Trump raped her. Kelly, pointing out that Ivana later recanted, seemed to take Trump's side in the segment, but Trump was still furious that Kelly covered it at all. Ailes suggested that Kelly give the candidate a call to smooth things over.

She did, but it didn't help.

"O'Reilly didn't put it on *his* show," Trump thundered through the receiver. He screamed at Kelly, threatened to unleash his "beautiful Twitter account" against her, and hung up.

The first GOP primary debate of the season was one week away. And Kelly was one of the moderators.

The August 6 debate is remembered as a point of enormous pride inside Fox. To this day it is the highest-rated program in the network's history, with 24 million viewers. Naturally, Trump took credit for every eyeball. Outside Fox, the debate is mostly remembered as the trigger for an epic Trump rage bender.

Murdoch was pleased to see Trump challenged on stage. Ailes was not. When Kelly asked her infamous question about Trump's disparaging treatment of women, Ailes sat up and said "What the fuck is that?"

Contrary to many people's suspicions, he was not pulling the debate strings. He wasn't even in the control room; he was watching the debate on the couch at home. Right after it ended, his phone rang. Trump was furious. "I thought you were my friend, Roger," he said, before lighting into Kelly. Her sin this time? Quoting Trump's own words back to him: "You've called women you don't like 'fat pigs,' 'dogs,' 'slobs,' and 'disgusting animals' . . ."

According to Kelly, Ailes objected to the "fat pigs" question and told her, "No more female empowerment stuff!" Others in Ailes's orbit said he didn't object to the question, per se, but to the order of the questions—he thought it was the wrong way to start the debate. Now he knew he was going to be warring with Trump for the foreseeable future. And he was exhausted just thinking about it.

Trump's campaign-within-the-campaign started minutes after the debate, when he walked by Kelly's live shot location and yelled "Megyn Kelly is not nice!" His rant continued all night long. "Wow, @megynkelly really bombed tonight," he tweeted at 3:40 in the morning, still amped up about his performance and still pissed off at her completely fair questions. "People are going wild on twitter! Funny to watch." He retweeted people who called her a "biased" "overrated" "bimbo." His lawyer Michael Cohen retweeted an account that called for a boycott and said "we can gut her." This misogynistic behavior justified the very question that Trump was so mad about.

Ailes worked the phones the next day while touring the Civil War battlefields of Gettysburg with his son. He deployed Hannity and his No. 2 exec, Bill Shine, to, in the words of one source, "just get it to stop." But no one could. Twenty-four hours after the debate, in a phone interview with CNN's Don Lemon, Trump implied Kelly was having her period ("blood coming out of her wherever") and called her every name in the book. Journalists at Fox were disgusted. Ailes was too, on a personal level, but he took a measured approach. He had Kelly in one ear, expecting Fox to back her up, and Trump in the other ear, demanding that Kelly get in line or be thrown off the air.

Megyn or Donald? Megyn or Donald?

Ailes was loyal to his talent.

But he also liked the Trump show.

Ailes stayed silent and Shine directed other anchors not to de-fend Kelly. What Ailes wanted was peace. He knew that "war" would cause further threats against Kelly and would drive a wedge between the GOP's leading candidate and its leading network. So he tried to calm Trump down in a phone call, and his magic worked for a few days, but then it wore off and Trump started up again. Every so often, when Trump resumed the cyberbullying, Ailes had to hit back. One of his knock-it-off-Donald statements called Trump's behavior disturbing, crude, and unacceptable. Another time he said Trump "doesn't seem to grasp that candidates telling journalists what to ask is not how the media works in this country."

To most people, Trump's attacks were meaningless. Look to the ratings for proof: Kelly's audience barely budged when Trump told America to stop watching. If anything, his attacks stirred more in-terest in her show. But among Trump's super-fans, his words were dogma. His insults stoked enough hate and fury to make Kelly's life miserable. Her family had to bring an armed bodyguard along to Walt Disney World. Her daughter, Yardley, said she was afraid of Trump because "he wants to hurt me." In response to Trump's boycott call, Fox News PR boss Irena Briganti wrote Fox's stron-gest statement yet, decrying Trump's "deplorable" abuse: "Donald Trump's vitriolic attacks against Megyn Kelly and his extreme, sick obsession with her is beneath the dignity of a presidential candidate who wants to occupy the highest office in the land."

I miss that version of Fox—the version that stood up to Trump and schooled him about the media. The truth is that many longtime Fox execs miss it too. Standing up to bullies and defending free speech is in the Fox News DNA. But those traits regressed due to the company's business interests. "Roger was really terrified of los-ing the *Breitbart* wing of Fox's audience," an insider explained. He could feel that the Fox base was pulling for Trump. That's why, in hindsight, the GOP primary season was the beginning of the end of Kelly's time at Fox, and the beginning of Fox's "deference to Donald," as one anchor described it.

Trump wanted full control. He wanted to tell journalists what to ask. He was already getting away with it on air with his friendliest "interviewers," so why couldn't he tell others? In private, he actively played Fox hosts off each other. For Trump, the First Amendment was always about putting him "first." If you're pro-Trump news, you're good. If you cross Trump, you're bad, and as of 2016, "fake," and as of 2018, a "hoax."

This was a direct result of his narcissism. In business, it was innocuous enough, but in politics, it became downright dangerous, because he modeled anti-media behavior that cast a chill on press freedom all around the world. Aspiring autocrats from Brazil to Malaysia took inspiration from Trump as they passed "fake news" and "false news" laws to suppress investigative reporting.

On one level this was ironic because Trump lived and died on media attention, especially from "elites." That's why he cared so much about Kelly's show. He could tell she was a huge star beyond the conservative media universe that Fox inhabited. Kelly was the first Fox News host ever to appear on the cover of *Vanity Fair*. Trump thought Melania should be on there. He wanted to be wooed and respected by magazine editors and assorted media bigwigs.

Trump's media relationships were so transactional that you could move from bad to good in the space of a minute. I noticed this when I conversed with Trump at the TIME 100 gala. On *Reliable Sources* I scrutinized his loose relationship with the truth every week; no one could mistake *Reliable* for a pro-Trump talk show. But when Trump saw me, he smiled and pointed and said, "Good show. Good numbers." He meant the ratings, which were way up thanks to campaign coverage. I took it as an attempt at flattery. The TIME gala was on a Tuesday, which meant there were primary races underway in five states. I showed him some of the latest results on my iPhone. He was winning by 50 percent, 60 percent—and "don't forget," he said, "that's with three people" in the race. Well-wishers oohed and ahhed at the results. He asked me to refresh the screen. This black tie affair was exactly what Trump wanted—he had a throng of politicos and TV anchors and stars crowding around him. He never even touched his dinner. "I'm trying to book him!" Gayle King shouted. A reporter from Page Six scribbled notes. Before Trump left, he looked at me again. "Keep it up. I love your show."

THE CANDIDATE

"He's out of control"

It is hard to imagine now, but there once was a time when Rupert Murdoch sternly told Trump to "calm down."

The date was February 18, 2016. The octogenarian mogul was gradually giving up on Jeb and giving in to Trump. His reluctance was palpable for all to read on Twitter. When Trump flipped out at Kelly after the first debate, Rupert defended Fox's moderation and said "friend Donald has to learn this is public life." On December 15, 2015, he tweeted that Donald "seems to be getting even more thin skinned!" He wondered, "Is flying around the country every day tiring him?"

All campaign season long, aboard Trump Force One and atop Trump Tower, the candidate watched Fox to get talking points, used Fox to vanquish his rivals, and complained about Fox to manipulate the coverage. He was constantly on the phone with Ailes ranting about perceived slights, which Rupert then heard about.

"You're showing the wrong polls!"

"When are you going to fire Karl Rove?"

"Why is Megyn such a bitch?"

And he ranted in public too. On February 17, 2016, he claimed Fox didn't want him to win. The next day he accused Murdoch of rigging a scientific poll. That's when Rupert talked down to Donald like a grandparent soothing a toddler.

"Time to calm down," Rupert tweeted. He observed that if he was running an "anti-Trump conspiracy" then he was doing a "lousy job!"

Rupert "always craved a relationship with the U.S. president. And he really craved it when it could help his business," according to a family friend. Rupert wanted the ability to strut into the Oval Office at a moment's notice. He wanted the state dinner invites and the policy briefings. Trump could be his ticket, if only the fellow could settle down.

If only.

Trump continued to come up with new ways to attack Kelly. Fox execs fumed—at Trump, at the RNC for not corralling the guy, and at the press for delighting in the so-called "feud." They weren't feuding—Trump was just wildly thrashing around, trying to cull Kelly from the Fox herd and make an example out of her. Almost every week during the primaries, I heard from a Fox exec or anchor who groused about the GOP front-runner.

"He's nuts," one Fox exec complained to me.

"He's out of control," said another.

"Fuck him," said a third exec.

But their complaints rang hollow for this reason: Whenever Trump wasn't pissing on Fox and Fox producers weren't cursing over him, he was live with Hannity or O'Reilly or Greta Van Susteren or *Fox & Friends* or *Special Report* or *Fox News Sunday*. And his rallies were being carried live on Fox and all across cable TV. His campaign was fought mostly on television, with the rallies serving as elaborate stages for the show.

Kelly noticed all the interviews and rallies and live shots. She felt like Ailes did the bare minimum to defend her. Other insiders saw it the same way. Ailes, on the other hand, wasn't sure what more Kelly expected from him. He was like an ego juggler, having to keep up with a dozen multimillionaire stars and Trump too, and he wasn't as nimble as he used to be. For all the talk of him as an all-powerful and sinister force in politics, what was not well understood is that he was, according to ex-employees and even friends, "losing it" in his final few years. "It was so sad, seeing him lose his fastball," one confidant said. He simply didn't have much fight left.

And his history of abuse was finally, *finally* catching up with him.

"Me too"

When Gretchen Carlson sued Roger Ailes on July 6, 2016, Trump thought the lawsuit was a hoax.

It turned out to be a history-maker.

With one bold legal filing, Carlson exposed Ailes's predatory tactics, dragged Fox News into the twenty-first century, affected Trump's presidential race, and lit the match that led to the modern-day #MeToo movement. The Ailes scandal led *The New York Times* to look more deeply into Bill O'Reilly, which led other *Times* reporters to ask around about Harvey Weinstein, and now Weinstein is behind bars and the world is at least a little bit more equitable.

Here's the part of the story almost nobody knows: The plan stretched back many years. Carlson's suit accused her former co-host Steve Doocy of "severe and pervasive" sexual harassment too. Somehow Fox has successfully memory-holed this part of her complaint—as far as I can tell, the claims against Doocy were never thoroughly investigated. But Carlson said Doocy's misconduct went on for years. In fact, it's the first thing she brought up when she called attorney Martin Hyman in 2014.

By then, she was off *Fox & Friends*. In 2013 Ailes bumped her from the morning show and gave her the 2 p.m. hour. In case it wasn't clear enough that this was a demotion, he also cut her pay. Carlson tried to make the most of it, and she booked Trump as her inaugural guest, leveraging her a.m. show connection from his weekly phone calls. "Gretchen will be a big success!" he tweeted. Well, sort of. Carlson held her own, but at one of the lowest-rated times of day. She felt underutilized by the company and disrespected by Ailes, who ogled her and flirted like an ogre. Carlson also experienced what another one of Ailes's targets, Alisyn Camerota, called "emotional harassment"—bullying that was intended to show who's boss and keep everyone in the right-wing line. Toward the end of her time at Fox, "I started refusing to go to Roger's office," Camerota told me.

Carlson continued to go, but she started to bring a tape recorder with her.

First she consulted with Hyman and told him about Doocy and the atmosphere at Fox. She said she was worried that Ailes would exercise a one-year "out" in her three-year contract and dump her overboard. She wanted advice. Hyman said she should be measured in her meetings with Ailes.

"Be careful with what you say," he said. "Remember he might be tape recording you."

"He can do that?"

Hyman explained that certain states, including New York, were one-party consent states, meaning one person could tape without telling anyone else.

"Ohhhh," she said, with her eyebrows raised.

Her tapes were eventually Ailes's undoing.

Carlson wasn't the first Fox anchor to gather evidence against Ailes to be used in case of termination. But in this case, Hyman's co-counsel Nancy Erika Smith said, Carlson intended to sue even if Ailes kept her on the air. In June 2016 Hyman and Smith sketched out a plan for filing suit in September and started to draft the paperwork. But Ailes decided to can her on the day her contract expired, June 23. Bill Shine and the top lawyer at Fox News, Dianne Brandi, called Carlson in and told her she wouldn't be allowed back on the air to say goodbye.

Carlson had a vacation scheduled, so she asked Shine and Brandi for time to process the news before signing her exit papers, and they agreed. She left the building, called her legal team, and told them to prepare for battle. The legal filing two weeks later so blindsided Ailes that it took him all day to come up with a public response. Privately, he erupted: "She's a crazy bitch," he told associates, and "her ratings suck."

Trump was incensed too—not about the possibility that Ailes had assaulted and harassed women for decades, but about his perception that Carlson was trying to take down a great man. The lawsuit landed a couple of months before women spoke out en masse and accused Trump of misconduct. "This is sad," Trump said to an associate. "What can we do to help Roger?" Then he fired up his old-fashioned social network.

Many of the men in this network subscribed to their mutual friend Roger Stone's rule: "Attack, attack, attack." That's how Ailes built Fox, that's how Hannity built up his profile, and that's how Trump won the GOP primary. And these men constantly talked with one another. Since Carlson filed suit in New Jersey Superior Court, Trump told Ailes to hire attorney Michael Sirota, who'd helped resolve Trump's Atlantic City casino woes. Sirota's specialties were bankruptcy and corporate restructuring, so the recommendation didn't really make sense, but Sirota, wanting to help somehow, called a crisis PR person named Karen Kessler.

When Kessler and her partner Warren Cooper drove over to Ailes's Cresskill, New Jersey, home, they found Ailes "in this humongous chair, larger than life, hooked up to an IV stand," Kessler said. A male nurse was dispensing . . . something. Rudy Giuliani was on the phone in another room of the house. Rudy wanted to steer Fox's internal investigation so that Ailes would be cleared and Carlson would be humiliated. But Rupert Murdoch's sons wanted this matter to be taken seriously. James and Lachlan had differing politics and very different views about how Fox News should evolve, but they agreed on this point: Ailes was a pox on 21st Century Fox's house. Both sons had fought with and lost to Ailes before. This was their chance to get even and get control of Fox.

Ailes explained this family drama to Trump in one of his calls with the candidate.

"Those boys, those punks are not going to get me," Ailes said.

Ailes and Trump's instincts were the same: to destroy Carlson. Trump sided with his friend publicly, saying Carlson's claims "are unfounded just based on what I've read."

"What he read" was planted by Ailes's PR machine to smear Carlson as self-absorbed and flirtatious and unpopular. It was character assassination. Fox PR people transcribed Carlson's past praise of Ailes and publicized the weak ratings for her 2 p.m. hour. Reporters covering the case received long emails with sections labeled "RATINGS DETAILS" and "HISTORY OF SUPPORTING WOMEN." Some of the emails even included 21st Century Fox's stock chart. "The stock has gone up following the news," a PR exec wrote. "That, coupled with the ratings, show business has not been impacted."

But dozens of other women knew what Ailes had done to them. The phones at Smith's law firm lit up with other women registering complaints about Ailes, some dating back to the 1960s. "Please tell

Gretchen to hang in there." "Thank her for speaking out." "I can't come forward, but . . ." "It happened to me too."

Still, stars like Hannity were firmly in Ailes's corner. Hannity told me on July 9, "He is loved by the overwhelming majority, 99 percent. Just a fact."

Kimberly Guilfoyle was the head of Team Roger. She was on the phone with his wife Beth constantly, exchanging info about who was cooperating and who was not. "You'd better stick with Roger," Guilfoyle told colleagues. "I'm taking notes."

Multiple insiders said Guilfoyle coordinated all of this with programming exec Suzanne Scott. "It was at Suzanne's behest," one of Guilfoyle's best friends said. (A source close to Scott firmly denied this.)

Guilfoyle's cheerleading for Ailes confused some staffers, since Ailes was known to be dismissive of her in private. According to unsubstantiated allegations in a lawsuit filed by former Fox cohost Julie Roginsky, Ailes once said to her that Guilfoyle would "get on her knees for anyone."

One explanation for Guilfoyle's allegiance proffered by sources: She likely believed Ailes would prevail and believed she'd be rewarded with her own show. "Remember, we all thought Roger would survive. We figured he was invincible," a well-known host reminded me.

Which is one of the reasons why Megyn Kelly stayed silent at first. When Kelly was a new reporter at Fox, Ailes had hit on her, offered to trade sex for career advancement, and tried to kiss her. Kelly firmly shut him down and sought help from her supervisor in the DC bureau. Ailes got the message and moved on to other targets. They went on to have a perfectly normal, mutually beneficial, very profitable working relationship. But she wasn't going to lie and pretend that he was incapable of what Carlson alleged.

Kelly saw stories pop up on Ailes-friendly websites calling her "selfish" for not defending him. She knew Ailes's minions were behind it. She also knew, from a source, that Rudy and Ailes's other allies were trying to limit the scope of the Fox investigation. Briefly, they succeeded: Talent would be excluded from the internal review, Kelly learned, and just a small circle of people around Carlson would be interviewed. That's when she decided to come forward. Three days after Carlson sued, Kelly called Lachlan and told him the truth. His first words were "I'm sorry."

Kelly's call had an immediate impact. Soon came word that the Murdochs had hired law firm Paul, Weiss to interview staffers about potential misconduct. Additional evidence of Ailes's misdeeds was uncovered almost every hour. What ultimately mattered was the pattern and the pervasiveness of his behavior, backed up by so many accounts. One week after Carlson's lawsuit was filed, the Murdochs were in agreement that Ailes had to go. There was nothing Trump or anyone else could do to save him.

Everything came to a head during the GOP convention in Cleveland, Ohio. When the convention began on Monday, July 18, Ailes was still convinced he could survive Carlson's "attack," as he called it. Hannity still supported him. Guilfoyle still leaned on reluctant colleagues to get on Team Roger, tempting them with promotions she couldn't actually deliver. "Dana is dead," Guilfoyle told one of her on-air colleagues, casually tossing *The Five* castmate Dana Perino overboard because Perino had refrained from backing up Ailes publicly. "Her seat can be yours," Guilfoyle added.

But Guilfoyle didn't have power anymore and neither did Ailes. Rupert called on Monday morning and urged him to step down. Agree to resign, he said, so that this doesn't have to get any messier. When the call leaked, the entire Quicken Loans Arena in Cleveland lit up with the news. "This feels like a coup that's actually succeeding," one Fox exec texted me. "How fast will Ailes launch a Fox rival?" another wondered.

The next morning, Tuesday, Ailes joined Fox's 9 a.m. editorial call and acted like it was a perfectly ordinary day. He was able to keep pretending until noon, when *New York* magazine reporter Gabriel Sherman revealed that Kelly had been interviewed by Paul, Weiss and had described Ailes's harassment in detail. Her testimony guaranteed nonstop coverage, just the kind of juicy scandal that Murdoch had built his empire on. But many of her colleagues were still in denial. "Don't believe the crap about" Ailes, Geraldo Rivera tweeted. "Only ones talking dirt are those who hate #FoxNews & want to hurt network that's kicking their ass."

Fellow anchors were furious at Kelly for opening her mouth. Flanked by security, she silently entered and exited the arena. Once she found a corner for privacy near Fox's set, she called a friend who had also been harassed by Ailes and interviewed by Paul, Weiss. They were both in shock about the leak. "I just want to crawl in a hole," Kelly said. Paul, Weiss had promised that the interviews would remain confidential, but now her name was out there, and she was about to saddle up and co-anchor hours of convention coverage alongside men who, she told her friend, had literally turned their backs on her. Kelly wondered: Who leaked, and why?

The leak seemed to come from Murdoch's inner circle—from James or Lachlan or people acting on their behalf to force Ailes out. Ailes finally got the message when, on Wednesday morning, his chauffeur pulled up to Fox News HQ and was told to circle the block. Ailes found out the Murdochs had locked him out—literally, they had deactivated his badge.

The man who had built Fox News could no longer get in the building. Before giving in and signing the separation agreement, he sought Trump's counsel via phone. Trump cussed out Ailes's accusers and said it was terrible how a powerful man could be wounded like this. Ailes told Trump the agreement barred him from joining a competing network, but contained a silver lining: It allowed him to help with Trump's campaign. *Wouldn't they work well together?* In an interview with *Meet the Press*, Trump suggested he might hire the disgraced political operative: "We'll see!"

Ailes signed the paperwork, but he had one additional demand— he wanted to meet with Rupert in person. He said Murdoch owed him that much. The men met for lunch at Rupert's $72 million triplex apartment on East 22nd Street along Madison Square Park. It was awkward but not outwardly confrontational: Ailes accepted $40 million and a muzzle while the Murdochs accepted his immediate resignation. Ailes also got to claim that he'd still be "advising" Rupert, although that was just a face-saving lie. The deal was announced at 4 p.m. on Thursday, July 21, almost overshadowing Trump's coronation in Cleveland. One bully boss of the GOP stepped down while the new bully boss stepped up. It was Trump's party now.

At 10 p.m. I watched Trump's doom-and-gloom speech from the rafters of the arena. "There will be no lies. We will honor the American people with the truth, and nothing else," he said, while making two dozen misleading statements. His depictions of extreme violence threatening "our very way of life" made little sense in an America where crime was on a decades-long decline. But it rang true in Fox's America, where crimes by illegal border crossers and attacks on police officers were regular themes on *Hannity* and *The O'Reilly Factor.* Ailes's fingerprints were all over this speech, so it made sense that Ailes's creation was the most watched channel on all of television, even ahead of the broadcast networks, on the night Trump took over his party. Ailes was one of the 9 million Fox viewers who watched at home in the dark.

"Business suicide"

On the day Ailes was forced out, some Fox staffers were in tears. Yes, he was a tyrant, but he was also the only leader they'd ever known. They wondered if Fox would survive the loss. They wondered if they would still have jobs. When asked about the mood, one staffer texted me back, "utter disbelief."

James and Lachlan Murdoch were much more composed. They agreed that Ailes needed to go, and they'd gotten it done in just two weeks' time. But now they disagreed about everything else.

James wanted to hire a new Fox News head from the outside. His first choice was David Rhodes, the president of CBS News, who had previously held exec positions at Fox and Bloomberg. James thought Rhodes was a shortcut to making the news division stronger and reorienting the network to the middle. That's what James wanted above all else—less Hannity, more Shep Smith. He shared the same world view as his wife, Kathryn Hufschmid, now Kathryn Murdoch, an environmentalist who'd once worked for the Clinton Climate Initiative. They were both tired of having Hannity and O'Reilly's regressive beliefs tarnish their family's name.

Rupert and Lachlan were both fond of Rhodes—but there was no way they were hiring him. Changing direction would be "business suicide," Rupert said later in the year. "It would be foolish of us" to mess with what's working, Lachlan said.

Plus, they didn't trust James to be anywhere near Fox News. In their view, Kathryn had caused James to lurch to the left. They wanted to keep James away from the channel and keep gas in Ailes's tank.

Rupert addressed employees in New York and said he would run Fox News temporarily, taking Ailes's CEO title to give everyone a sense of stability. The eighty-five-year-old ignored questions about his complicity in Ailes's crimes and commenced a long-overdue housecleaning.

Rupert found that Ailes had kept all sorts of people on the payroll at Fox. Ailes was just like Trump in this way—both men kept fixers and yes-men close at hand. Private investigator Bo Dietl, once dubbed "Roger Ailes's top goon," was under contract as an on-air contributor at Fox. His contract was not renewed. Other "friends of Roger" were sending monthly invoices to Fox for mysterious consulting work. Rupert put a stop to that too. Every day, something new cropped up. Three of Ailes's personal lawyers who counseled him in July were also longtime Fox legal analysts. One of them even filled in on *Fox & Friends*! Not anymore.

But Rupert was in the odd position of relying on Ailes's lieutenants to clean the general's messy house. The problem was that Ailes had never groomed a successor. Most people explained this by saying he thought he'd run the joint forever. He encouraged rivalries to form on the second floor, where his executive team worked. Now the same execs who'd carried out Ailes's orders, who'd sat on the couch and laughed at his racist and sexist remarks, who'd claimed not to notice when he leered at young staffers, remained in place. In some cases, they were promoted. On August 12, Rupert named Bill Shine and Jack Abernethy copresidents of Fox News. They would report to him. Two other Ailes loyalists were one rung lower on the ladder: Jay Wallace, the newsroom boss, and Suzanne Scott, whose new title was EVP of programming and development. They would both report to Shine. All four executives were Fox News originals—and had the baggage to prove it.

After Shine became copresident, his name came up in multiple lawsuits, with repeated allegations that he enabled Ailes's misconduct. These suits kept Fox lawyers busy for more than a year and cast a permanent shadow over the management team. Rupert, undeterred by the concerns about management's awareness of Ailes's abuse, gave Abernethy and Smith multiyear contracts on September 15.

"If I stay here, I'm going to get cancer"

For Hannity, Trump was a shortcut to renewed relevance. Eight years of Obama-bashing was awfully repetitive. His eponymous show was a snooze and his producers knew it. That's why, back when Ailes was still in charge, some of the execs mused about sticking Hannity with a cohost again. They thought a younger female liberal host would make the show more interesting.

Then along came Trump, the most interesting story of the decade. It was a match made in TV producer heaven and a solution to the "Hannity problem." Trump was pushing the same GOP policy goals and culture war battles that Hannity promoted every day. "Hannity was Trump before Trump was Trump," one of Hannity's friends observed. He continued to have his own solo radio gig in the afternoon, which meant that he was more in touch with "the base" than other Fox hosts. His nightly TV commentaries reflected the bitter feelings of his radio callers. It was a vicious circle—his audience's anger made him angrier, which made them angrier, and so on.

Trump took his cues from what he heard from Hannity's show. And like Trump, Hannity had no one to check him anymore—no one to stop him from following his own worst instincts.

"Ailes wanted us to step right up to the line, but not cross it," one of Hannity's sparring partners said.

Without Ailes around, Hannity was free to indulge Trump's looniest lies about voter fraud and about Hillary Clinton's health. It was a difference of feet: Instead of tiptoeing up to the line, the way Ailes had taught him, Hannity strode right past it. He helped Trump sow doubts about election security without a shred of evidence. "You said in a speech today you're afraid this election is going to be rigged," Hannity said in an August interview. Instead of asking a question, he simply cued Trump to start talking. "Yes, well, I have been hearing about it for a long time," Trump claimed. From whom? Hannity didn't ask. He just lapped it up as Trump predicted the election "is going to be rigged." Any self-respecting executive producer would have gotten in Hannity's ear through the IFB (one-way communication from the control room) and demanded that the interviewer follow up. Probe further, push back, do something—Trump's claims were Third World dictatorship stuff. But Hannity simply wrapped the interview and thanked Trump for his time.

This was a prime example of how Hannity did Trump and their audience a disservice. Hannity had tried to back up Trump's BS by citing a *Philadelphia Inquirer* report that said Mitt Romney did not get a single vote, "not one," in fifty-nine separate precincts in Philadelphia in 2012. Come on, Hannity, I said in my retort on CNN—a simple Google search showed that there were also precincts in other states, like in Utah, where Obama did not get a single vote. Hannity wielded his megaphone irresponsibly.

In response, Hannity came after me on Twitter and changed the subject, asking, "Is HRC a liar?" Given Trump's pathological lying, I thought it was cute that Hannity claimed to value honesty. He simultaneously used misleading videos to advance the "Hillary is secretly sick" conspiracy theory in front of millions of people. One night he even asked a Fox News doctor if she could be suffering from a traumatic brain injury or a stroke. When I spoke out against this, Hannity called in to *Fox & Friends* and called me a "little pipsqueak." Trump and Hannity both name-called their way through life.

One month earlier, when Ailes was at the precipice, Hannity

had led a brigade of Fox hosts who threatened to follow him out the door, using the "key man clause" that Ailes had inserted in their contracts. The clauses were like get-out-of-Fox-free cards. They were originally Ailes's idea, so that if he ever left, his stars could leave with him. "He viewed them as a poison pill, to protect himself in case the Murdoch family ever came after him," a longtime Fox News exec said. From a corporate governance standpoint, it's irresponsible to let everyone go down with the CEO's ship. But Ailes had so much autonomy that he tried to ensure his invincibility. Once word got around, stars started asking for the clauses to be added to their contracts. According to an agent who did business with Fox for decades, the clauses turned into loyalty tests: "Roger wanted talent to want the clause." And most hosts did.

When Ailes was ousted, several Fox stars *did* look around. Shep Smith and Bret Baier's agents both put out feelers, just to find out their clients' worth in the TV marketplace, and executives at other networks were startled to hear how much money they made. "Roger overpaid," a VP quipped. "He bought people off," another exec said.

Hannity wasn't serious about leaving. There was nowhere else for him to go. But Greta Van Susteren eyed the exit with more sincerity. She felt embarrassed about having defended Ailes back in July. If she was going to stay, Greta and her husband, lawyer John Coale, wanted Fox to pay a price in the form of a huge raise. Rupert was furious at the maneuver. He felt that Greta was trying to hold the network hostage at a moment of weakness. "I can't believe they just threatened me," he said after a tense phone call with Coale. In early September, when Fox's lawyers officially rejected her contract demands, she gave notice to leave. Murdoch responded harshly: He dispatched a courier to her home in northwest Washington with two letters that said her time on Fox was over, immediately.

Coales told me Greta volunteered to stay in the anchor chair for a few weeks to help with a smooth transition. Rupert had other ideas. She wasn't allowed back in the building to say goodbye to viewers. Within hours, her biography was removed from FoxNews.com. It was like she was deleted from Fox's history. Within hours too, Rupert reached out to weekend host Tucker Carlson about taking over her time slot after the election.

"Cable news is a snake pit," Bill O'Reilly warned Megyn Kelly when she moved to prime time in 2013. He knew because he was the biggest python of them all. But Kelly could bite too: Years later, another Fox host told me "I've never known someone with as many enemies as Megyn Kelly."

Those internal enemies existed long before Kelly spoke to the Paul, Weiss lawyers about Ailes's sick treatment of women. Here's why: When someone goes from a correspondent gig to the anchor desk and then to her own two-hour show and then her own prime time spot and a $15 million-a-year contract, others are going to feel passed over. And they're going to hiss and moan. But Ailes picked the time slots, not the anchors. Kelly resented the fact that others resented her for being good at her job.

Then came the Ailes scandal. The perception that Kelly ratted out the old man further tarnished her image inside Fox. Some colleagues refused to speak to her. "If I stay here, I'm going to get cancer," Kelly told a friend in late 2016 as she weighed what to do with her career.

Kelly had a "key man" clause, but unlike the others, she also had a contract coming due in July 2017. Normally her contract window wouldn't have "opened" until early 2017, but Lachlan did something unusual: He "opened her contract in September and said, because of extenuating circumstances, you're free to look around," a source explained.

The week of September 12, executives from ABC, NBC, and CNN rotated through the Manhattan offices of CAA, Kelly's talent agency, for meet and greets. ABC courted Kelly for *GMA*. CNN offered her a 9 p.m. talk show to go up against Fox. NBC said she could do pretty much whatever she wanted. She wasn't looking to leave Fox right away, not with an election right around the corner, but the possibilities were tantalizing. Lachlan countered with a four-year contract renewal worth $100 million, putting Kelly on par with O'Reilly. He believed O'Reilly's best days were behind him, and Hannity was reliable but predictable. Kelly, on the other hand, was capable of bringing in a new audience to Fox. She was youthful and unpredictable. He thought *The Kelly File* would be Fox's signature show of the Hillary Clinton years.

The bosses wanted Kelly to sign on the nine-figure dotted line before Election Day. Rupert publicly urged her to hurry up and make a decision when he told his *Wall Street Journal* that other stars would "give their right arm for her spot." Instead of hurrying up, Kelly tapped the brakes, as talent tends to do—she wanted to get through the release of her memoir first. Launch day ended up being the day she decided she had to leave Fox.

"I'm a newsman"

In the immediate aftermath of Ailes's expulsion, the man was portrayed in the press like a nuclear weapon pilfered by a rogue state. There were numerous reports that Ailes was advising Trump ahead of the debates. Clinton campaign aides talked about what kind of advice Ailes might be feeding her opponent. But they didn't need to worry. While Ailes did run a very informal debate prep in Bedminster, his coaching was of limited value, partly because he babbled about past debates and bragged about his past victories—a sure way to lose Trump's attention. Besides, as Ailes once said, his talent was in getting people to loosen up and be themselves on TV. "If you see them at home," he said of typical politicians, "they're laughing and they're physical and they could move. And as soon as you put them on television they turn into stiffs and they're boring." So his go-to move, he said, was to "peel the layers back so they could be themselves." Trump definitely didn't need that advice. There were no layers. What you saw on TV was what you got.

So Trump didn't really need Ailes. Neither did Fox. The network kept humming along without him. The Murdochs and Shine and Abernethy were moving the network from a dictator model to a committee model of leadership. They didn't try to improve the content; they just kept a good, profitable thing going. The summertime scandal had proven that everyone was replaceable, even Roger Ailes.

Trump was in charge of the television wing of the GOP now and had all the deputies he needed. Rudy Giuliani was at debate camp along with Fox commentator Laura Ingraham and assorted friends. Hannity was at Trump's beck and call. And *Fox & Friends* spewed toxic waste at his opponent every day. On October 25, Rudy told Brian Kilmeade that "we've got a couple of surprises left," and added, "I do think that all of these revelations about Hillary Clinton, finally, are beginning to have an impact." Rudy had heard that FBI agents in New York were in possession of a laptop with a new cache of Clinton-related emails. The agents—some of whom detested Clinton—wanted to crack it open. Rudy alluded to "surprises" again the next day in an interview with Fox's Martha MacCallum. It appeared as though he was getting leaks from current FBI agents (although he later claimed the info came from "former agents"). And it sure seemed like he was spreading the info on Fox to pressure FBI director James Comey into reopening an investigation in the final inning of the election. If that was the plan, it worked: On October 28, Comey took the highly unusual step of disclosing that investigators were examining the new cache of emails. "I think his decision to publicly reopen the case, rather than investigate quietly, was certainly driven in part by the fear that news of the laptop would leak," Josh Campbell, Comey's special assistant at the time, told me in 2019.

Clinton was exonerated by the FBI, but convicted by the Fox echo chamber. The words "Clinton" and "emails" were paired together like peanut butter and jelly in the critical closing days of the election. Comey's "October surprise" tightened the race and, according to some political scientists, likely cost Clinton the election. And Fox was at the center of it all.

There was a moment, after Ailes lost, before Trump won, when Fox News could have gone in a different, truthier direction. Ryan Grim, the DC bureau chief of the *Huffington Post*, wrote a pivotal October 2016 story about what might have been. It was titled "Is Shep Smith The Future of Fox News?"

Shep was a hero to the Fox newsroom. He was unlike every other newsman on the air. First people noticed his boyish good looks and Mississippi drawl. Then his unflappable delivery. He exuded an electricity. Without shouting, he made viewers want to listen. A reporter once called Shep "the Red Bull of TV news anchors."

Shep came from the Walter Cronkite "that's the way it is" school of journalism—which, as Fox made its rightward turns, increasingly clashed with Hannity's "this is the way I want it to be" school of spin. Shep stood for journalism while Hannity tried to tear down journalism. How could they possibly share airtime? How could they coexist? Eventually, in the Trump age, they couldn't.

But in October 2016 Fox was planning for the Clinton age. Smith and others on the news side of Fox News "were hoping that with Ailes collapsing and Murdoch coming back in, that this was their moment," Grim told me. "And perhaps with Hillary winning the White House—perhaps it was a moment for them to pivot."

Trump was behind in the national polls. The GOP was bracing for a face-first collapse. The Fox brand was facing a reckoning. "I think they thought that perhaps Trump was going to discredit all of the energy that had been building since the Tea Party by getting annihilated at the polls," Grim said. "Clinton's victory—that was the world they expected to be living in." So consider that world while you digest these quotes. Smith told Grim all about his recent meeting with Rupert, recounting it in great detail. "He wants to hire a lot more journalists, he wants to build us a massive new newsroom, he wants to make more commitments to places like this," Smith said as he showed off his massive Studio H facility with its mine-are-bigger-than-yours screens.

He said it could get even bigger.

Murdoch wants to "just enlarge our news-gathering," he continued. "When the biggest boss, who controls everything, comes and says 'That's what I want to do,' that's the greatest news I've heard in years. And he didn't mention one thing about our opinion side."

I could practically hear the journalists at Fox leaping to their feet and cheering. Smith recalled Murdoch saying, "I'm a newsman. I want to be the best news organization in America." These words were inspirational to the oft-overlooked scribes at Fox. One of the network's most-respected correspondents, Conor Powell, who left Fox in disgust in 2018, told me that the *Huffington Post* story was a signal moment for him and his colleagues. "If Murdoch is going to come in here and say we're gonna double down on reporting," he recalled saying, "this will be fantastic."

It could have been. It might have been. But then America started to vote.

"Is this really happening?"

Everyone has their own Election Day story. Let me tell you mine.

It was three in the morning, and I was in a small studio, what we call a "flash cam," on the fifth floor of CNN's New York office. Trump and Clinton were both coming home to New York after holding late-night election eve rallies. Trump landed at La Guardia at three in the morning and slipped into an SUV for a lonely ride back to Trump Tower. There were no photos, no made-for-TV moments. His campaign staffers were already acting like losers. Clinton's campaign, on the other hand, staged a welcome-home rally at Westchester County Airport. When her plane touched down at three-thirty, two hundred well-wishers surrounded her on the tarmac. I remember commenting on CNN that it was a brilliant bit of stagecraft—one final "winning" image for the morning shows to play on a loop. Trump only countered with a phone call to *Fox & Friends.*

"If I don't win," he told the cohosts, "I will consider it a tremendous waste of time, energy, and money."

Points for honesty, I suppose.

Like Trump and almost everyone else, staffers at Fox headed into Election Day assuming that he would lose. Many news anchors and line producers and ad sales execs honestly wanted Clinton to win. Trump was, in a word, exhausting. And he had made media bashing a centerpiece of his entire campaign. While Hannity loved it, a lot of rank-and-file Fox journalists knew it was damaging and needed to stop.

There were business considerations as well. Network executives thought that four more years of a Democratic president would be good for ratings and outrage. Hey, maybe Trump's consolation prize would be a show on Fox: *Trump & Friends*! Some of his campaign aides, expecting to be out of work, were already calling Fox execs about possible commentator gigs after the election.

The anchors filled the day talking about Trump's long-shot paths to victory. In the afternoon he called in to chat with Martha Mac-Callum and stoke spurious fears about voter fraud one last time before the polls closed. Setting up an excuse for his loss, Trump confidently said there were "lots of complaints" about voting machines casting Republican votes for Democrats: "It's happening at various places today, it's been reported." That was a lie, but Mac-Callum just let him say it without asking for any proof. An hour later, Shep Smith stepped in and said straight up, "We've seen *no* evidence of that, no evidence from authorities."

Shep had voted in Greenwich Village first thing in the morning. His 3 p.m. opening monologue made clear his disgust at the bitter nature of the race: "A campaign season filled with name-calling, personal attacks, federal investigations, accusations of sexual assault, suspected interference from Russian hackers, false claims of widespread voter fraud, and the airing of dirty laundry from decades ago. And now, at last, it's almost over." The relief was palpable in his voice.

At 5 p.m. Megyn Kelly, Bret Baier, and a raft of producers gathered for a final pre-show prep meeting. "We were all around this long table, Rupert at the head of the table, and all of the producers and anchors on both sides of it," Chris Wallace told me later. "They gave us the first wave of exit polls. While it didn't flat out say Clinton was going to win, if you read it you had to think Clinton was going to win.

"In fact," he added, the sheaf of paper even said "it was likely that we would make the call between eleven and eleven-thirty." The networks never called the election before West Coast polls closed at eleven, so this was another sign of Clinton's apparent strength. The forecast called for an early night.

An exec at ABC News, Chris Vlasto, shared the early exit poll results with the Trump campaign. Jared Kushner and Ivanka Trump told the patriarch that the data looked bleak. "We're not going to win," Donald told Melania. But several of the president's strategists, like Brad Parscale, insisted otherwise. The Trump clan worked the phones throughout the early evening, doing last-minute hits on radio stations in the Florida panhandle and other key battlegrounds, urging supporters to get out and vote.

The early exit poll findings informed the tone of the early evening TV coverage. But by 8:30 p.m., as actual votes poured in, the picture started to change, just as Parscale had expected. "The sweep that the exit polls had predicted just wasn't happening," Wallace recalled. "Now we were down to counting individual votes."

There were no immediate calls in states like Michigan or Wisconsin. Wallace factored that in as, on-air at 9:05, he told Kelly that he was becoming "open to the possibility that Donald Trump could be the next President of the United States." His voice betrayed his own amazement at the words. It was a pivotal moment in the coverage of the night because he said aloud what others had until then been saying only to themselves. "I'm kind of proud of it," Wallace told me, "in the sense that it altered our coverage a little bit."

It sure did. The crowd outside Fox's sparkling new $20 million street-level studio started to cheer. "I turned around toward them and said, 'I'm not saying he's going to win, folks, but it's possible,' " Wallace recalled. Trump's election night party was five short blocks up the street at the Midtown Hilton, so some people strolled back and forth between the Fox broadcast and the ballroom. Pirro,

Ingraham, and former Fox contributor Sarah Palin all hung out at the Hilton. Trump was still ensconced in Trump Tower, wondering whether to believe Parscale's insistence that they could pull this thing off. Wallace's comments had an immediate impact. There were tears of joy and tears of fear in Trump's inner circle. Chris Christie, who was in charge of the transition team, sensed that Trump was scared shitless.

Trump watched from a room on the fourteenth floor of Trump Tower, which was actually just the sixth floor in a building full of exaggerations. Around midnight he went upstairs to his residence to come up with an acceptance speech. Once it was clear that Trump was going to win, Hannity called in to Fox and called the result a "modern-day political miracle." At 2:41 a.m., Fox News was the first TV network to officially project that Trump was the president-elect. Baier credited him with winning "the most unreal, surreal election we have ever seen." Wallace looked across the studio, where one of the oversized screens flashed "TRUMP ELECTED PRESIDENT," and he shook his head, the way you try to wake yourself up from a nightmare or a dream. "Is this really happening?"

"There's nothing more exciting for a political reporter," Wallace said, "than when things go off-script."

Kelly looked into the camera and wondered if she could remain at Fox.

Ailes watched from the sidelines from his mansion and took comfort in a bag of chips.

Closet liberals at Fox cried the night of November 8, 2016, while the network's biggest Trump boosters partied until sunrise the next morning. Pete Hegseth and Jesse Watters walked around like they owned the building. They were drunk with power. And not just metaphorically drunk: Watters, once described as a "human Jäger bomb," celebrated the election results at the boozy Hilton party and then stumbled back to work with Emma DiGiovine, a staffer on his show and his future wife. Watters high-fived and hugged his colleagues.

When Fox's special coverage finally wrapped up, two hours later than planned, Baier and some others convinced Connolly's, the Irish pub on 45th Street near the office, to stay open. "We just all had a beer and toasted the night being a broadcast success and how surreal the whole thing was," Baier recalled a year later. "I remember telling people that night, 'Well, at least now it will slow down.' I was wrong."

Hannity rubbed the win in the faces of the "elite media." The overnight ratings showed that CNN topped Fox during prime time, 13 million viewers versus 12 million, but a greater number of Fox viewers stayed awake later as Trump's victory looked more and more likely. In the immediate aftermath, Fox's ratings stayed elevated. Carlson's show debuted at 7 p.m. a week after the election, and one of his first guests was Laura Ingraham, who was in talks to become Trump's press secretary. "I wanted to get you on before you get drafted by the Trump people," Carlson wisecracked.

But Ingraham wanted to be more than just a hairsprayed spokeswoman for the president's policies. She was willing to do battle in the briefing room only if she also had a seat at the policy-making table on issues like immigration and trade, to achieve the protectionist and nationalist goals she'd been pursuing for years. The competing factions on the transition team couldn't agree on how to make room for her, and Sean Spicer was hired instead.

Tucker talked about Trump's election as a peasants' revolt— "a reaction against the people in charge," against elites, he said the morning after. The conventional explanations of Trump's win made even less sense once the popular vote totals were finally complete. How much of a rebellion was it, really, when 3 million more people voted for Clinton? I thought a buzzer should sound every time a Fox commentator invoked "the people"—e.g., "the people voted for a wall," "the people voted for a travel ban," "the people voted for corporate tax cuts." The people were hopelessly split almost in half and the election proved it. Carlson did acknowledge this by bringing up the saddest part of the exit polling: 94 percent of Trump voters said they'd be scared or concerned about President Clinton while 95 percent of Clinton voters said they'd be scared or concerned about President Trump. "So there really is a real divide here," Tucker said.

Yes, everyone felt it—but Fox stars seemed incapable of looking inward at their own contributions to the divide. And unwilling to admit that there were very good reasons to be concerned about the Trump presidency.

Trump suddenly needed to assemble an administration, so he turned to the people he knew best: Fox personalities. The revolving door between Fox and the Trump administration began to spin. On Friday, November 11, Dianne Brandi called up Fox Business weekend cohost Anthony Scaramucci and said he had to leave his show since he was being appointed to the Trump transition team. He was also making $88,000 a year as a contributor, and that deal had to end too.

"We have to cancel your contract," Brandi said.

Fox management enforced a rule: No one could work for the network and Trump at the same time. Most outsiders laughed at this demarcation since so many of Fox's stars helped Trump in so many ways. Still, they had to draw a line somewhere, and money, instead of, say, journalistic integrity, became the backstop.

"Loyalty is good"

"In the weeks and months after Roger was fired, Fox was pretty rudderless—no one was in charge," correspondent Conor Powell said. "Nothing was approved, nothing was rejected. In theory Rupert was in charge, but he wasn't really around to make many decisions." When Powell flew from Jerusalem to New York for a visit to the mother ship, news boss Jay Wallace told him the management team was "just trying to keep the place afloat."

I could sense it from the outside—in the fall of 2016, sources began whispering, "the inmates are running the asylum." The execs were, according to numerous sources, simply afraid to deal with the hot-air-balloon egos in prime time. Which explains what happened on November 15, the day Kelly released her memoir, and the same day O'Reilly was on *CBS This Morning* to promote *his* next book, even though it wasn't coming out for another week. O'Reilly had been a staunch defender of Ailes, and on CBS that day he went further, saying he'd "had enough" of people treating Fox News like a "piñata."

When the anchors asked about Kelly's allegations against Ailes, O'Reilly said "I'm not that interested in this."

Norah O'Donnell interjected: "In sexual harassment? You're not interested in sexual harassment?"

O'Reilly: "I'm not interested in basically litigating something that is finished, that makes my network look bad. Okay? I'm not interested in making my network look bad. At all. That doesn't interest me one bit."

O'Donnell: "Is that what she's doing?"

O'Reilly: "I don't know. But I'm not going to even bother with it."

This old white guy culture was still deeply entrenched at Fox even though Ailes was gone. Kelly, disgusted by the CBS appearance, wrote an email to management around three in the afternoon that called out O'Reilly's "history of harassment."

"His exact attitude of shaming women into 'shutting the hell up' about harassment on grounds that it will disgrace the company, is in part how Fox got into the decades-long Ailes mess to begin with," Kelly wrote. She urged them to intervene—to defend her—and to defend the other women O'Reilly insulted.

According to Kelly, Bill Shine called her and promised to "deal" with O'Reilly. But he didn't. O'Reilly went ahead and pretaped his 8 p.m. show and included another shot at Kelly. Her executive producer Tom Lowell caught wind of it early in the 8 p.m. hour and alerted her.

"We've got a problem," he said. "I just looked at his rundown. At 8:50, he's going to double down."

Lowell tried to get through to Shine. O'Reilly was on tape, but Lowell had an idea for a breaking news insert that could replace the offending segment and stop the 8 p.m. host from attacking the 9 p.m. host. You'd think that the copresident of Fox News would call back and thank him—*Yes, Tom, please break in, thank you for alerting me to this, I'm sorry I didn't take action sooner*—but that's not what Shine said. He said, "The segment stands." Lowell had to go tell Kelly.

At 8:50, O'Reilly devoted his "Factor Tip of the Day" segment to the Kelly fracas—disguising it, barely, as being about the subject of "loyalty"—by saying that "if somebody is paying you a wage, you owe that person or company allegiance. If you don't like what's happening in the workplace," he lectured, "go to human resources or leave! I've done that. And then take the action you need to take afterward."

This was beyond audacious, coming from a man who was credibly accused of sexual harassment in a 2004 lawsuit, and who had—unbeknownst to his viewers—settled multiple cases with other accusers. "Loyalty is good," he concluded, condescension dripping from his voice.

Loyalty to whom? The Murdochs knew, from the law firm investigation, what Ailes had done. They had approved of Kelly writing about her experience. Her book was for their publishing house! Kelly was in disbelief and almost in tears. When she went live at 9 p.m., she hid her shock from O'Reilly's drive-by shooting, but she mentioned the Murdochs at the end of the hour: "Like me," she said, "they believe that sunlight is the best disinfectant."

Right then, Kelly knew she was done with Fox. Done with these executives, done with this place. That night, she told friends, was the "final straw." She wondered: Was the decision to allow O'Reilly's drive-by made by Shine? Or did he consult with Rupert and Lachlan? Were they afraid to intervene because they were trying to sign O'Reilly to a new contract? Were they just ignorant? She never found out the answer. But the episode spoke to a basic lack of leadership that would hobble the network for years to come.

Lachlan truly wanted to keep Kelly in the fold. He offered her a $100 million contract plus all the sweeteners she could ever want. "When Trump won, Lachlan thought, 'We need her more than ever,'" an insider told me. His theory was that *The Kelly File* would be the X factor of the Trump years—the unpredictable, buzzy hour that would make Fox News stand out.

But deep down inside, Kelly knew that she probably couldn't be what the Trump-era Fox would need her to be—a PR flack pretending to be a fiercely independent journalist. What she really wanted was a more hospitable climate at work, a better schedule for her family, and fewer excuses for Trump to bully her. By Christmas, she had a deal with NBC. But she didn't formally tell Lachlan until January 3, mere minutes before *The New York Times* broke the news of her historic defection. When Shine heard about the paper's request for comment, he sputtered, "You've got to be kidding me. *This* is the way she tells us?" But from Kelly's perspective, Shine gave notice to *her* back in November, when O'Reilly was allowed to shame her and all of Ailes's other targets.

I was at a dinner with Lachlan the day after Kelly decamped for NBC. We were both in Las Vegas for the CES tech convention, and we both attended a presentation by Hulu, the streaming TV service, in one of Restaurant Guy Savoy's dimly lit private rooms somewhere in the belly of Caesars Palace. I loved Hulu, but I wanted to talk about Kelly. Lachlan told me, "I wish she'd stayed, genuinely." I believed him. But I think he also knew that Fox was unstoppable with or without her. He said he viewed CNN as being "soft left" and MSNBC as "hard left," leaving a huge space, the "middle right," for Fox. But there was nothing "middle right" about the increasingly extreme rhetoric that emanated from his network. Journalism at Fox was being suffocated. In hindsight, Kelly was just the first of many Fox journalists to jump ship in the Trump era. When she packed up, she took almost everything out of her office, but left one thing: a sign that said "You don't have to be crazy to work here. We have on the job training!"

And it was about to get so much crazier.

THE COMMANDER

"Self-brainwashing"

How many times have you heard someone say "What's wrong with those people?" while referring to Hannity's groupies? Or say "What's wrong with *those* people?" about Rachel Maddow's fans?

Whether they're wrong or right, they're different. For all the pandemic-era talk of togetherness and common humanity, there are massive differences between the liberal and conservative tribes—and Fox and Trump both exacerbate those differences. Look no further than the studies that show variations in brain chemistry between conservatives and liberals. Some people really are hardwired to value tradition and preservation. They are more likely to perceive threats from outsiders. One study showed frightening images to participants—maggots in an open wound, a spider on a man's face, a crowd fighting with a man—and found that conservatives reacted more strongly to the images than liberals. I think about that now when I notice Fox's fear-based appeals.

Up until Election Day in 2016, Fox fans, when compared to the public at large, were far more pessimistic about America's future, far more critical of Obama's performance, and far more fearful of a Clinton presidency. (Common denominator: fear.) Fox's highest-rated shows reinforced this point of view night after night. "The conservative entertainment news complex has constructed an alternative reality so all-encompassing that the chance of conservatives happening on any sort of good news is virtually nil," Jason Sattler wrote in *USA Today*. This foreboding view of the world benefited Trump.

A Suffolk poll in October showed that people who trusted Fox over other networks were way gloomier about the health of the economy than, say, people who trusted CNN or CBS the most. Only 11 percent of Fox devotees said America was in an economic recovery, when the recovery had been going on for years. Fox loyalists were also more likely than other news consumers to say they were concerned about political corruption, media bias, and the bogeyman of voter fraud that Trump kept talking about. Many of these viewers were primed to lose, which made Trump's victory all the more shocking. Now they felt like they were gaining power for the first time in years, in the most surprising of ways, with the most surprising of leaders. Fox felt like the home team, with one of the network's super-fans ascending to the presidency. Like many of Fox's super-fans, he was resentful of news outlets that didn't reflect his view of the world. Now he had the unique power to do something about it. Trump was determined to delegitimize anyone who stood in his way.

While he was still president-elect in January 2017, Trump seized on the term "fake news"—which was coined by reporters and researchers to describe made-up stories on social media—and co-opted it as a bludgeon, a diversion, and a punchline. "Fake news" meant Russian propaganda and clickbait, but for his base Trump defined

it as "news you shouldn't believe." It was probably the most important thing he did during the presidential transition period. Turning
"fake news" into a slur fit perfectly into Trump's permanent campaign of disbelief, as best conveyed by his 2018 statement that "what
you are seeing and what you are reading is not what's happening."
He suggested with disturbing regularity that everything could be a
hoax. It was straight out of George Orwell's *Nineteen Eighty-Four*:
"The Party told you to reject the evidence of your eyes and ears. It
was their final, most essential command."

Disbelief of, and disdain for, the news media was the cornerstone
of Fox's business model in 1996, and it became the cornerstone of
Trump's presidency. But the anti-media posture was part of something even bigger: The utter transformation of the Fox-fueled Republican Party. The anti-intellectual positioning of the party, the
resistance to settled scientific fact, the contempt for intelligence
agencies—"it's all one thing," as media scholar Jay Rosen liked to
say, all part of the same rejection of expertise and resentment of
anyone who claims to know better. These observations didn't just
come from liberals like Rosen. In 2012 the straight-edge DC think
tankers Norm Ornstein and Thomas Mann described the GOP as
"ideologically extreme" and "unpersuaded by conventional understanding of facts, evidence, and science." They said "asymmetric polarization" afflicted the country, meaning conservatives had
moved more radically to the right than liberals had to the left, and
accused Fox of being partly responsible. Some veteran members of
the GOP establishment, like former Reagan and Bush aide Bruce
Bartlett, were equally outspoken about this radicalization and also
faulted the Fox echo chamber.

"Like someone dying of thirst in the desert, conservatives drank
heavily from the Fox waters," Bartlett wrote in 2015. "Soon, it became the dominant—and in many cases, virtually the only—major

news source for millions of Americans. This has had profound political implications that are only starting to be appreciated. Indeed, it can almost be called self-brainwashing—many conservatives now refuse to even listen to any news or opinion not vetted through Fox, and to believe whatever appears on it as the gospel truth."

This had dangerous consequences during the coronavirus outbreak in 2020. At that time, Bartlett argued that "Murdoch and the Fox brainwashing operation are risks to public health."

By then, the president had been telling people to suspend belief for three full years.

The first time he did it, he was in a rage against the U.S. intelligence community's conclusion that Russia intervened to help him win the election. As Obama ordered a full review of the Russian plot, Trump was in denial about it, telling Fox's Chris Wallace in December that "I think it's just another excuse. I don't believe it." Under pressure from the press corps, Trump eventually said he accepted the intel agencies' consensus view that Russia that was behind the cyberattack. Then came CNN's exclusive about the Steele dossier on January 10: "Intel chiefs presented Trump with claims of Russian efforts to compromise him." The story was airtight—the meeting happened as described—and it shook Trump to his core. "FAKE NEWS—A TOTAL POLITICAL WITCH HUNT!" he tweeted a few hours later. He brought the term "fake news" with him to a previously scheduled press conference the next day.

The dossier, thirty-five pages full of allegations of Trump's links to Russia, was all anyone could talk about. CNN did not publish the dossier's contents, since the info was unvetted and some of it was virtually impossible to confirm, but *BuzzFeed* did publish it—even the part about Trump supposedly paying Russian prostitutes for a "golden showers" show at the Ritz-Carlton in Moscow in 2013. *BuzzFeed*'s rationale was that the dossier's claims had already "circulated at the highest levels of the US government," and Americans should be able to read it and "make up their own minds." Anchors at CNN criticized *BuzzFeed*'s decision, but that didn't matter to Trump—he attacked both news outlets and acted like CNN had printed the salacious claims. He used his press conference to praise other outlets, claiming to distinguish between "good" and "bad" media like a regulator saying this product is approved and that one is banned.

Some people at Fox saw through the act. "CNN's exclusive reporting on the Russian matter was separate and distinctly different from the document dump executed by an online news property," Shep Smith said at the end of his show. "Though we at Fox News cannot confirm CNN's report, it is our observation that its correspondents followed journalistic standards and that neither they nor any other journalists should be subjected to belittling and delegitimizing by the president-elect of the United States."

Shep claimed to be speaking for the network—"we at Fox News"—but he couldn't truly speak for the network because Hannity felt a proverbial thrill up the leg as Trump spoke. "Trump's press conference today was the single greatest beat-down of the alt-left, abusively biased mainstream media in the history of the country," Hannity declared. He one-upped Trump's attacks and told his viewers to "be prepared" because "they're going to try to destroy the president." By "they," he meant the media.

Hannity and Trump worked hand in hand to tar practically the entire American news media as "fake." Both men's hypnotic message was that Fox was the only legit network while everyone else was fraudulent. Hannity reinforced this position on every episode of his show. Every night, he served the exact same meal, made from the same ingredients—mashed-up videos of commentators saying things he didn't like, graphics of cherry-picked information from

Clinton campaign chair John Podesta's stolen emails, slogans like "media mob." Hannity took examples of individual journalists acting friendly with the Clinton campaign, ignored the fact that the same coziness happened on the Trump side too, and alleged "all these major news organizations" were "colluding with Hillary." This rubbish, repeated every night, was pure propaganda in service of Trump's campaign of disbelief. Hannity's effect was to say to viewers, You can't trust anyone or anything but me. There was nothing equivalent to this on the left. Nothing even close.

Jay Rosen described it as an "information loop" where all the information about Trump came from Trump or his approved surrogates. "It's as if one-third of the public has been broken off from the rest of the electorate and isolated in an information system of its own," he told me. "It's not only that they are inclined to trust the president more than the news system, it's that the White House and Trump himself are trying to eviscerate the whole idea of a public record or of an independent source of facts on which the country can disagree and argue about. And I think that goes way beyond the notion of bias in the media or 'look skeptically at what you are told.' It's actually an authoritarian news system that is up and running in the country that is known for having the freest press in the world."

The system delivered un-news while trying to destroy traditional sources of news. And the president-elect preferred the authoritarian approach.

"The crowds were much, much smaller"

From the day of his inauguration, Trump was the say-anything president. He valued feelings over facts. And he needed his two Seans, Hannity and Spicer, to do the same.

The president's early morning TV watching hurt him on his

very first day waking up in the White House. Most people don't know this, but the inauguration crowd size debacle started because Trump was watching CNN's *Early Start* the morning after the inauguration. At 5:19 a.m. anchor John Berman turned to journalist Josh Rogin and said, "One thing people are discussing today, Josh, and I think it's just worth showing the picture, is the difference in crowd size.

"I mean, Donald Trump leading up to this had been calling on people to come here and said they were going to break records with the crowds. It doesn't look like they did," Berman said. "If you look at the difference—"

On screen, a CNN.com graphic showed Obama's historic 2009 crowd on the left and Trump's sparse crowd on the right. "You can see, along the Mall, there were empty spaces this time around," Berman's co-anchor Christine Romans said.

Yes, Rogin said, "the crowds were objectively smaller." Rogin was right, but he was also sympathetic to Trump. He pointed out that many of Trump's supporters hailed from faraway states and couldn't take off work to travel to DC. But, he concluded, "there's no doubt that the crowds were much, much smaller."

Trump heard this accurate comment about his crowd size and blew a gasket. He called and screamed at Sean Spicer, who in turn called and screamed at CNN DC bureau chief Sam Feist around 9 a.m. Feist found video of the segment in question, and saw that it was fair. But Trump remained enraged.

"We need to figure something out," Spicer told Sarah Huckabee Sanders and other aides.

Spicer, at this point, was still tethered to reality. He was a reasonable Republican comms guy with a twenty-year record of spinning but not lying. He was trying to fall in line and serve the president his party had elected—but it was excruciating. A 5:19 a.m.

segment seen by half a million viewers had lit a presidential fuse. CNN had mentioned it again an hour later with the banner: "TRUMP DRAWS SMALLER CROWD THAN OBAMA FOR INAUGURATION." And *The New York Times* posted its own compare-and-contrast widget. For the news outlets, this was just one small item out of dozens of stories and segments, but for Trump, it was all that mattered. Nothing of his could be smaller than Obama's. "He wants me to say it was the largest crowd to ever witness an inauguration," Spicer told his aides.

In my view, this absurd Saturday set the tone for Trump's entire presidency, including his relationship with Fox and other television networks. Because after he watched *Early Start*, Trump flipped to Fox and soaked up *Fox & Friends* praise for his "American carnage" speech. He tweeted a thank-you to @FoxNews. It was already clear that Fox was going to be his safe space, a humiliation-free zone, while the other channels were going to burst his bubble.

Since Trump demanded that his press secretary retaliate, the White House announced that Spicer would address the press corps in the briefing room at 4:30. I was on an Amtrak train to DC, so I turned on a CNN livestream on my phone, curious to see what was about to happen. But CNN didn't carry Spicer's tirade live. Why? Because Feist had been dealing with this issue all day, so he knew Spicer was going to come out and lie to the press corps. Why amplify that lie without any context? Instead, CNN producers showed the press conference on a tape delay and the anchors refuted Spicer's comments with facts.

Was that the right way to handle a livestream of wrongness? Discussions about journalism in the age of alternative facts lit up newsrooms in the early days of the Trump presidency. What were the best ways to fact-check the White House's lies? What about the times when Trump aides came on network shows and deceived the public? Should those aides continue to be booked? Was it just plain irresponsible to show Trump's rallies live? These questions consumed journalism conferences for months. But the decision-makers at Fox barely had these debates. Fox carried every second of Spicer's stunt live. It was a metaphor for the next few years: Fox watched what the other networks did and did the opposite. Call it being contrarian . . . or call it being part of the cover-up.

For the Murdochs, it was a business calculation. Fox filled a void in the marketplace and fomented a cult following. For the producers, similarly, it was a ratings maneuver. And for some of the hosts it was a political strategy, advancing a GOP agenda. The result: Inexcusable stupidity, duplicity, and treachery got excused. Inauguration weekend illustrated it perfectly.

Feist was in the briefing room when Spicer went out to the podium. Afterward, Spicer brought Feist back to his West Wing office and lectured him. Then Spicer told his aides to leave and asked the White House operator to patch in the president. Trump proceeded to yell at the CNN executive for close to half an hour. Trump cared so much about this coverage from five in the morning that he was still venting about it at six in the evening. Trump's rage and Spicer's presser turned crowd size into a top story for the rest of the weekend. So Trump's narcissism ruined his first days on the job.

In my estimation, the say-anything president lost the benefit of the doubt somewhere between January 21, when he said that the skies became "really sunny" right after his inaugural address, when in fact it remained cloudy with occasional sprinkles, and January 24, when he claimed that 3 to 5 million people voted illegally in the election that he won. He proved that his words were worthless, yet they were taken so seriously by his converts, and thus they remained newsworthy.

This was true in 2017 and it remained true in 2020. So much of what came out of Trump's mouth was inaccurate, illogical, or incoherent. But Fox's shows still generally took his words seriously. Segments were centered around his point of view, even when his point of view made no sense. On Fox, his failures were treated gently. His lies were ignored almost completely.

For Hannity and his acolytes, it was pretty easy to perform this way, because they believed the No. 1 story Fox sold: That no matter what, the Democrats were worse. But other hosts had to swallow hard and come up with different justifications for their jobs. "We speak the conservative language," one anchor said, in an attempt to explain the bullshit. With all the anti-Trump conservatives seeking refuge on CNN and MSNBC, Fox defaulted to the pro-Trump language. "We're a business," another anchor said. "It's as simple as that." There was no big behind-the-scenes meeting, no single moment when new marching orders were delivered. There was just a capitulation. "The Republican party was co-opted by the Trump movement, and that's what happened to Fox too, in the absence of anyone at the top setting any other direction," a producer who was on the inside for decades said.

When Ailes was the ruler, everyone knew who they were trying to impress. The channel was produced for an audience of one. Without him, "there was a power vacuum, and everyone was afraid to fill it," a former host said. So the channel was still produced for an audience of one—but now it was for Trump, not Ailes.

How did it come to this? Ask *Fox & Friends*.

"You're getting much better"

The first time I found myself at a way-too-fancy party in Manhattan, one of my editors at *The New York Times* trotted out the old "fake it till you make it" aphorism. It was new to me at the time. "That's what we all did, faked it till we made it," he said, whispering like it was an actual secret. It applies to so many conservative commentators too, like Heather Nauert.

An Illinois native, Nauert wanted to be in DC and wanted to be on TV. She broke through in 1995 with a job on *Youngbloods,* a long-forgotten talk show on a channel that no longer exists. It was a perfectly fine starting point for Nauert because television hits are about repetition. You've gotta do your reps and gain muscle memory, just like an athlete. That's what she did. When the Clinton-Lewinsky scandal broke, there was a huge demand for young female analysts on the news. As *The Washington Post's* Paul Farhi put it, conservative "pundettes" satisfied "a market need: a telegenic group of women who were predictably anti-Clinton."

During the Clinton impeachment, Nauert landed a commentator job at Fox, in large part thanks to Hannity's pal Bill Shine, who was then the top producer for prime time programming. On the air, Fox conferred an impressive-sounding title on her: GOP strategist. The only drawback was that she had never strategized for the party or for any campaign. "They need a label, I guess," Nauert told Farhi.

And if you think of segments on Fox as free strategy sessions for the party, well then, she was a GOP strategist, all right!

Farhi was so intrigued by Nauert that he wrote a profile of her in 2000, when she was thirty. The notion of a full-time talking head was still new and strange back then. Nauert comments on "an astonishing variety of political and public-policy issues," he wrote.

"Sometimes—especially now, the political season—she'll pop up three or four times a week. The Fox people think she's going places, although it's anybody's guess where."

It's safe to say no one guessed spokesperson for the State Department. That's not a knock on Nauert; it's a knock on what happened to the GOP.

Around this time, post-Lewinsky and pre-9/11, people started taking notice of cable's color palette. "Blondes make for better TV," a cringey *New York Post* story declared. The story named "blond gabbers" Ann Coulter, Kellyanne Fitzpatrick, and Laura Ingraham and said "the new wave of blond pundits continues the conservative line with the likes of Heather Nauert and researcher Monica Crowley." Nauert felt affronted enough by the *Post* to issue a denial. "Has my hair color helped me? No," she declared.

Nauert decided to cross over from commentary to reporting and enrolled at Columbia Journalism School. She earned her master's degree, became a correspondent for Fox, defected to ABC for a couple of years, then returned to Fox as an anchor as well as correspondent. In 2013 Ailes asked her to join *Fox & Friends* as the show's news headline reader. He said the show needed a "serious" person.

It should be obvious at this point just how many of the Fox Newsers and "pundettes" of the late 1990s and early 2000s wound up playing a significant role in the Trump inner circle: Kellyanne Fitzpatrick (now Conway) became counselor to the president; Bill Shine became communications director; Monica Crowley became an assistant secretary of the treasury; Ann Coulter became one of the loudest voices in Trump's ear about restricting immigration.

Nauert became a Trump lieutenant after a January meeting with the president-elect at Trump Tower. She avoided the main entrance, where there were TV cameras, because she didn't want the attention. Nauert's job reading news headlines on *F&F* was a bore, and it was never quite the right fit. She told friends she had outgrown Fox, especially in the wake of the Ailes scandal, and all the infighting that ensued. The Trump Tower visit turned into a job interview: "What would you want to do in the administration?" She named the State Department.

What Nauert lacked in foreign policy credentials, she made up for in Fox face time. She had covered the war in Iraq, the genocide in Sudan, and other international matters as a journalist. Trump offered her a job on the spot, though it was subject, he said, to incoming Secretary of State Rex Tillerson's approval.

While she waited for the slow gears of government to catch up to their conversation, Nauert continued reading the news on *F&F*—and one February day she publicly criticized Nordstrom for dropping Ivanka Trump's brand from its stores and "caving to liberal pressure." Forget that the decision was based on sales, not pressure. Nauert went even further, wearing clothes from Ivanka's line on the air. Was she trying to appeal to Ivanka's father?

Nauert interviewed with Tillerson at the State Department after his confirmation. Though he remained skeptical, Trump was sold, and the deal was done. She gave up a $500,000-a-year job on Fox for a $179,700 government salary but gained a much higher profile and a big new challenge, fielding sensitive questions from some of the toughest reporters in the world. She mostly held her own: She could be snippy at times, but was careful not to alienate the press corps the way Trump and Spicer did. Her hardest relationship was with Tillerson, who rarely let her travel with him and ignored her advice. He dismissed her as a "White House spy." "Rex disliked anyone POTUS endorsed," an insider said.

After one year, Tillerson was fired through a presidential tweet and Nauert remained. Circumstances changed. Nauert was welcomed into new Secretary of State Mike Pompeo's inner circle; he promoted her to "acting undersecretary for public diplomacy and public affairs." In one year, she went from Fox anchor to high-ranking State Department diplomat, traveling the globe, counseling the leader of the free world.

Nauert was the first full-time example of the revolving door of the Fox-Trump Temp Agency, so it made perfect sense that she came from *Fox & Friends*. Within days of the inauguration, White House reporters had to wrap their heads around the fact that the Fox morning show had supplanted the president's daily intelligence briefing. West Wing aides and lawmakers and lobbyists had to start watching the show so they could follow Trump's tweets and orders.

The *Fox & Friends* A-team started at 6:00 a.m. sharp, and Trump planned his day accordingly. Steve Doocy, Trump said, was a 12 out of 10. Brian Kilmeade was a 6, but later earned an upgrade to a 9. Yep, Trump really scored the hosts. When word got around, it became a running joke at the show. Trump graded Kilmeade to his face in a 2019 interview: "I used to say you, you were a solid 6, maybe a 7, but you're getting much better." Most journalists would be embarrassed to be graded by a powerful person they covered every day. But Doocy and Kilmeade occupied that strange space where so much of Fox News thrived—they talked about the news, they interviewed newsmakers, they covered breaking stories, but they didn't hold themselves to the news standards that journalists try to meet. Fans like Trump didn't just tolerate this, they embraced it, since they purported not to trust traditional newspeople anyway. They were predisposed to believe the worst about the NBCs of the world.

That's why I used to think *Fox & Friends* was an uncomfortable environment for Ainsley Earhardt. See, Earhardt had worked her way up in local news before joining Fox. She used to close her eyes and envision herself on NBC's *Today* show; in her sophomore year at the University of South Carolina, she stood out on the *Today* plaza with a sign that read "Will you marry me, Matt Lauer?" She graduated in 1999 with a journalism degree and the speak-truth-to-power attitude that comes with it. She wanted to report, but most of her work in local TV was news-reading. By her own admission she "did not know the first thing about politics" before arriving at Fox. So she learned from right-wing teachers like Hannity. Shine cast her on a regular segment called "Ainsley Across America" on Hannity's show, and she leaned on her newfound Fox friends while divorcing her first husband.

Earhardt's professional success was entirely her own; even her detractors conceded that. But as her second marriage came and went, there was chatter in the building about a possible romance with Hannity. The rumors were an open secret in and around *Fox & Friends*, to the point that on-air staffers assumed everybody else knew about it too. Some gossipers called it an affair, but Hannity was separated from his wife, Jill, and heading toward divorce. He was keen to keep his marital status a secret. (When I fact-checked the reporting for this book in June 2020, Hannity's team leaked information about his divorce the very next day. Nearly a dozen articles popped up on the web, all saying that the breakup was amicable and that Sean and Jill are great co-parents. A week later, the Earhardt dating rumors came out, but both sides insisted they were just friends.)

In any case, everyone could see why Earhardt fit right in at a show that was the a.m. edition of *Hannity*, a show that ran interference on Trump's behalf and mocked news outlets like *The New York Times*. She had a knack for channeling Hannity and undermining her J-school degree, like the day when she defended Trump's sickening description of the non-Fox media as "the enemy of the people."

"He's saying if you don't want to be called the enemy, then get the story right, be accurate and report the story the way I want it reported," she insisted. Her bachelor's degree in journalism must have spontaneously burst into flames.

The *F&F* mission in the Trump age was to make hosts and guests forget what they knew about journalism. That's how you became a "friend." On *F&F* Trump's agenda was America's agenda. Immigration was something to be feared. White Christian culture was something to be protected. The media, other than Fox of course, was something to be defeated.

And Trump's score for Hannity's angelic protégée? A perfect 10.

Earhardt's colleagues uniformly told me she is a lovely person. "She's very sweet," one said, "but"—of course there was a "but" coming—"this is not someone with a core set of political beliefs."

"It's not just Ainsley," the source added. "What you have to understand is, a lot of these people were basically blank slates. Blank canvasses."

Every morning in the car on the way in to the studio, Earhardt listened to hymns and read from the daily devotional book *Jesus Calling*. In the makeup chair, she leafed through the prepared research packet of printouts from right-wing websites. In the host seat, she was curious but not pushy. As one of her colleagues said, "She knows what she's there for." A magazine profile once likened Earhardt to a "wedding-cake figurine come to life," with a smile "glorious enough that when it flashes it feels like nothing in the world could be wrong." With the Trump White House in perpetual crisis, and *F&F* tasked with pretending it wasn't, that smile was worth millions.

In one of his last big talent moves before his past caught up to him, Ailes promoted Earhardt to the weekday job while she was on maternity leave with her newborn daughter. The schedule was a dream come true. She was done at 9 a.m., which meant she could spend most of her day with Hayden. When Earhardt separated from her second husband, in 2018, she issued a statement that said "I am grateful to Fox for their support and allowing me to spend all day, every day after the morning show with my child." Don't discount that—because she definitely didn't. When outsiders wondered how people at Fox tolerated the network's many fuckups and flaws, insiders pointed to the personal reasons—the friendships, the flexible schedules, the sense of "family," the respect for faith. Fox gave Earhardt a rainbow full of dresses in her office closet, managed by a stylist; a Bible study show on the web; and a chance to put out children's books through Fox's sister company. All of this made it a lot easier to wake up at 3 a.m. and come up with excuses for Trump's sins. She is "zenful," one of her best friends said.

That's why Earhardt stopped dreaming about the *Today* show. Years ago she had a high-powered agent who could have made it happen. But those doors aren't open anymore, and Earhardt's not trying to knock on them anyway. She looked at the map and saw a media landscape divided into red and blue. The theory went like this: There's no way to appeal to the entire country anymore, not if you're talking about politics. There's no space for a Dan Rather or Katie Couric or Peter Jennings anymore, if there ever was—conservatives always derided them as liberals anyway. And there's almost no way to cross over. If you want to be a TV star, you have to pick a side and stay there. If you imagine yourself to be in the middle, there's precious little space for you. If you doubt this, just look back at Megyn Kelly.

"The bandwagon"

The president's first time cribbing from *Fox & Friends* was less than a week into his presidency, on Thursday, January 26. He was glued to *Fox & Friends First*, the 5 a.m. hour that preceded the main event, from a cozy corner of his White House residence. Host Abby Huntsman (whose dad would go on to be Trump's ambassador to Russia) read a short news item about Chelsea Manning, whose thirty-five-year prison sentence had been commuted by Obama before Trump took over. Manning had penned an op-ed for *The Guardian* that predicted "darker times ahead" under Trump. She also criticized Obama's stabs at compromise with the GOP. Fox only mentioned the latter part.

Manning is "slamming President Obama as a weak leader with few permanent accomplishments," Huntsman said, while the words "UNGRATEFUL TRAITOR" appeared at the bottom of the screen. Fourteen minutes later, Trump tweeted that "ungrateful TRAITOR Chelsea Manning" was calling Obama weak. "Terrible!" he said.

Newsrooms scrambled to figure out why Trump suddenly cared about Chelsea Manning. I had a feeling I knew. I logged in to a service called TVEyes, which contains rough closed captioning data from all the major networks, and typed in the word "traitor." Huntsman's 5:50 a.m. segment popped up instantly. This was the first of hundreds of times that POTUS stole from *F&F*, and it was a strange sensation, even for some Fox staffers. Huntsman only found out about the "ungrateful traitor" rip-off when I tweeted about it.

So did the producers of *F&F* reckon with their newfound power? Did they triple-check their facts to make sure the president was fully informed? No. They continued to rip stories off fringe right-wing blogs and promote conspiracy theories and play into the president's worst partisan impulses. They took the cheaper partisan path. This was the show's natural setting, but suddenly the stakes were profound: Trump was making policy decisions based on what random TV pundits told him to do. "People claim Putin is Trump's puppet master but it appears that role is actually occupied by *Fox & Friends*," *The Intercept*'s Glenn Greenwald remarked. It sure seemed like the producers of *F&F* had more power than the CIA. And they used that power to feed him resentment news and nonsense about voter fraud and random stories about leftists on college campuses. To put it bluntly, the president's media diet was poisoned . . . and he gobbled it up.

As for the hosts, they played their newfound power for laughs. "I asked the president to blink the lights on and off if he was watching," Brian Kilmeade said at 7 a.m. on January 27. "Now clearly he's awake," Kilmeade said as the control room showed a live shot of the White House, where lights in an upstairs bedroom appeared to be flickering.

"Good morning, Mr. President!" Ainsley Earhardt said, joking that the flashing lights were a "Mayday" or an "SOS."

It was actually a prank concocted by a control room staffer. "It's a video effect," Steve Doocy told the audience. "Just having a little fun." HAHAHAHA.

A video clip of the prank zipped around Twitter, without the explanation, and many people thought it was real—because it could have been. Every single day, Trump either tweeted about Fox or talked to Fox hosts or cited Fox's coverage of how well he was doing. "Turn on Fox and see how it was covered," he said to ABC's David Muir after Muir brought up widespread criticism of Trump's self-aggrandizing speech in front of the CIA's Memorial Wall. Earlier in the interview, when Muir challenged Trump's discredited belief about voter fraud, Trump justified his lie by saying that "millions of people agree with me.

"If you would've looked on one of the other networks," he continued, clearly talking about Fox, "and all of the people that were calling in, they're saying, 'We agree with Mr. Trump. We agree.' They're very smart people."

Day by day, tweet by tweet, the country came to grips with the fact that presidential statements—which used to really mean something—were now just the misinformed and misspelled rants of an elderly Fox fan. No one was going to turn off Trump's TV set or stop him from tweeting. This realization sunk in for me on February 17, the first time he lobbed an "enemy of the people" grenade at the media. Up until that point I thought that Spicer and chief of staff Reince Priebus, old Washington pros, people I trusted to some degree, would intervene before things got that bad. I was wrong. Spicer and Priebus knew that the Stalinist "enemy" language was dangerous, but they didn't stop it from happening. After leaving the White House, Priebus's successor, John Kelly, said, "the media, in my view, and I feel very strongly about this, is not the enemy of the people. We need a free media." Yes—but he should have said that while working for Trump. Kelly also commented, in his post–West Wing life, that "you have to be careful about what you are watching and reading, because the media has taken sides. So if you only watch Fox News, because it's reinforcing what you believe, you are not an informed citizen." Another veiled critique of the president—but past the point when it mattered.

I asked people like Hope Hicks why aides didn't step in when the president used morally reprehensible rhetoric to disparage the free press. The answer basically boiled down to: "He's the president."

"You weren't elected. I wasn't elected. He was," one aide said.

That's what Fox's biggest stars told themselves too. If Trump wanted to ignore his actual PDB, short for the CIA-produced President's Daily Brief, and treat *F&F* like his No. 1 intel source instead, who were they to judge him? "He's the president."

"The untold story," a former Fox host told me, "was how one by one the hosts jumped on the bandwagon." The Trump train, if you will.

By the time Trump took over the GOP, Doocy and Earhardt and Kilmeade were already big deals at Fox. Doocy's lucky break came when Ailes's deputy Chet Collier tapped him to be the *F&F* weatherman in 1998. Kilmeade was a sideline reporter for the MSG Network, covering soccer matches, when Collier called him up for the morning show. "The joke around the office is that he'd be a soccer coach in Massapequa if it weren't for Chet," a Fox veteran said. "Now he's writing history books!"

The point this person made was, "it's not about the lucky break—it's what you do with that break." Once someone is on the ladder, they've got to hold on for dear life. Otherwise, Doocy might have been working behind the counter at an Avis car dealership, not behind an anchor desk.

Trump's election was the ultimate way to grow the "Friends" and gain newfound relevance, just like it was for Hannity and Jeanine Pirro. "Hosts realized, 'This is a real opportunity for me too,' " an insider said. Within weeks, it became clear to Doocy and the others that they had a real ability to impact policy-making. "We started to make decisions for Trump, meaning a lot of the decisions that were made on stories to cover were based on the fact that he was watching," a former host said.

When government officials couldn't get a face-to-face meeting with the president, they jostled for bookings on *F&F*. Corporations bought ads on the show, sometimes addressing "Mr. President" directly, because it was cheaper and more effective than hiring lobbyists. (What they didn't realize was that Trump usually muted or fast-forwarded straight through commercials.) Some Fox hosts started to greet the president by name. They understood that if Trump stayed happy with their shows, viewers would stay tuned. It created an incredible and perverse incentive structure that was completely at odds with journalistic values. Everyone at Fox could see that the way to get attention, to get promoted, to get ahead was to hitch a ride with Trump and never look back. This ethos trickled out from *Fox & Friends* to the shows before and after.

Take the early morning anchor Heather Childers. Before he ran for office, Trump used to tweet compliments to Childers. "You are doing a great job Heather!" "You do a great job on Fox!" In another universe, Trump would just be one of those guys posting comments to her Instagram page, pining for her attention, gazing at Fox's anchor desk with a hole in the middle that blatantly showed off her legs. But in the Trump age, the roles were reversed. Fox hosts yearned for *his* attention.

At first Childers's show started at 5 a.m., but then CNN's *Early Start* crept up on Fox in the key 25–54 demo. *Early Start* had a 4 a.m. start time for the same reason that so many local TV stations start their morning shows at 4 or 4:30: The earlier you start, the longer you can build audience as the morning goes on. In early 2017, when interest in all things Trump was sky-high, CNN's 4 a.m. live show topped Fox and MSNBC's repeats in the demo. So, in a wholly predictable move on the cable news chessboard, Fox moved Childers and *Fox & Friends First* to 4.

"Guys," TV critic James Poniewozik joked the day the earlier show was announced, "Trump has to sleep at some point."

The time shift wasn't just a response to CNN, it was also part of a post-Ailes plan to add more live hours of programming and push the ratings even higher. "It was an arms race," CNN's 4 and 5 a.m. anchor Christine Romans said. "No, literally, an arms race," she joked, alluding to the sleeveless sheath dresses encouraged by Fox's wardrobe department.

With Childers live at 4, Fox quickly returned to first place in the demo. Natural order was restored to the cable news universe. As that veteran producer said, "Ratings are the only thing that matters." But I would add an asterisk to that quote: After Inauguration Day, Trumpiness mattered too. Childers's show shared a name and topic selection and tone with its big brother, but it was merely Trump-friendly, not Trump-slavish. The president preferred the shows that were 100 percent sycophantic. He craved the purest form of the drug. More importantly, so did Fox's base. Hosts like Childers could sense this craving in 2017. Producers responded by booking Trump-ier guests and downplaying bad news about Trump. But Childers wasn't a total Trump bootlicker, and management wasn't fond of her, so her star didn't rise. She stayed in the same predawn hosting gig she'd had when Trump was hosting *The Apprentice*. Meanwhile, the Fox personalities who went full Trump (Hannity, Pete Hegseth, Maria Bartiromo) got rewarded with his affection and better time slots and bigger promo campaigns and fatter contracts. For a while, one man bucked this trend: Bill O'Reilly.

"I want the O'Reilly lighting"

In January 2020 I was on the phone with one of Fox's household names who said, with complete sincerity, "I think it would be good for the country right now if Roger Ailes were still in charge of Fox and Bill O'Reilly were still on the air."

Before you say "which country?" you should know that Ailes nostalgia was very real and very deep at Fox, even three years after his exit. Many insiders believed Fox would be better off with Ailes at the helm.

But O'Reilly? I didn't detect much longing for the return of Bill. He was not well liked when he was on at 8 p.m., and he was not missed when he was fired. So why would it be good for America to have *The O'Reilly Factor* still on Fox?

"Because O'Reilly would tell the truth," they said. "O'Reilly would sit down with Trump and call him a jerk to his face. Hannity will never do that."

I conceded the point. O'Reilly viewed himself at least partly as a journalist and acted at least quasi-journalistically. He had a complex relationship with Trump. Yes, they hung out at Knicks and Yankees games, but they also ticked each other off. O'Reilly was never all the way in—he was "three-quarters in" for Trump, one of his producers commented. "In Bill's mind," another source said, "he believed he could have his relationship and still give arm's-length political observations about the man. He didn't see himself as a complete hack, in bed with Trump." In fact he mocked Hannity for bedding down with the candidate. And this mattered because in 2015 and 2016 and early 2017, O'Reilly was still No. 1 in the ratings. Of all the Fox interviewers at the time, O'Reilly challenged Trump the most.

O'Reilly was known to book him personally. Trump was on *The Factor* all the time, though there were dry spells when they had beefs with each other. They'd usually work it out by phone or pass notes back and forth, though the spats occasionally spilled out on TV. After a Fox primary debate in March 2016, O'Reilly needled

Trump, asking, "Do you get mad at guys like me when I ask you the negative questions?"

"Well, you know, I think you've become very negative, I do think—"

"Me? Why, why would I do that?"

"I don't know, who knows, you'll have to ask your psychiatrist."

O'Reilly just chuckled. He knew how to appease Trump when need be. One producer told me that O'Reilly used to post-game his Trump interviews by talking with Trump critic Charles Krauthammer right afterward. But the candidate hated it, so O'Reilly eventually moved Krauthammer out of that immediate post-interview spot. "Remember, we were competing with Hannity, we were competing with other networks," the producer said. O'Reilly didn't think he could risk being cut off by the GOP front-runner, so he placated him. The goal, a source commented, was to "do an interview that was tough but not too tough."

It worked, because O'Reilly—not Hannity, not one of the "Friends"—landed the much-sought-after Super Bowl Sunday interview with the newly inaugurated president. Questions swirled about Trump's ties to Russia. At the heart of the matter: Why in the world was Trump always defending Vladimir Putin? The two leaders had just spoken by phone, so O'Reilly had a Putin question near the top of his list. The interview was scheduled for Friday, February 3, two days before the big game. Trump, as always, was very interested in how he looked.

"I want the O'Reilly lighting. I always look best with the O'Reilly lighting," Trump told Hope Hicks.

Don't worry, she said, "the O'Reilly team is coming."

The same crew that set up their Trump Tower interviews was at the White House this time. There was always a monitor facing Trump's seat, so he could see the shot as soon as he sat down. There was also "a little bit of trickery involved," a source confessed years later. "We always tried to make him think he looked better on our show." But it was all psychological—they weren't really lighting him differently.

The interview started, and O'Reilly brought up Russia. "Do you respect Putin?"

Trump said yes—"it's better to get along with Russia than not"—and then O'Reilly posed the kind of follow-up that Hannity never would. "He's a killer, though," O'Reilly said. "Putin's a killer."

Trump looked away and thought for a second. There are "a lot of killers," he said, turning back to O'Reilly. "We've got a lot of killers. What, you think our country's so innocent?"

The eyes of the O'Reilly crew members lit up. Did Trump just defend Putin and say America is guilty of the same sins as Russia? Russian state poisonings and arrests and occupations came to mind.

While O'Reilly hesitated, thinking about how to respond, Trump said it again: "You think our country's so innocent?"

"I don't know of any government leaders that are killers in America," O'Reilly said.

"Wellllll," Trump answered, "take a look at what we've done too. Made a lot of mistakes."

O'Reilly moved on, declining to challenge Trump's vague remark. He had pushed back a bit, which is more than Hannity would've done, but then he dropped the subject before eliciting a real answer. Was Trump thinking about CIA-led coups and assassinations? Was he referring to the Bush administration's responsibility for death and destruction in Iraq predicated on lies about WMDs?

Most likely Trump was thinking of nothing more than defending Putin. But viewers didn't know because O'Reilly never followed up. Instead, the "newsman" sat there slack-jawed and allowed Trump to get away with a sinister and yet sweeping accusation of murder perpetrated by his own government. This is what it meant to be "three-quarters in."

Hicks was the sole White House staffer in the room, and she was glued to her phone, overwhelmed by the never-ending spigot of press questions and requests. She should have known that Trump's defense of Putin was going to be a big problem—but she had so many other problems at any given time. "They did not have their act together," a Fox staffer observed. "The White House knew that comment was going out to the world. They could have gotten in front of this. They never did." Fox released the damaging sound bite on Saturday to promote Sunday's Super Bowl interview. Democratic congressman Adam Schiff, the ranking member of the House Intelligence Committee, said that Trump's comments were "inexplicably bizarre" and a "gift to Russian propaganda."

It wasn't like O'Reilly was out to hurt Trump. Arguably he was there to *help* Trump. But even when seated with a friendly interviewer, Trump found ways to hurt himself.

When hosts on other networks called out Trump for kowtowing to Putin, the Fox wingmen said the real scandal was the media's abusive treatment of Trump. The hourly anti-media shtick was best understood this way: Fox was a 24/7 ad for Fox. Every insult hurled at CNN and NBC doubled as a reminder not to change the channel. Every segment about some other news outlet's screwup doubled as a declaration to only trust Fox. "The secret sauce for Fox," MSNBC's Chris Hayes observed, is that "it's better for ratings to be in opposition, but if the media is the enemy then you're always in opposition!" It was as effective as it was cynical, and Trump helped by battering Fox's competition every step of the way.

It was hypocritical too. Trump called the news "fake" but pined for journalists' attention. O'Reilly constantly griped about the "mainstream media," but no one was more "mainstream" than he was. He was the most watched man in cable news, and he was welcomed on all the broadcast networks every time he wanted to sell a book. Yes, O'Reilly had some legitimate grievances about the liberal values of some major news outlets. But in the Trump years most constructive sorts of media criticism were replaced by destructive attacks. They didn't even buy what they were selling half the time: The same Fox talkers who called *The New York Times* "failing" relied on it for story ideas and background information. The same hosts who bashed CNN texted me links to their latest segments, hoping for coverage from CNN.

Sometimes I wondered if stars like Jesse Watters would have anything to talk about were it not for the Big Bad Media. Watters was an O'Reilly creation: He had started as a production assistant, joined *The Factor*, and turned into the show's go-to ambusher, showing up at the homes and offices of O'Reilly's targets. Viewers loved the on-camera confrontations and Watters's shit-eating, Trump-loving grin. Fox rewarded him with a *Watters' World* show, which started on the weekends once a month and then became weekly at the start of the Trump presidency. When called out for his offensive segments, like an outright racist segment interviewing residents of Chinatown, he claimed he was a "political humorist." He paired well with a new president who claimed "sarcasm" to get out of tight spots.

Six weeks after O'Reilly's interview with Trump, Watters was offered an Air Force One ride and an on-air chat. He asked Trump tough questions, like: "Chuck Schumer, the president of CNN, and Alec Baldwin. If you had to fire one person right now, who would you fire?"

In a rare show of diplomacy, Trump wouldn't choose one. He

said he was "disappointed" in all three. At the end of the chitchat, Watters prompted Trump to review several other people. "Last one: Jesse Watters," he said, like every great newsman who knew that he was the real story. We all remember when Mike Wallace looked the Ayatollah Khomeini in the eye and said, "Rate me."

Although Trump had ducked Watters's earlier question, he happily answered this one. "Tremendous future. Tremendous potential," Trump said. "Should be making good money, your agent should be very happy, and I enjoy your show. And honestly, you've been so nice to me, that this is why I turn down the biggest shows on television, and here I am: *Watters' World*."

When they posed for a photo, both grown men flashed a big thumbs-up to the camera. Watters was giddy. More than almost anyone else, the thirty-eight-year-old knew that this was a huge win in Foxworld—posing with POTUS, sucking up to power, covering up for corruption (not necessarily in that order). Trump's compliment to *Watters' World* hit on an essential truth: He skipped higher-rated TV shows like *60 Minutes* and favored lower-rated shows that were "so nice" to him.

If Watters saw that as the way forward, so did veteran journalists at Fox. Their response was not a thumbs-up. Instead, some started to pack up their things and send out their résumés.

"It's going to be a catastrophe"

Carl Cameron just couldn't take it anymore.

Every Fox fan knew Cameron as "Campaign Carl," the nickname given to him by Shep Smith. Cameron logged hundreds of thousands of miles covering twenty years of campaigns. He definitely earned the nickname. Younger reporters looked up to him—and not just reporters at Fox. Cameron was friends with the campaign junkies at the other networks too. That's how it works . . . or at least that's how it used to work. In 2016, Trump diehards jeered when Cameron socialized with CNN and NBC reporters at rallies. The sight of a Fox star fraternizing with the enemy? Unbelievable!

The venom and hypocrisy of the rallies exhausted Cameron. He was planning to leave Fox long before Trump won the GOP nomination, but the prospect of a Trump presidency sealed the deal. "There's no way I'm going to cover Trump the president," he thought to himself. "It's going to be a catastrophe."

During Trump's first few weeks in office, Cameron filed a handful of reports, then sat on the sidelines until his contract ran out in August 2017. He walked out the door and never looked back. Guys like Watters and Hannity didn't miss him. But Shep, Bret Baier, and Chris Wallace did. Those three anchors knew that Fox was losing one of its fig leaves of respectability.

Cameron was a Fox original who had worked for the Fox Broadcasting Company's embryonic news division even before Ailes arrived. Cameron sometimes quipped that he was "grandfathered in," but he was part of Fox's success. He was eternally proud of what he helped build, proud to train a generation of Fox reporters, and proud to work for Rupert Murdoch.

"In 1996, when we launched, I didn't see any bias at all," Cameron told me. Plenty of others did—critics argued that Fox was invented with a deadly defect—but Cameron just saw a scrappy news organization trying to take on CNN. He ticked through the daytime schedule circa 1998 and pointed out all the hours of straightforward news coverage that were later replaced by slickly packaged opinion shows. In the late nineties, the strategy was to beat CNN with news coverage, not commentary. But by 2017, he said, "entertainers" had taken over. "The access that some at Fox have, in the entertainment side, to the president is questionable if not dangerous," he said. He stopped there, but I could tell he had more to say.

Cameron didn't change over the years; the network changed around him. He met his second wife, Moira Hopkins, on the job, and they became a traveling pair, covering Bush and Kerry in 2004, Obama and McCain in 2008, Obama and Romney in 2012. He reported the stories while she ran the audio and video equipment, making sure everyone could hear him. It was a sweet and well-paying setup, but they constantly talked about post-Fox, post-trail life. They knew it was just a matter of time. Cameron dated the changes at Fox back to 2003, when the network's stars tried to paper over the Bush administration's lies about the Iraq invasion. He thought it got worse after Obama was elected. He watched as the network adopted a more aggressive approach that emphasized red-hot opinion over news. Bureaus went dormant. Reporters went long stretches without getting on the air. "The news muscles atrophied a lot," he said, while the entertainment muscles flexed. Cameron saw younger journalists sizing up Fox's reward structure and making calculations about their careers. Many people, some of whom still work at the network, made similar observations to me. "A lot of these guys realize that if they want to keep the money coming, they have to host a talk show," one said. The phrase "golden handcuffs" was invoked more than once. One veteran of the network said that up-and-coming talent "know they're not going to get hired by CBS or CNN because they've said so much stupid shit on Fox," so they stay put and keep talking and talking.

In private, during the 2016 primaries, Cameron likened Trump to a con man and reminded people of all Trump's documented fraudulent activity. He pointed out that Fox was owned by Murdoch, a phenomenally successful businessman who'd built a global media empire, while Trump merely sold his name to other people's projects. During the grueling campaign season "I was increasingly uncomfortable—and voiced it," Cameron said. He recalled several times that he hung up on editorial meetings—then scrubbed any trace of his point of view out of his scripts for Baier's show *Special Report*. That was his job, or rather, that was how he kept his job. There wasn't much of a market at Fox for fact-checks about Trump's checkered business past.

"The problem with Trump, speaking about him as a political journalist, is that his showmanship buffoonery is absolutely addictive," Cameron said. "Grizzled old TV producers would prefer to basically just take reporters out of the mix, run a montage of all of Trump's sound bites, and go to the panel. The sound bites generate instant outrage. Think about it: You get two different ad breaks out of that. Lots of ads for Geico. It's cheap and it's fast and it feeds everybody's biases."

But wait, I said to Cameron. Decent panelists, on Fox and every other channel, called out Trump's lies and performative victimhood. I went back and read hundreds of transcripts and stories. The 2016 campaign coverage was far tougher on Trump than people recall. Cameron allowed the point, but said it didn't matter. "All Trump wants is to be remembered," he said. All he wanted was attention. "He just had to say something nuts, and it completely absorbed everything."

When Trump emerged as the big story in the 2016 cycle, Cameron's wife said "fuck that." She finagled an assignment on Capitol Hill to get off the campaign trail. Cameron wanted out too. He was completely physically and emotionally drained. The rallies were the worst. "People would come up to me and parrot their excitement from a morning *Fox & Friends* falsehood, and I would have to say, 'No, that's not true,'" he recalled. How demoralizing for Cameron, to have his own colleagues responsible for so much pollution in the political atmosphere.

Cameron's dedication to truth was shared by hundreds of Fox journalists, most of whom toiled behind the scenes. Every time Steve Doocy got a story wrong, he undermined his coworkers. Every time Hannity said "journalism is dead" and real news is "fake," he actively insulted his own colleagues. And they noticed.

Reporters like Cameron lodged complaints about this. So did anchors like Shep, Baier, and Wallace—but they were advised by upper management to worry about their own shows. These men had enough sway to speak out publicly about the toxicity too, though their comments didn't result in any meaningful changes. Right after he signed a contract to keep hosting *Fox News Sunday* in 2017, Wallace told the Associated Press that the anti-media attacks from his colleagues bothered him, though he was careful not to name any names. "If they want to say they like Trump, or that they're upset with the Democrats, that's fine. That's opinion. That's what they do for a living," Wallace said. "I don't like them bashing the media, because oftentimes what they're bashing is stuff that we on the news side are doing."

Not to mention all the times that prime time propaganda undercut the interviews Wallace and Baier had conducted earlier in the day. Cameron felt sympathy for the folks he was leaving behind. "All I can say is to my friends in the news division: Good for you," he said. "Hang in there. Keep your sanity."

For Wallace, that wasn't so hard. Happily ensconced on Sunday mornings, he rarely crossed paths with Hannity. But he said of the media bashers, "I don't think they recognize that they have a role at Fox News and we have a role at Fox News. I don't know what's in their head. I just think it's bad form." And it got more extreme each and every year. Pre-Trump, Hannity corrected anyone who labeled him a journalist, commenting in October 2016 that "I'm not a journalist, jackass." But in the Trump age he embraced the J word. "I'm an advocacy journalist, or an opinion journalist," he said in a November 2017 interview with the *Times*, the same newspaper he likened to toilet paper.

So Hannity said he was a journalist at the same time he declared that "journalism is dead." He needed to have it both ways to keep his illusion alive. Adam Serwer of *The Atlantic* once observed that "the way to understand conservative media's hostility towards the rest of the press is that they think it operates the way many of their reporters and outlets do—that they take money to make shit up."

Hannity posed as the head of a shadow news operation that reported the *real* news that Shep and others ignored. He regularly cited his "investigative reporting team"—made up of far right commentators and freelancers who would never get hired by Rupert—and pretended his people were Fox-approved. His insistence on calling commentator Sara Carter an "investigative reporter," for example, spurred complaints from Fox's actual reporters.

"We know it's a problem. We are trying to stop him," an exec told me. But Hannity was defiant. Clearly management wasn't trying hard enough. The schism between opinion and news was growing ever wider, like a scene in a disaster flick where a dormant fault ruptures and splits the land into two halves.

Baier, Wallace, and Shep felt they were working from the inside to preserve some space for news as Trump and Hannity gained power at Fox. Baier told people he had "horse blinders on," which was supposed to mean he was solely focused on his *Special Report* hour.

When people at hoity-toity DC dinner parties questioned why he worked for a propaganda machine, Baier told them to give his newscast a try and see if it seemed fair. He said he studiously avoided getting "emotional," as he thought too many other news anchors were, even though he was confounded and frustrated by Trump's conduct.

Staying unemotional—that was the way to stay sane as a newsman at Fox. But emotion flooded through the opinion shows—and to be honest that's what people have been hardwired to prefer from storytellers, ever since ancient peoples gathered around fire pits and told tales passed down through the generations. In this war on truth, passivity was a sure way to lose.

Critics of Fox said that anchors like Baier and Wallace were used to disguise Fox's true propagandistic purpose. Wallace was confronted about this at a Columbia Journalism School event on February 25, 2020. An audience member asked: "Do you ever think that Fox News is using the quality of your work to truth-wash prime time?"

"I think that you're underselling the intelligence of the viewer," Wallace responded. "I think the viewer knows that what goes on in prime time is opinion." And there's a "firewall" between news and opinion, he insisted, even though the wall had been dismantled by 2020. I watched it come down brick by brick—as in March 2017, when Judge Andrew Napolitano sparked an international incident.

"You should be talking to Fox, okay?"

What better way to wow your friends than to get the president of the United States on the phone?

One night, while out drinking with friends, Fox's senior judicial analyst Judge Andrew Napolitano was being overly humble about his access to President Trump. So a friend decided to put it to the test. He Googled the White House switchboard number and called the operator.

"I'm calling on behalf of Judge Napolitano," he said, trying to reach the president.

The phone rang just a few minutes later. It was one of Trump's secretaries. "Can the president call you first thing tomorrow?"

And sure enough, Trump did.

Napolitano's friendship with Trump stretched back thirty years, back to the 1986 day they met at the memorial service for Roy Cohn, Trump's consigliere and Napolitano's occasional collaborator. A year later, Napolitano was named a New Jersey Superior Court judge. Napolitano and Trump's sister, a federal judge, once worked a trial together. Napolitano's eight years on the bench transformed his political thinking, from a "law-and-order conservative" in his youth, he said, to a "true libertarian." Police officers lie; prosecutors cheat; governments steal. Citizens must defend themselves against tyranny. This was the world view he brought back to private practice in 1995 and brought to Fox in 1998. The title of judge distinguished him in a sea of legal commentators, and appearances on *Fox & Friends* catapulted him to power in the Trump age. "The president loves you," Roger Stone told him. Trump often brought up Napolitano's analysis with his actual lawyers. He once told the judge, "Everything I know about the Constitution, I learned from you on *Fox & Friends*." Napolitano was both flattered and horrified.

During the transition period Trump invited him to Trump Tower twice for lengthy meetings, about ninety minutes each time, where the president-elect free-associated about the Supreme Court and gay marriage and Syria and so on. Hanging out in Trump's office with VP-elect Mike Pence and Newt Gingrich and others, the two men talked about Trump's list of potential replacements for

Antonin Scalia, and as Napolitano described the type of person he thought should be on the bench, Trump interjected: "Sounds like you're describing yourself."

"No, no," Napolitano begged off, "I'm describing Neil Gorsuch."

Trump was having fun. "All right," he said, leaning in, "give me a spiel as to why I should put you on."

And that's how a Fox commentator wound up auditioning for the Supreme Court.

Napolitano later said, of the surreal exchange, "Who would turn that down?"

Trump wasn't exactly serious, but he enjoyed flattering his friend. Age sixty-six at the time, Napolitano was too old to be considered for the court anyway, as seventy-three-year-old Gingrich pointed out: "The judge is a little long in the tooth."

"Fuck you," Trump shot back at Gingrich. "I'm four years older than the judge and I'm about to become president!"

Napolitano's chats with Trump continued after the inauguration, which led to speculation—never confirmed—that the president was one of his sources for a story that upset America's closest ally.

Egged on by radio host Mark Levin, Trump was tweeting wild-eyed claims that "Obama had my 'wires tapped' in Trump Tower just before the victory." This accusation was false, but it was welcomed on the right, where a new narrative was taking shape—a narrative that maintained the real scandal wasn't the Russian attack on the election, it was the way the "deep state" investigated the Russian attack in a desperate attempt to stop Trump. It was like saying *We're not gonna report the crime, we're just gonna report on those who care that a crime was committed.* It was worse than a cover-up. Fox eventually coined a catchy name for this: "Investigating the investigators."

First and foremost, Trump needed some backup. He was getting hammered for the wiretap lie. Napolitano rode to his rescue. "Fox News has spoken to intelligence community members who believe that surveillance did occur, that it was done by British intelligence," he said on the talk show *Outnumbered*.

If, he went on, "if" Obama did this, "we have a very, very, very serious criminal issue on our hands." Napolitano couched this explosive claim with the word "if" again later in the day. But the next morning he went on *Fox & Friends* and erased all doubt. Instead of saying his sources "believed" it happened, he made it sound like his sources knew. The way he worded it is important: "Three intelligence sources have informed Fox News that President Obama went outside the 'chain of command'—he didn't use the NSA, he didn't use the CIA, he didn't use the FBI, and he didn't use the Department of Justice. He used GCHQ," short for Government Communications Headquarters, the British intelligence agency. Thus, "there's no American fingerprints on this."

Napolitano looked at cohost Brian Kilmeade, who delivered the takeaway line: "So Trump might be right, except for the fact [of] who did it. Unbelievable."

Kilmeade said the judge did a "great job," but Fox's head of news Jay Wallace was aghast. Who were Napolitano's sources? What the hell was he doing, stating as fact that Obama used the British to spy on Trump? The judge was making it sound like the network had landed a big scoop, when it hadn't. No one vetted what Fox's top legal expert said on air to millions of viewers.

This was a typical Trump-era conundrum: The "Trump was right, Obama did it" segments bolstered Napolitano's standing with the president, but hurt him professionally. Wallace intervened and said Napolitano couldn't keep going on the air and citing secret "sources" who were "informing Fox News" about a scandal, because that made it sound like Napolitano was speaking for the network's news division, and he was not.

This episode might have stayed contained to the newsroom, but Sean Spicer changed that. Napolitano had given the White House some sketchy support for Trump's tweets, so Spicer had to run with it. He read Napolitano's "report" aloud at a press briefing, which prompted public rebukes from the Brits. "Nonsense," GCHQ said in an extremely rare statement. "Ridiculous," a spokesman for the prime minister said. While State Department officials tried to smooth things over, Trump defended Spicer: "We said nothing. All we did was quote a certain very talented legal mind." At a press conference he called Napolitano a "very talented lawyer on Fox" and told the reporter who asked about it, "You shouldn't be talking to me, you should be talking to Fox, okay?"

I did. Fifteen minutes after the presser, the network's head of PR told me that the judge "stands by his report on *Fox & Friends*." But did Fox stand by it, with the weight of the network and its credibility on the line? No. Even Napolitano's longtime friend Shep Smith chastised the report after the presser. "Fox News cannot confirm Judge Napolitano's commentary," Smith said. "Fox News knows of no evidence of any kind that the now President of the United States was surveilled at any time in any way. Full stop."

The White House ignored this correction, of course, and Trump kept on believing what he wanted to believe. But this incident was a big deal inside Fox: Even the Murdochs became involved. Rupert's top priority at the time was winning his takeover bid for British Sky Broadcasting. Regulators were torturing him, questioning whether he would be a "fit and proper" owner, as the law required. He'd already lost out on Sky before. The last thing he needed was Fox News pissing off the British government. He wanted Napolitano's segments disavowed loud and clear. That night, Baier looked into the camera and stated, "We love the judge, we love him here at Fox, but the Fox News division was never able to back up those claims." Fox execs benched Napolitano for a little while—because the ultimate punishment in TV is to starve someone of airtime. They also leaked this reprimand to reporters. Media critic Erik Wemple summed up the episode best: "Dear Fox News," he wrote, "How does it feel to be taken very, very seriously?"

"Stench"

With Napolitano on leave, Rupert and his committee of managers strategized about their next crisis. *The New York Times* was about to take down the network's biggest star.

When Ailes was forced out, the *Times* caught wind of secret settlements between Bill O'Reilly and women who accused him of harassment. Fox execs knew about the impending *Times* story for months. They knew about O'Reilly's reputation all the way back in 2004, when producer Andrea Mackris sued him for sexual harassment. They also knew about at least some of the settlement deals when, in February 2017, they renewed O'Reilly's contract for an astonishing $25 million a year, up from about $18 million previously. His ratings power was unparalleled. His show was still growing in popularity. So the deal was supposed to keep O'Reilly in place as the cornerstone of Fox News through all four years of the Trump presidency.

Extending his contract nearly a year before it was set to expire was the ultimate show of support for a broadcaster who felt besieged. It sent a message that nothing could bring him down. Hey, "sometimes that's what you have to do," an exec mused, challenging me: "*You* try keeping talent happy for a day." There's that word again—talent. With employees, rules are followed and standards are enforced. But in the immortal words of Donald Trump, "When you're a star, they let you do it. You can do anything."

O'Reilly, dubbed "Billo" by his detractors, tested that proposition. The *Times* story, released on Saturday, April 1, said five women "received payouts from either Mr. O'Reilly or the company in exchange for agreeing to not pursue litigation or speak about their accusations against him. The agreements totaled about $13 million."

Skittish sponsors reacted to the *Times* story by telling Fox to move their ads away from *The Factor*. Fox hoped to ride it out, but by Monday night, Mercedes-Benz had publicly disowned the show, and dozens of additional advertisers bolted the next day. The producers responsible for loading in the commercial break times noticed the ad loads getting lighter each day. Viewers noticed too, and loved it, because it meant more time for Billo's content, but it also meant millions in lost revenue for the Murdochs. In response, O'Reilly used his show to bash the media—"deception is everywhere," "there are few standards left"—and praise the Murdoch-owned *Wall Street Journal*. It was a cheesy, desperate, and obvious ploy to suck up to management. "In the end, it's math," a rival host said as the scandal deepened. "If it costs them more than it gets them, he's gone."

O'Reilly's defenders claimed he was just your average sixty-seven-year-old man with a flirty streak. "He is a good person," Trump told the *Times* in an Oval Office interview on April 5. "Personally, I think he shouldn't have settled. Because you should have taken it all the way. I don't think Bill did anything wrong." At that point, Hope Hicks interjected—"Can we get to infrastructure?"—and other aides laughed.

At least Hicks knew Trump should shut up. One of the women paid off by O'Reilly, former Fox Business host Rebecca Diamond, tweeted her disappointment at the president, saying "such comments tell women they won't be believed." O'Reilly was becoming a serious liability for the network. The *Times* reporters had more info about other O'Reilly payouts that they couldn't quite report, yet. And former host Julie Roginsky had just filed a damning lawsuit against Fox, Ailes, and Shine, alleging that Shine—the current copresident of Fox News—"aided and abetted" Ailes's harassment and retaliation. "Shine and other senior executives kept Ailes' conduct secret and enabled it," the suit asserted.

The Murdochs fretted about how all of this was affecting the Sky deal in Britain. Looking back, an O'Reilly ally told me, "Here's what people didn't appreciate: The Murdochs were desperate to get the Sky deal done. They thought Bill was a hindrance."

By the end of the week, a replay of the Ailes drama was underway. "There was a huge divide internally," one of Rupert's lieutenants said. "Those who thought O'Reilly should be ousted were actually secretly pushing advertisers to boycott." That wing was led by James Murdoch, who wanted O'Reilly out right away. Rupert was taking his time, weighing all the *Factor* factors, including the Sky transaction. Lachlan was siding with his dad over his brother, saying he was reluctant to cave to the "liberal media." O'Reilly was hearing all of this second- and third-hand, and he was coming unglued. Rupert tried to calm him down, and said his job was secure. But there was an X factor: The law firm Paul, Weiss was about to review new claims against O'Reilly that were being phoned in to the company hotline.

Time was on the company's side because Billo had a preplanned vacation coming up. Yes, it was truly preplanned. There have been other times when Fox "vacations" were actually punishments after bad behavior or cooling-down periods amid scandals, but *Factor* staffers had known about this vacation for months. On April 13 O'Reilly flew to Italy for R&R and leaned on Cardinal Timothy M. Dolan, the archbishop of New York, to line up a VIP meeting with Pope Francis at the Vatican. Maybe he thought only the Pope could save him now.

Back in New York, staffers chuckled when they walked by the oversized ground-floor poster of O'Reilly that said "NOBODY MOVES THIS MAN." The man was at risk of being removed any day. What ultimately doomed him was the new complaints that Paul, Weiss evaluated, according to sources involved in the matter. "Rupert just wanted to rid Fox of the stench," a Fox lifer said.

O'Reilly was in denial. Just like Ailes nine months earlier, he tried to throw around his power, even as it slipped away. O'Reilly wrote to his lawyers on April 18 and acted like he owned the 8 p.m. time slot: "You all should know that I will not put up with much more from FNC" (an abbreviation for Fox News Channel).

But in Rupert's mind, *The Factor* was already canceled. Tucker Carlson was already in line to take over the time slot. Billo didn't own 8 p.m., Rupert did.

On the morning of April 19, O'Reilly shook hands with the Pope in St. Peter's Square. At 2:30, back in New York, programming exec Suzanne Scott summoned the nervous *Factor* staff into a second-floor conference room. Before she could get the words out, some of the producers looked up at the TV monitors and saw CNN's banner: "BILL O'REILLY OFFICIALLY OUT AT FOX NEWS." In other words, the Pope gambit had failed. And just as Rupert didn't let Ailes address the staff on the way out, O'Reilly was not afforded a chance to say goodbye on the air, but—and this may be the biggest "but" I've ever uttered—he was given a $25 million parting gift.

The next day workers removed the O'Reilly poster so people would stop snickering at it. O'Reilly landed back in New York and retreated to his Long Island mansion, where he launched a podcast and hoped someone would listen.

Trump, having again sided with the loser, did what he always does: dropped him and moved on. Trump had absorbed the key lesson of the Ailes scandal: Fox was so much bigger than any one person. Trump needed the network, but he didn't need every individual. Besides, O'Reilly was critical of him sometimes. Hannity was now the undisputed biggest star at Fox, and a much more dependable ally.

Hannity's loyalty even extended to Billo. Back when Hannity was the ratings runner-up, he and O'Reilly loathed each other. But when *The Factor* and its host were booted from Fox, Hannity actually felt some sympathy for the guy. On September 27, 2017, he brought the disgraced ex-host back into the Fox News HQ for a special prime time interview. And when O'Reilly promoted Hannity's ratings, Trump happily retweeted the news. Management told Hannity "never again" when he broached the idea of a second interview. The whole thing was an embarrassment. Later on, when Hannity said O'Reilly should "go back on Fox," there was an uprising in the ranks. One of the staffers who emailed me called Hannity's idea "despicable."

"What message does Sean send to our female colleagues here when he's openly inviting someone who used his position to prey on women? This is not about Democrats vs. Republicans," the staffer wrote, "this is about basic human decency."

It was cringeworthy to see Hannity act like nothing had changed when so much had. O'Reilly was gone. Ailes was gone. Greta was gone. Kelly was gone. Fox was Hannity's network now and he needed to act like it. Instead, he just kept booking O'Reilly on his radio show instead of on TV.

Career-wise, Hannity was in the I-don't-give-a-shit stage: He had made it to the top, and now he could coast for a while. Most days he portrayed himself as a carefree guy, "just having fun," he said, while taking advantage of his access to the president. But Trump's public and private rants and raves were a burden.

Hannity occasionally called in very personal favors. He was a family man, his separation from Jill notwithstanding, and when his son Patrick's tennis team at Wake Forest won an NCAA men's championship title, he was the "driving force" behind the team's special visit to the White House, the university said. "Patrick is back there," Trump said during the event, making sure to single Junior out for praise. Trump even joked that Patrick's team could borrow the presidential tennis court, first installed by Theodore Roosevelt in 1910.

That was a fun day. Hannity had a lot of fun days. But being No. 1 had some serious drawbacks too. "Think about it," an exec remarked to me. "No. 2 is a fun spot to be." Picture a pro cyclist drafting behind the leader. "But when you're No. 1, life is much harder," the exec said. It was all riding on Hannity now.

"Tell Sean to knock it off"

Certain restaurants in Manhattan are made for celebrating. Marea on Central Park South is one of them. The sunken dining room, the Poltrona Frau leather banquettes, the braised-octopus-and-bone-marrow fusilli—it's all meant to spark joy. But Rupert used the restaurant for a different purpose on Monday, April 24, 2017. He took Shine and Abernethy for $39 plates of spaghetti and some tough talk about pushing past the O'Reilly scandal and pulling Fox out of crisis mode. There was a photographer waiting on the sidewalk when they finished dessert—something Shine wanted, because he needed Rupert's backing. When the photos hit the wires, the press interpreted the very visible lunch as a public show of support for the embattled execs, but it was actually the beginning of the end for Shine, and his glum face gave it away.

Up until this point, Shine had been a Fox News success story. The son of an NYPD officer, Shine graduated from college in 1985, found a TV production assistant gig on Long Island, worked his way up to director, and parlayed that into a producing position at a channel named Newstalk. Hannity called in to the channel and filled in for the hosts often enough that he got to know Shine in 1995. They both wanted to be so much more than minor leaguers. When Ailes recruited Hannity for the launch of Fox News, Hannity recommended Shine as producer. Then they grew up at Fox together. Shine was a company man through and through, commuting into Manhattan on the Long Island Rail Road and staying as late as Ailes needed. "He was Roger's bag man," a friend of both men said. And Hannity's best man: They golfed and took family vacations together.

Shine was a Republican, but he cared far more about ratings than political rhetoric. He was affable, he was steady, though not a natural born leader with killer TV instincts like Ailes. Shine and the rest of the gang were more like caretakers who, when solving problems, asked themselves "What would Roger do?"

They flailed about and moved shows around the schedule to replace O'Reilly. Tucker went from nine o'clock to eight. The 5 p.m. talk show *The Five* filled the empty nine o'clock slot. O'Reilly's frat-boy sidekick Jesse Watters was added to *The Five*, replacing Eric Bolling, who stayed at 5. Right when O'Reilly's exit was announced, Bolling was called to Ailes's old conference room, where Rupert was seated at the head of the table. Shine and Suzanne Scott were with him. "Congratulations," Rupert said, "you're our new five o'clock host." But it wasn't something to celebrate.

Ailes had invented The *Five* in 2011 when he needed to replace Glenn Beck in a hurry. Shine joked that the name wasn't a reference to the time slot, "it's because Roger came up with this brilliant idea in five minutes." Ailes put five rotating cohosts around a table, creating a right-wing version of *The View* with one token liberal for the others to beat up. Ailes was proud of his casting abilities and said each character had a specific role to play: Bolling was the jock, Dana Perino was the straight-A student, Bob Beckel was the left-wing crank, Greg Gutfeld was the cutup. Rounding out the five was a "hot chick," in Ailes's words—two actually, Kimberly Guilfoyle and Andrea Tantaros, who took turns sitting at the end of the table so the wide shot showed off their legs. That was the "leg chair."

From a talent management point of view, this ensemble setup worked wonders: It meant that none of the hosts ever had too much leverage in contract talks. There was always someone mad about something, but "everyone was replaceable and everyone knew it," as a *Five* regular put it. So when the bosses decided to move *The Five* to 9, all the cohosts hated it—no one wanted to stay at work until 10—but all they could do was complain. Mostly they protested to their agents, but in Guilfoyle's case she also griped to Trump. Fox management could barely keep track of which personalities had which relationships with the president at any given time.

This lent credence to the arguments that Trump was practically running Fox and colluding with top talent. The man who was supposed to be in charge, Shine, felt off-balance and unsupported by the Murdochs. As scandals kept erupting and lawsuits kept hitting, further besmirching his name, he wanted Fox to put up a fight and issue statements defending him . . . but got almost nothing. Julie Roginsky's lawsuit was full of serious charges against Shine for retaliating "because of her complaints of harassment and retaliation" and because Roginsky "refused to malign Gretchen Carlson and join 'Team Roger' when Carlson sued Ailes for sexual harassment." Shine denied this, and his people (execs always have "people") pointed out that he had never been accused of sexual harassment by anyone. Still, Shine's history as Ailes's enforcer was a real problem, and the Murdochs were in no mood for further scandals.

One day after the Marea lunch, longtime anchorman Kelly Wright added to the pile of lawsuits and accused Shine and other Fox execs of racial discrimination. Wright, incredibly, was still on the air as a reporter and weekend anchor at the network. Now his name was added to a class action suit alleging discrimination and harassment. The lawsuit said Fox had asked Wright "to perform the role of a 'Jim Crow'—the racist caricature of a Black entertainer." Shine, the suit alleged, "demonstrated an obsession with race when it comes to discussions with Mr. Wright, including regularly asking him, 'how do Black people react to you?' and 'how do you think White viewers look at you?'" It also claimed that Wright complained to Shine and other execs that Fox is "too blonde and too white," but his concerns were ignored.

Other people of color at Fox agreed with Wright, but never said so in public. One exception was Eboni K. Williams, who briefly cohosted with Bolling during this tumultuous period. After she left the network, Williams, who is black, decried Fox as racist and fear-based. The entire programming strategy, she said, was to address conservatives' fears "of the intrinsic devaluation of whiteness in this country." White identity politics, in other words. Williams said she joined Fox to "talk to the people in the middle," but she was mostly talked over.

As the lawsuits showed, there was a growing target on Shine's back. He was deeply hurt by Wright's charges. Colleagues said he retreated from his work and wore the stress on his unshaven face. On Thursday, April 27, Gabriel Sherman popped a story that signaled a management change was imminent. Shine's leadership, he wrote, "has angered many Fox News employees, especially women, who view him as a product of the misogynistic Ailes culture."

Hannity read the story and hit the roof. "Somebody HIGH UP AND INSIDE FNC is trying to get an innocent person fired," he tweeted. He huffed and puffed and threatened to quit in solidarity with his best friend. He said Shine's exit would be "the total end of the FNC as we know it. Done." He even tweeted a hashtag, #IStandWithBill, and when some people wondered if he meant he was supporting the disgraced Bill O'Reilly, he changed it to #IStandWithShine.

Outbursts by talent are the sort of thing that a strong boss would prevent—or at least punish. But there was no such boss at Fox. "There's no one in the building, except maybe Rupert, who can tell Sean to knock it off," an exec told me. Rupert thought Hannity's conduct was childish but never thought Fox was at risk of losing him. Where would he go? Fox's wannabe rivals like Newsmax or One America News had such weak distribution and so few viewers that they weren't even rated by Nielsen. Hannity had just become the No. 1 host on the No. 1 network, and he wasn't going to give it all up for his BFF.

Rupert was right about that. One week after the lunch at Marea,

Rupert decided to relieve Shine of his duties. It played in the press like Shine's decision, but "he was whacked," an insider said. For his discretion, he received $15 million in cash and bonuses on the way out, the equivalent of roughly ten years' pay.

Hannity watched his friend go over the edge and then stepped away from the cliff: To calm his staff's nerves, he ordered pizza for his show team the next day and reassured them that he wasn't going anywhere. Still, Hannity wasn't about to completely abandon Shine. He immediately began lobbying Trump to hire his newly unemployed pal.

Bolling's show debuted a few hours after Shine's exit was announced. Some viewed the show as a reward for Bolling being one of Trump's top boosters on the network: The message was, put in the time, put in the pro-Trump effort, and you get your own hour. Rupert told him "it's your show," and the press release about O'Reilly's departure said he was the solo host. But three days before launch, the exec committee added two women to host with him: Williams and Kat Timpf. Suddenly, Bolling was just the cohost of a lesser *The Five*. The trio didn't gel, the experiment was a flop, and the show was canceled months later, but programming exec Suzanne Scott somehow dodged the blame. In fact, none of her bad decisions (or lack of decision-making) seemed to hurt her standing with Rupert. She was in line to be the first-ever female CEO of Fox News.

"Wardrobe enforcer"

"Tits up, hair back." That's what Ailes said he wanted Suzanne Scott to deliver for him.

"She was the wardrobe enforcer," a former Fox host told me.

That's why my phone lit up with texts when Suzanne Scott was named president of programming on May 1. Staffers couldn't believe that she was being promoted again.

"Suzanne Scott? She's the worst of all of them. Give me a break," a female Fox talking head wrote. By "worst," she meant Scott was an accomplice of Ailes.

Scott has never answered detailed questions about whether she was complicit in his abuse. The closest she came to commenting was in an interview with the *Los Angeles Times*, when she said "I had no clue on what was going on in Roger Ailes' office." Some staffers had a hard time trusting her.

Here's what Scott absolutely did know: that Ailes, for all his charm and power, was a racist and a misogynist with a warped and outdated view of the world. He wanted a certain southern beauty queen look from the women on his channel. And, according to current and former Fox anchors and commentators, he wanted Scott to deliver it.

Sometimes Scott would convey his messages directly, by telling new hires to "let hair and makeup do their job." She wanted more glam, longer eyelash extensions, shorter skirts, bronzer legs. Some of the Fox makeup artists called it the "Barbie doll look."

"Suzanne's job, straight up, was to enforce the dress code," a male Fox anchor told me. "She told women how short their skirts had to be." Scott typically did this indirectly, by sending word to a show producer who would then call a makeup artist to the set. Hosts and guests were told the "second floor" ordered a change. "She would call the control room and say, 'Fix her necklace.' Or change which way my hair was parted," recalled Alisyn Camerota, who left Fox for CNN in 2014.

The source who dubbed her the "wardrobe enforcer" said, "Suzanne would call and say, 'I don't like her shade of lipstick. It looks like shit.' The poor makeup people would rush out on set and change my lipstick." Personalities who objected to the cosmetic adjustments would sometimes be asked, "Don't you want good ratings?"

Television is a visual medium, so there are certain expectations, but some staffers charged that Scott took it to the extreme. Griping about facial hair is one thing, but she was known to tell men to shave even when they were in the middle of a breaking news marathon. It's hard to find a razor while on the scene of a mass shooting.

Scott's allies bristled at the description of her as a "wardrobe enforcer" and said that when she did place those calls, she wanted a professional look on the air—the opposite of "tits up." But no one believably denied that she was a good soldier for Ailes, who trained her to keep the ratings up, keep the profits up, and keep the shareholders happy. Scott learned from the best and the worst.

Scott joined Fox News at its founding in 1996 as an assistant to Chet Collier, one of Ailes's deputies. Collier said he believed that TV news had to tap into the "best elements of the entertainment world." People watch people, he said, a basic concept that producers sometimes forget when they try to fill the screen with videos and graphics and gizmos. "People watch television," he said, "because of the individuals that they see on the screen."

Collier died in 2007. By then, Scott had snagged a producing job, helped to launch Greta Van Susteren's prime time show, and became Fox's vice president of programming. "Chet taught me talent puts themselves on the front lines for this place. They need to be well managed and taken care of," she told the *Times*.

By paying hosts exorbitant sums of money and letting some of them host from home, Scott did take care of talent. But "well managed"? That's questionable. Ailes hated what he called "pissing inside the tent," the kind of host-on-host violence that got all the wrong kind of press attention. With Scott in charge, the tent was soaked.

Almost no one I interviewed depicted Scott as a strong leader. And those who did have positive things to say couched their comments by bringing up her weaknesses. "She has no vision," said one host who worked closely with her. "She's living off of Donald Trump and Roger Ailes."

I thought that was a harsh assessment. In the aftermath of the Ailes scandal, Scott pushed for multiple women to be promoted, like Dana Perino and Harris Faulkner. She championed workplace equality initiatives and improved interoffice communication. "I wanted to do everything I could to heal this place," she said.

I noticed that women at Fox were more critical of Scott than men—perhaps due to the "wardrobe enforcer" legacy of the Ailes years. At least ten female sources said things that would've sounded misogynistic coming out of a man's mouth. "All she did was provide Roger cover so that there was a woman on the management team," one longtime host said. The woman who texted me on the day of Scott's promotion, calling her the worst, went on to write, "They wanted a woman, I guess, but she's in waaaay over her head."

"It's all so complicated"

Throughout all of this turmoil, where was Roger Ailes? Like many seventy-six-year-olds, he was living a restless retiree's life in Florida. Unlike most seventy-six-year-olds, he purchased a $36 million mansion at the edge of Palm Beach's Billionaire's Row. He paid cash for the modernist six-bedroom, ten-bathroom home after receiving his $40 million payout from Fox. The real estate splurge was based on more than a love of modern architecture. As *Variety* explained at the time of the sale, "Floridian courts cannot force the sale of one's home to pay off judgments." His legal burdens were considerable.

Ailes was right down the road from Mar-a-Lago, but he was

no longer in touch with Trump. He could tell that Rupert was in Trump's ear and vice versa. This made his grudge against the Murdochs even bigger. He still reserved most of his disdain for the sons, James and Lachlan, telling author Michael Wolff in an early May phone call that "they got the memo."

What memo?

"If you strike the king, you better kill him."

Ailes lost some weight in Florida with his wife Beth's help, but otherwise had little to show for his post-Fox phase. Roger Stone had predicted that without Ailes, "Fox will be surpassed by a new conservative network," but that was hyperbolic and wrong. Ailes was more replaceable than anyone thought.

Some days Ailes stared out at the Atlantic and stewed. Friends like Matt Drudge came to visit. Suitors reached out, wondering if Ailes could help launch something Foxier than Fox, and he took the calls, scratching an itch that never subsided. He was bound by his noncompete deal, so "I can't call," he told Wolff, "but I can't stop people from calling me." Ailes had lots of ideas about where to find a billion dollars for a new network. He said he might get Steve Bannon involved. Maybe they could poach Hannity and O'Reilly and leapfrog Fox with its own talent. This was fantastical talk, but it was a way to pass the time. Wolff reported that Ailes was scheduled to meet with billionaire tech mogul and Trump backer Peter Thiel about a possible network venture in mid-May. But on the afternoon of May 10, he slipped and fell in one of his bathrooms. When the ambulance crews arrived, he was hemorrhaging blood from his head. He was put into a medically induced coma and never came out.

Thiel later denied that there was a meeting on the books. But in a 2020 documentary, *Man in the Arena*, Beth confirmed that Roger was contemplating a comeback just before he collapsed. "He toyed with the idea of doing something to compete with Fox News," she said. "He had that street-fighter mentality, he was not one to give up, so he was going to come back."

Beth was fiercely protective of her husband's privacy and furious at the Murdochs for throwing him overboard. So no one at Fox knew about his fall or his hospitalization in mid-May. If they had, they probably wouldn't have issued a press release on May 17 about Fox's decision to take a sledgehammer to Ailes's infamous "second floor." In place of the executive suites would be a state-of-the-art newsroom. Rupert announced it himself, intending to boost morale by moving Fox staffers out of the network's much-hated office space in the basement and into a light-filled showcase. He said the new space would befit "the most important media outlet in America." The symbolism wasn't lost on anyone: Ailes's lair was being demolished.

The next morning, shortly after 8 a.m., Ailes took his last breath. Beth took a final jab at his old network by sharing the announcement with Drudge instead of Fox. When the *Drudge Report* posted Beth's statement, *Fox & Friends* broke in with an alert and, in a rare display of journalism, credited the website with the scoop.

Ainsley Earhardt's voice quavered as she processed the news. "Roger, rest in peace," she said. At the end of the broadcast, one of the many employees Ailes had propositioned, Janice Dean, joined the cohosts on the couch and wiped away tears with a tissue. "I wouldn't be here without that man," she said. "He will be missed on this channel. He will be missed."

She was right. In spite of the sexual abuse and misuse of company resources, Ailes was admired and loved. Shep Smith wept on the air for the "media genius" while briefly acknowledging his "now well documented flaws."

Ailes had been Shep's guardian. The tears reflected the fact that

Shep now felt alone and isolated at the network. Scott said talent needed to be "well managed," but Shep wasn't being managed at all.

Ailes "left the company, and the rest is history unfolding," Shep said at the end of his on-air tribute. "To the true victims, respect and comfort. It's all so complicated. Everything here was and is, as he was."

In his will, Ailes left $250,000 for his brother, $100,000 for his former bodyguard, and $30,000 for his former assistant Judy Laterza. Most of his estate went to Beth and their son, Zachary, seventeen at the time. The Palm Beach funeral almost looked like a Fox event, with Hannity front and center along with Ingraham and Guilfoyle and news anchor Bill Hemmer. The group had flown down from New York on Hannity's Gulfstream. They mourned not just the Fox News CEO, but the end of the era when Roger ruled. The casket was draped with an American flag. Ingraham's website *Life-Zette* reported that Zachary spoke at the funeral service and invoked Wyatt Earp in the 1993 film *Tombstone*: "I want all the people who betrayed my father to know that I'm coming after them, and hell is coming with me."

Trump never called with condolences for the family.

"Anti-journalism"

On May 9, 2017, the day before Ailes slipped and fell, Trump fired FBI director James Comey and threw the ultimate wrench into the Russia probe. Official Washington was in crisis mode. By the day of Ailes's funeral, the DOJ had appointed a special counsel. "This is terrible," Trump said, lambasting Jeff Sessions for letting Robert Mueller in. "This is the end of my presidency, I'm fucked."

But he was wrong about that. It wasn't actually the end of his presidency—because he had Hannity and the Fox base. Ailes was gone, but his troops knew what to do: Make Mueller enemy No. 1, make sure Trump could keep rolling back regulations, and make sure the GOP could keep appointing judges to remake the federal judiciary.

On May 10, Trump invited Russian officials into the Oval Office and bragged about firing Comey, whom he called a "real nut job." Trump told them the Russia cloud—pressure from the probes into his Russia ties—would now dissipate. The opposite was true: Intelligence officials were leaking. Lawmakers were freaking. White House lawyers were researching impeachment procedures. Viewers could sense that the Trump presidency was in serious trouble. While MSNBC and CNN's ratings soared, Fox fell to third place in prime time in the 25–54 demo, a place the network hadn't been in seventeen years. Bad news for Trump was bad news for the Murdochs and their investors.

Fox's top shows responded with three techniques: deny, downplay, and distract. Hannity chose the path of greatest resistance: denialism. He sowed all those "fake news" seeds of doubt so that he could harvest them at a moment like this. The "destroy Trump propaganda media" are getting their facts wrong again, he proclaimed, linking reporters to Democrats and the "deep state" and Never Trumpers and every other bogeyman he could conjure up. "The truth does not matter to people that call themselves journalists," he lied.

Tucker Carlson took the easy media-bashing route too, leading his pretaped show with a lament about liberal media bias, while CNN and MSNBC led with breaking news about Comey preparing to testify. Tucker was excited about a Harvard study showing overwhelmingly negative coverage of Trump's first one hundred days.

The only problem was that Tucker had insulted the same researchers a year earlier, dismissing them as "political hacks posing as journalists" back then.

Tucker insisted he was a journalist, not a hack, but he showed shockingly little interest in covering Trump's scandal parade. He told his producers he just didn't think Donald was all that interesting. A perfect hour of his show never mentioned the president by name at all. Tucker said he wanted to "fill in the gaps that no one else is covering." A fair attitude—but by not covering Trump's mishaps and misstatements and misconduct, he was covering *for* Trump.

Hannity also came up with a demented way to change the subject. There's a "MURDER MYSTERY," his show exclaimed, while all of his rivals tried to figure out the Trump-Russia web. And this alleged mystery conveniently allowed viewers to think that there was no "collusion."

First, the facts: Russian hackers targeted the Clinton campaign and the DNC. They stole thousands of emails and other materials. Then, via WikiLeaks, they dumped the documents at specific times to help Trump win the election. Trump and his associates welcomed these dirty tricks. Roger Stone may have gone even further and coordinated with WikiLeaks. Some campaign aides believed that Trump and Stone talked about WikiLeaks dumps ahead of time, though neither man has ever admitted it. Russian operatives tried to help Trump in other ways, including through a torrent of online propaganda, but the DNC hack was critical. Hannity and his supporting actors didn't think twice about touting stolen emails in their effort to tarnish Clinton. Hannity taunted me for not covering the WikiLeaks emails more.

Those are the facts, but Hannity glommed on to a fiction about Seth Rich, a DNC staffer who was murdered in DC on July 10, 2016. Police concluded that he was the victim of a botched armed robbery, but the Russians seized on Rich's death to cover their hacking tracks: A Russian intelligence agency planted a conspiracy theory that Rich was a whistleblower who'd pilfered the DNC emails. In other words, they framed a dead man. This "inside job" theory was promoted by RT (also known as Russia Today, a Russian government–funded television network) and retweeted by Russian bots and embraced by far right–wing Trump fans who wanted to get their guy off the Putin hook. And in one of the most shameful episodes in Fox News history, the theory traveled from the Russian disinformation universe to *Fox & Friends*. Fox embraced the Seth Rich lie to "advance President Trump's agenda," veteran Fox commentator Rod Wheeler later alleged in a lawsuit.

This misconduct was incredibly cruel to the Rich family, for it compounded the misery of losing a loved one. Fox's coverage was "another extension of just this absolute hijacking of this horrible event that happened to our family, that we've never been able to process properly," Seth's brother Aaron said. Aaron felt like he never had a chance to properly grieve because he was on the defense against the ghouls who used his brother's body for political gain.

Wheeler got caught up in it through Malia Zimmerman, a FoxNews.com reporter, and Ed Butowsky, a money manager, Republican donor, and occasional Fox guest, both of whom were pursuing the "inside job" theory. Wheeler, a former DC police detective, agreed to help. Butowsky used his Trump White House connections to get a meeting with Sean Spicer, where, according to Wheeler, they told Spicer about their "investigation" into Rich's murder. Wheeler tweeted a picture from the press briefing room podium after the meeting and wrote, "Doing my part to Make America Great Again!!"

A few weeks later, after Zimmerman shared drafts of her story, Butowsky called Wheeler and told him "we have the full, uh, attention of the White House, on this." Butowsky claimed in a text that "the president just read the article. He wants the article out immediately." Butowsky later told NPR that he was just kidding about the president's involvement, but Wheeler didn't know that. He was under intense pressure to back up the Moscow-instigated conspiracy theory. And he was feeling underutilized by Fox. He wanted to get on TV more often, and this was a way to get on.

Wheeler wound up being the only on-the-record source in Zimmerman's story. He was quoted asserting that "multiple sources" said Rich "had contact with WikiLeaks." Wheeler later said his quotes were fabricated, but he also advanced the theory in multiple TV interviews. For *Fox & Friends*, this was enough to hit the gong.

"Hitting the gong" was an internal term for a "FOX NEWS ALERT." No matter what you were doing, the gong sound and the blazing red graphics made you look up at the television screen. This was the network's way of signaling breaking news (whether the news was actually breaking or not).

Fox wasn't singularly guilty of this tactic. The truth is that almost everybody in cable news abused the term "breaking news" from time to time. (I've overused the label myself and regretted it later.) Executives occasionally told their producers to cut back, to use the label a little bit less, to reserve it for really breaking news, and the producers did—for a week or two—until they couldn't resist anymore. Some producers swore they could prove that hitting the gong gave a fractional increase in ratings. Others had a very loose definition of "breaking." And others just didn't give a shit. The incentive was not to inform—it was to excite and enthrall so that everyone stayed put. The onus was on the viewer not to fall for it. But let's be real: If you're flipping between channels, and one screen is screaming "BREAKING" and the other isn't, which will you stop and watch?

At 7:17 a.m. on May 16, 2017, the director in the *Fox & Friends* control room cued the gong. "Another Fox News Alert," Ainsley Earhardt said, "a huge bombshell in the murder of this DNC staffer." The cohosts acted like the story was rapidly developing, and they hinted at a cover-up. "If that is true, and we don't know yet, looks like Russia didn't give it to WikiLeaks," Doocy said.

Doocy had been fed that line by Butowsky, who had emailed all the *Friends* hosts and top producers ahead of time to hype the story. "This is a massive story," Butowsky wrote, and "one of the big conclusions we need to draw from this is that the Russians did not hack our computer systems." He was explicit about it: "There was no collusion."

This was all predicated on a shoddy FoxNews.com story that should have never been published. While the opinion shows ran wild with the "MURDER MYSTERY" for a full week, this was originally a failure of Fox's news operation, the part run by Jay Wallace, the man who was supposed to protect the brand from this sort of embarrassment. Officials in the DC bureau were howling as soon as they saw the story. Reporters who actually covered the Rich case were outraged. Wallace pinned some of the blame on the heads of FoxNews.com. Eventually Fox retracted and removed Zimmerman's story because, the company said, it didn't meet the site's "standards." But there was no way to erase Hannity's smears and insinuations. If Rich was the leaker, he said, sounding just like Butowsky, "wouldn't that blow the whole Russia collusion narrative . . . out of the water?" Hannity brought it up day after day on his radio show and night after night on TV, even after reporters like CNN's Oliver Darcy proved it was bogus. The Rich family begged Hannity to stop. They even wrote a letter to his executive producer and shared it with the press.

Many of Hannity's own colleagues thought his conspiracy-mongering was disgusting. Other shows steered clear of it. "I'm not covering that," Tucker remarked to a friend, "because I'm not crazy." Let that sink in—a conspiracy too "crazy" for Tucker.

The Murdochs tried to ignore this fiasco, but grew concerned that Hannity's behavior would be used by UK politicians to sink the Sky deal. James was furious with how far Fox News had fallen. What was the point of owning these world-class brands, he thought, if Hannity and Trump tainted everything? On May 23, Suzanne Scott finally intervened to tell Hannity about the online retraction and leaned on him to take Rich's name out of his mouth. Hannity claimed not to be influenced by anyone, but he went on TV that night and asserted that he would stop talking about Rich "out of respect for the family's wishes."

Hannity was so afraid of pissing off his viewers—the ones who wanted to believe that Rich, not Russian hackers, was the culprit—that he added this, tantalizingly: "I am not going to stop finding the truth." This was two-faced Hannity at his absolute worst—saying journalism was dead on one side, but invoking reporting and truth-telling on the other side.

Fox hoped people would forget that Hannity's handling of the matter was morally reprehensible. His behavior served several Trumpian purposes—it distracted from the real-life Russia investigations, gave the MAGAsphere an alternative explanation, and fixed blame on a Democrat who couldn't speak in his own defense. Real people suffered. Aaron Rich just wanted time and space to grieve—but he had to play conspiracy Whack-a-mole instead. "When the stuff is really ridiculous," he said, "the number of times I've wanted to pick up my phone, and describe this absolutely ridiculous situation that's going on, um . . ." He paused.

"The person I would call would be my brother."

In March 2018 Rich's family sued Fox, Zimmerman, and Butowsky. "We hope to help prevent this kind of malicious and reckless behavior in the future so that others can be spared the hell the Riches have had to endure," the family's lawyers said. The legal jockeying took more than two years but was eventually resolved in their favor. Fox reached a multimillion-dollar settlement with the Riches and wished the family well. According to *The New York Times*, the deal was done on October 12, 2020, but Fox insisted on a provision that kept the settlement secret until after Election Day. Why, media columnist Ben Smith asked, was it important to Fox that "one of the biggest lies of the Trump era remain unresolved for that period? Was Fox afraid that admitting it was wrong would incite the president's wrath? Did network executives fear backlash from their increasingly radicalized audience, which has been gravitating to other conservative outlets?" No answers were forthcoming.

At The New York Times and CNN and other established news organizations, there are departments with names like "standards and practices" and rows of editors who supervise what's being produced and published. Their assignments and processes differ a bit depending on the newsroom, but the mission is the same—to uphold basic standards about sourcing, fairness, and accuracy. In practice this sometimes means they third-guess and fourth-guess the reporters who have already second-guessed their own work. Now, these news outlets still make mistakes, no doubt. Even the best-designed systems still fail. But the systems are like a shield that tries to protect reporters and their institutions. In the heat of the moment, when three news outlets all have the same scoop and they're racing to be first, and some editor in some other time zone is nitpicking the conditional clause in the fourth paragraph, the shield can seem self-destructive. Reporters sometimes curse the process under their breaths. I certainly have. But I've also been thankful that somebody tapped the brakes and helped me avoid crashing the car. Tap, tap, tap, just to keep everyone safe. That's what standards editors and fact-checkers and media lawyers do.

The Seth Rich debacle happened because Fox operated without brake-tappers. It lacked a traditional standards department. And most viewers generally had no idea. When I brought it up with journalists elsewhere in the industry, they were usually surprised too. Journalists who work at big-time, big-name national news outlets are used to having their stories and scripts eyeballed and reviewed and revised. But at Fox, one veteran anchor said, "I was never never ever asked to get a second source." Not once. Sure, individual journalists at Fox know they need a second source for scoops and other sensitive stories—"but that is a self-regulated experience," the anchor said. Only one show, Baier's *Special Report*, enforced a multi-step review process for stories, and that was only because Baier and his executive producer insisted on it.

So that's why Hannity was on the air all the time citing his "sources," oftentimes the president, without any review or scrutiny. On March 19, 2018, Hannity told viewers to expect "criminal charges against Andrew McCabe," the former FBI deputy director, for unspecified crimes. Hannity kept his viewers' hopes up until February 14, 2020, when the Justice Department formally said McCabe would not face charges. That night, Hannity didn't admit he was wrong, he just shifted the goalposts: "My sources," he said, "the same sources that I've been using for you in getting the story right for three years," claimed that Attorney General Bill Barr "is now focused on something much bigger" than McCabe. There was no accountability for his errors. And he would say anything to keep people watching for another day.

It was a demoralizing experience, the veteran anchor told me, "attempting to do journalism in a place that's anti-journalism." It was doable, yes, but there were few incentives to do it. It's no wonder why daytime anchors and correspondents headed for the exits. Jenna Lee, one of the network's most talented anchors, signed off on the day her contract expired, June 2, 2017.

Lee was a natural at Fox. Her on-air demeanor oozed red state values. Her husband was a decorated U.S. Navy SEAL. Still, she chose not to re-up. "I love being a journalist. I believe it's what I'm called to do," she said in her farewell to viewers. Left unspoken was this: Why couldn't she live up to her calling at Fox?

Lee declined to comment, even years later. She truly appreciated her time at the network and didn't want anyone to think otherwise. But when she left, she told friends that she could tell "the real estate for real journalism was shrinking" at Fox. She saw colleagues like Ed Henry slowly but surely assuming more political personalities, trying to be what viewers wanted them to be. It was clear to everyone that the network wanted less news and more "programming," the favored word inside Fox for yak-fests like *The Five* and *Hannity*. The news side was being muzzled while the pro-Trump opinion side was being handed a megaphone cranked up to 11. And that's exactly what Trump needed.

"Why all these lies?"

Walk into a green room at Fox in the Trump era, where guests drink stale coffee and wait their turn for a live shot, and you might find Rudy Giuliani chewing over an anti-Mueller conspiracy theory. Or you might hear Jeanine Pirro down the hall shouting at a White House aide through the phone. "I spoke with POTUS," she bellowed on more than one occasion. "He *said* he would come on my show!"

And Trump did, over and over again. As Mueller investigated Russian interference and reporters chased leads about a collusion-y Trump Tower meeting, Trump let Fox in and kept the rest of the press out. One day he chatted with Ainsley Earhardt; the next day, Pete Hegseth. And Trump's kids were on Hannity's show so often, they should have had badges to the building.

The sad truth was this: Hannity wasn't in the news business, he was in the stop-the-news business. He coordinated with virtually every power broker of the Trump era: One minute he was texting with Donald Trump Jr.; the next minute, Paul Manafort. He knew about Don Jr. and Manafort's infamous June 9, 2016, "dirt" meeting at Trump Tower more than a week before *The New York Times* revealed to the world that Don Jr. had allowed a Russian lawyer who was offering anti-Clinton opposition research to pay a visit. Emails in advance of the meeting promised that the anti-Clinton dirt was part of "Russia and its government's support for Mr. Trump." Trump's presidency was forever tainted by the revelation.

Hannity was in the loop about the meeting by late June of 2017. If he felt any loyalty to his Fox colleagues, he would have tipped off the DC bureau. Instead, he strategized with the Trumps about how to keep it from coming out, and what to say if it did. Why, Hannity wondered, was this Russian lawyer even allowed in the country? Maybe, the president said, this was all a setup. This was talking-point collusion.

The *Times* broke the news on July 8, 2017. Day after day, the headlines were astonishing:

- "Trump Team Met with Lawyer Linked to Kremlin During Campaign."
- "Trump Jr. Met Russian for Dirt on Clinton."
- "Trump Jr. Was Told in Email of Russian Effort to Aid Campaign."

Hannity stuck to his talking points and stayed on tape while the news was breaking everywhere else. All of the real action was happening off-camera—Hannity with his phone glued to his ear, counseling Don Jr., telling him to come on TV and clear the air. They came up with a plan. At 10:50 a.m. on July 11, Fox announced Hannity's "exclusive interview" with Junior. Ten minutes later, Junior released all of the emails in question, preempting another *Times* story that was about to hit. That one of the emails offered the campaign info that would "incriminate" Clinton, as part of Russian "support for Mr. Trump" was Category 5 news. I was on set with Kate Bolduan while she anchored on CNN, and she didn't take a commercial break for an hour. Same thing on MSNBC. But Fox's newscast merely mentioned the emails, then moved on to other stories, acting like Junior's willingness to collude was no big deal. That was the party line all day and night. "The real journalists at Fox News must be disappointed that Don Jr. is talking to Hannity, not them," I tweeted. Hannity replied, "Lol. At least Fox has real journalists."

They did then. They have fewer now, due to the conduct of crusaders like Hannity.

Shep punctured the Trump-Hannity narrative on his afternoon show. "If there's nothing there," Shep asked on the air, "and that's what they tell us, there's nothing to this, and nothing came of it . . . if all of that, why all these lies? Why is it lie after lie after lie?" He called the deception "mind-boggling. And there are still people out there who believe we're making it up. And one day they're gonna realize we're not."

I think Shep was too optimistic about that. In 2020, three in ten Americans still described Trump as honest and trustworthy, despite tens of thousands of falsehoods to the contrary. But Shep was right about the mind-boggling nature of the lies. In response, Hannity took a swing at his colleague: "Shep is a friend, I like him, but he's so anti-Trump."

Shep did not return the friend compliment when he snapped back, "Sometimes facts are displeasing. Journalists report them without fear or favor."

Shep could report all the facts he wanted during his hour, but unfortunately he wasn't empowered to stop the opinion folks from humiliating themselves the rest of the day. While every other morning show was scrutinizing the Trump Tower meeting, *Fox & Friends* jumped on a story from *The Hill* about Comey, one of the show's chosen villains. "RPT: COMEY LEAKED CLASSIFIED MATERIAL," said the on-screen banner, even though *The Hill* didn't actually report that. The show's Twitter feed shared the erroneous news, and then Trump did too, without bothering to credit Fox. "James Comey leaked CLASSIFIED INFORMATION to the media," Trump tweeted. "That is so illegal!"

Trump was so wrong, and it was Fox's fault. The network was guilty of actively misinforming POTUS. *Fox & Friends* should have run a correction immediately, but instead the network started covering Trump's leak allegation like it was legit news, and not just a regurgitation of their morning show's screwup. It was lie-laundering. It took a full twenty-four hours for the "Friends" to sheepishly admit "We were mistaken." There was never any acknowledgment that the network had deluded Trump, and he never walked back his Comey smear, even when the DOJ's inspector general confirmed in 2019 that Comey never leaked anything classified. Comey sent a tweet "to all those who've spent two years talking about me 'going to jail' or being a 'liar and a leaker'—ask yourselves why you still trust people who gave you bad info for so long, including the president." And, he could have added, Fox's biggest stars.

Before interviewing Junior on July 11, Hannity played the child's game "I know you are but what am I," flipping the charges against Trump back on his accusers. He said the press was guilty of "collusion" and Trump's critics were "frothing at the mouth." And then he brought up something that didn't seem to matter at the time, but had huge significance in retrospect. He said the media had "completely ignored an example of actual election interference." He quoted a story from *Politico*—which, last I checked, is part of the "media" Hannity pretended to hate—headlined "Ukrainian Efforts to Sabotage Trump Backfire." He was clearly psyched to have this story to wave around. "UKRAINIAN COLLUSION!" he said. This was one of Hannity's typical techniques: He liked to claim that critical info was being suppressed, when in fact news outlets were just exercising good old-fashioned judgment. And he loved to attack those same news outlets while waving around their reporting. *Politico* did, in fact, report that some Ukrainian government officials tried to help Clinton and undermine Trump before the election. But the story was limited in scope: It described what former ambassador Marie Yovanovitch later called "isolated incidents" by individuals in Ukraine. It did not allege a top-down campaign of Ukrainian meddling, because there wasn't a top-down campaign of Ukrainian meddling. But Hannity needed to imply there was, so he waved the headline around. He brought up Ukraine to Junior and again, later in the hour, to Trump attorney Jay Sekulow. Ukraine became one of Hannity's fallbacks—one of the talking points on the index cards he carried everywhere. Little did his viewers know that Hannity's show and the other right-wing sources of Ukraine conspiracy theories would ultimately lead Trump to the edge of the impeachment cliff.

"Willing to be accomplices"

Trump famously had a red button on the Resolute Desk to summon a Diet Coke. Starting in 2017 he basically had a Rupert Murdoch button too.

"Get me Rupert," Trump shouted to his personal assistant on a regular basis, beckoning the elder Murdoch for advice or gossip. And Rupert happily obliged.

Murdoch had never believed Trump would beat Clinton. So when it actually happened, he worked through Jared Kushner to reach what one Murdoch family friend called a "detente" with the president-elect. Think of all the things they could accomplish together, he said. "There was something in it for both of them," the family friend observed. "At the end of the day, business trumps ideology. Business trumps principle."

Rupert still mocked Trump's inadequacies behind the man's back. "Rupert calls him a fucking idiot," a Murdoch insider told me. "Rupert knows Trump is crazy," another insider said. And Rupert's wife Jerry Hall was known to call Trump a "pig." But the media mogul craved proximity to power, and with Trump, he had it. Perhaps it was his own inadequacy.

By mid-2017 the two men gabbed on the phone several times a week. Rupert proffered advice for calming the Trumpworld chaos. He thought chief strategist Steve Bannon should be fired, for example. And Rupert sometimes bent Trump's ear about AT&T's pending takeover of CNN and the rest of the Time Warner media empire, a deal that both men opposed. At a campaign trail stop on October 22, 2016, Trump said his administration would not approve the deal. One year later, sure enough, Trump's DOJ sued to halt it. AT&T executives saw Rupert's hidden hand at work, and they had good reason: Rupert was acting like Trump's consigliere.

On May 16, AT&T CEO Randall Stephenson received an out-of-the-blue call. It was Rupert.

If you have to sell CNN to get the deal done, he said, I'm interested.

Stephenson was not interested. And he wondered about Rupert's agenda. Murdoch had a longing for CNN and a loathing for founder Ted Turner dating back decades. He had tried to buy CNN on at least two occasions in the past. What was he coming back around for now? One theory that made the rounds: He wanted to scoop up CNN and neuter it to curry favor with the president.

Stringing the letters C, N, and N together were a surefire way to get Trump going. He huffed and puffed about the network and its president Jeff Zucker, whom he previously counted as a friend. He wanted Zucker fired and he wanted CNN brought to heel, and it seemed like Rupert could help. Trump was really starting to like this friendship. He was overheard telling Maria Bartiromo that "Rupert's been a lot better to me than Roger ever was."

The back-patting and back-stabbing at the top of the media world was truly something to behold. Take Anthony Scaramucci, the hedge funder and former Fox Business host. In January 2020 he told me the president is a "demagogic leader trying to split the country into two or three tribes." Trumpism was a cult, he now believed, and his former employer was propping it up. "What I can't understand," he said, "is why good people are willing to be accomplices to this nightmare."

But The Mooch had been an accomplice himself, during his blink-and-you-missed-it stint as White House communications director, and Hannity remained one of his closest friends. They called each other on Christmas.

"Sean has done a very good job of dividing his political opinions and compartmentalizing them from his friendships," The Mooch said.

They are business partners too, and they don't want Trump to hurt business. "He gets my beef with President Trump," said Scaramucci. "But at the same time, Sean's got a commitment to thirty years of Republican-style politics. We can debate whether Trump is a Republican. But Sean is."

When Scaramucci was up for the comms director job in the summer of 2017, Hannity vouched for him. Trump wanted a plumber—someone to come in and plug the leaks that were exposing White House chaos. The Mooch mostly tried to do it by yelling at the pipes. On day three of his tenure, he went on TV and told White House aides "You're either going to stop leaking or you're going to be fired." On day six, he dined with the president, the first lady, Hannity, Bill Shine, and Kimberly Guilfoyle, and he was targeted by a leak. Reporter Ryan Lizza tweeted about the meal before dessert was even served. The Mooch called up Lizza and demanded to know his source, already convinced it was chief of staff Reince Priebus, whom he called a "fucking paranoid schizophrenic." Lizza recorded the insane call and wrote about it. Priebus resigned a couple of days later, and incoming chief of staff John Kelly made shit-canning The Mooch his first official act. It was day eleven.

Over on Fox, Greg Gutfeld cracked a tame joke about The

Mooch, then said, "I don't want to hammer him too hard, he may end up working here." Speculation swirled that Shine or Laura Ingraham might become the new comms director. The door occasionally slowed but never stopped revolving. By mid-2020, there were twenty known cases of Fox-to-Trump moves. "He always wanted to create Trump TV, so he's turning the White House into it," comedy writer Nick Jack Pappas joked. Production assistants became West Wing aides. Right-wing commentators became ambassadors. In one of the most dramatic examples, longtime Fox contributor Richard Grenell jumped from the TV network to the U.S. embassy in Berlin to the cabinet-level position of acting director of national intelligence. One thing never changed: the leaking.

A day after the Scaramucci Show was canceled, Rupert flew to DC for dinner with Trump, John Kelly, and Jared Kushner. Unlike the prior week's meal, this one didn't leak for a full week, when I broke the news on *Reliable Sources*. Rupert and Trump had plowed through their steaks and talked about their boys, their businesses—and that pesky AT&T deal. Trump was determined to stop it. And he bought into the fantasy of Rupert somehow buying CNN. "They'd finally be fair to me," he said.

On August 7, 2017, AT&T exec John Stankey was quoted in the press saying that the company would not sell CNN. Nonetheless, Rupert came back around the next day, calling Stephenson and alluding to some inside information. He said he had heard AT&T might have to shed CNN as a condition of the deal passing government muster. Conditions are imposed on mega-mergers all the time, but the political ramifications of this particular possibility were huge and troubling. Would the DOJ really take revenge for CNN's coverage of Trump by making AT&T divest the news channel? The possibility hung heavy in the air when Rupert once again said he'd acquire it. We're not interested, Stephenson said for a second time.

Rupert was still in a deal-making mood. And he was scheduled to meet with Disney CEO Bob Iger the next day. Iger paid a visit to Rupert's winery in Bel Air for a catch-up session, and the first question out of Rupert's mouth was "Are you running for president?"

Iger was seriously thinking about it at the time, but he played coy with Rupert, not knowing what the Trump ally's true agenda was. Talk turned to their respective businesses—all of the ways that Disney and 21st Century Fox were both being disrupted by Netflix et al. Rupert wanted to plant the idea of a deal but wanted Iger to think it was his idea. And his maneuver worked: Iger came away from the conversation believing that Rupert might be ready to part with his beloved brands like FX and the Fox Searchlight film studio. But one brand was certainly not for sale: Fox News, his all-powerful connection to the current president.

"Out of bounds"

"This is high school. This is like 'The Real World,'" a Fox host said. "Of course they're hooking up with each other, because they're all basically trapped in a house together."

When the host put it that way, I guess the extramarital affairs at Fox made some amount of sense. But the affairs still belied the faith and family values that Fox claimed to represent.

Pete Hegseth was the most brazen example. He cheated on his second wife, Samantha, with Jennifer Rauchet, one of the top producers of Fox & Friends and a rising star at the network. "Jennifer was favoring Pete with airtime. She kept putting Pete on TV," an exec said.

Rauchet disclosed the relationship to HR when she got pregnant at the end of 2016. Hegseth was still married at the time. Management moved Rauchet—demoted her, really—to the weekend show *Watters' World* so that the couple wasn't working together anymore.

It was ironic that Rauchet ended up on *Watters' World*, because Jesse Watters, with wife Noelle and twin girls at home, was also dating in-house. Colleagues said his relationship with Emma Di-Giovine was an open secret around the office—they were posting vacation photos on social media—but management apparently looked the other way until November 2017, when Watters went to the aforementioned HR department and disclosed the relationship. At that point, Emma was transferred to Laura Ingraham's show. Fox's PR shop mostly kept a lid on both extramarital affairs. Hegseth and Watters were valuable assets despite their asshole antics.

Both Watters and Hegseth were warriors for Trump just like Trump was for them. He had ample experience with the sort of expensive divorce both men were going through. His version of offering comfort: bringing them to the White House for dinners. When Watters proposed to DiGiovine, Trump tweeted congratulations with five exclamation points. Don Jr. and Eric Trump flew to the wedding in Naples. And when Hegseth married Rauchet at Trump National Golf Club Colts Neck in New Jersey, the whole family donned hats that said "MAKE WEDDINGS GREAT AGAIN."

Hegseth was a latecomer to the Trump movement. Trump had been third on his dance card: Hegseth first backed Marco Rubio in the primaries and then Ted Cruz. But once he belatedly fell in line with Trump, he fell hard. "I had a conversion moment," he explained. Hegseth found mind-bending ways to connect disparate problems—say, murders of cops and offshoring of jobs. Trump was the solution to all of it, he claimed, hooking viewers with a simple story he told over and over again. "Look," one of Hegseth's friends at Fox said, when

I asked about his conversion. "It's pretty simple. You can convince yourself of almost anything." And the perks were considerable. Undying support for Trump translated to face time with him. Those White House suppers. Invites to policy calls. And on-camera interviews that were doled out like Ronald Reagan doled out jelly beans.

Hegseth's brand became all about flaunting his Trumpiness and pissing people off. "I love the fact that it must drive liberals nuts that they have to report what he tweets," Hegseth told an interviewer in 2017. "Owning the libs" increasingly came to define most of Fox's talk shows.

Trump was consuming more and more cable TV. And more and more of it was being tailored to him. During commercial breaks on *Fox & Friends Weekend*, Hegseth peeked at his phone, checking to see if Trump had tweeted about the show yet. He was thrilled when Trump picked up on something he said, and he made sure everyone around him knew it. His cohosts Abby Huntsman and Clayton Morris felt like he was putting on a show specifically for POTUS—because Hegseth was angling to become veterans affairs secretary.

Hegseth wasn't the only television host choosing his words carefully with the knowledge that the president might be listening. I did it myself when the Unite the Right rally stormed the city of Charlottesville. On August 12 all the cable news channels covered the violent clashes between racist alt-right adherents and counterprotesters who wanted the racists to leave. Commentators criticized Trump for not denouncing the violence right away. I tried to be forward-looking when I spoke on CNN in the minutes before the president was supposed to hold a press conference. Heather Heyer was dead. Other counterprotesters were seriously hurt. The town was a tinderbox. I said Trump could bring healing to Charlottesville—and I hoped he was listening to the advice. But his speech made things much worse. He condemned "hatred, bigotry, and violence on many sides, on many sides," equivocating between the racists who marched with torches and the activists who marched to stop them. He did not condemn white supremacists by name. He begrudgingly addressed the criticism at a press conference three days later and said there were "very fine people, on both sides," digging the hole deeper.

Once again, Fox had done him a disservice. Throughout the Charlottesville crisis, Trump repeated exactly what he heard from Fox. On August 14 Fox's Martha MacCallum asked about which statues would be targeted for removal next: "You could make an argument for Thomas Jefferson or George Washington. Are you going to change the name of the Washington Monument?" At his presser, Trump echoed her: "Is it George Washington next week? And is it Thomas Jefferson the week after?"

The morning after the disastrous presser, the "Friends" attempted cleanup on his behalf. Steve Doocy said Trump's real "mistake" was taking questions from the dastardly press in the first place. Then the hosts turned to viewer emails for backup. "Trump was right," the first handpicked message said. "No matter what he says, he will always be condemned," the second one said. This was the language of defeat. The language of nihilism. It was heard every day on Fox. Day in, day out, viewers heard that dark forces were conspiring to destroy the president. They heard that Trump would never win over the elite media and evil Dems, no matter what he said or did, so why should he bother trying? Some supporters later claimed that the media narrative about Charlottesville was a "hoax"—but Trump's odious words had aired on live TV.

Charlottesville was a tipping point—a low point of the Trump presidency and also for his Fox defenders. Correspondent Conor Powell, at Fox's Jerusalem bureau, said he "watched in horror as many of my Fox News colleagues initially defended or stayed quiet about what happened in Charlottesville."

Powell hailed from Virginia. He and his wife, Atia, both had fond memories of Charlottesville, so the pictures on TV were especially painful to see. "I always felt that if Fox News wanted to debate healthcare, tax or environmental policy, that was a legitimate part of the American political conversation," he told me. But this atrocity—this strain of white identity politics and all-out defense of the president's indefensible remarks—"seemed so out of bounds I just couldn't stomach it."

Powell was already ambivalent about being at Fox in the Trump age. But his journalist friends had been telling him to stay. Their argument was that viewers needed real reporting on Fox. "Even if they only got a few minutes a day," Powell quipped, it was better than the alternative. He usually agreed with this line of thought, but it was getting to be too much. Powell was going through the same thing Shep was. He reacted to the Charlottesville commentary by heading home and telling his wife he was going to quit.

"I didn't get into journalism to have coworkers defend neo-Nazis and white supremacists," he told her.

Powell ultimately waited until the following summer, so that their son could finish his first year of school in Jerusalem, but Charlottesville was the spark for his resignation.

Fox & Friends Weekend cohost Clayton Morris came to the same decision. According to colleagues, he felt queasy going on the air the morning after the riot and listening to pro-Trump commentators try to rationalize what had happened. There was a hellish undercurrent to Fox's coverage, and a sense of normalizing white nationalism as acceptable. "Spin it to the statues," the show's producers said, "say it's about the statues," i.e., the Confederate memorials in Charlottesville and across the South. But Heather Heyer was dead, and this wound in America's heart was about so much more than hunks of granite.

Three weeks after Charlottesville, Morris announced that he was retiring from TV to focus on his real estate business. Everything seemed hunky-dory on the air. Abby Huntsman and Pete Hegseth wished him well. What nobody knew was that Morris still had two years left on his contract. He was quitting in protest, though the terms of his contract didn't allow him to say so.

Morris was a jovial, easy-to-wake-up-with morning host. He was better suited for the pre-Trump Fox. He had started thinking about leaving several months before Charlottesville erupted, when the death threats (for criticizing Trump on air) and talking points (kooky stuff about immigration) got to be too much. With the scenes from Charlottesville blanketing the airwaves, his wife, Natali, tried to explain the controversy to their son, and he asked her, with an unbelievably innocent voice, "Is Daddy a white supremacist?"

That was it. Morris called his agent the next day and said "I'm done." But he never talked publicly about any of this. Like other former Fox hosts who'd signed NDAs, he declined to comment to me.

Trump's failures in the wake of Charlottesville appalled James Murdoch enough to write a letter to staffers rebuking the president. It was read by some as a rebuke of his father and brother too, for lending Trump so much support. Earlier in the year, when Trump instituted the travel ban, James had wanted Fox corporate to issue a full-throated statement in support of its Muslim employees and in opposition to the policy. Lachlan watered the statement way down, but at least signed his name that time. This time, it was James speaking alone at the urging of his wife, Kathryn. "I can't even believe

I have to write this: standing up to Nazis is essential; there are no good Nazis. Or Klansmen, or terrorists," James wrote. "Democrats, Republicans, and others must all agree on this, and it compromises nothing for them to do so."

James lauded 21st Century Fox's diversity and praised movies like *12 Years a Slave*, which Fox distributed. He didn't mention Fox News at all. He announced a $1 million donation to the Anti-Defamation League. His dad was working on a different kind of statement: a prime time show for Laura Ingraham, one of the biggest purveyors of white identity politics in America. James held the title of 21st Century Fox CEO, but he was being kept out of Fox News. The Ingraham move proved that Rupert and Trump were really in charge.

"We print money in the basement"

Charlottesville turned the whispers about Trump's fitness for office into full-blown shouts—on other TV channels. At Fox, people were still just whispering, and only off the air.

"I really do think he's lost it," an exec remarked to me on August 19, 2017. This person wasn't speaking colloquially; they genuinely questioned the president's sanity. And they weren't alone at Fox. The following month, after a drink or two, a prominent Fox anchor admitted their concerns about Trump's mental health and well-being. "He is not well," they said to me, in the same concerned tone that people use while talking about their grandfather.

When the family patriarch is sick, the entire family suffers. That's what America was experiencing by late 2017. For some journalists, including at Fox, the president's mental health was a running line of speculation. Narcissistic personality disorder was the most comforting explanation because the other possibilities were far more frightening. Words like "delusional" and "dementia" were invoked in private. For Hannity, however, these sincere concerns—shared by some of his colleagues—were catnip. "They want you to think he's crazy!" he exclaimed on the air. He subscribed to the "crazy like a Fox" argument instead . . . at least in public.

Other Fox stars learned to mimic Hannity's offensive line strategies. Maria Bartiromo was the best example. "Of all the people at Fox," one of the network's top commentators said, "Maria is the one who's changed the most."

In the nineties, working for Ailes, Bartiromo had endeared herself to CEOs and CNBC viewers alike. She brought credibility and two famously sharp elbows to Fox Business when she defected in 2014. Ailes awarded her a six-year contract, a bold move since most stars only commit to two or three years at a time. I interpreted it to mean that Bartiromo knew there was no going back to CNBC or other major media enterprises. That once she entered the Fox orbit, she was in for the rest of her career.

Bartiromo skillfully co-moderated a GOP primary debate in late 2015, showing no particular favoritism toward Trump or anyone else. But then something changed. When Bartiromo's name came up in conversation with her old CNBC colleagues or Wall Street sources, people usually said the same thing: "What happened?" They worried that she had tripped and fallen down a far right rabbit hole, but she'd gone willingly. She had known Trump for years. She had a knack for booking him. And she had a crystal clear sense of what her audience wanted. By Election Day she cribbed his language and trashed Hillary Clinton and said Trump would be better for the stock market. After the election she backed Trump's conspiracy theories, retweeted some of her own, and stacked her shows with MAGAsphere sycophants. She even defended Trump in the wake of Charlottesville. A few months later when a guest brought up Trump's record of sexual harassment she shut the guest down by saying "there are no allegations against the president." Critics responded with a collective "huh?" and "what happened to Maria?"

Part of the answer had to do with her media diet. As she waded deeper into the world of right-wing news, of *Breitbart* and *The Daily Caller*, of "fake news" and "witch hunts," she learned the language of conservative victimhood and grievance politics. A former Fox exec told *The Daily Beast* she did it "because she knows the best way to move up the ladder at Fox News is to keep saying far-right bullshit." Bartiromo was offended by the quote, but it was one of the most common explanations of the past few years. She was a Davos regular, suddenly raging about globalists! Why? Because that's what she was incentivized to do. As one of Fox's famous faces said to me in an unguarded moment, when you're inside Fox, "I think your brain gets cooked after a while."

When Bartiromo's six-year contract came up in 2019, Fox put a new deal on the table that paid six million a year. She told Trump it was another six-year deal. "Great news. @MariaBartiromo just renewed," Trump tweeted. "I don't care how much they paid her, they got a beautiful bargain. Congratulations to both!" She replied to the president with a red heart emoji.

A grossed-out Fox employee showed me the heart emoji on her phone. We were at a bar, talking about what had changed at Fox, who changed the most, and why. Some anchors, this employee said, hadn't succumbed to the Trump BS. There were standouts like Shep, Neil Cavuto, Arthel Neville, and Jon Scott. And there were superb correspondents like Trace Gallagher, Laura Ingle, Steve Harrigan, and Bryan Llenas who played the news straight. But everyone was affected by the Trump-Fox merger in one way or another. Everyone shared the same studios, rode the same elevators, and felt the same ratings pressures. Everyone paid attention to programming changes and read the scheduling tea leaves for clues about Suzanne Scott's plans for the network. Nearly every change tilted in a Trumpier direction.

Rupert and Scott made adjustments to the prime time lineup in the fall of 2017, mostly for defensive reasons. MSNBC's Rachel Maddow was beating *The Five* at 9 p.m. and CNN was doing well with live programming at 11. So *The Five* moved back to 5 where it belonged and Hannity moved to 9, officially becoming the network's tentpole. Now "the whole thing is riding on my back," he said to friends. Hannity agreed to do the show live most of the time, even though he much preferred to tape it. Laura Ingraham took his 10 p.m. spot. Daytime news anchor Shannon Bream went live at 11. The people rewarded with time slots and fat new contracts were the people who gave Trump shelter from the storm.

Bartiromo existed at one end of a spectrum, next to Hannity, Jeanine Pirro, and Lou Dobbs. Others at Fox justified their evolutions by saying they weren't quite as sycophantic as them. Take the funny guy from *The Five*, Greg Gutfeld. Trump liked watching him on TV and called one day to say hi. One call led to another, and by 2014 Gutfeld was hitching a ride from Mar-a-Lago to New York on Trump's plane. When Gutfeld gained a weekend comedy show on Fox, Trump was one of his first guests, just a couple of weeks before escalator day. Trump told Gutfeld that he would make a good press secretary. Ha ha ha.

But Gutfeld was nowhere near submissive enough for Trump's taste. Once the campaign began, so did the criticism and the cutting mockery. Gutfeld called him a "first-class asshole" and a "conspiracy freak" with a "nest of hair." He was so disgusted by the infamous

July 18, 2015, insult of John McCain ("He's a war hero because he was captured. I like people that weren't captured") that he kept bringing it up for months afterward. "If Eric Holder had said this—Fox News, we would be covering it 24–7, and we would be demanding resignations and investigations," Gutfeld said. "We have to hold Donald Trump to the same standards." He said Republicans should not nominate a person whose comments constantly had to be explained and defended.

Back then, Gutfeld believed critiques of Trump were like guardrails—making everyone safer and better. "Donald's not to blame for being Donald," he said. "The fault lies with those who yield to his rules," e.g., his colleagues on *The Five* and all around Fox.

Gutfeld needled conservative viewers by saying Trump's cult of personality was even bigger than Obama's. On November 24, 2015, he said that "Trump pisses me off—mainly because his gaffes and exhausted repetitions are a product of laziness and pettiness. Meaning, they are preventable." He brought up McCain again, plus the "creepy" attacks against Megyn Kelly and so much more. He said Trump fans would impeach Obama for the exact kind of shit they were cheering Trump to do. This point about hypocrisy was made all the time on CNN and MSNBC—but rarely on Fox. Gutfeld was a heretic. Often he was more disappointed in his cheerleader colleagues than the candidate; he ridiculed people like Kimberly Guilfoyle for constantly making excuses for inexcusable conduct. On December 2, when Eric Bolling tried to defend Trump's lie about seeing thousands of American Muslims cheering in Jersey City on 9/11, Gutfeld snapped, "If Bernie Sanders said there were thousands of pro-lifers cheering the Colorado shootings, everybody at Fox would go, 'show me the proof.' " On December 22, when Trump said Clinton was "schlonged" in the 2008 primaries, Gutfeld said

"We're not even allowed to use the word that he said, but somehow we're going to have him on our network all the time." Gutfeld distilled his exhaustion in one sigh of a sentence: "I'm sick of hearing people defend this stuff."

But all of these righteous moments did little except to excite left-wing bloggers who only watched Fox for the gotchas. Gutfeld was at risk of alienating himself from the audience that actually liked Fox. A Facebook user named Angela browsed Gutfeld's website in late 2019 and commented on one of the old posts, "I had NO idea you hated Trump AND his supporters so much. What made you change your opinion on virtually every aspect of Trump? You are completely opposite now."

True. Gutfeld was a holdout all throughout the campaign season, but he found a path forward after Trump's victory. He returned to his first love: hating the media and the Democrats. He rededicated his career to trolling. He truly enjoyed watching Trump get a rise out of people. When I watched Gutfeld, I was reminded of what Michael Caine's character said in 2008's *The Dark Knight*: "Some men just want to watch the world burn."

Gutfeld convinced himself that Trump was the Comedy Central roast master version of a president. The "war hero" smear, he now said, was a sick burn, perfect for a roast of John McCain. Gutfeld was in the position he had previously warned against: the position of defending and excusing Trump.

Trump noticed and approved. At one of his rallies where he listed various Fox personalities for praise, he said Gutfeld "wasn't good to me" before, but had now earned a shout-out.

The alternative could have hit Gutfeld in the wallet. Fox made him a millionaire several times over—between his TV shows, the books he promoted on TV, his ticketed speaking gigs across the country—so "Greg has made a cynical calculation," an insider said. "There's no point in being anti-Trump."

Financial motivations drove Fox's corporate leaders too. Rupert's bid for Sky Broadcasting was still being held up, partly by progressives' fears that he would "Foxify" the global broadcaster, but he had a new ambition now: A deal with Disney to sell most of 21st Century Fox's assets, including his studios and global entertainment brands, such as FX. He would hold on to Fox News and Fox Sports. When the $52.4 billion deal was announced on December 14, Trump instantly phoned Rupert to congratulate him, and Sarah Huckabee Sanders touted the transaction from the White House press briefing room stage. She said Trump "thinks that—to use one of the president's favorite words—that this could be a great thing for jobs." Business journalists knew that was nonsensical. Disney told Wall Street to expect $2 billion in synergies, which was code for cutbacks and job losses. So Sanders was ignorant to invoke job gains. Thousands of people were about to lose their jobs as a result of the deal. Even James Murdoch!

Well, no, Rupert wasn't literally laying off his son. And James was a champion of the Disney deal at first, believing that he had a shot at running the combined Disney-Fox someday. He negotiated with Iger about what sort of senior role he could take at the company, but couldn't come to terms. Unwilling to accept anything but a top job, James walked away with a chip on his shoulder.

Elder son Lachlan wasn't happy either. He had been pissed ever since he caught wind of the August meeting at the winery. His father had been grooming him to run a media colossus—but then went off in secret and sold most of the company. Now it seemed like he'd be a caretaker for the leftover channels. Iger acknowledged the tension, gently, in his memoir: "They'd watched their father build the company since they were kids, hoping and assuming that someday it would be theirs. Now he was selling it to someone else. It wasn't an easy situation for any of them."

No, it was not. It was made easier on one level, however, by Rupert's collaboration with POTUS. At least the family could be confident that the deal would get approved by the Trump administration.

Good-government advocates looked at the administration's divergent treatment of media mergers with suspicion. AT&T's takeover of Time Warner was held up in the courts by Trump's Justice Department while Disney's acquisition of the Fox assets was fast-tracked by the same department. It was exactly what it looked like. Approval of the Disney deal meant all the Murdochs would get paid, which meant the brothers could go their separate ways.

This was one of the key reasons why the Fox-Trump merger was beneficial to Rupert: It resolved years of family drama. James could take his $2 billion from the Disney deal and invest in start-ups and liberal news outlets. Lachlan could run the slimmed-down Fox Corp and do some deals of his own. Rupert could sail around the world with Jerry Hall and pull all the political strings he wanted, like a one-man nation-state. And Rupert and Lachlan would still have Fox News throwing off nearly $2 billion in profit a year. "You know," an executive joked, "we print money in the basement."

THE CULT

"Fake freak"

"You're not Making America Great."

The emails and tweets came by the dozens. They bore all the hallmarks of a coordinated campaign. And they intensified as Trump time went on. The MAGAsphere targeted journalists who pointed out Trump's falsehoods and flubs. Fox's truth-tellers faced some of the most vociferous attacks because they were perceived to be turncoats. Fox insiders said the hate emails became nastier as Trump's public loyalty demands became more and more extreme. Some news anchors tried to filter it out, while Neil Cavuto went a different way: He read the emails on the air.

"You, snap-on hair, you're the fake freak who's lying to the people, not the guy sitting in the White House," a viewer named Paul wrote. Cavuto read it on air and took the opportunity to teach Paul a thing or two about journalism. Cavuto did not think highly of Trump, or of Hannity, for that matter. He thought Trump got bad advice from the prime time players, and he used his 4 p.m. show to urge restraint. Don't go to war with Senate Republicans. Don't tweet out "tacky insults" to critics. Don't scapegoat reporters. "Mr. President," he said one afternoon, "it is not the fake news media that's your problem. It's you."

The base did not take kindly to these suggestions. Paul's nasty-gram to Cavuto said "Trump will never talk to you now" because he knew the anchor was "fake news." Cavuto replied by saying that he had never asked for a sit-down with the president, because he didn't think he would get that much out of it. Cavuto recognized what Hannity would never admit in public—so much of what Trump said in interviews was uninformed or untrue.

Trump had a knack for looking people straight in the eyes and lying, even if, as Kellyanne Conway told me in July 2017, he didn't "think" he was lying. When I said it was scandalous that the president was lying about voter fraud and wiretapping, just to name two issues, Conway said, "Excuse me? He doesn't think he's lying about those issues, and you know it."

Trump also had a tendency to flip-flop, to flounder, to contradict himself. All of this degraded the value of interviews with him and, I confess, aides like Conway too. But most of Fox's stars held tight to the notion that presidential interviews were inherently newsworthy. Cavuto was an outlier by opting out. Fox's intramural competition to book Trump was fierce: Various friends slipped ratings reports to the president, sometimes verbally by phone, other times more formally by faxing and emailing printouts to various aides. Hannity, for example, wanted Trump to know that his show was much higher rated than Bret Baier's show, so that Trump didn't stray. Some of this ratings chatter was also about boosting Trump's ego. In his mind, if Fox was doing well, it meant he was doing well. He interpreted Fox's popularity as evidence of his own popularity.

After Trump's first State of the Union address, in January 2018, he tweeted congratulations to himself for a ratings record: "45.6 million people watched, the highest number in history. @FoxNews beat every other Network, for the first time ever, with 11.7 million people tuning in."

Fox did rank No. 1, but it wasn't the "highest number in history" for a SOTU, not even close. In a story for CNN.com, I wrote that eight other SOTUs were higher rated, including Obama's first address of his presidency. That's the part that irked Trump. A White House aide emailed me a few minutes after the story went up. He asked to speak on background and I agreed not to use his name. This aide said the president "was referring to the highest in cable news history. That's why he mentioned Fox News as well."

But that's not what the president said. He said "45.6 million people watched, the highest number in history." Then he mentioned Fox's record separately. This was a stupid sequel to crowd-size-gate. So I pressed for an on-the-record explanation and asked: "Why hasn't he issued a correction tweet?"

"There's not much to correct," the aide replied.

"His tweet was incorrect," I said. "You're saying he meant to say something else. Can you put this on the record?"

"It's not incorrect," the aide said. "He mentioned Fox News in the sentence immediately after."

I was stuck in an alternative facts wormhole. But it reflected Trump's priority: the ratings.

About a year into the Trump presidency, his speeches and interviews lost the pizazz that generated huge ratings. He started to phone it in, both literally and figuratively. When an interview "made news," it was usually because Trump felt so comfortable with the hosts that he blurted out something inappropriate, like the time he said he tried to "stay away" from the Justice Department, "but at some point I won't." His aides tried to intervene and stop these chats from happening, but they felt they could only tell him no so many times in a row. The end result: his April 2018 call to *Fox & Friends*. Trump hijacked the *Friends* conversation from the get-go; when the hosts tried to ask him about his dealings with Michael Cohen, who had just been raided by the FBI, he railroaded them; and when they eventually tried to wrap the president, he kept rambling. "We're running out of time," Steve Doocy said. "We could talk to you all day, but it looks like you have a million things to do," Brian Kilmeade said a couple of minutes later, trying to be polite. But no—the president just wanted to keep talking. When it was finally over, Kilmeade said, "We'll see you next Thursday, Mr. President," alluding to Trump's weekly segment in the past. "The phone line's open!" White House aides groaned. They were worried about his troubling admissions that could come back to hurt him in court, but Trump tweeted that he "loved" being on the show.

Later in the year, he called the "Friends" again and defended his decision to hold a political rally at the same time a major hurricane was bearing down on the Florida panhandle. Earhardt saved her most important question until the end.

"Give me a nice one," Trump said.

"So," she said, beaming, "today is my father's birthday."

The president was in the White House residence, watching his three friends talk with him on TV—Earhardt in a tight, low-cut dress—and he knew just what to say.

"And your father's first name is what?"

"Wayne Earhardt. Coach Earhardt."

"And is he in South Carolina?"

"Yes, sir."

"Well that's a great place. So Wayne, I just want to say you've done a fantastic job with Ainsley. I want to congratulate you. That is not easy, but she is a terrific human being and just a great person. Happy birthday and great job. Great work."

"Thank you, Mr. President," Earhardt said.

Doocy jumped in with a perfectly timed joke: "Mr. President, my neighbor is having an anniversary next week . . ."

"I know, I know, we could do this for ten minutes," Trump responded.

Kilmeade thanked him for calling in, and Trump laid the praise on thick: "Thank you all, your show is a fantastic show, just keep it going."

Then Doocy leaned in with the four wisest words of the whole conversation: "Go run the country."

But Trump didn't. His "Executive Time" that day continued until 11:30 a.m., when he Sharpied a couple of bills and lunched with Kanye West. In Trump's mind, watching Fox *was* a key part of running the country. He rarely interacted with average voters, so *Friends* was the connection to his base. With some rare exceptions, the "Friends" went easy on Trump and Trump went easy on them.

Past presidents never had a space as safe as this, a place to turn for constant reassurance and reinforcement. Fox made it safer by signing up more pro-Trump commentators—not just to please the president but to please his super-fans. Execs and producers employed other deck-stacking tricks too, like setting up folksy diner segments called "Breakfast with Friends" where patrons were interviewed about politics and culture war issues. When it seemed like the interviewees were just repeating Fox and Trump's positions right back to the interviewer, that was because the rooms were packed with Trump promoters. "The producers would strategically pick counties or towns that Trump won," an insider told me, "to get the pulse of the people." Well, one specific subset of people. When a hater interrupted one of the feel-good segments by holding up a "FOX LIES" sign and shouting "fake news," Fox security escorted him out of the restaurant.

The Washington Post tracked down the protester, Bob Reams, who said "I just couldn't help myself" when he found out that Fox was coming to town. "They have brainwashed so many of my friends and believe in just conspiracy theories and bullcrap," he said. "It's just sad to see my friends just turned into idiots." In the Trump age, left-wing blogs filled up with stories about families torn apart by a loved one's Fox News addiction. I heard those stories from staffers too: Some of their relatives resented what they did for a living.

"I feel like Fox is being held hostage by its audience," a veteran staffer said. "The audience has been RADICALIZED," a longtime commentator texted me, in all caps, as he scrolled through his Twitter feed after a live shot on the daytime show *America's Newsroom*. The amount of vitriol staggered him. Any momentary break from Trump was penalized. Decades of nuanced debates about the role of government and taxation and immigration were all distilled to a single question: Were you with Trump or against him?

The Fox brand was with him, but not every minute, not every hour, and that offended the viewers who believed Trump was owed complete obedience. At a 2018 rally, Trump himself even complained about the dissenting voices that showed up on *Hannity*.

"Do we love Sean Hannity, by the way?" Trump said to rally-goers in Montana. Trump had figured out that he could always revive a bored crowd by shouting out the names of Fox stars. "I love him," Trump said over the cheers, in a scene that was being shown live on Fox during Hannity's hour. "But here's the only thing. He puts up all these losers that say horrible things! I've got to talk to him [about it]."

What was he talking about? Hannity hardly ever booked Dems

anymore, but Trump said there was "one after another," saying things like "Donald Trump, he's lost it up here." And then it hit me: He was griping about the clip montages that Hannity's staffers strung together, usually showing people on CNN and MSNBC criticizing Trump. These montages were the raw fuel for the right-wing resentment engine. Producers assembled them with the help of a private Twitter account, shared by the show team, that provided a daily "pool of ideas" for the show, Hannity's executive producer Porter Berry explained to *The New York Times*. The team had until nine o'clock each day to "pull it all together" and "build that argument." Without those montages, without those foils from other channels, without those out-of-context clips, Hannity would have nothing to talk about. When my face popped up in the montages, my Twitter replies tab filled up with invective from his viewers, repeating whatever derogatory thing the feckless host had just said. "Humpty Dumpty!" "Stenographer!" Hannity's more authoritarian-minded fans said things like "you should be arrested for treason" and "get fucked you commie piece of shit." His most cultish viewers looked up my Gmail address and hurled insults there, and when I replied, they were often stunned to hear back from me. I think they forgot their hate object was a real live human being. I wanted to remind them.

"Clueless"

"I don't want Pete fucking Hegseth taking my time slot."

When Shep Smith was weighing whether or not to sign a new contract in early 2018, his potential replacement was a big factor.

Hegseth wasn't literally up for the job, but Shep actively imagined all the things Suzanne Scott could do to take the teeth out of the 3 p.m. hour. Scott said she wanted him to stay, and he believed the network would be worse off without him. That's why he committed to three more years. "I wonder," he told *Time* magazine, "if I stopped delivering the facts, what would go in its place in this place that is most watched, most listened, most viewed, most trusted? I don't know." But he had his suspicions, and those were scary enough to convince him to sign on the dotted line. Fifteen million a year helped ease his concerns too.

Shep had struck his first $15 million deal back in June 2013 when Roger Ailes was still cutting the paychecks. The stunning raise was a consolation when Shep lost his 7 p.m. show. Ailes called all his stars into his conference room to talk about the new schedule. Greta and Hannity were both about to move time slots to make way for Megyn Kelly at 9. Shep was the odd host out—a decision that reflected Ailes's view that the audience wanted red meat, not straight news, at dinnertime. So Shep was getting paid more to do less. Ailes also threw $10 million at a new studio just for Shep, dubbed the Fox News Deck, with walls of screens for the anchor and oversized iPads for the producers. That's where Shep would continue to anchor his 3 p.m. hour, now with his name in the title, *Shepard Smith Reporting*, and that's where he would anchor breaking news cut-ins during other people's shows—all part of an effort to appease him and make the demotion look like a promotion.

But everyone around the conference room table knew what this really was. "We knew right then, this was never going to work," a person in the room recalled.

It did work once in a while, when mass shootings and other horrors required hours of rolling live coverage. But Ailes's other stars fought the "Fox News Deck" approach. They said they could handle any breaking news just fine by themselves. TV airtime was like water for these stars, necessary for survival. TV executives some-times derided this as "red-light syndrome," named for the light that shone atop the camera when it was live. "Everybody got very ter-ritorial very fast," an insider said. "It took a huge toll. It changed everything." The rest of the network didn't want him, so he didn't want them. He leaned into his happy life off-camera.

Shep had stopped dating in 2012 when he settled down with Giovanni "Gio" Graziano, a production assistant on his team who was twenty-three years younger. Gio was transferred to a job at Fox Business to avoid the obvious conflict. By the time Gawker revealed the relationship and outed Shep in 2013, Gio was gone from the company altogether.

Shep was the most prominent gay anchor at a network with an ugly history of antigay commentary. He later said he didn't think he needed to "out" himself because "I didn't think I was in." It's true that his coworkers and New York City neighbors knew about his personal life, but his viewers generally didn't. He started to talk publicly about "the gay," as he once jokingly called it, in 2016, while denying another Gawker report that claimed Ailes tried to keep Shep in the closet. He nonchalantly told a group of college students in 2017 that "I go to work, I manage a lot of people, I cover the news, I deal with the holy hell going on around me," and then "I go home to the man I love, and I go home to family." And the family part is what he prioritized as he felt the channel lurching further to the right, caring less about news and more about views he reviled. He cut back on work travel and booked vacations with Gio instead. He developed a reputation as one of those anchors who came in two hours before airtime on slow days. "He's in at 1 and out at 4:15," a source said. It's no wonder why—the halls of Fox News HQ were not a happy place for him to be. Other hours of the Fox day were increasingly hostile to what he reported. Shep's show was an island under siege. "When something is reported on Shep's show, it doesn't make it past the commercial break on Neil Cavuto's four o'clock show," Conor Powell said. "There wasn't a continuous line of reporting" the way there was at other networks. Each time slot was someone's fiefdom.

Before Trump was elected, a former colleague of Shep's said, "he told me it was all about the money." But once Trump took over the executive branch and much of Fox, it wasn't "about the money anymore. It was about saying he's holding down the mantle of journalism."

Reporting the truth about Trump put Shep at odds with Hannity and the others who, Shep said, were there "strictly to be entertaining." He talked about the opinion-slingers in ways that were deeply insulting to them. "I don't want to sit around and yell at each other and talk about your philosophy and my philosophy," he told *Time*. "That sounds horrible to me."

What Fox did all day sounded horrible to him.

Shep's jabs at prime time caused a stir, just like he intended. Hannity swung back at him in a tweet: "While Shep is a friend with political views I do not share, and great at breaking news, he is clueless about what we do every day." Clueless! Yikes. "Hannity breaks news daily," he insisted, speaking in the third person and listing the Trumpworld obsessions that Fox used to counterprogram and contradict the Mueller probe. Laura Ingraham also defended her staff. "Always liked Shep," she wrote, "but his comments were inconsiderate & inaccurate."

This was the "pissing in the tent" that Ailes always guarded against. Shep saw the tweets and laughed. He liked to get a rise out of people. Sometimes he did it by declaring that politics, the fixation of most cable newsers, was "weird and creepy." His disdain bled through the TV screen. He'd rather cover a hurricane or a car chase. He absolutely loved the day two runaway llamas led Arizona police on a chase during his 3 p.m. hour. But there hadn't been any South American escapees lately—or much time for non-Trump drama of any type.

"I miss doing that thing I used to do," Shep said, "but I like this thing I'm doing now. I just wish everyone weren't so angry about it all. I wish that we could have lighter moments and not always be on guard with each other." He predicted that the cable news climate would get worse. In private, he blamed Trump for the madness and wondered why Hannity sold out. Was there more to the alliance than the public knew? Shep perked up his ears on Monday, April 16, 2018, when Michael Cohen's lawyer was forced to reveal that Hannity was one of Cohen's clients. Cohen's team had tried to keep Sean's name under wraps. But Cohen only had two other clients—the president and a Republican financier, Elliott Broidy, who hired Cohen to buy a *Playboy* Playmate's silence. So what secrets was Cohen stowing away for Hannity? Did the Fox host have a woman problem? Did Trump know, and use the knowledge as leverage?

The news about Hannity's connection with Cohen broke just before the start of Shep's show. A reporter awkwardly mentioned the Hannity revelation at the top of the hour, but moved on as fast as she could, so Shep brought it back up. "Hannity's producers are working to contact him," Shep said. "Since it's now part of the story, we'll report on it when we know the rest of it." Then he added with a smile, "A lot of people here know his number."

Hannity was supposed to be hosting his radio show, but instead he was watching Fox's coverage while texting with pals about how to handle this embarrassing disclosure. His radio producers scrambled to fill air. Hannity worked up a response that stated Cohen never "represented me in any matter." Hannity had merely sought his pal's legal advice, mostly about buying real estate, not about burying an affair. Reporters discovered that Hannity was, in fact, a mini real estate mogul: *The Guardian*'s review of public records linked Hannity to $90 million worth of investments on more than 870 homes in Alabama, Florida, Georgia, New York, North Carolina, Texas, and Vermont.

The newsman wanted to know: Had his opinion counterpart told anyone in management about the extent of his relationship with Cohen? The answer was no—Hannity hadn't disclosed a thing. He had the power to get away with it. Hannity pestered Fox for a statement clearing his name, and got one the next day. "We have reviewed the matter and spoken to Sean and he continues to have our full support," the network said. What Shep had told *Time* magazine rang true once again: "They don't really have rules on the opinion side." Every night Hannity railed against "elite" media types, like George Stephanopoulos, who, he said, had inappropriately cozy connections with the people they covered. Then he was proven to be exactly the kind of person he criticized. And nothing came of it.

Hannity's pals said the Cohen connection was overblown. "Cohen gave him some advice once," a family friend shrugged. He had an entire thicket of real lawyers, including David Boies, the Democratic lawyer of *Bush v. Gore* fame, and his agent David Limbaugh, brother of Rush. The Limbaugh connection extended to his office at Fox: Hannity's assistant was David's daughter Christen Limbaugh Bloom. Christen was like conservative radio royalty: The biggest talker in the country was Uncle Rush to her, and the No. 2 host was her boss. Christen wrote regular columns for Fox's website. A sample column: "How to pray even bigger in the year ahead."

Hannity rarely talked about his own faith, except for his nightly invocation of John 14:1, "Let not your heart be troubled," which Jesus told his disciples before being crucified. Hannity usually uttered the words at the end of his show as he vowed to continue protecting the president.

On May 17, 2018, "wardrobe enforcer" Suzanne Scott was promoted to CEO. This was (1) a historic moment in TV news, the first time Fox News had a female CEO, and (2) another symbol of right-wing opinion winning and news losing.

Jay Wallace was promoted on the same day, to president of Fox News, reporting to Scott. They were almost equals, but Scott was on top, and that meant the talk shows known as "programming" were on top. "That's what she prefers," a news anchor grumbled to me. "She believes 'programming' is what works." Scott took steps to make some of the newscasts talkier. She encouraged more segments with partisan guests. She liked when daytime newscasts played clips from *Fox & Friends* or Limbaugh's radio show. In short, she promoted all the things Shep lobbied against.

Shep was on the record as saying "I think we have to make the wall between news and opinion as high and as thick and as impenetrable as possible. And I try to do that." But his own bosses undermined him. Chief national correspondent Ed Henry, supposedly a rising star of the news division, became better known for his mornings on *Fox & Friends* and his nights filling in for Tucker Carlson. If there was a wall between news and opinion, Henry was walking through one of those "big, beautiful doors" Trump was always pledging to build. I spoke with numerous correspondents who thought it was outrageous. "Ed found a way to get ahead, it's that simple," one said. "And Suzanne loves him."

Shep professed not to watch *Fox & Friends*, but Henry's back-slapping on the show was precisely the problem. Shep used his new contract and his *Time* magazine interview to speak out about it. The solution, he said, was steadiness: "If we start making changes, if ratings go down or viewers scream too much and we make changes to accommodate, we are in extreme dereliction of duty. I cannot do it. I will not do it. I'll quit. I'll stop doing it completely."

To that threat, Hannity might have responded, *Please do.*

"Shadow chief of staff"

In the halls of the White House and in the pages of *The Washington Post*, Hannity acquired a new nickname: "Shadow chief of staff."

The I-don't-give-a-shit, just-having-fun Hannity was gone. Yeah, he was all smiles while golfing with Trump and Bill Shine at Trump International Golf Club, but Hannity's friends said he was feeling the stress that came from counseling Trump at all hours of the day. There were many days when the unpaid position was a source of tension—like a needy friend who called and called but never took advice. "He doesn't know how to get out of his own way," Hannity complained to a colleague.

Setting aside whether any of this was appropriate for a TV performer to be doing, it was intense work. Hannity thought Shine could help calm the White House seas, and he wanted to rehab his out-of-work pal's career, so he ramped up his campaign to get Shine hired after Hope Hicks left the White House in March.

Given his proximity to the president, Fox executives had serious concerns about whether Hannity's phone was being targeted by foreign governments. He took precautions, but it was a huge problem for the corporate IT department. Hannity had the access and attitude of a White House aide without any of the government protection. Many people wanted to know what he and the president were gabbing about. And this didn't just apply to Hannity: I know of a prominent Fox host who found spyware on their phone and traced it back to a nosy foreign ally.

In June 2018 Hannity flew to Singapore for the overhyped summit between Trump and North Korean dictator Kim Jong Un. Back in New York, *Fox & Friends Weekend* host Abby Huntsman was narrating live coverage of Trump's arrival when she accidentally called POTUS a dictator. No one in the control room noticed her "meeting between the two dictators" gaffe, and neither did her guest. But Twitter erupted with laughter. She really didn't mean to say it, but sometimes, she had to admit, Trump sure acted like a dictator wannabe.

All the cable newsers went wall-to-wall with summit coverage. Chris Wallace and Bret Baier led Fox's news coverage from Singapore, but Hannity scored the exclusive post-summit sit-down with the president and worked to spin the trip in Trump's favor. Through these promotional Q&As, "the first snapshot of history gets filtered through a sympathetic lens," *Politico* pointed out.

Reporters who covered the White House marveled at Hannity's ability to *stop* Trump from making news. Whenever Hannity would be granted precious time with Trump, the say-anything president would just repeat his greatest lines and lies. According to *The Daily Beast*, Trump sometimes mocked Hannity "for being such a suck-up," specifically calling out "the low-quality laziness of the host's questions." Trump wanted a little bit of a challenge! But he kept saying yes to Hannity's interview requests.

After taping with his best man, Trump held a rare press conference and took real questions from real reporters. Hundreds of credentialed journalists streamed into the ballroom at the Capella Hotel and hoped to be called on. Their attention was Trump's power source, and he didn't even try to hide it. When he called on One America News, he heaped praise on the channel's "beautiful" coverage of him. When he called on *Time* magazine, he asked, "Am I on the cover again this week? Boy, have I—so many covers."

There was a seat in the front row with a piece of paper labeled "government official," reserved for Hannity. Journalists snickered about it, but there was nothing they could do about this perversion of norms. Well, nothing except document it and try to convince people that this was not normal or right. And ultimately not good for the country.

While in Singapore, Baier bombarded Sarah Sanders with interview requests. "We flew all the way here," he said. Baier was the opposite of Neil Cavuto—he believed presidential interviews were paramount. He lobbied the West Wing constantly and he was ticked off that his opinion peers landed all the interviews. This was a sign of weakness on Trump's part, he thought. Trump eventually gave Baier ten minutes on board Air Force One before taking off. It was a repeat of the O'Reilly Super Bowl Sunday interview: Baier pointed out that Kim "is a killer. I mean, he's clearly executing people." And Trump responded with false equivalencies. "He is a tough guy," and besides, he said, "a lot of other people have done some really bad things."

The news cycle was unforgiving. Trump one-upped himself every hour, dodging this scandal or that screwup by delivering some other shock. "In the Trump era," Brian Kilmeade told an interviewer, "there are three major stories every day. It used to be one big story every three days." Cable news shows live and die by the rundown, a computerized list of every script and guest and graphic and video clip, but in the Trump age the rundown was "thrown out," in TV parlance, so often that it became a running joke among show teams. "Trump just tweeted, throw out the rundown!"

But certain stories still managed to break through. When Trump returned from Singapore, it was the forced separation policy. The administration was breaking up thousands of families for crossing the southern border into the U.S. The utter inhumanity of the policy catapulted it to the top of the national news agenda—and another Fox host reached her breaking point. This time it was Huntsman.

Huntsman told friends that she had lots of "hard days" on the curvy couch, lots of days when she struggled to figure out how to defend the administration's actions and antics. Kids in cages was too much. Huntsman's seven-month-old daughter, Isabel, was on her mind. Her cohost Pete Hegseth was a father of four—and this was unfolding on Father's Day weekend—but he somehow stuck to Trump's talking points. "They're getting school and soccer and video games and three squares and two snacks," he said, taking the word of a government that lied incessantly. Later reports revealed that some of the migrants were in squalid conditions, with inedible food, overflowing toilets, and deficient medical care. "Treated worse than dogs," one seventeen-year-old Honduran boy said. But *Fox & Friends* stayed on its default setting—outrage at the way other media outlets were covering the story. That was sometimes the only way to skate by shameful Trump news. But Huntsman slipped in how she really felt, as subtly as possible. "Where we are right now is not sustainable," she said. "The United States has always been the good guy. We've always been the ones—"

Hegseth interjected: "We're still the good guy!"

Yes, but that's "why we need to figure this out," she said.

Huntsman had been quietly talking to ABC executives about

leaving Fox and joining *The View*. But she'd been on the fence, feeling grateful to Fox, feeling reluctant to give up what she had. Family separations tipped her off the fence and onto ABC.

Why did so many others stay? That's the question I am asked most often. After Hannity became the face of Fox News and indulged in offensive conspiracy theories, after the network turned a blind eye to Trumpworld's mendacity and hypocrisy, after it resorted to self-censorship to avoid angering the base, why didn't others follow Carl Cameron and Clayton Morris and Conor Powell and Abby Huntsman out the door?

For some it was about absolute devotion to the Trump cause. They cared about remaking the courts. Rolling back abortion rights. Taking on China. But for many it was about money. Anchors and correspondents making more than $1 million a year don't think they'll make that much money anywhere else. They worry that they're not really marketable to other networks, and they're usually right.

The money was just part of it. "We have a strong sense of family. We protect each other," an anchor told me. "When someone's going through a tough time at home, Fox takes care of them. Don't underestimate that." When Bret Baier and his family members were in a serious car accident after a ski trip in Montana, Suzanne Scott immediately offered to send a plane from 21st Century Fox's private fleet.

Numerous employees also cited the investments Rupert and Scott made to clean the place up. New HR executives and protections against workplace harassment—hotlines, training sessions, councils—were tangible if imperfect evidence of change. Gleaming new studios and luxurious new offices were a big morale boost. The new second-floor newsroom opened in January 2018 and Studio J debuted in June. Upstairs on the twentieth and twenty-first floors, renovated offices for the talent were a huge deal. Anchors were able to design their own offices with standing desks, big closets, and couches for naps between live shots. "We all came in and said, 'This is a game changer,' " a daytime host said.

For talent too there were all the fringe benefits that come from being a major-league player at a media conglomerate, like $10,000 wardrobe budgets and priceless Super Bowl tickets. For those who could stomach the Trump cult and could navigate the internal fiefdoms, it could be a happy place to work. And there was no denying the influence of the platform. When the head writer of *Fox & Friends* quit, about twelve months into the Trump presidency, there were whispers around the office that he couldn't stand the Trump sycophancy anymore. He told his ex-colleagues he was "mentally beat down." Fox posted a job wanted ad for his replacement, and Vox.com declared, "the most influential job in America is open."

"Desperate"

On July 5, 2018, Trump gave in to Hannity's pleas and hired Bill Shine as his deputy chief of staff for communications. Shine's first assignment was small but supremely important to the president: Fix the lights.

The president hated the way his events looked on TV. So on July 9, the night Trump nominated Brett Kavanaugh to the Supreme Court, Shine got to work. He fiddled with the camera angles and fretted over the backdrop. According to Axios, "he showed the president three different lighting options and Trump selected his favorite."

It was a made-for-Fox event. The White House held an unveiling at 9 p.m. Eastern, introduced on Fox by Hannity, who called it "one of the most important and consequential decisions in American history."

A key function of right-wing media was counterprogramming. With the family separation policy stoking outrage, the special counsel hard at work, and the Democrats poised to make gains in the midterms, the Kavanaugh news gave the Trump-Fox conservative base something to cheer about. Laura Ingraham watched the announcement in the East Room, then conveniently walked out to the North Lawn to host her 10 p.m. show. She was grinning from ear to ear.

Ingraham was a steady ally for the nomination fight, and far from the only one. Whenever the White House needed help with the nomination, Shine phoned his former network. Kavanaugh's pivotal interview defending himself from Christine Blasey Ford's sexual assault allegation was awarded to Fox's Martha MacCallum. Trump reminded his Twitter followers to tune in. MacCallum's questions were tough, but most of Fox's commentary around Kavanaugh's combative confirmation hearing was in his favor. A female staffer told me that several of her colleagues were so troubled by the tenor of the Kavanaugh coverage that they brought it up in therapy. Overworked television producers seeing therapists is nothing new, or in any way unique to Fox, but the rah-rah win-at-any-cost defense of Kavanaugh was triggering for some.

Supreme Court watchers said Kavanaugh's use of the Fox airwaves was extremely unusual and at odds with his commitments to neutrality and nonpartisanship. "The Supreme Court must never be viewed as a partisan institution," Kavanaugh said at his confirmation hearing, leading NBC's Chuck Todd to ask: "How impartial can a Supreme Court nominee be when he goes on Fox News—of all possible platforms—to defend himself?"

Blasey Ford was a credible witness. But Kavanaugh bulled his way through the hearing and told the world about his frat-boy love for beer. During a break in the testimony, Andrew Napolitano said the judge "dug himself *out* of the hole" he was in. Another Fox commentator got himself buried: Right-wing personality Kevin Jackson tweeted that the Kavanaugh accusers were "lying skanks," and "TO HELL with the notion that women must be believed no matter what." The tweet went viral, and Fox management went looking for Jackson's phone number. Before the hearing was over, his contributor contract had been terminated. Fox said his reprehensible comments "do not reflect the values of Fox News," raising the question, did all the other smears reflect the values of Fox News?

After Kavanaugh was sworn in on October 6, 2018, Trump claimed that Blasey Ford's allegations were part of "a hoax set up by the Democrats." The word he always wielded to vilify the Russia probe ("Russia witch hunt hoax") suddenly had a new application.

"I think it is important to understand that the use of the word 'hoax' cues a particular cognitive frame," Georgetown University sociolinguist Jennifer Sclafani told me. "Democrats and Republicans use frames to talk about political issues in different ways, and the choice of words activates a particular understanding or frame of the issue. For example, whether we talk about 'gun control' or 'Second Amendment rights,' we are talking about the same political issue. But our choice of terms tells the audience where we stand on the issue."

Sclafani said Trump used "hoax" to discredit the Democratic framing and reinforce his own political identity. "His use of 'hoax' works in the same way as his repetitive claim that any news that undercuts his authority is 'fake' news," she said. "While both these words have denotative (literal) meanings of falsehood, their connotative (contextual or social) meaning is to undermine the authority of the person or organization peddling the news."

Poll after poll showed how scarily effective this was. Through "hoax" and "fake news" and "witch hunt," Trump and Fox changed the language of politics. Everything existed along a pro/anti dividing line. The Bush years weren't consumed with talk of "pro-Bush" versus "anti-Bush" factions. The Obama years weren't defined by "pro-Obama" or "anti-Obama" lingo. But in the Trump age, the "pro-Trump" and "anti-Trump" labels were everywhere. Partisans expected everyone to pick a side, and for those who abstained, a side was picked for them.

Trust in institutions was low and getting lower, especially among Republicans. "We are careening dangerously from a high-trust to a low-trust society," libertarian editor Matt Welch wrote in November 2018. The reasons were innumerable, but the Foxified portrayal of fellow citizens as enemies undoubtedly was a factor. Trump's media allies worked to convince the base that everyone was a lying liar, so Trump's sins weren't that bad, and at least Trump was on their side. And Trump led a hate movement against media outlets that weren't on his approved list. After a rousing rendition of "CNN sucks" from the crowd at a West Virginia rally, Trump said, "They really do stoke the fires of resentment and chaos," while he stoked those same fires himself. One of the big problems was that he was surrounded by people who didn't call him out on the hypocrisy or the dangerous rhetoric. In exchange, those loyal wingmen were rewarded with soft landings.

In October 2018, at Trump's recommendation, Hope Hicks was appointed chief communications officer for Fox News's corporate parent. Hicks barely knew a thing about Hollywood PR or corporate earnings, but she knew the right people. And she came quite highly recommended by reporters on the Trump beat. Plus, the job gave her an excuse to move to L.A. and get a Land Rover. She interviewed for the job with Lachlan Murdoch, who would be the CEO of Fox's remainders once Disney took control of the entertainment assets. The company was in limbo, and the current heads of PR were leaving because they didn't want to work for a suddenly-much-smaller company. But for Hicks, who needed someplace to ride out the Mueller probe, it was a cushy landing. Her new office, right down the hall from Lachlan's in Building 88 on the Fox studio lot, was four times the size of her White House cubbyhole. She hung a 2017 inauguration proclamation on her wall.

Hicks didn't have anything to do with the news channel headquartered in New York, but the eventual Mueller report contained a passage that revealed a ton about her assessment of Fox. Interviewed by Maria Bartiromo one month before he fired Comey, Trump was questioned whether it was too late to ask Comey, who was four years into a ten-year term, to step aside. "No, it's not too late, but you know, I have confidence in him. We'll see what happens," Trump said. After the interview, according to Mueller, "Hicks told the president she thought the president's comment about Comey should be removed from the broadcast of the interview, but the president wanted to keep it in, which Hicks thought was unusual." Hicks's belief that she could unilaterally cut a chunk out of a Fox interview was never explained.

For a sign of the synergies between Fox Corp and Trump, one had to look no further than Hicks's very first press release in the new job. It was an announcement of corporate support for the First Step Act, the prison reform act supported by the president, the ACLU, the Kochs, and Kim Kardashian West, among others. Hicks later testified that Jared Kushner called her and "asked if this would be something that Fox would be interested in supporting." Insiders interpreted Hicks's press release as a nudge at Mitch McConnell, who was holding up the bill in the Senate. Once he allowed a vote, it passed, and Trump hailed it as a grand achievement, a useful weapon in his reelection war chest.

Bill Shine also symbolized the Trump-Fox soft landing arrangement. Incredibly, he was still paid by Fox even after joining the Trump administration, thanks to his generous multiyear severance agreement with the Murdochs. He cashed $3.5 million from Fox in 2018 and another $3.5 million in 2019.

Once he fixed the lights, Shine tried to get a grip on the White House comms operation. His main contribution was the end of Sanders's daily press briefing. Reporters wondered what he did all day. Trump called him "No Shine" behind his back and soured on him, just as he did with so many other new hires. Shine's soft landing was a gig on the reelection campaign.

Kimberly Guilfoyle had a more successful transition into the Trump orbit. She was forced out of Fox in mid-2018, though in retrospect her days were numbered as soon as Ailes was forced out. The leader of "Team Roger" had generated quite a few HR complaints that couldn't be ignored by the Murdochs. The top lawyer for 21st Century Fox, Gerson Zweifach, had to get involved. Chief among the accusations: that Guilfoyle went around the office showing off dick pics on her phone. She claimed the pictures were from her male suitors. One of the people who saw the pictures told me, "I thought, 'She's single, he's single, what's the big deal?' But flaunting it at work was a violation."

There were other issues too—and sources pointed out that most of the complaints were lodged by women. The bottom line, one colleague said, was that "she was very open about her sex life. *Too* open." An HR investigation dragged on for months. "If Kim were a man, she would have been out much sooner," a person with knowledge of the investigation said. (Guilfoyle's lawyer said, "Any accusations of Kimberly engaging in inappropriate workplace conduct are unequivocally baseless and have been viciously made by disgruntled and self-interested employees.")

In the spring of 2018 Guilfoyle made her Trump love literal. Depending on who's telling the story, she either seduced Donald Trump Jr. or he decided to pursue her. Junior's impending divorce from Vanessa, the mother of his five children, was first reported in March, and when he was first seen in public with Kim in May, Page Six said they had been dating "for a few weeks" already.

Guilfoyle "knew how to use sex to get ahead," in the words of one friend, and some of her colleagues suspected that she was hitching herself to Junior for more than purely romantic reasons. According to them, Guilfoyle had been told months ahead of time that her last day at Fox was July 1. Undeterred, she fought to stay on the air. "She had Trump calling Rupert, lobbying on her behalf," one well-placed source said. "She thought Rupert would do nothing to her once she was with Trump Jr.," another source said.

In June, I asked Fox PR how the president's son's girlfriend could feasibly cohost a show about politics. Fox dodged the question because the answer was, she couldn't. Maybe it was true love—but *l'affaire* Don Junior also supplied an alternative story line on the day she departed Fox, several weeks after the original deadline. Guilfoyle said she was leaving to go campaign with Junior. That's when Yashar Ali, writing for *HuffPost*, published a story saying she did not leave voluntarily. Ali had been chasing rumors about Guilfoyle's behavior for months. She knew he was working on a story, and before the end of the day Guilfoyle's lawyers were threatening to sue him and *HuffPost*. Ali followed up a week later with a detailed accounting of her workplace escapades, noting the Junior angle: "Some people at Fox News were concerned that easing her out of the network would be slowed or halted due to the Trump family's close relationship with Murdoch." Alas, Rupert hated feeling like someone was manipulating him. Guilfoyle's time was up. She went out on the campaign trail with Don Jr. and hosted streaming video shows and extolled all things Trump. The mostly male members of Trump's inner circle thought she was a huge asset. In the words of former campaign aide Sam Nunberg, "Those legs got ratings, and I think those legs can get votes."

Guilfoyle wasn't missed at Fox. To the contrary, there were awkward rumblings whenever she came back to Fox HQ with her boyfriend, whom she nicknamed "Junior Mints" for his alleged sweetness. She tagged along on his interviews with Hannity and others, prompting one Fox insider to say, "It's not a good look. She seems desperate."

"Executive Time"

Once unbound from the shackles of truth, Fox's power came from what it decided to cover—its chosen narratives—*and* what it decided to ignore. Trump's immature, erratic, and immoral behavior? His sucking up to Putin? His mingling of presidential business and personal profit? Fox talk shows played dumb and targeted the "deep state" instead.

Conservative media types were like spiders, spinning webs and trying to catch prey. They insisted the real story was an Obama-led plot against Trump to stop him from winning the election. One night Hannity irrationally exclaimed, "This makes Watergate look like stealing a Snickers bar from a drugstore!" Another night he upped the hysteria, insisting this scandal "will make Watergate look like a parking ticket." The following night he screeched, "This is Watergate times a thousand." He strung viewers along, invoking mysterious "sources" who were "telling us" that "this is just the tip of the iceberg." There was always another "iceberg" ahead, always another twist coming, always another Democrat villain to attack after the commercial break.

Hannity and Trump were so aligned that, on one weird night in 2018, Hannity had to deny that he was giving Trump a sneak peek at his monologues after the president tweeted out, twelve minutes before air, "Big show tonight on @SeanHannity! 9:00 P.M. on @FoxNews." Political reporters fumbled for their remotes and flipped over to Fox en masse. Hannity raved about the "Mueller crime family" and said the Russia investigation was "corrupt" and promoted a guest who said Mueller "surrounded himself with literally a bunch of legal terrorists," whatever that meant. Some reporters who did not watch Fox regularly were shocked at how unhinged and extreme the content was. But this was just an ordinary night in the pro-Trump alternative universe. Night after night, Hannity said the Mueller probe needed to be stopped immediately, for the good of the country. Trump's attempts at obstruction flowed directly from his "Executive Time."

Trump granted himself more "Executive Time" and watched more TV as the years went by. He outfitted his upstairs residence with multiple TVs and DVRs, and lingered there in the morning, out of sight of the potential leakers who worked for him downstairs. He typically watched shows like *Fox & Friends* on a bit of a delay, which meant he could zap through the commercials with the DVRs. He channel-surfed to Fox Business and Newsmax and the broadcast networks. For all of his professed hatred for CNN and MSNBC, he kept a close eye on those channels too. I knew it for a fact because my *Reliable Sources* guests occasionally heard from the president after saying supportive things about him on my program. One of the biggest lies he ever told, measured by its distance from the truth, was "I do not watch much television." He watched so much that he sometimes fell asleep with Fox still on, like the truly hardcore fan that he was.

The DVRs were the critical part of his television setup. He called TiVo "one of the great inventions of all time" and said television was "practically useless without TiVo." But TiVo, which was invented in 1999, was just the brand name for a generic concept, like people who "Xeroxed" a paper on a different brand of copier. Trump said he had "Super TiVo" in the White House, but he actually had the DirecTV Genie HD DVR, a whole-home system that recorded multiple channels at the same time and let users watch those recordings from any screen in the home. It was genuinely awesome technology for a TV junkie. With the Genie, he could flip through hours of Fox in his residence, hit pause, walk downstairs to the Oval Office, and resume watching right where he left off. When he moved in, contractors also installed a sixty-inch TV above a fireplace in his private West Wing dining room, steps from the Oval. That's typically where he caught up on cable news during the workday before retreating back upstairs in the evening. Obama only kept a small TV in the dining room, mostly tuned to ESPN, as Trump told visitors when he mocked the size of Obama's screen and pointed out his replacement unit.

Other TV monitors were scattered about the West Wing, many of them set on one of the "four box" screens that showed four different networks simultaneously. The most popular version was the "four cable boxes," with Fox News, Fox Business, MSNBC, and CNN all represented. Another four-box carried Washington's broadcast TV stations. A third variation included C-SPAN, CNBC, and Bloomberg. Trump was, as you know by now, most keenly interested in the "four cable boxes."

He also received packets full of TV news screenshots so he could see who was on cable talking about him, and what the chyrons said, during the rare hours when he wasn't watching. The packets also included transcripts of TV segments and, according to *Vice*, "sometimes just pictures of Trump on TV looking powerful."

Time magazine reporters who spent time watching TV with Trump in 2017 said he watched the screen "like a coach going over game tape, studying the opposition, plotting next week's plays." Sometimes this meant rewatching his rallies and interviews; other times, it meant watching his Democratic rivals. The DirecTV Genie was the key.

The joke around Fox was that Trump watched more of the network's programming than management. Now that Hope Hicks was out of the White House and working at Fox Corp, she knew there was some truth to the joke. But she hated the drumbeat of stories about the president being glued to Fox News. She thought it made him look ill-informed and small.

The problem was, the stories were accurate.

White House director of social media Dan Scavino was tasked with making sure the MAGAsphere saw Trump's favorite Fox segments. He tweeted so many videos ripped from Fox's shows that his Twitter page sometimes resembled an official network account.

Fox is "not just an echo chamber. We see it as a CMS system on steroids," a former White House aide told me, referring to the content management systems that websites use to publish content. He depicted the network as the ultimate CMS—a content creation engine that past presidents would have killed to have. It's about "pulling clips and having social influencers blast them out where millions of people will consume them," he said. "It's getting friendly news sites to do first- and second-round write-ups. It's giving the party ammunition for their opposition research books. It's allowing campaigns the ability to cite something like *Breitbart* or *Daily Caller* in TV ads and mailers. And all of that comes from Fox."

"Don't be a baby"

On Monday, October 15, 2018, Fox launched its midterm campaign for the GOP. "Expose the deep state" took a break. The racist and sadly effective "Fearing immigrants" took its place.

"To the southwest border we go," news anchor Bill Hemmer reported. "Another caravan apparently is heading that way." Earlier in the day, when the president was watching, *Fox & Friends First* said the caravan was "exploding," getting bigger. The news and opinion shows held hands and jointly hyped the threat of traveling migrants who were making their way from Honduras through Guatemala toward Mexico and the U.S.

"Caravans," providing strength and safety in numbers, had been traveling through Central America for years. Activists sometimes organized these trips specifically to call attention to the plight of migrants. In the run-up to the 2018 midterms, Fox converted this act of protest into something to fear and set it up perfectly for the president, who weighed in on Tuesday and threatened to withdraw all aid money to Honduras. Trump's warning gave Fox another hook to cover the story every hour. See how that worked? A perfect loop of distorted information and fearmongering.

On Tuesday night Laura Ingraham linked the migrants to the midterms explicitly. While a graphic over her shoulder screamed "BORDER RUSH AND POSSIBLE ELECTORAL CRUSH," she asserted that Republicans had failed to lock down the border, but a Democrat-led House would be much worse. She warned that her loyal viewers were at risk of being "replaced"—conjuring up the racist Great Replacement theory that imagined that whites were being replaced by people of color in some sort of grand conspiracy. "Of this, my friends, you can be sure," Ingraham said, "your views on immigration will have zero impact and zero influence on a House dominated by Democrats who want to replace you, the American voters, with newly amnestied citizens and an ever-increasing number of chain migrants."

The election narrative was set. The midterms, in this telling, weren't a referendum on Trump's temper tantrums—they were a life-or-death fight for the future of white America. It seemed like the old local TV axiom "if it bleeds, it leads" needed an edit: On Fox, it was more like *"if it bleeds, and an immigrant is the suspect, it leads."*

On Wednesday night, Newt Gingrich told Hannity that two words would define the 2018 election: "One is Kavanaugh and the other is caravan." On Thursday Trump stole Gingrich's line: "This will be an election of Kavanaugh, the caravan, law and order, and common sense." When Trump invoked the "caravan" at a Montana rally, he said, "You know what I'm talking about," and the crowd, primed by Fox, did indeed. The banner on Tucker Carlson's show warned of a "MASSIVE MIGRANT CARAVAN ON THE WAY" at the same time the banner on Chris Hayes's MSNBC show said "REPUBLICANS STOKE FEAR AND RESENTMENT AHEAD OF MIDTERMS." Fox supplied the raw material. Everyone else just tried to play catch-up.

Reporting was no match for migrant fearmongering. When *New York Times* reporter Emily Cochrane asked Trump to back up his made-up-out-of-thin-air claims that the "caravan" was full of "hardened criminals," he responded, "Oh please, please, don't be a baby."

Trump continued to spread misinformation that he picked up on *Fox & Friends*. A crumb of information from Guatemala's president about his country's past deportation of immigrants with links to terrorism—shared in an apparent bid to impress the U.S.—was whipped by right-wing websites into a lie about the current "caravan." This lie was transmitted from the web to *Fox & Friends* by Pete Hegseth on Monday, October 22. "They caught over a hundred ISIS fighters in Guatemala trying to use this caravan," he said, falsely. Hegseth infected Trump, who tweeted during the show and said "criminals and unknown Middle Easterners are mixed in" with the migrants. He didn't attribute this to Fox, he stated it as fact, and said, "I have alerted Border Patrol and Military that this is a National Emergency."

A lone voice on Fox tried to correct him. It was Shep, of course.

"Fox News knows of no evidence to suggest the president is accurate on that matter," Shep said at three o'clock. "And the president has offered no evidence to support what he has said." He came back around to the subject the next day and pointed out that the "caravan" was one thousand miles away from the U.S. border. That's "a 353-hour walk, says Google. At 8 hours a day, 7 days a week, they are at least 44 days away at minimum."

But Shep's fact-checks were trampled by the fearmongering every other hour.

Fox even dispatched reporter Griff Jenkins to Texas, where it looked like he was waiting for the migrants to arrive any minute. Since he had a lot of time to kill, he went hunting for other border-crossers. *Fox & Friends* showed him hiding in the bushes with his eyes peeled on the Rio Grande. When a small group started to cross in a raft, he shouted questions and the smuggler turned the raft around, a moment Fox celebrated with a banner: "GRIFF FOILS ILLEGALS' ATTEMPT TO CROSS BORDER."

News anchors at Fox hated being lumped in with the network's prime time crusaders. As Bret Baier put it, "I don't spend a lot of time analyzing what the opinion shows are doing." Chris Wallace claimed he didn't watch the shows either. But if that was true, it was borderline irresponsible. Look at Jenkins: He was a correspondent assigned to Baier and Wallace's DC bureau, but he was playing Border Patrol agent for the amusement of *Fox & Friends*.

White identity politics were suffused all throughout Fox, whether staffers wanted to recognize it or not. Countless segments preyed on racial anxieties and the perceived loss of status of white Christian America. Fox shows were talking about this well before Trump the candidate was—just think back to Bill O'Reilly and the "War on Christmas."

"It was exactly these kinds of fears about cultural change, cultural displacement, and immigration that were the key drivers of support for President Trump," Robert P. Jones, the head of the Public Religion Research Institute, told me. Those fears were sown and stoked by the media machine Murdoch and Ailes created. Jones depicted America as a dining room table and said white Christians used to control who sat at the table and where, like the head of the family. Now, in an increasingly multicultural country, no single demographic group controls the table. Everyone is welcome to take a seat. And that feels "deeply unsettling" to the group that used to be in charge, he said. Thus: "Build a wall." Polling by Jones's organization, PRRI, found that only one in three Republicans believed immigrants strengthen American society. The other two out of three said immigrants threaten American values. In the Trump age, Fox increasingly spoke to the latter audience.

Carlson and Ingraham made cultural displacement a theme of their shows. They vocally sympathized with their viewers' sense of whiteness being under threat. Carlson said that "reckless immigration policies" caused demographic changes—e.g., an influx of Hispanics—that were "bewildering for people." In a much-derided segment in March 2018, he cited the coal-mining town of Hazleton, Pennsylvania, where the Hispanic population grew from 2 percent in 2000 to 52 percent in 2016. "People who grew up in Hazleton return to find out they can't communicate with the people who now live there, and that's bewildering for people," he said. "That's happening all over the country. No nation, no society has ever changed this much, this fast."

The source for Carlson's commentary, an article in *National Geographic* magazine, said "few communities have seen the kind of rapid change that Hazleton has." Writer Michele Norris was drawn to Hazleton for that reason. The headline of her incisive article could have been about Fox: "As America Changes, Some Anxious Whites Feel Left Behind."

Nostalgia was one of the products Fox sold. "The America we know and love doesn't exist anymore," Ingraham declared in August. "Massive demographic changes have been foisted on the American people, and they are changes that none of us ever voted for, and most of us don't like."

Ingraham's words went viral when a researcher from Media Matters flagged them on Twitter and said her anti-immigrant rant was "ripped from white supremacists." Fox executives hated when the left-wing media watchdogs caused headaches like this. Just as firmly as Media Matters staffers believed Fox was a stain on the country, Fox execs believed Media Matters was a shadowy arm of the DNC that was trying to blow up their network. The group opposed Fox, yes, but it was just pointing out what Ingraham had said. No one could deny that she said it. White supremacist David Duke said Ingraham delivered "one of the most important (truthful) monologues in the history of" the media. The next night Ingraham called Duke a "racist freak" and denounced white nationalism. She insisted her comments weren't about race or ethnicity, even though she specifically said "massive demographic changes" were disturbing to her and to her viewers. Amid the blowback, she didn't bring up "demographics" again for a while.

Other hosts on Fox distanced themselves from Ingraham and Carlson. They told me they wished Carlson would drop the "white supremacist shit" because it tarnished the entire network. At one point he trolled his critics by saying the threat of white supremacy was a "hoax. Just like the Russia hoax. It's a conspiracy theory used to divide the country and keep a hold on power." There was a big audience for what he was selling and a much smaller audience for Shep Smith's retort on the air: "White nationalism is without question a very serious problem in America."

Hannity noticeably did not talk about the browning of America the way the other two prime time hosts did. But I wondered if he realized what he was saying when he proclaimed himself to be a proud "deplorable." He said it all the time, night after night, reminding viewers of the 2016 comment Hillary Clinton wished she could take back. But if Hannity stopped to think for just a second, he would have realized he was telling on himself. Clinton said there were two baskets of Trump supporters. One was full of people "who feel that government has let them down, nobody cares about them, nobody worries about what happens to their lives and their futures, and they are just desperate for change." She empathized with them, in contrast with the other basket, which was full of "deplorables" with "racist, sexist, homophobic, xenophobic, Islamophobic" views. Clearly that distinction was lost on Hannity, and on most of his viewers.

October's "caravan" was convenient in that it was a coded way to appeal to conservative white anxiety. Fox's coverage was dehumanizing. Ingraham warned that the migrants might be diseased. Carlson alluded to an "invasion" as early as October 16. "This is an invasion," Newt Gingrich said. "We have to treat this as an invasion," Representative Steve Scalise said on Ingraham's show. "Invasion" was used on Fox News more than sixty times, and another seventy-five times on Fox Business, in October.

Again, Shep tried to push back. On his October 23 broadcast he read a tweet from a viewer who told him, "Sorry, Shep. We are not falling for your fake story. This is an invasion." Smith tried to tell her that Trump was preying on her fears.

But that same night, Ingraham referred to the migrants as an "invading horde."

Shep thought the rhetoric from his right-wing colleagues was shameful. He thought someone—like the CEO of the network—should intervene, but he believed Suzanne Scott was too weak to take action. "They're not actually managing anything. The place is on cruise control," a Fox producer told me. "Tucker and Hannity are more managerial than Jay and Suzanne." Others at Fox blamed the executive vice president for prime time programming, Meade Cooper, and said she didn't have firm enough control over the content. In my view, the responsibility was shared, so the blame was as well. When I shared this reporting with two of the best TV talent managers I know, they said the job is really quite easy: It's about saying yes whenever possible and no whenever necessary.

"People need to understand who's in charge," he said.

"You have to say no to your stars sometimes," she said.

"You have to praise them when they do well and you have to say 'Why the fuck did you just do that?' when they fuck up," he said.

"You can't be afraid of them," she said.

"That's right. You can't be afraid of them," he said.

Fox management seemed afraid.

Apocalyptic "invasion" rhetoric ricocheted all around the right-wing media world. The calls from spitting-mad listeners to talk radio and the hateful comments on hyperpartisan websites were worse than what was being spouted on Fox—but it was all connected. In Pennsylvania, forty-six-year-old anti-Semite Robert Bowers posted a message on a seedy Twitter alternative called Gab: "I noticed a change in people saying illegals, they now say invaders. I like this."

Bowers fixated on HIAS, a Jewish refugee agency which gave life-changing help to refugees in America. On October 27 he wrote that HIAS "likes to bring invaders that kill our people. I can't sit by and watch my people get slaughtered. Screw your optics, I'm going in." Then he walked inside the Tree of Life synagogue and shot eleven people to death.

There was no official link between the "invasion" talk on Fox and the bloodbath in Pittsburgh. But some people at the network suspected there was. "We know that the rhetoric that we're hearing now can't be helpful," Shep said on the air on October 29.

"No, I don't think there's a coincidence," his guest, criminologist Casey Jordan, told him.

Shep's voice was low, mournful. He spoke straight to Fox viewers, those who could still stand to watch him: "There is no invasion, no one's coming to get you, there's nothing at all to worry about."

In prime time, Tucker rebutted him: "The migrant caravan is a real thing, despite what they may be telling you on television." Ingraham interviewed the president, who said "we're being invaded," two days after a sicko said the same thing to justify slaughtering innocents.

Trump's campaign made the imaginary "invasion" its closing message for the midterms, and tried to buy ad time for a racist, anti-immigrant thirty-second spot. CNN refused to run it because the ad was racist. NBC did run it, then stopped amid a backlash from viewers. Fox News pulled the ad too . . . after it ran about a dozen times. And the network never really covered the controversy on the air—never told its viewers that it had rejected one of Trump's ads.

In the closing days of the midterm campaign, Barack Obama made a prediction: "Right before the election, they try to scare the heck out of you," he said. "And then the election comes, and suddenly the problem is magically gone. Everything's great. 'I'm sorry, what did we say?' " This, Obama said, "is what happened in 2010, this is what happened in 2012, what happened in 2014, just over and over and over again, they'll just run these same stories and then after the election, suddenly they're not interested anymore."

In 2010, it was "death panels." In 2014, it was Ebola. Obama didn't have to blast Fox by name—his audience knew who he was talking about. "There's a certain news station," he said, "that they just, their business is ramping up these scare tactics, that's what they do." But he said the CNNs of the world were also part of the problem: They amplify "lies over and over again, even when they don't intend to," by repeating what Republicans were talking about.

Obama had a point. Lots of journalists regretted their excessive "caravan" coverage in late October. But not Carlson and Ingraham—for they were on a mission.

"No one can stop us"

On October 26, 2018, I flew to the Bojangles' Coliseum in Charlotte, North Carolina, for one of Trump's final rallies before the midterms. Walking up to the arena in the driving rain, I saw that a projection screen told everyone to sign up for "real news" by following Trump on Twitter and Facebook. I met up with a private security guard assigned to me by CNN for the day. This had become an unfortunate custom for the network's news crews covering Trump rallies. The other CNN correspondent at the rally had a guard too. The retired cops kept an eye on the crowd and made sure nothing got out of hand.

At the risk of stating the obvious, Fox correspondents did not travel to Trump rallies with private security.

I never felt threatened at the rally, but there were legitimate reasons to be vigilant. Back in July, a man in State College, Pennsylvania, called in to C-SPAN's open phones show and threatened me and my colleague Don Lemon. "It all started when Trump got elected," the man said. "Brian Stelter and Don Lemon from CNN called Trump supporters all racists. They don't even know us. They don't even know these Americans out here and they are calling us racists because we voted for Trump? Come on, give me a break. They started the war. I see them, I'm going to shoot them, bye." Then the caller hung up on the host.

None of the man's rant made any sense. Don Lemon and I started a war? Maybe against hair products, but that's it.

I never called all Trump supporters racist. So when I heard this phone call on C-SPAN, my first question was, what made this man so angry? I hadn't even said anything recently about race. It seemed like his attack came out of nowhere. I searched news websites and

TV transcripts—and then I found something. Hannity had gone on a tirade the night before about Trump critics in the media. He played a two-year-old clip of me asking if racial anxiety was a factor in Trump's rise. A *two*-year-old clip! At the time I was merely asking the question, but since then it has been well established that the answer is yes—racist beliefs and resentment of minorities did drive some support for Trump. That's not the same as calling all Trump supporters racist, but the timing of this C-SPAN caller's rant was suspicious to say the least. Hannity blasted me on Thursday night and I got a death threat on Friday morning.

I didn't blame Hannity then, and I don't blame him now. Hannity is unfortunately on the receiving end of threats too. But I'd be a fool not to wonder about the connection. And Hannity would be a fool not to admit that racial anxiety was a factor in Trump's rise.

Back to the rally. Inside the fenced-in area for the press, I felt like a penguin at the zoo. I sat at a folding table next to Fox correspondent Kevin Corke. Some rallygoers gawked at us, showed off their anti-CNN shirts, and shouted "fake news" insults in my direction. Most, however, just wanted to take selfies.

I saw how these rallies were social gatherings—chances to see friends and share stories with no resemblance to reality. Cesar Sayoc, the man who sent mail bombs to CNN and prominent Democrats, had been arrested earlier in the day, so I listened in as one woman told other Trump fans that the suspect was actually a "liberal." In fact, Sayoc was a hardcore right-winger and an obsessive fan of Trump and Fox. Sayoc's lawyers admitted that the bomber planned "his morning workout to coincide with 'Fox and Friends' and his evenings to dovetail with Hannity." During the day he lived on Facebook, where right-wing friend groups used Fox as a source of content. "Many of these groups promoted various conspiracy theories and, more generally, the idea that Trump's critics were dangerous, unpatriotic, and evil. They deployed provocative language to depict Democrats as murderous, terroristic, and violent. Fox News furthered these arguments," Sayoc's lawyers said. "For example, just days before Mr. Sayoc mailed his packages, Sean Hannity said on his program that a large 'number of Democratic leaders [were] encouraging mob violence against their political opponents.' "

Sayoc believed outlandish reports—like the kind that this woman was spreading about him, right in front of me at this rally. She said, "He was anti-Trump on his Facebook." That was a lie. As for Sayoc's van, which was plastered with pro-Trump and anti-Democrat memes, the woman proposed a full-blown conspiracy: "They put stickers on his van, like, last night." She shouted this to anyone who would listen. And several people did.

A few minutes later, a rallygoer approached the fence and asked me, "Is Sean Hannity going to be here?" No, but he did show up on occasion. At Trump's invitation, Hannity attended another rally a few days later, on the eve of the midterms. The Trump campaign dubbed him a "special guest." That struck me as odd, so I asked Fox PR what was going on. Bill O'Reilly was never a "special guest" at a George W. Bush event—Ailes would have never allowed that. "Hey," I texted a Fox News spokeswoman, "can you remind me Fox's policy re: people like Hannity doing political rallies?"

"Hannity will be hosting his show from that location and interviewing the president," she responded.

"But the rally literature portrays Hannity as a speaker and sponsor of the rally," I said.

"He is not sponsoring the rally nor is he campaigning," she said.

I stifled a laugh. Hannity campaigned for Trump every night. But management told him that he couldn't give a speech at the rally.

The news division would go nuts if he did. And Hannity accepted their terms: "To be clear," he tweeted, "I will not be on stage campaigning with the president."

What happened next was inevitable. Hannity received a hero's welcome at the rally. He and Trump buttered each other up in a televised chat, then Trump took the stage and thanked the special guests who, in his mind, worked for him. He beckoned Hannity to the podium and gave him a man hug. The first words out of Hannity's mouth were "By the way, all those people in the back are fake news."

The crowd cheered and the Fox staffers in the press pen cringed. They were just trying to do their jobs, and the network's biggest star was insulting them. I texted the Fox spokeswoman three face-palm emojis. She didn't reply.

Trump called Jeanine Pirro to the stage next. Pirro "treats us very, very well," Trump said, promoting her to "Justice Jeanine," like she was a member of the Supreme Court. She soaked up the affection.

Offstage, Hannity and Shine high-fived at the brazen display of Hannity's power. He defied his bosses while all of Trumpworld watched and cheered. Fox journalists were aghast, and that made the moment even more scrumptious for Hannity. "No one can stop us," he commented to a friend. His excuse to management was that the president asked him to come up on stage. He asked: "Am I supposed to tell the president no?"

Fox was supposed to be showing off its news talent on Election Day, but November 6, 2018, was overshadowed by Hannity and Pirro's high jinks.

"Fox News still has news in its name," Bret Baier told Scott and

Jay Wallace at a lunch that should have been celebratory but instead turned contentious.

"They embarrassed all of us," Chris Wallace said.

This meeting had been scheduled long in advance, to get everyone together for Election Day, but the timing was fortuitous; the anchors needed to vent about the rally.

"That can never, ever happen again," Baier said.

Scott said it wouldn't. But the newsmen wondered how she would make sure of that.

Around this conference room table, it was evident to everyone how much Trump had altered Fox. Wallace and Baier wanted to report the way they always had. But Hannity and Pirro wanted to be a part of Trump's never-ending campaign, and a greater number of viewers sided with them, rejecting old-fashioned rules about independence. Pirro hosted as many private fundraisers for GOP candidates as she could possibly fit into her calendar. (In fact, she got ticked off when management blocked her from accepting $20,000 checks to host state GOP fundraisers.) Hannity hobnobbed with Trump and told him whom to hire. None of this was helping Fox's reporters; they had no idea what Trump was confiding in Hannity or vice versa, and they groaned when competitors assumed they did. "Other White House crews always come up to us asking questions, like we know everything," a staffer grumbled to me. Too often, the Fox team stationed at the White House knew *less* than their rivals. On any given day CNN and NBC had more staffers on the property than Fox did. "That's why we were behind on stories," I was told. Sometimes a manager would ask: "We're supposed to have this special relationship. Why are we behind on this story?" The "special relationship" didn't apply to the news side.

Rupert's allies insisted that he genuinely cared about the news operation. For all of his faults, he was a news junkie, the kind of guy with newspaper ink smudges on his thumbs, who liked owning the *New York Post* even though it lost money, because he could call in tips to Page Six. When one of his teenage daughters Instagrammed a photo of him reading his *Wall Street Journal*, I remembered season 2, episode 4 of *Succession*, the obscenely entertaining HBO drama about a Fox-like media empire, when the Rupert-like character played by Brian Cox tried to take over a CNN-like channel by pitching himself this way: "I'm a hairy old bastard who everybody hates, yadda, yadda. But I fuckin' love news and newspeople."

That was Rupert. He fuckin' loved news. As the U.S. newspaper industry took a nosedive, he looked at buying all the big chains (Tribune, Gannett, McClatchy) because he wondered if he could swoop in and help them survive. At Fox, he wanted Baier and Wallace on Fox's air and needed the credibility they proffered. He even stopped by Baier and Martha MacCallum's Election Day rehearsal. Sources said he referred to Baier's *Special Report* program as "the news," occasionally telling Scott about the show, "I saw on the news last night . . ."

But as much as Rupert loved news, he loved his profits more. Scott's job was to keep the ratings up. Keeping the ratings up meant making sure Hannity and Pirro were made up and miked up at 9 p.m. to fire up the Trump faithful. So her team drafted the meekest possible reprimand—more a light tap than a wrist slap. Rupert and Lachlan OKed it. The statement said, "Fox News does not condone any talent participating in campaign events," and called the rally "an unfortunate distraction." It did not even name Hannity or Pirro. But it enabled Scott to tell her irate news anchors that something (weak) had been done.

Hannity was MIA on Fox's election night broadcast, even though the network had said he would pop up during the prime time coverage. Insiders said he refused to appear, as payback for Scott's statement.

"Fix this"

Every so often Robert Mueller's prosecutors dropped bombs that exploded the news cycle but barely made a dent at Fox. At the end of November Michael Cohen pleaded guilty about lying to Congress. This is just the "tip of an iceberg," Judge Andrew Napolitano said on Fox, and "where is the rest of that iceberg? In Bob Mueller's office."

Napolitano was like a pesky teacher who refused to grade on a curve while everyone else handed out A's. He liked Trump personally but liked the rule of law more—and believed every politician should be held to the same high standard. Napolitano was always talking about the seriousness and thoroughness of Mueller's probe, while most of Fox's other personalities called it a "hoax" like Trump wanted.

No wonder Trump could barely stand seeing his old pal on TV anymore. The two men fell out of touch. Trump's last phone call to Napolitano had been back in June, after the legal scholar testified at a congressional hearing on "War Powers and Federal Spending." Napolitano's warning against executive branch overreach so surprised Senator Bernie Sanders that he approached afterward and said, "Do you really work for Fox News?" The two men were photographed together, and Napolitano's phone rang later in the week. "How's your new pal Bernie?" asked the Queens-born voice on the other end.

Trump trash-talked Napolitano in his calls with Hannity, but it wasn't like the two Fox motormouths ever crossed paths or cared about each other. They might as well have worked at different networks. Hannity only booked Trump-approved lawyers who toed the anti-Mueller line, not Napolitano. The judge told friends he didn't care—he was such an early riser, he was getting ready for bed by nine o'clock. But his bookings earlier in the day were drying up too. And that was getting to be a problem.

When the Mueller noose tightened, Fox's talk shows pressed the fear button and fell back to the imaginary "invasion." Banners screamed about the "BATTLE FOR THE SOUTHERN BORDER." It was good television, but it was bad politics for Trump—most Americans weren't nearly as panicked about the border as Fox led the president to believe. He didn't even have 50 percent support for further wall construction. But he convinced himself that he had 80 percent support—and told his aides to recite that fake stat—through his constant viewership of TV shows that called out his failure to deliver funding for the wall. This ever-present feedback loop led him to pick fights that were politically damaging.

On December 11, 2018, Trump said he would be "proud to shut down the government for border security." He sounded tough in front of Chuck Schumer and Nancy Pelosi; his fans loved it. Hannity and his guests used the word "fight" fourteen times in under an hour. They cheered for their fighter—until he basically backed down a week later and accepted a Senate-brokered compromise to keep the government open through the holidays. He was "bowing to political reality," *The Washington Post* said. But right-wing media wanted no part of reality. Ann Coulter lit into Trump so hard that he unfollowed her on Twitter. Hannity communicated his concern more discreetly. "Our viewers will hate this," he warned Trump by phone, according to a West Wing source.

On the morning of December 20, every hour of *Fox & Friends* was outwardly critical of both the House GOP and the president. "This is going to be a problem for Republicans," guest host Jedediah Bila said. "You see a lot of people around the country saying, 'Wait, hold on a second; you told us that you weren't afraid to shut down the government, that's why we like you. What happened? You just gave in right away.' "

Was he a fighter or a folder? Trump was going back and forth every hour, his mood dictated by what Fox put on the air.

"Fix this," he told aides, pointing at a Fox segment paused on his DVR.

Bill Shine worked the phones, reassuring surrogates that Trump was still committed to wall funding no matter what. In the afternoon, Trump took matters into his own hands, sending word to Rush Limbaugh that he was not going to accept the compromise. Limbaugh read the message on air: "You tell Rush that if there's no money in this, it's getting vetoed."

No new wall funding equaled no funding for the government. The Trump Show built suspense to a dreadful season finale on December 21, the darkest day of the year, when time and money ran out and the third partial shutdown of the year took effect at midnight. It was not an exaggeration to say that right-wing media— and its obsessions with "caravans" and "invasions"—shut down the government. The result: Government employees went without paychecks right before Christmas. The shutdown was a self-inflicted wound, one that embarrassed Trump when he eventually surrendered. But at this moment, Fox's millionaire hosts—who'd have no trouble paying for Christmas presents—were pleased. Jeanine Pirro gave Trump a pep talk through the TV. "Mr. President," she said, "I understand the pressure that you are under from every side, but the wall at our southern border is a promise that you made, ran on, got elected on, and must keep."

"I am pleading with you," she said, to "get it done." Meaning, keep the government closed until Democrats caved and ponied up money. "This is your moment," she snarled, "JUST DO IT."

Trump was watching, of course. He was all alone at the White House while his family was in Florida.

On New Year's Eve, Trump crawled back inside the television by calling into the Fox News countdown show and chatting with Pete Hegseth. Even there, Hegseth pressured him to hold steady: "Are you willing to continue the shutdown if that money does not come?"

"We are," Trump said. "We have no choice."

Trump was feeling the pressure from Fox.

So the shutdown continued into the new year.

On January 10, 2019, day nineteen of the government shutdown, Pete Hegseth asked a MAGA hat–wearing, toast-eating woman in Texas, "Would you describe it as a crisis?"

"It *is* a crisis," she said, because "we" in Corpus Christi "have so many problems with illegals."

When Hegseth tossed back to the studio, Doocy said the president's supporters "do not, as we just heard, want him to cave."

Trump heard him and tweeted straight to Doocy: "I won't!"

He did cave a few days later. A few of his Fox fans admitted they were disappointed: Lou Dobbs went on the air with his strangely hypnotic voice and said Pelosi "has just whipped the president of the United States." But others gave him a very long rope. Hannity, playing the inside game as he always did, dutifully spread Trump's spin that the government was merely reopening temporarily. Don't worry, he reassured viewers, Trump will win in the end. His fall-back message was always to say "stay tuned."

"Prostitutes"

Right-wing TV stars couldn't inspire government shutdowns and influence foreign policy without inspiring a resistance. I came to view Lieutenant Colonel Ralph Peters as the canary in the coal mine. Peters proudly worked at Fox News for ten years. He was a believer in Fox's conservative mission and he was vicious toward Obama . . . but he wasn't impressed by Trump either, so he didn't fit in anymore. On March 20, 2018, he wrote a scathing memo to colleagues calling Fox a "propaganda machine for a destructive and ethically ruinous administration." He said he was ashamed to work there, and he quit, dynamiting the bridge on his way out.

"What Fox is doing is causing real harm to our country right now," Peters told me. He described his former colleagues as "prostitutes" and said the president was "a danger to the republic."

These were the words of a man who felt he'd lost his party and his network. "Fox isn't immoral, it's amoral," he concluded. The network's merger with Trump "was opportunistic. Trump was just a gift to Fox and Fox in turn is a gift to Trump."

Peters even condemned Fox's core fans, calling them "couch potato anarchists" who wanted to "tear things down. They want vengeance." I'd never heard a former Fox employee talk in public about the network this way. But I had heard it in private—even from executives at 21st Century Fox. Some of them reached their own breaking points.

Joseph Azam had joined Fox's sister company News Corp in the fall of 2015. He was a senior vice president overseeing compliance. He was proud to represent brands like *The Wall Street Journal*, but his exposure to Fox News—just by being in the same building and working for the Murdoch family—troubled him greatly.

Around the time of the 2016 election, "it became very profitable to kind of fall in line with the anti-immigrant, anti-refugee, anti-Muslim rhetoric, and I was affected by that," he said.

Azam, an Afghan-American immigrant, was so disgusted by one of Tucker Carlson's anti-immigration commentaries, on June 29, 2017, that he responded to Tucker's question on Twitter asking "Why does America benefit from having tons of people from failing countries come here?" Azam replied: "If you come upstairs to where all the executives who run your company sit and find me I can tell you, Tucker." Azam didn't have a big Twitter following, but I did, so when I retweeted him, tens of thousands of people saw his message. Unbeknownst to me or anyone else, Azam's boss, the general counsel of News Corp, David Pitofsky, hauled him in for a talk.

"You're getting close to the line," Pitofsky said, telling Azam not to assail the Murdoch empire's biggest stars.

Azam took down the tweet, but the episode contributed to his decision to leave. He hadn't paid a lot of attention to Carlson before joining the company, but now he keyed into what the guy was all about. He believed Carlson was a "bona fide white supremacist." He resigned from the company in December 2017.

Some people who worked on the Fox News floors of News Corp HQ shared Azam's views. There was a bona fide resistance in the ranks. Correspondents and producers told me that they wished management would rein Carlson in. They cited examples like his December 2018 comment that mass immigration "makes our country poorer, and dirtier, and more divided." Liberal activist groups raised hell about that one, and advertisers bailed, but Lachlan Murdoch texted Tucker to buck him up.

The alliance between these two men said everything about the state of Fox News two years into Trump's term. There were a couple of factors at play: Lachlan shared his father's contempt for being bullied by the "liberal media." He didn't want to appear to give in to left-wing ad boycotts. Also, he thought Carlson's overarching message about immigration was worth protecting. He was rather fond of Carlson—both men fancied themselves contrarians and enjoyed philosophical conversations. They were only two years apart in age. They dined together when they happened to be in the same city.

At Lachlan's direction, Fox PR trotted out its usual statement: "We cannot and will not allow voices to be censored by agenda-driven intimidation efforts." Emboldened, Carlson doubled down: He defended his "dirtier" comments by contending that mass immigration has an environmental impact on the desert. He aired images of trash at the border and said that "thanks to illegal immigration, huge swaths of the region are covered with garbage and waste that degrade the soil and kill wildlife." Cherry-picking? This was trash-picking. But it worked for his viewers.

Holding steady was the Fox game plan as more and more offensive things happened on the air. For Lachlan it was about both business and politics. His team called the boycott efforts "economic harassment" designed to put Fox News out of business. "We don't hang talent out to dry," an exec told me, "because once you cave to these lunatics, you won't have any shows left." The rank-and-file Fox staffers who said they loathed Carlson were just "social justice warriors," this person said, using the pejorative term for progressives that was in vogue among conservatives.

This is what people misunderstood about Lachlan: His politics aligned pretty closely with the retrograde programming on his network. Michael Wolff used to write about Rupert's "liberal sons" like they were equally enlightened, but that was just a reflection of what Ailes believed. There were actually huge differences between Lachlan and James's world views.

Lachlan was always more conservative-leaning than James, "in part to ingratiate himself with his dad, in part to separate himself from his brother," a Murdoch confidant said. Lachlan's conservative instincts were buttressed by the people he surrounded himself with—like Hope Hicks, and the Bush White House veteran Viet Dinh, best known for drafting the post-9/11 Patriot Act, who was Fox Corp's powerful head of legal and policy.

When I interviewed Azam about his decision to leave that world, to resign from Murdoch's empire, he was careful to draw a distinction between fact-based conservative media and ferocious fact-free attacks.

Stories and columns from a conservative perspective were needed, he said, but smears were not. He saw "dehumanization" taking place on some of Fox's opinion shows and an absolute lack of decency. The resistance types who remained at the company agreed with him in spirit, but most didn't have the courage or the financial independence to say it or act on it. So they leaked instead.

A Fox News executive, who had defended the brand fiercely for a decade, looked at the prime time lineup and said, "I don't recognize the place at all anymore."

"Right-leaning is fine," a news anchor remarked to me. "But we're not leaning, we've fallen over."

"Without Roger here, this place is losing its compass," another anchor said.

The Ailes compass was crooked, but at least it existed. Ailes had had such a vise grip on the pre-Trump Fox that "what would

Roger do?" was still a subject of debate two years after his death. Some thought Ailes would have maintained some distance from Trump; others thought he would have bent to Trump's will for the sake of business. The ghost of Ailes still hovered over the channel's content—it was gut-level politics, black and white, good and evil. The channel was more "anti-Democrat" than "pro-Trump," which was convenient whenever Trump hit a rough patch.

"When you're with Tucker and Sean and Laura one-on-one, they won't defend Trump, they'll tell you how bad Democrats are," a former commentator said, which mirrored my own experiences with Fox talent. On Fox, "evil" Democrats were the default justification for any awfulness on the GOP side. "If," the former commentator postulated, "the liberals are evil and they're ruining America and they're turning your children gay and they're persecuting Christians, then aren't you justified in the way you're behaving?" It was an endless game of trumped-up whataboutism—a technique some scholars attribute to Soviet-era propagandists—that exhausted everyone except the players. The Russian political activist and Putin foe Garry Kasparov once described it this way: "If you're a thief, accuse your enemies of thievery. If corrupt, accuse your rivals of corruption. If a coward, accuse others of cowardice. Evidence is irrelevant; the goal is to dilute the truth and the case against you with 'everyone does it.' "

Propaganda, in other words.

By 2019, Fox News was many things—a vitriolic virtual community, a beleaguered news operation, a thriving right-wing website—but more than anything else it was a propaganda machine the likes of which the United States had never seen before. The pollution from this machine showed up in poll after poll. When NBC and Murdoch's *Wall Street Journal* asked if the president had been "honest and truthful" about the Russia probe, only 1 percent of regular CNN viewers said yes. Among regular Fox viewers, 84 percent said yes, he'd been truthful. His lies were so voluminous and so well documented that only one thing could explain this gap: The omnipresence of TV hosts like Hannity.

The propaganda worked.

THE CONTROL FREAK

"Hate-for-profit racket"

"Thank you, Queens," a Fox producer texted me in January 2019. "Thank you for AOC!"

When the Democrats took control of the House after the 2018 midterm elections, it was a win for Fox too, because the network was always most comfortable as the opposition. Fox's shows obsessed over the emergence of AOC, aka Alexandria Ocasio-Cortez, who represented parts of both Queens and the Bronx. The head-turning twenty-nine-year-old congresswoman and her promotion of a "Green New Deal" were like gifts from the right-wing news gods. In the first few weeks of the new term, Fox helped make her into a hate object and sowed fear of the climate change legislation. Research in March showed that most Republicans had heard a lot about the "Green New Deal," and those who had heard, hated it. Most Democrats had only heard a little about it, but wanted to know more. This was the Fox effect in action. Another name for it is "asymmetrical intensity"—when there's much more intense passion on one side than the other. I asked AOC how she was handling all of the, umm, passion on the right. Was she debating whether to appear on Fox and take her attackers head-on? She said she was. So were other Democrats. The network was actively courting them for a very specific reason: to impress the advertisers who abhorred the bad press that came from the white identity politics of prime time.

That's why Jane Mayer's timing was so damaging to Fox. On March 4 Mayer dropped a bomb in *The New Yorker* magazine. Her unflinching look at Fox and the Murdochs—on the eve of the Disney deal getting done—gave prominent Democrats a fresh reason to demand that Fox be excluded from the primary debate process.

Frankly, it surprised me that Fox was ever in contention at all. The network hadn't held an actual Democratic primary debate since 2004, and the channel had moved far to the right since then. Still, Jay Wallace was serious about securing a debate in the 2020 campaign season. Bret Baier and Martha MacCallum, who tag-teamed election coverage, pressured him to make it happen.

Wallace still insisted there were clear divisions between the two sides at Fox, even though most observers could see that those divisions were melting away due to ratings pressures and the audience's demands. Take the 5 a.m. hour of *Fox & Friends First*. It looked like a newscast sponsored by the Trump reelection campaign and Froot Loops—it was a brightly colored, artificially flavored sugar rush anchored by Jillian Mele and Rob Schmitt. Mele kept her politics to herself, but Schmitt was clear about where he stood. Anyone who wanted lessons for fitting in at Fox could just scroll through Schmitt's Instagram page. There he was hitting a hole-in-one at Trump Golf Links at Ferry Point. Then a picture of him grinning with Rudy Giuliani. Then a joke about "Russian collusion" in a caption and a vacation snapshot praising Japan for having "very strict immigration" and "almost no litter." Trumpism permeated everything. Anchors who were at Fox during the Bush years said it was never this pervasive back then.

Anchors who resisted the pressures said they could see the rightward bent at almost every hour. Bill Hemmer and Sandra Smith gave the late morning hours of *America's Newsroom* more of a conservative edge than it had had before. Harris Faulkner treated Trump with kid gloves on *Outnumbered* at noon. Baier's 6 p.m. *Special Report* panel became two on one, with two right-wing guests and a lone dissenter who was often a straitlaced news reporter. (He defended this by saying he wanted "left, right, and Trump" every night, noting that "right" wasn't always the same as Trump anymore.) At 7 p.m., MacCallum made her program *The Story* Trumpier through topic and guest selection. Clinton loyalist Philippe Reines, an occasional guest on Fox, observed that guests "do much of the dirty work in peddling misinformation even during news hours." And that's exactly right: The bookings kept the programming on Trump's side.

Staffers referred to shows like MacCallum's as "hybrids" or "borderline shows" because Fox counted them as news, but the product looked and sounded like opinion. Viewers by and large didn't care about these nuances as long as they heard what they wanted to hear about their president. But it mattered internally and externally because Fox wanted to be seen as a powerful media brand, not a propaganda arm. Mayer's article undermined all of that.

DNC chair Tom Perez succumbed to pressure from the left and publicly banned Fox from the debate process, citing "recent reporting in *The New Yorker* on the inappropriate relationship between President Trump, his administration and Fox News." Mayer simply pointed out what Fox's viewers already knew and liked about the network, but the article propelled Democrats to re-ask: Is Fox a legitimate news operation or strictly a political opponent?

Some Democratic candidates swore off appearances on the channel. Elizabeth Warren called it a "hate-for-profit racket." But other Democrats argued that if you're not on Fox, you don't even have a chance of persuading Fox's America. Former DNC spokesman Mo Elleithee believed this so strongly that he signed a contract with Fox back in 2016. It was a flip-flop of sorts, because when he was running comms at the party, he believed Democrats should shun the network. "I never went on Fox and I never put a surrogate on Fox," he recalled. When he left the committee in 2015, he began to see things differently. "I realized it had been a mistake to neglect the network," he said, citing math: "We're leaving a lot of people on the table."

By appearing on Fox, "I feel like I'm showing those viewers that Democrats are not the caricature Hannity makes them out to be," Elleithee told me. "That's why I keep pushing Democrats to go on: I say, 'You can define the Democrats or you can let Tucker or Hannity define the Democrats.' "

Elleithee liked to tell a story about the day a burly biker dude made a beeline for him. It was a holiday weekend in 2018 at the Dutch Wonderland amusement park in central Pennsylvania. The man stopped Elleithee's family as they were walking in between rides. "Aren't you that Democratic dude on Fox?" Elleithee's wife put her arm around their two kids and took a step back, fearing the worst. Then the viewer said, "You are wrong most of the time, but I appreciate what you have to say." The lesson, to hear Elleithee tell it, was that Democrats "need to do a better job of listening and talking. And Fox is one way to do that."

Still, he harbored reservations. Like countless other Democrats, he detested Lou Dobbs's xenophobic segments and Carlson's white nationalist dog-whistling. When Carlson claimed white supremacy was "actually not a real problem in America"—after a radicalized loner slaughtered Hispanics at a Walmart in El Paso—Elleithee tweeted, "You know who else believes white supremacy is not a real problem? White supremacists."

"Iceberg problem"

The lights burned out for Bill "No Shine" on Friday, March 8, when Shine resigned from his post. There was all the usual hand-wringing about the significance of the communications director leaving, but it didn't really mean anything.

"The *Titanic* did not have a communications problem, it had an iceberg problem," Democratic strategist Paul Begala said on CNN. "The Trump presidency has an iceberg problem. He can run through six more communications directors" if he wants, and it won't matter. "He has to do a better job as president and he'll get better press then."

Shine wasn't really missed at the White House. Without a daily briefing to study for, Sarah Huckabee Sanders had time to handle the tasks that fell to Shine. Later in the year Sanders left the White House and landed a higher-paying gig with Fox. Her successor, Stephanie Grisham, never held a briefing and almost exclusively gave TV interviews to Fox and other right-wing outlets like Sinclair. She pointedly went to the Fox bureau across town for most of her hits instead of standing at Fox's live shot location on the North Lawn like Kellyanne Conway did. White House beat reporters concluded that Grisham was going out of her way to avoid being questioned by them after her Fox appearances. "I've covered Obama and Trump and it's insane to me that we only see the press secretary when she's on Fox News," a veteran on the beat said. It gave Fox yet another advantage.

Sanders and Grisham admitted that they would resume briefings if Trump said so. He called all of these shots and the comms staff just had to keep up. Dysfunction was the result. Fox's Steve Hilton found out his long-standing request to interview POTUS was being granted with just one day's advance notice. He flew from L.A. to

DC on the next available flight. Hilton was a Rupert pal and a former adviser to British prime minister David Cameron who hosted Fox's Sunday night show *The Next Revolution*, promoting what he called "positive populism," and became more bullish about Trump as the years went on. He was one of those *he should stop tweeting* conservatives who thought Trump's words were wrong but his actions were right. The more Hilton praised those actions on the air, the more Trump watched on Sunday nights, and that's what led to this seemingly sudden interview.

The White House press shop told Hilton that he would get fifteen minutes with the president. But Trump was in a talkative mood and went on for forty-five minutes. "I think your people are actually going to kill me if I don't stop now," Hilton said as aides tried to wrap him.

"Don't worry about that, that won't happen," Trump said.

These interviews were almost like an extension of "Executive Time." According to data collected by presidential historian Martha Kumar, the Hilton sit-down was Trump's sixty-fifth interview with Fox. He averaged one chat on Fox every two weeks. Other national TV interviews were few and far between. Trump wasn't trying to appeal to CNN or ABC viewers—he just wanted to keep Fox viewers satiated. But as Shine's underwhelming performance at the White House showed, the Fox obsession kept backfiring on Trump. He was so fond of Heather Nauert, for example, and so desperately in need of a replacement for Nikki Haley, that he wanted to tap Nauert for U.S. ambassador to the UN. She "looks the part," he told associates, referencing her made-for-TV good looks. Nauert turned Trump down at first, but relented when he pushed her to accept. For all his faults, he had a good way with people he wanted on his team—he went out of his way to ask about Nauert's kids, who were still back in New York.

On the night Trump announced her nomination, Nauert fumed as she watched me (and many others) on CNN describing her as unqualified. She told friends that she thought the coverage was sexist, but I believe that any man with the same TV-centric résumé would have been labeled as equally unqualified for a UN ambassadorship. Nauert's nomination was never officially sent to the Senate because Republican senators signaled that she didn't stand a chance of being confirmed. So after two awkward months, she dropped out. There was no going back to Fox. But Trump found a plum job for her on the Fulbright board—another soft landing for one of his "Friends."

The revolving door continued to turn as Morgan Ortagus, a Fox News contributor, was named as Nauert's replacement as spokesperson at the State Department. On the day of the announcement, Ortagus was annoyed with the headlines that focused on her Fox role. She was a U.S. Naval Reserve officer. She brought experience as an intel analyst for the Treasury Department and a public affairs officer for USAID. But the headlines were about Fox because that's how she landed the State Department job. Trump looked at his TV screen and told Shine he wanted her on staff. Shine recruited her and floated multiple jobs, even White House press secretary. Ortagus was flattered but knew she fit better at State. Shine set up a meeting for her with Pompeo. "Fox News was her interview process," a source said. By the time she started work, Shine was gone.

"They'll fire me"

On the afternoon of Sunday, March 10, Suzanne Scott had an Islamophobia-induced headache.

Jeanine Pirro, triggered by one of AOC's colleagues in the freshman progressive lawmaker "Squad," Ilhan Omar, wrote an anti-Muslim rant and read it on the air on Saturday night. Pirro questioned Omar's patriotism and asked whether the Somali-American congresswoman's "Islamic religious beliefs stand in opposition to the US Constitution." She pressed down hard on one of Fox's favorite fear buttons: Sharia law. And she demonized and other-ized Omar even more than her weekday colleagues had.

Trump thought it was a fair question to ask.

Scott thought Pirro was out of line.

Shep Smith, overseas on vacation, read about the "Judge Jeanine" segment and said he didn't want to work in the same building as a woman like that. Hufsa Kamal, a young Pakistani-American producer on Baier's staff, tweeted straight at Pirro, "Can you stop spreading this false narrative that somehow Muslims hate America or women who wear a hijab aren't American enough? You have Muslims working at the same network you do, including myself."

Kamal was a relative nobody—a desk assistant turned producer with two hundred followers on Twitter. Still, her tweet went viral. Her message spoke for so many invisible journalists at Fox who were sick of the hatred spewed by Pirro and others. Refreshingly, Kamal received support from higher-ups. "Good for you," Fox's DC bureau chief told her. Correspondents came up to her and thanked her. Colleagues worried that Kamal would get in trouble, but no one ever sanctioned her for the tweet. Baier supported her and emailed Scott: *There's an issue here.*

Scott agreed. She needed Pirro to issue an apology, but Pirro refused to budge—reminiscent of Trump's incapability of apologizing for anything. "The viewers have my back," she said.

Furious, Scott decided that Fox would issue a statement instead. "We strongly condemn Jeanine Pirro's comments about Rep. Ilhan Omar," Fox rightfully said Sunday night, though it took more than twenty-four hours to say.

Scott suspended Pirro, not for her offensive comments ("No one at Fox ever gets in trouble for what they say," a news anchor ruefully told me) but for insubordination. Scott hoped that benching Pirro would take the heat off the show at a critical time. The network was about to hold its annual schmoozefest for advertisers—and it was taking place at Fox News HQ for the first time ever. Manhattan was covered in billboards that proclaimed "America is Watching." The message was that corporate America couldn't afford to ignore Fox's big audience, even if young leftie ad buyers had to hold their noses while buying airtime. The Fox News head of ad sales, Marianne Gambelli, was holding her own nose—other execs claimed that she detested the prime time shows she was in charge of selling. Soon she would take a bigger role running all of Fox Corp ad sales, so the ad boycotts would be someone else's day-to-day problem. But on March 13, she was on a mission to shift attention to Fox's plain vanilla newscasts and "borderline" shows like *The Story*. That's why anchors like Baier, Faulkner, and Cavuto were featured at the event. The only problem? Their shows were much lower-rated than the prime time propagandists, and thus a lot less valuable to advertisers.

As the ad execs arrived at the corner of 48th Street and Avenue of the Americas, there were dozens of protesters outside holding signs with messages like "FOX NEWS IS TOXIC." Media Matters and other left-wing groups set this up to remind the advertisers what they were subsidizing.

In the days leading up to the ad event, Media Matters released old audio clips of Carlson calling in to the "Bubba the Love Sponge" radio show and making misogynistic, racist, and homophobic comments. In one clip, Carlson joked about wanting to invade Canada, while Iraq, on the other hand, "is a crappy place filled with a bunch of, you know, semiliterate primitive monkeys—that's why it wasn't worth invading." In another clip, he said he loved Bubba "in a completely faggot way." (He also joked about Rupert Murdoch in one of the clips, saying "I'm 100 percent his bitch. Whatever Mr. Murdoch says, I do.") This is "faux outrage," a Fox exec said at the time, claiming it was all stirred up to "harass our advertisers." The ad buyers entered through a different entrance, so the effect was muted. "The voices of a few shouldn't stop you from marketing to consumers who will buy your brand," Gambelli told them. Her appeal to capitalism worked.

I covered the newest Carlson controversy on CNN's air, which caused Tucker to retaliate. While I reported his past statements, he called me names, including "eunuch." (Google it.) His fans picked up the insult and ran with it. A year later, I still received tweets every day that called me a "eunuch." (Mission accomplished, Tucker.) He also sent someone over to CNN's New York office with a Dunkin' Donuts delivery for me. I threw out the dozen jelly donuts and decided to ignore the fat-shaming attempt, but Tucker made sure everyone knew by tipping off the right-wing website he founded, *The Daily Caller.* By the end of the week Page Six had called me for comment. I said I would accept the donuts if Tucker accepted my interview requests.

Why did any of this matter? Because this shit was what appealed to Carlson's audience. Millions of people loved to watch his high jinks every night. As the Bubba controversy swirled, Fox senior statesman Brit Hume defended Carlson by pointing out that he was in first place in the ratings, even ahead of Hannity on some nights. "Doing well is the best revenge," Hume said. Clinton-era White House press secretary Joe Lockhart, a CNN analyst, responded to Hume by expressing regret that "bigotry and misogyny sells so well."

"It's a stain on our country," Lockhart wrote. "Ratings don't trump values, and I know you know that."

I hoped Hume did, but I wasn't so sure. This is what Fox always did: The network wielded The Scoreboard like a sword and shield, like an excuse for even the very worst types of behavior. But the advertiser exodus was a severe problem for Carlson's show, costing the network tens of millions in potential revenue.

While Pirro served her two-week sentence, she called Trump. She wanted him to know why she was missing from Saturday night's schedule. Trump responded exactly as she had hoped. "Bring back @JudgeJeanine," he tweeted on Sunday morning, shortly before I broke the news that she was actually in trouble at Fox.

Scott was straddling a line by punishing Pirro privately but not confirming the suspension publicly, so I had to rely on anonymous sources for my story. Pirro herself copped to it later, telling former Fox News contributor Sebastian Gorka in a hot mic moment, "I'm worried that that suspension was the basis to tee up" further action. "Anything I do wrong," she said, "they'll fire me."

Trump related to the victimhood script that Pirro and Carlson followed. Hell, he practically wrote the script. "They have all out campaigns against @FoxNews hosts who are doing too well," the president tweeted, sounding like ever the concerned fan. "Fox must stay strong and fight back with vigor," he wrote. "Stop working soooo hard on being politically correct, which will only bring you down, and continue to fight for our Country." He almost sounded like a motivational speaker: "Your competitors are jealous—they all want what you've got—NUMBER ONE," Trump wrote. "Don't hand it to them on a silver platter. They can't beat you, you can only beat yourselves!"

This was a return to the days of the 2016 campaign when Trump employed Twitter to punish Megyn Kelly, keep the network in line, and tell his fans what to watch. He needed cheerleaders like Pirro and trolls like Tucker on the air, and he needed the network's remaining journalists to be sidelined, suffocated, squeezed out. He was doing some of the squeezing himself: On a Sunday afternoon, St. Patrick's Day, while Fox was covering the possibly imminent release of Mueller's report and North Korea's threat to exit nuclear talks and restart missile testing, Trump insulted Shep for the first time in four years and said he should be working at CNN, not Fox. Trump called Shep "their lowest rated anchor," which was technically true, judging by the weekday ratings—but tongues immediately wagged about who'd reminded Trump of the ratings race. Who pointed him to The Scoreboard this time? Was it Pirro? Hannity? Hegseth?

Along with Shep, Trump also attacked Fox weekend anchors Arthel Neville and Leland Vittert. Later in the afternoon, he retweeted a fan who'd told him that "when those three" news anchors "show up, I turn @FoxNews OFF!" The result was a wave of hate and vitriol at all three anchors, particularly at Neville, one of the few black women on Fox's airwaves. Threats and racist screeds filled up her inbox and her Twitter mentions—from her own viewers. That was the remarkable, crazy thing about Trump's power. As a CNN anchor I wasn't surprised to get hate emails from Fox viewers. But it's another thing to get hate mail from your *own* viewers. That's what happened when Trump told people to attack journalists like Neville. Fox execs checked in with the anchors and made sure they were not too rattled by the attacks. They were fine—"just doing my job," Neville said—but the venom still stung.

"The times ahead will test all of us"

Amid all the craziness, Shep was the journalistic backbone of Fox. On the same day of the advertiser shindig, the same day that protesters lined up outside Fox News HQ, Shep was in DC accepting a First Amendment Award along with CNN boss Jeff Zucker and ABC News boss James Goldston. Shep's speech was one massive subtweet of the prime time lineup. "Being accurate and honest and thorough and fair is our primary mission," Shep said. "It's our professional calling. And everyone on my team takes it extremely seriously." His emphasis on "my team" struck me as an obvious jab at guys like Hannity, who was on the air at the very same time, running defense for the president.

Smith invoked advice from one of his Ole Miss journalism professors about telling the truth, no matter what. "I personally believe this is the duty not only of journalists but of every person who has the honor of a platform of influence," he said—again aiming straight at the prime time players with their huge platforms. "We must never manipulate or invent," he said. "We must never knowingly deceive. Because to do so is a disservice to our audience and potentially injurious to our society." He said he was convinced that "history will poorly reflect" upon those who intentionally misinform. "The times ahead will test all of us as finders and disseminators of accurate information," he warned. "My team and I, like you and yours, will strive to remain on task, trying our very best to ignore the Twitter trolls and others who relentlessly pursue us, daily, and to get the facts to the people. *All* of the people. In every place, in every corner where information is taken in."

Audience members whispered to each other about Shep's clear

disdain for his colleagues. "Good night," Shep concluded, "and get it right."

At white-tablecloth settings, Shep won applause and attention, but inside Fox, his admonitions were met by sneers and eye-rolls. Carlson, Hannity, and Ingraham thought he was pompous and condescending, and so did a surprising number of the network's news anchors, maybe because he was making them look weak by comparison. Shep was calling for an accountability and fact-checking form of journalism when it was needed most, at the place least empowered to do it.

Shep's internal critics said he was letting his biased left-wing stripes show. Executives said to each other that this situation—Shep versus the rest of Fox—was unsustainable. Someone was going to snap. "He's tired of the viewers, he's tired of the harassment," one veteran staffer said. He's acting like a left-wing pundit, "trying to balance out the entire prime time lineup," another vet said, amused by the attempt. The description conjured up an image of one puny kid on the playground trying to climb on a seesaw while the three biggest bullies in school confidently sat on the other side. Shep didn't stand a chance.

On March 18 Fox hired an actual left-wing commentator, former DNC interim chair Donna Brazile, sticking it to the Dems who wanted Fox to be blacklisted. She said there was "an audience on Fox News that doesn't hear enough from Democrats." Her arrival unsettled Juan Williams, the lonely liberal voice on *The Five*, and one of the only other African American commentators at the network. "Juan is freaking out about her being there," one of his confidants told me.

There were no signs that Scott actually considered replacing Williams with Brazile, but the whole point of a show like

The Five was that everyone was replaceable. Trump critics were among the most vulnerable, because the audience jeered them on a minute-by-minute basis. "Everyone else has fallen in line and is coming up with the most outrageous excuses for the president's unhinged behavior," the friend said. For the few holdouts, like Williams, it feels as if "you have fallen through the looking glass, where reality is entirely distorted. It's mentally exhausting having to prove over and over again that the earth is round, provide satellite imagery from NASA to back up your contention that the earth is round, and still have to deal with colleagues who insist, despite all evidence, that the earth is flat."

Williams told friends that he felt he had the "Fox taint" on him, making him all but unhirable elsewhere. "He understands that this is his last big payday," the source said.

The word "taint" came up uncomfortably often in on-background conversations. Officials at NBC and other networks received lots of résumés from Fox staffers who wanted out—but "they're tainted, no one wants to hire them," in the words of an NBC exec. There were a few talent-based exceptions, but in general, Fox is "in a different line of work," the NBC insider said. "They're a lifestyle brand." Ironically, that's not so different from Disney, the mighty empire that was swallowing up the Fox assets.

On March 19, the Disney deal began to take effect. The Murdochs spun off their new, slimmed down Fox Corp, and former Speaker of the House Paul Ryan, a longtime pal of Rupert and Lachlan's, joined the Fox board of directors. He received $330,000 a year for the gig and chaired the company's nominating and corporate governance committee.

On March 20, with most of the family's prized possessions now in Mickey Mouse's hands, all six of Rupert's children—Lachlan and James plus Prudence, Elisabeth, and teenagers Grace Helen and

Chloe—were officially billionaires. About $12 billion in proceeds from the sale were divided equally among the six. Lachlan was in charge of keeping Fox humming along. James was happy to be out. Elisabeth was busy with her own media ventures. Prudence wanted nothing to do with Fox. But they all remained in the fold because all four adult children held shares in both Fox and News Corporation through the Murdoch Family Trust. They were bound together by the trust for as long as Rupert lived.

With Fox Corp spun off on its own, relying on Fox News for most of its quarterly profits, the "lifestyle brand" would now subsidize the Murdochs' lavish lifestyles even more directly.

The day of the deal's completion was, coincidentally, also the day that Fox mainstreamed the Ukraine conspiracy theory that got Trump impeached.

"Breaking tonight," Hannity declared, "according to *The Hill*'s John Solomon, we now have major evidence of election collusion in 2016, real evidence to back it up." Whoa. Hannity continued: "This collusion surrounds Hillary Clinton and a top Ukrainian government official that wanted her elected."

Hannity had dropped these Ukrainian bread crumbs back in 2017 to distract from Trump's firing of Comey. Now he was coming back around. This was where impeachment started.

Hannity was in league with his longtime buddy Rudy Giuliani, who was laundering this Ukraine bullshit through Solomon's workplace, *The Hill*, an allegedly nonpartisan news source. Giuliani's fixer Lev Parnas, who would later be arrested by the feds, set Solomon up to interview Ukraine's deeply corrupt prosecutor general Yuri Lutsenko. In the interview, Lutsenko made all sorts of sordid allegations. He said, for example, that U.S. ambassador to Ukraine

Marie Yovanovitch gave him "a list of people whom we should not prosecute." That was a lie, but it got Hannity and Trump's attention. So did the claims that the Ukrainians were the real meddlers—and they had tried to help Clinton win. Trump had heard this nonsense before, on Hannity's show, back in 2017. Now it was back, with Ukraine's version of the attorney general claiming it warranted a criminal investigation.

Yovanovitch later speculated that the corrupt prosecutor was trying to help his boss, Ukrainian President Petro Poroshenko, win reelection. It was already looking like Volodymyr Zelensky was going to defeat Poroshenko, which meant Lutsenko would be out of a job. Sure enough, after the April elections, he was. But none of this was explained when Solomon went on Hannity's show and shared Lutsenko's ludicrous claims. Trump was so happy, he tweeted out what one of the on-screen banners said: "John Solomon: As Russia Collusion fades, Ukrainian plot to help Clinton emerges."

Like O.J. pledging to track down the real killer, this was a chance to portray Ukraine—not Russia—as the real attackers, and a chance to demean the "deep state" to boot. One of Hannity's other banners bleeted: "COLLUSION NARRATIVE CRUMBLES, AS MEDIA IGNORES THE REAL DEEP STATE SCANDAL." Solomon was joined by Joe diGenova and Victoria Toensing, a husband and wife pair of lawyers Trump had previously tried to hire. They now defended Trump for free on TV. DiGenova brought up Yovanovitch twice and claimed she had "bad-mouthed the president of the United States to Ukrainian officials and has told them not to listen or worry about Trump policy because he's going to be impeached."

DiGenova: This woman needs to be called home to the United States.
Hannity: Oh, immediately.

DiGenova: For consultation.
Hannity: Immediately.

Ingraham joined the chorus and attacked Yovanovitch two days later. By the end of the week Donald Trump Jr. was referring to the ambassador as a "joker." A month later, she was told to "come home on the next plane." Only later was it revealed that Secretary of State Mike Pompeo called Hannity and asked him to back off the ambassador.

Joe Biden's name didn't come up during the introductory segment on March 20, but Fox's Chris Wallace later reported that diGenova and Toensing were "working off the books" to help Giuliani dig up dirt that would hurt the former vice president and political rival to Trump. "Only the president knows the details of their work," Wallace said. And it would stay that way. But the seeds of the Ukraine scandal were planted in public view at 9 p.m. on Fox News.

The month of March 2019 concluded with the release of William Barr's letter summarizing the Mueller report and falsely exonerating Trump. The right treated it like a sequel to election night—with ratings to match. Trump called in to Hannity's show for a victory lap, and said he noticed that Hannity's ratings were way up while his rivals' had "dropped." And, he added pointedly, he hoped Pirro would be back soon. Sure enough, she returned on March 30, bitter as ever, and she used her monologue to allege an attempted "coup." The plotters, she warned, will try again "unless we stop them." She called for "behind-the-bars justice"—meaning, "lock them up." This sort of authoritarian rhetoric was now a mainstream Republican talking point. Fox's newest board member, Paul Ryan, claimed to be uncomfortable with the Pirro wing of Fox News, but he told friends there was nothing he could do about it . . . because this was what Fox's audience wanted. Max Taves, a media adviser and blogger, put it this way: The media business is about *commercial* correctness, not political correctness. Critiquing Trump "risks alienating their core consumers/viewers. In many ways, Fox News is hostage to its base consumers."

"They owe *you* an apology"

On April 18, 2019, three long weeks after the misleading Barr letter, the text of the Mueller report was released.

"A really great day for America!" Trump tweeted.

He may not have wanted Americans to read all 448 pages, but he did want them to watch his friends' coverage. Sounding more like a deep-voiced TV announcer than a president, he promised "a special evening tonight on @TuckerCarlson, @SeanHannity & @IngrahamAngle."

Some guests earlier in the day on Fox told the truth about what Mueller had found—widespread Russian interference, troubling but not illegal contacts between Russians and Trump aides, and Trump's repeated attempts to curtail Mueller's investigation into all of it. Mueller found ample evidence of obstruction but declined to say whether it legally amounted to obstruction of justice, in effect punting the issue to the DOJ and Congress. "He's out of legal jeopardy, but he's certainly not out of political jeopardy," Judge Andrew Napolitano surmised. Chris Wallace called out Barr's role, saying "the attorney general seemed almost to be acting as the counselor for the defense, or the counselor for the president, rather than the attorney general."

But these reality checks were drowned out by the right-wing media's "exonerated" blitzkrieg. "Victorious, exonerated, vindicated," Lou Dobbs said, shouting down the special counsel's explicit statement to the contrary. On the subject of obstruction, Mueller wrote, "While this report does not conclude that the President committed a crime, it also does not exonerate him." Trump declared "total exoneration" anyway, and with the help of the wingmen, the lie worked. In a Washington Post/ABC News poll, 61 percent of Republicans said Mueller had cleared Trump of all wrongdoing. Eighty-seven percent of Democrats said Mueller had not. NBC interviewed a GOP voter in Michigan who said she was "surprised to hear there was anything negative in the Mueller report at all about President Trump." She watched Fox most of the time, and she said, "I hadn't heard that before." The quote whipped around the interwebs as alarming evidence of America's alternative universes.

In prime time, much of Fox's coverage was about the media "melting down" because there was "no collusion." One of the chyrons on Laura Ingraham's show blared, "MUELLER REPORT EXPOSES LIBERAL MEDIA ALLIES." Another asked, "WHERE IS THE LEFT'S APOLOGY TO FOX NEWS?" Every day, in every way, the producers and hosts told viewers not to trust anyone else.

Trump tweeted out video clip after clip after clip of support in his hermetically sealed Twitter chamber. And at the end of the week he got back on the phone with Hannity to celebrate some more. They chatted for forty-five minutes, with Trump repeating Hannity's talking points back to him. "This was a coup," Trump lied. "This was an attempted overthrow of the United States government."

Fox was the gas station where Trump stopped to fill up his tank of resentment. At one point, Sean asked Trump, "Do you think the news media in this country and their coverage on this, owes you an apology?"

Trump: "Well, they do owe me an apology. A big one. They owe *you* an apology."

Everyone could see why this relationship was of immeasurable value to Trump. Obsequious didn't even begin to describe it. Hannity routinely put up a scrolling graphic of the president's self-proclaimed accomplishments. It was better than any ad Trump 2020 could produce because it was packaged like "news."

Hannity's "Dear Leader" performances made him a punchline outside the Fox universe. When I brought this up with Hannity's allies at Fox, they said I should have some sympathy for the guy. They admired his discipline and his decades of broadcasting strength. "Sean's a workhorse," one of his loyalists said. "He works his ass off."

But to what end besides ratings?

To deal with the "shadow" chief of staff stress, Hannity doubled down on his martial arts workout regimen and lost weight. He also straightened out his personal life. His separation with Jill was amicable—she threw him a birthday party at the end of December 2018 at the Naples penthouse they shared—but it was past time to file the papers and make the divorce official. Sources told the tabloids that Hannity's "workaholic" streak "broke his marriage."

I sensed that Hannity put on some of Trump's paranoia as time went on. Keeping his divorce filing a secret was just one of many examples. He saw threats in every direction—including inside Fox—and railed against "snakes" and "pretenders" who opposed the president. Hannity wasn't totally off-base about that: There *were* some key managers and anchors who despised Trump. "The president is a complete maniac," one exec remarked to me. But the internal Trump opponents didn't have a tenth of the power Hannity had. Trump wanted the dissent shut down anyway, and target No. 1 was the judge.

Napolitano tried in vain, all week long, to point out that the facts in Mueller's report contained evidence of obstruction and campaign finance law violations and other outrages. In an op-ed for Fox's website, Napolitano wrote that "Mueller laid out at least a half-dozen crimes of obstruction committed by Trump—from asking former deputy national security advisor K. T. McFarland to write an untruthful letter about the reason for Flynn's chat with Kislyak, to asking Corey Lewandowski and then-former White House counsel Don McGahn to fire Mueller and McGahn to lie about it, to firing Comey to impede the FBI's investigations, to dangling a pardon in front of Michael Cohen to stay silent, to ordering his aides to hide and delete records.

"Depending upon how you look at them," he added, "it might be enough to prosecute."

Napolitano made the same points in a video for his Fox web show, and it went viral on social media. Liberals were thrilled—here was the senior judicial analyst for Fox News telling the truth about Trump's crimes! Napolitano said Trump's acts were "immoral, criminal, defenseless, and condemnable." But he was on the outside—literally—as his video was recorded outside Fox News HQ, in a handheld, shaky-cam style the judge liked, making him look like a renegade. The video garnered so much attention that *The Ingraham Angle* sought to rebut it—not by booking Napolitano and challenging him, as a normal network would do, but by playing a clip, and then giving Alan Dershowitz plenty of time to reassure everyone that the president was innocent. Trump noticed. "Thank you to brilliant and highly respected attorney Alan Dershowitz for

destroying the very dumb legal argument of 'Judge' Andrew Napolitano," Trump tweeted the next day. "Ever since Andrew came
to my office to ask that I appoint him to the U.S. Supreme Court,
and I said NO, he has been very hostile! Also asked for pardon for
his friend."

The judge denied asking for a SCOTUS appointment, and no
reasonable person believed that he actually did. Napolitano recognized what most other Fox figures refused to admit: that Trump
lied through his Twitter teeth each and every day. Trump had just
hit the 10,000 mark in *The Washington Post*'s count of false and
misleading statements, including 45 falsehoods in his most recent
45-minute chat with Hannity. That's a piece of misinformation
every single minute. But his professional excusers on television said
he simply had a unique style of communicating.

The craziest thing of all was that Fox didn't issue statements of
support for its talent when Trump attacked them. The executives
didn't want to dare risk the president's wrath. Shep was incensed by
this show of weakness. On more than one occasion, sources said,
he pressured Scott to put out a statement rebuking Trump's attacks.
But she didn't.

It had a bad effect on morale among the people Trump targeted—
and it emboldened him to keep taking shots. "Like any bully, Trump
knows they're not going to fight back, so like any bully, he piles
on," a longtime exec said.

Were the Murdochs caught between a rock and a hard place?
No, they weren't caught, because they chose this spot. Most Fox
shows continued to avoid Trump's immature, erratic, and immoral
behavior. They played dumb . . . which also emboldened him to
keep doing what he was doing. He grew more and more intolerant
of any accurate reporting on Fox and raged against the reporters.
Sometimes, as he fast-forwarded through shows on his Genie DVR,

he griped about details as specific as the graphics at the bottom of the screen. On one occasion he even called Scott and denounced the network's coverage. He wanted control. Scott's response: Sit down for an interview with Baier.

An interview with Baier would have been a show of strength. Scrutiny makes people stronger. Sycophancy makes them weaker. But Team Trump thought it was the other way around. Trump stuck close with Hannity and *Fox & Friends* instead. The length of Trump's phoners became something of a punchline among rank-and-file staffers. "When Trump was booked for 8:10, and we had an assignment for 8:40, we didn't bother writing it, because we knew he'd talk until the end of the hour," a morning show producer said.

"What do you think?"

Different Fox auxiliaries used their influence in different ways. Laura Ingraham pressured Trump to get the border wall built. Lou Dobbs goaded him to crush China. Mark Levin urged Trump to blow up the Foreign Intelligence Surveillance Court. Pete Hegseth pushed pardons for members of the military accused of war crimes.

Fox & Friends executive producer Gavin Hadden used his show's presidential power as a retention tool. In at least one case, when a staffer made noise about wanting to leave the morning show, they were reminded that the president consistently tweeted their stories, sometimes word for word. "They thought it was a good thing," a producer told me after leaving Fox. "I thought it was unhealthy."

Tucker Carlson used his 8 p.m. perch to push against Trump national security advisor (and Fox veteran) John Bolton and other hawks who wanted aggressive action in Syria and Iran. In June 2019, Carlson and Fox military analyst General Jack Keane were credited with stopping Trump from bombing Iran. (I find it hard to believe that I just wrote those words.)

Trump was, by his own account, "cocked and loaded" to strike Iran in retaliation for the downing of a drone. Warplanes were in the air, but Tucker's publicly aired views weighed on him.

Earlier in the day, Trump had phoned Tucker, wanting a more personal assessment of the situation. "What do you think?" the president said, his voice blasting through the receiver on Tucker's end.

To his credit, Carlson held to what he'd been saying on TV: It would be "crazy" to respond to Iran with force. "That's not why the voters elected you," he said.

Unlike Hannity, Carlson never initiated calls to POTUS, but when the White House switchboard called, he answered. Whether through the calls or his television platform, his isolationist views and contempt for Bolton-style neocons got through to Trump, and he could tell that at least part of Trump agreed with him. "He's conflicted," Tucker told a pal. "All I can do is remind him of what he thinks."

General Keane was also persuasive—whether he intended to be or not. Hours before the planned strike, he appeared on Fox and reminded everyone about the fogginess of war. "Our viewers may have forgotten, but during the tanker war in the late eighties when Reagan did take some action, we actually made a mistake," Keane said. "We had a USS warship shoot down an Iranian airliner in Iranian airspace. Two-hundred ninety people killed. Sixty-six of them were children. And we took that for a Tomahawk F-14. That was clearly a mistake by the ship's crew in doing that. And we acknowledged that we made a horrific mistake." *Politico* reported that Trump was "spooked" when he heard Keane tell that story. Trump brought up Iran Air Flight 655 repeatedly later in the day and eventually called off the strike shortly before 8 p.m.

Carlson was relieved. His reward was an exclusive interview with Trump one week later during the president's trip to Japan for the G20. Carlson traveled along as a "guest member" of the White House staff. Tensions with Iran remained high, and Iranian officials knew how to push Trump's Fox buttons. Not long after Trump and Carlson got back from Japan, on July 3, an adviser to Iranian President Hassan Rouhani tweeted at Trump saying he "can listen to Pompeo and we'll make sure he stays a one-term President" or "he could listen to @TuckerCarlson and we might have a different ball game." What a world. "I feel safer having Tucker in charge of the country than Sean," a Fox commentator joked in a text.

As a weekend TV anchor, I paid especially close attention to the president's Twitter feed on Saturdays and Sundays. I noticed that he tended to lash out at Fox on those two days of the week. He did it again in early July, saying that "watching @FoxNews weekend anchors is worse than watching low ratings Fake News @CNN, or Lyin' Brian Williams." He accused Fox of "loading up with Democrats" and said Fox "is changing fast, but they forgot the people who got them there!" A TV exec emailed me with a theory: "He hates Fox on the weekends because Steve and Brian and Ainsley and Tucker and Sean and Laura aren't there to help him."

Evidently Pete Hegseth and Jesse Watters and Jeanine Pirro weren't enough. But they tried so hard! On July 27, 2019, the Saturday edition of *Fox & Friends* set off a weeklong battle over the city of Baltimore that showed just how baldly and badly it could misinform POTUS.

It all started with the oversight work of Maryland congressman Elijah Cummings, who was examining the Trump administration's treatment of migrants at the border. The administration was trying to block Cummings from obtaining documents and witnesses. So a wannabe conservative commentator swooped in with anti-Cummings talking points and Trump glommed on by posting racist tweets that insulted the congressman's entire district of 700,000+ people. He called the district a disgusting rat-infested mess and said "no human being would want to live there."

The whole thing made me, a Maryland native, want to scream. Trump had no idea what he was talking about. He expressed no sincere interest in the city of Baltimore or its surrounding suburbs. He just wanted to score points against Cummings, and *Fox & Friends* was more than eager to help him, thanks to an occasional guest named Kimberly Klacik. Fox labeled Klacik a "Republican strategist," but I could find no evidence that she had ever worked for a campaign. She was an aspiring broadcast journalist who took a right-wing detour into propaganda and retained a TV booking firm to get her face in front of Fox producers. With Cummings's oversight work in the news, she recorded videos of trashed lots and ruined row houses in impoverished parts of West Baltimore. The message to Cummings: Clean up your own backyard. Klacik provided a ready-made segment to Fox's producers—she supplied videos and photos and a Cummings-is-a-hypocrite frame for the conversation. "There is a crisis at the border, but there's also a crisis in Baltimore," she said. Trump heard her and began a tweetstorm that lasted for days. Klacik was thrilled. "The President saw my work. This just made my day," she tweeted.

The *Fox & Friends* crew was thrilled too. At a post-show meeting on Sunday morning, the producer who had pitched Klacik, Jennifer Merwitz, was given a pat on the back in front of everyone. "Good job," the weekend executive producer said, "the president is tweeting about your story."

A single propaganda segment on *Fox & Friends Weekend* sparked dozens of follow-up segments and debates. Fox called it the "BATTLE OVER BALTIMORE" and talked about the city like it was a foreign country. Instead of sending news crews to interview residents and assigning investigative journalists to examine the city's real crises, talking heads jabbered about the failures of Democrat-led cities. Most mystifying at all, almost none of Fox's coverage acknowledged its own role in lighting the fire. That was by choice, according to sources at the network. "At a certain point, we stopped showing his tweets if he tagged @FoxAndFriends," a producer said. Fox spoon-fed bullshit to Trump but then acted like his tweets came out of nowhere. It was the same approach Trump took to his job: As he infamously said during the pandemic, "I don't take responsibility at all."

Fox hosts bristled when guests dared to bring up the network's responsibility. When former Obama senior adviser David Plouffe appeared on *Fox & Friends* to promote a book, he commented that "Trump's got this network, he's got his unofficial campaign chairman Vladimir Putin, he's got billions of dollars—"

"That is not right," Brian Kilmeade interjected. "He doesn't have the whole network. Every show here is different . . ."

"This is his happy place," Plouffe shot back. "It's like his own political *Westworld* where he can be the man he wants to be, not the man he is."

"He knows it's the number one channel in America," Kilmeade said.

Plouffe shut him down: "This is not a debate. Media outlets should hold the powerful to account—not the account to the powerful."

Kilmeade was frosty to Plouffe after the cameras stopped rolling. Later in the day, Plouffe glanced at his Twitter mentions for amusement, and told me his takeaway was that "the MAGA folks really don't like their alternative reality disturbed."

Why bother finding real stories to cover when you could invent a conflict? It was cheap and easy to do, but it did come with a cost. Episodes like the "BATTLE OVER BALTIMORE" were extraordinarily demoralizing for the Fox staffers who wanted to travel the country and cover actual news. Management left the news division in neutral; the correspondents who remained at Fox rarely produced packages or feature stories. Show producers generally didn't *want* reported packages—they preferred personalities and pundits. "We just sat around and waited for something horrible to happen," said one veteran correspondent who ultimately left because he felt like Trump had suffocated everything the network used to be.

Reporters felt like they had little power. "When I push back on a dumb *Fox & Friends* idea," said another disillusioned correspondent, "they just say, 'We're not going to do this hit,' and they book someone else." In other words, they were motivated to play along, because someone else would just gobble up their airtime otherwise.

Shep Smith had diagnosed the problem in his 2018 interview with *Time* magazine. Fact-based reporting at the network was "available for people who want it," he said, but "I don't know how badly they want it." Fox had trained its viewers to crave the "BATTLE OVER BALTIMORE" instead.

Shep was depleted. Colleagues said he was withdrawing from work. "Instead of giving counsel, and nurturing coworkers, and helping the rest of the network, he just focused on his hour," one of his former friends complained.

This had been true to some degree for years. Correspondents

and anchors elsewhere at Fox were proud to call him a colleague, but said he ran hot and cold. One minute he'd be generous, recommending his therapist to a producer in need; the next minute he'd be vindictive, canceling a planned live shot from a correspondent who was on his shit list. Shep was like a "tyrant," one of the correspondents on his list said. "If he thought you were anywhere close to being conservative, you were blackballed," a second correspondent said. But his allies said he was simply upholding high standards.

Everyone agreed that Ailes had been the Shep whisperer. Ailes knew how to tamp down the newsman's volatility and bring out his talent. With Ailes buried, and with Trump burying any semblance of shared truth, Shep felt "unprotected and vulnerable," according to one insider. "He just got madder and madder and madder. And he aired it on the channel."

Shep had hit a breaking point. Unbeknownst to even his closest friends at Fox, he called his agent Larry Kramer and said he wanted out of his barely one-year-old contract. "There wasn't just one reason, there were a hundred reasons," an insider said. Shep's grievances with the network's programming went back years. He was perturbed by the Trump-Murdoch-Hannity alliance. He was outraged that so many colleagues stayed silent while Trump gaslit the country. He was disgusted that Trump-loving pastor Robert Jeffress, known for his anti-LGBTQ views, was a paid contributor on the network. He was bothered that no one else seemed to be bothered by things like that. He had loved the place and hated seeing it sink into the Trump swamp. "Shep tried to wait out Trump," a producer said, and "eventually he gave up."

"He couldn't work at state-run TV anymore," a close friend said.

Fox was not literally state-run TV, a term that called Soviet Russia to mind, but it was getting alarmingly close. The best term for it was state-supported TV, the likes of which we'd never seen in the United States. Trump and his aides granted the network special access and promotion—and in exchange, Fox was "supporting-the-state TV."

Executives at the network bristled at these descriptions, but Trump let the cat out of the bag more than once. He talked about Fox like it *was* state-run TV that he just wanted run *better*. Fox "is so different than it used to be," Trump sighed. What he hated most was when anchors like Baier gave airtime to his Democratic rivals. After Fox held a highly rated town hall with Bernie Sanders, Trump said something "very strange" was afoot and chastised the network for insufficient loyalty. "So weird to watch Crazy Bernie on @FoxNews," he tweeted. "Not surprisingly, @BretBaier and the 'audience' was so smiley and nice. Very strange, and now we have @DonnaBrazile?"

His use of the word "we" revealed exactly what he thought of Fox.

Just before Labor Day, Trump did it again, contending that Fox "isn't working for us anymore!" For *us*.

This form of Trump whiplash—attacking Fox one minute, seeking its affection the next—was triggered by his impulsiveness and need for attention. He was a control freak. Rupert Murdoch never paid much mind to the attacks, though he did marvel at the incongruity. "He's always unhappy, but I'm always being told I'm kissing his ass," the mogul shrugged to a friend.

"You're going to be called on, Sean"

In September the Ukraine scandal erupted all around Trump. Impeachment went from improbable to inevitable in what seemed like a matter of hours. Mid-eruption, Lachlan Murdoch and his wife, Sarah, flew to DC for a special occasion on Friday, September 20:

Trump's state dinner with Australian prime minister Scott Morrison. Loyalists Maria Bartiromo and Lou Dobbs also joined.

To this point, Lachlan had not yet met the president. He didn't relish U.S. politics the way his father did. He didn't want a personal relationship with the current president or any other. But he didn't mind a White House party invite.

At the party Trump gave the impression that everything was hunky-dory, but evidence of his plot to pressure Ukraine's president into investigating Joe Biden's son had seized the world's attention. Trump insisted that his July 25 call to the Ukrainian president was "perfect," which challenged his TV minions to yet again defend the indefensible. As Geraldo Rivera said to Hannity one night, "You are going to be called on, Sean, in ways you have not been tested yet. You'll stand up, you'll be strong, you'll be a pillar of strength for the president—he'll need you."

Geraldo embodied the conflicted life of Trump's wingmen at Fox. He felt loyalty toward his friend of nearly fifty years but struggled to explain his friend's tendencies toward racist rhetoric. His Trump allegiance "has cost me schisms in the family," he said; "my wife and I are constantly at odds about the president." Most members of Geraldo's family saw no redeeming value in Trump. But he swore his friend was treated unfairly by most of the media, and he defended Fox as a necessary counterweight. On September 27 Geraldo attacked the Ukraine whistleblower as a "rotten snitch—I'd love to whop him."

That's where many Fox News stars trained their sights—on the whistleblower. The real scandals, they said, were Biden's dealings in Ukraine and the whistleblower's anti-Trump agenda. But honest brokers like Judge Andrew Napolitano knew where this was really heading—toward an impeachment trial. The judge said that the emerging abuse-of-power case was "the most serious charge against the president" yet, "far more serious than what Bob Mueller dug or dragged up against him."

Shep also tried to lay out the facts: He said on his September 23 newscast that "the real issue" wasn't Biden, but the charge "that the president pressured a foreign leader to investigate a political rival." Steve Doocy, of all people, agreed that the circumstances looked really frickin' bad. "If the president said, 'I will give you the money but you have got to investigate Joe Biden,' that is really off-the-rails wrong," Doocy said, while grasping for a counternarrative to glom on to: "But if it's something else, you know, it would be nice to know what it is."

Doocy didn't have to wait long to get his talking points. The counternarrative was as cut-and-dried as Ailes's old crusades against Muslims. Anyone and everyone who challenged Trump, even his own appointees, was cast as unpatriotic. Hannity was insistent that the real problem was "psychotic anti-Trump hysteria." When Nancy Pelosi announced the Democrats' formal impeachment inquiry on September 24, White House aides said they didn't need to set up a "war room" the way the Clinton White House did in the nineties. They didn't explain why, but the reason was obvious to me—Fox *was* the war room.

Like jackhammers chiseling away at a city street so loudly you can't even think straight, the prime time shows insisted that Trump was innocent and the real guilty party was the whistleblower. "This was a professional hit on Donald Trump," Dan Bongino declared. "I have no doubt." Trump, in turn, shared video clips of Fox's reality-denying segments on Twitter. But in the reality-based universe, the big question was about Trump's legal and political jeopardy. Napolitano appeared on Shep's show and said yes, Trump committed a crime on the July 25 call.

Enter jackhammering, Trump-loving lawyer Joe diGenova. He

was booked on Tucker Carlson's show later in the day, September 24. Tucker invoked Napolitano and asked, "Is it a crime? You're a former federal prosecutor."

"Well, I think Judge Napolitano is a fool," diGenova said, "and I think what he said today is foolish. No, it is not a crime."

Tucker was choosing to use his own legal "expert" instead of Fox's official "senior judicial analyst." And diGenova didn't just say Napolitano was foolish, he called him a "fool," a distinction that led one Fox exec to tell me "it was out of line." There weren't many lines left to cross at Fox, but diGenova had found one.

Shep, incensed, wanted what he always wanted: some support from management. None was forthcoming. He thought carefully about what to say and hit back the following afternoon: "Last night on this network during prime time opinion programming, a partisan guest who supports President Trump was asked about Judge Napolitano's legal assessment, and when he was asked, he said unchallenged 'Judge Napolitano is a fool.' Attacking our colleague, who is here to offer legal assessments, on our air in our work home is repugnant."

In Shep's mind, Carlson was the one who "started" this, so Scott needed to end it. Bad blood between the two men stretched back several years; Carlson's *Daily Caller* website ran anti-Shep stories on the regular. So Scott had to do something. Right?

She didn't. After dark, Carlson brought back diGenova and kept the feud going. He said Napolitano's analysis wasn't news, it was opinion. He mocked Shep for acting holier-than-thou. "Apparently our daytime host who hosted Judge Napolitano was watching last night and was outraged by what you said and, quite ironically, called you partisan," Carlson said, basically calling Shep and the judge anti-Trump crusaders. "Unlike maybe some dayside hosts, I'm not very partisan," Carlson claimed. He later joked to friends that he gave Shep a "spanking." Shep hit the roof.

No one knew this outside Fox HQ, but Shep's staff thought in the wake of Tucker's comments that he would resign immediately. On Thursday he asked the team where they wanted to order food for a special Friday lunch. They chose Carmine's, the Italian mainstay on 44th Street just off Times Square, and they nervously awaited the enormous spread, thinking their trusted leader was going to quit right then and there. When the food arrived, Shep gathered everyone and gave a speech. "The news will always continue at this network," he said, as staffers exhaled just a bit, learning today wouldn't be the day. He still had to negotiate his way out. Looking back, "we knew right then that his mind was made up," a staffer told me.

On day three of the feud, Shep alluded to network unrest on the air by saying "there are two different information streams" in competition. On one side, he said, there were facts that the president had admitted. "Then there's this information stream of constant attacking of the facts that is . . . interesting to watch."

And, he should have added, exhausting to be a part of.

Vanity Fair's Gabriel Sherman reported that Scott and Wallace "communicated to Smith" to "stop attacking Carlson." Fox execs insisted that never happened. Part of the problem was that management wasn't communicating at all. But Shep had a sense—from Scott's silence—that the network sided with Carlson. A Trump flunky would be allowed to call Fox's senior judicial analyst a "fool" with no repercussions. This truly was Shep's last straw.

But nothing this expensive and this consequential could be done overnight. The Shep talks unfolded in secret for several weeks. Attorney Arthur Aidala, who had previously represented Ailes and was getting ready to defend Harvey Weinstein, was enlisted to do, or rather undo, Shep's deal. Fox executives tried to bargain with Shep's team;

they appealed to him to suck it up and stay. But deep down Shep knew there was no future for him at Fox. Colleagues said they had never seen him so low. "He was just beaten down," one ally said.

Television news contracts are essentially one-sided. Management can almost always come up with a reason to fire talent, or keep a person off the air while still paying what's owed to them, a peculiar situation known as "pay or play." But there's rarely an out for talent to just walk away and join a competing network. Shep's proposal—to abandon ship at the halfway point in his contract—was incredibly unusual. But so were these circumstances. According to two people with knowledge of the negotiations, the decision went all the way up to Rupert Murdoch. "If he doesn't want to work here," Rupert said, "he shouldn't work here."

One of the people involved also remembered Rupert saying "We'll replace him and get better ratings."

While the Shep negotiations were wrapping up, and Rupert considered who should take over the 3 p.m. time slot, his son James was at a book party on the Upper East Side. Radhika Jones, the editor of *Vanity Fair*, and Richard Plepler, the former head of HBO, were toasting former Obama State Department official Richard Stengel, whose book *Information Wars* was about the global battle against disinformation. Liberal lights like Arianna Huffington and Phil Donahue filled the room. James and Kathryn Murdoch's attendance was enormously symbolic of James's split from his brother and father. James barely spoke to them anymore. He leased office space in the West Village for Lupa Systems, a new media holding company with a progressive point of view, and made investments in companies like Vice Media. Later in the month, he went to the *Vanity Fair* New Establishment Summit, talked up Pete Buttigieg, and vented frustration with cable news shows that "just preach to the choir." He dropped hints but never expressed the true depths of his disgust for Fox News. "There's plenty of stuff on Fox News that I disagree with," he said uneasily, as he tried to spread blame for the country's gaping wounds, chiding talk radio for its "incredibly, crazily damaging" contributions to the discourse. Talk radio—the model for Fox News.

James saw little upside in bashing Fox, specifically, in public. But whenever reporters like me weren't listening in, he ripped into Fox's alternative reality and his brother's willingness to allow it to continue. He likened the network to a "sinking ship" and said some of the "rats" would drown while others would scurry off. One of the few hosts he could stand watching was Shep Smith.

"The truth will always matter"

At 3:59 p.m. on October 11, 2019, Shep signed off for the final time.

None of his viewers had any idea what was about to happen. Nor did most of his colleagues.

"This is my last newscast here," he announced. He thanked his bosses and producers and viewers. And he alluded to the weeks of negotiations: "Recently I asked the company to allow me to leave Fox News. After requesting that I stay, they obliged."

So this was a sudden and total split.

"Even in our current polarized nation," he said, "it is my hope that the facts will win the day, that the truth will always matter, that journalism and journalists will thrive. I'm Shepard Smith, Fox News, New York."

Fox staffers were shell-shocked. Some journalists rushed to his twelfth-floor studio to try and convince him to stay, or at least shake his hand, but Shep had a getaway plan. He went straight to the freight elevator and climbed into a waiting car in the basement garage. A friend told me he didn't want to see anyone on the way out the door because it would have been too emotional.

Shep's exit was more than the end of an era for Fox: It was also a sign of what was happening to the country. There was a great divide into two halves, and little tolerance for dissent within each tribe. Shep refused to be a part of it anymore. Colleagues and friends said the Shep of ten years ago would have held on; back then he felt supported by Ailes, and news was his life. Now, though, he had a home life. He had his partner, Gio, and a dog, Lucia, and a gracious house in the Hamptons. Gio had been encouraging him to leave Fox for months, insisting, "You don't belong there anymore."

He knew Gio was right. And he was relieved to be untethered to Fox for the first time in his professional life. "I feel free," Shep told me, when they returned from a post-resignation Fox detox in Mexico.

His ex-colleagues felt anything but free. On the occasion of Shep's first return to public life, as emcee for a journalism awards dinner in Manhattan, Fox's attendees were warned by management that I'd be there and were reminded that I'd be fishing for info for this book. I said hello to a few correspondents but kept my distance because I didn't want to give away which people I knew. At the after-dinner cocktail hour, I accidentally left my briefcase in a corner, and when a group of Fox producers moseyed over, they wondered who had left it there. When I came to claim my item, someone joked about calling it in as a suspicious package. By the end of the night, word had filtered back to management—a producer was worried that the case may have concealed a tape recorder to surreptitiously monitor their conversations for dirty laundry. Nuts?

Yes. But not far-fetched for products of the environment Ailes had fostered and his successors encouraged—an environment hostile to journalism.

The remaining reporters at Fox were heart-stricken by Shep's escape. I heard from them immediately after the shocking sign-off on October 11. More than one correspondent said that Shep's decision sowed doubts in their minds: "Is this worth it anymore?" "Should I stay?"

"To my Fox Friends," correspondent Laura Ingle wrote on Instagram the next day, "anyone else wake up this morning, open your eyes and forget for a brief moment what happened yesterday . . . then feel like you were hit by a bus?"

Rumors swirled about management's massive fuckup. "I heard they called HIM in but not Tucker," a news anchor told me. "Why didn't they fight harder to keep him?"

"I just can't shake the feeling that at the end of the day this company let him walk," a disgusted reporter said. He called his agent and explored his own options.

"They should have put out a statement defending him every single time" Trump or Carlson attacked, a deflated anchor concluded.

Others worried about who would be chosen to replace him. Would the time slot head in a Trumpier direction, as Shep had feared when he decided to re-up his contract? And honestly, wouldn't Fox viewers prefer that anyway?

"We are still committed to news," Jay Wallace said. Staffers didn't believe him.

The Shep shock was best understood this way: "Shep had power that almost none of us had." That's how a veteran staffer put it. Shep, they felt, was uniquely able to fact-check Trump and call out his lies. The remaining anchors felt powerless.

Trump changed the channel whenever Shep was on, so he missed the grand sign-off. Forty-five minutes after it happened, he departed the White House for a rally in Louisiana. One of the reporters on the South Lawn shouted a question about Fox, assuming the president already knew the news, given his addiction to the channel.

"Mr. President, did you or your administration pressure Fox News to get rid of Shepard Smith?"

"No, I don't know. Is he leaving?" Trump asked. "Oh, that's a shame."

He circled back a moment later and made fun of Shep's "terrible" Nielsens. "Is he leaving because of his ratings?"

Shouting over the whirring blades of Marine One, a reporter tried to ask Trump the same question *Vanity Fair* posed in an all-caps headline: "WHY IS WILLIAM BARR MEETING WITH RUPERT MURDOCH?"

A conspiracy theory linking Barr to Shep's exit was already circulating on far-left Twitter because the attorney general had paid a visit to Rupert two nights before. But Barr truly played no part in the move. Months later, I found out what had actually transpired between the two men. The meal was about several things—media consolidation, criminal justice reform, the maddening choices their adult children made, all the usuals. But it was also about Judge Andrew Napolitano.

The president was so incensed by the judge's TV broadcasts that he had implored Barr to send Rupert a message in person. According to a source, it was "about muzzling the judge." POTUS wanted the nation's top law enforcement official to convey just how atrocious Napolitano's legal analysis had been. (The DOJ denied this but did not divulge anything about the meeting.)

Barr's words carried a lot of weight. No one was explicitly told to take Napolitano off the air. These things always happened much, much more subtly. One day Fox re-allotted digital resources, which meant Napolitano no longer had the ability to tape web videos. Another day he disappeared from a daytime show's rundown. When the impeachment hearings began in earnest, Napolitano was nowhere to be found. He complained to pals at the network that "twenty-five-year-old producers" were keeping him off the air because they didn't think viewers could handle his analysis. A twentysomething staffer confirmed to me that Maria Bartiromo's show would usually only book him to talk about non-Trump topics, because the host would get too upset with him otherwise. Other employees justified the benching of the judge by claiming that viewers hated him: "Why are we going to book someone who kills our ratings?"

The shock of Shep's departure weighed on another Fox veteran who already eyed the exit. Catherine Herridge was a well-sourced correspondent in DC who, unlike Shep, appeared up and down the daily schedule, even on shows like *Hannity*. Critics at other DC bureaus said she had a conservative bent, but CBS News put a lucrative offer on the table. Herridge was the rare Fox talent who was able to get a bidding war going with another network. Her Fox contract expired over the summer, and she made her concerns clear: Management was not up to the moment. Execs were "afraid of the news," she said, in a time that called for tenacious coverage. It boiled down to this: "Programming is easy compared to news," she commented to a colleague.

Herridge defected for CBS on Halloween. Another correspondent in the DC bureau, Ellison Barber, gave notice in November. According to colleagues, she told Jay Wallace that she was worried about the direction of the channel, even more so post-Shep, and didn't feel comfortable there anymore. In April, she jumped to NBC.

Fox had no way to replace these seasoned journalists with stars from the outside—the way, say, *The Washington Post* poached from *The New York Times* or CNN stole from ABC—because so few of those stars were willing to entertain Jay Wallace's calls. Reporters from Axios and elsewhere passed. Scott focused on keeping her current lineup under contract, and she reached new long-term deals with virtually all of Fox's biggest stars, from Hannity to Chris Wallace.

As for 3 p.m., by the middle of November Scott settled on replacing Shep with Bill Hemmer, a fourteen-year vet of the network. Hemmer felt stuck in his morning spot, and tired of seeing all his women cohosts promoted into their own solo hours while he stayed put, so he welcomed the change. Everyone who hoped for a Shep-like truth-teller in the time slot was disheartened. The PR division came up with a list of times when, they claimed, Hemmer had challenged Trump officials, but none of the examples were as impactful as a single Shep fact-check, not a single one. Hemmer was professionally soft on Trump and personally conservative. He was known to be friendly with Rudy Giuliani. They golfed together at Maidstone. (The mere prospect of golfing with Rudy would have made Shep uneasy.) So the change at 3 p.m. represented yet another turn to the right. Six months after the anchorman's departure, at the apex of the pandemic, a high-profile correspondent confided in me: "I still miss Shep every day."

THE CRISIS

"Complicit"

In the Trump White House, Dr. Fiona Hill said, "the television was always on. And it was usually on Fox News." It was a direct hookup to a well of disinformation.

Hill was once Trump's most senior adviser on European and Russian affairs. She knew it was a risky position to hold. But she never expected to be a star witness in an impeachment inquiry. In her testimony, first behind closed doors and then on live television all around the world, Hill shared some of the most troubling evidence yet of Fox's influence on the highest levels of government. She said the "whirlwind" of Ukraine disinformation spewing from Rudy, John Solomon, and other Fox regulars made her job nearly impossible to perform.

"I would have to go home in the evening and try to look on the news to see what Giuliani was doing," she testified, "because people were constantly saying to me: 'My God, have you seen what Giuliani is saying now?'"

When Hill would meet with John Bolton in his office, and Rudy was live on Fox, Bolton turned up the volume to hear what he was saying. Hill observed that key parts of the pressure campaign played out right on TV for all to see.

A mountain of evidence showed that the blame-Ukraine scheme was seeded on, and then supported by, Fox. So did the president rethink the value of those friendships? No. As his gross misconduct vis-à-vis Ukraine was exposed in October and November, Trump needed Fox more than ever.

Hannity turned into a human word cloud of defenses and deflections, bashing the "total sham Schiff show charade" night after night. When Fox's well-respected polling unit said that 50 percent of Americans wanted Trump impeached and removed, Hannity overlooked the data entirely. Other shows also played their parts: Fox & Friends producers wrote wackadoo talking points like "MEDIA DECLARES TRUMP SHOULD BE IMPEACHED," as if the media were a single person. Ingraham assailed the Dems every night. Carlson made fun of other news outlets for taking the scandal seriously.

The result of all this: The House impeachment inquiry unfolded in two totally different news worlds. Weeks of damning testimony were met by weeks of insults directed at the witnesses. Fox's biggest stars tried to delegitimize the process and demonize the Dems. Hannity continued to claim that Ukraine interfered in 2016, creating a completely bogus equivalence between Russia's multi-pronged attack and the amateurish actions of some individual Ukrainians. The lies worked in the real world outside DC: Polling by Ipsos and FiveThirtyEight found that Fox viewers were more likely to say Ukraine interfered *and* less likely to say Russia interfered, versus people who predominantly watched other channels. Democratic lawmakers pointed out that the president's reliance on this alternative reality was part of the problem. Senate Minority Leader Chuck Schumer chastised Trump for buying into "baseless conspiracy theories told by known liars on Fox News." But Schumer's office also bragged about the number of Democrats who went on Fox to puncture the bubble and present evidence of high crimes and misdemeanors.

For Hannity, this was his second impeachment-go-round, and bashing Bill Clinton in the nineties was a lot more fun. The Trump impeachment was rote, and Hannity barely suited up for the fight. Sometimes he even faked his own show. While deep into the research for this book in December 2019, I ran into Hannity at a holiday party hosted by the TV news tracking website Mediaite. The party was upstairs at the Lambs Club, a stately Manhattan restaurant wrapped with red leather banquettes on 44th Street. Hannity greeted me by putting both his hands on my shoulders and exclaiming: "Humpty!" Oh, right, his nickname for me was Humpty Dumpty. I looked him in the eyes and asked if he ever felt bad about the name-calling. "No," he shot back. He took his hands off my shoulders and moved toward the bar.

It was eight o'clock, and Hannity worked the room like an old pro, dressed down in a Fox-branded hoodie zipped to his chest. He hugged CNN's Alisyn Camerota and chatted with media reporters and even said hi to Trump antagonist George Conway. This room was the embodiment of the so-called "media mob" he attacked every weeknight—and he looked like he didn't want to leave it. I marveled at the scene and wondered what Hannity's viewers would think if they knew he was here. At 8:30 his PR person pushed him toward the door, insisting to me that he had to get to the studio for his nine o'clock show. I later realized that the PR person had lied to me—Hannity had already pretaped his show before coming to the party.

Hannity preferred to tape his show whenever he could. Fox managers preferred that he be live. But he usually won out—

because not a single person in charge at Fox had the guts to tell him no.

That's why Fox looked so weak on the night of the final vote on two articles of impeachment, Wednesday, December 18. "After this day," Bret Baier said that afternoon, "we will never talk about the 45th president of the United States the same way again." Well, not if Hannity had something to say about it. The vote was completed in the 8 p.m. hour, so Hannity's 9 p.m. monologue was crucial sustenance for the viewers. He reassured them that the impeachment was a sham, a lie, a hoax, every word he could think of, but his heart wasn't in it at all. On a historic night, the third impeachment vote by the House of Representatives in American history, Hannity's show was on tape. He recorded everything before the vote actually happened.

Hannity's producers did everything they could to mask the fact that the show was stale. The control room threw up banners on screen with the results of the House vote. They added a box in the right-hand corner of the screen with live pictures of Trump holding a rally in Michigan. They left a forty-five-second hole for a live news update from a fill-in anchor. And Hannity left another hole for them to fill—at the end of the pretaped hour he tossed to a clip reel of the "best moments" from the rally, not knowing what they'd be. The producers inserted a few clips about tariffs and the military and the Space Force. Then the taped Hannity came back on camera and tossed to a very live Laura Ingraham in DC.

Ingraham didn't care what Hannity did as long as he kept delivering her a huge ratings lead-in for the start of her 10 p.m. hour. But people on the other side of the Fox fence, at the besieged news operation, were outraged by Hannity's lazy behavior. "When people in the news division found out Sean taped his show, they flipped," a DC source said. Bret Baier was especially angry. He could have been anchoring the network's live coverage, just like his counterparts on other networks were. In the past, he would have been in the anchor chair. But Trump had transformed Fox. What the network now valued most was the attention of Trump's America, news and facts and traditions be damned. Embarrassing or not, no one in Fox management really thought straight-edged news coverage would have out-rated Hannity's outdated charade. And that's what mattered most: The Scoreboard.

Apart from climactic moments like December 18, Baier kept his head down. Everyone in his social circle said the same thing about him—that he was the reasonable one left at Fox. "Thank God for Bret and Chris Wallace," an attendee remarked at a glittery party for Baier's new book in DC in the fall.

A friend of Bret's told me she was surprised to see a CNN anchor at a Fox anchor's party. She figured the atmosphere had become too poisonous to allow for such a thing. It almost had. Historically these backslapping kinds of events were the media version of bipartisanship—and, sure enough, at Baier's party I spotted Norah O'Donnell from CBS, Jonathan Karl from ABC, Mike Allen from Axios. But the poison was real. Some of Baier's Beltway friendships withered in the Trump years. Journalists at other networks told me they were disappointed by his "both sides"–type coverage in an era when one side, the Republicans, egregiously lied so much more than the other side. "He's complicit," these journalists typically said, writing him off as part of the problem. Fox's base believed Baier was problematic for a different reason: because he wasn't deferential enough to Trump. Fox's hour-by-hour ratings showed a widening gap between incredibly popular pro-Trump talk shows like *The Five* at 5 p.m. and *Tucker Carlson Tonight* at 8 p.m., and lower-rated news and hybrid shows like Baier's *Special Report* at 6 and MacCallum's *The Story* at 7. On a line graph, Fox's evening hours took the shape of a hammock, because so many Trump diehards turned off Baier and MacCallum and came back for Carlson at 8. "Bret and Martha have a real problem," one executive whispered, pointing to the audience's lukewarm interest in their shows. Let's put it this way: No one in television news wants to be a hammock.

Ever since impeachment was first floated as a remedy to curb Trump's misconduct, in 2017, historians and experts had brought up the Fox factor. Often it came up in the form of a hypothetical: If Richard Nixon had had Fox and an entire universe of right-wing media, would he have been forced from office, or could he have hung on?

In 2020, we found out the answer. The Fox war room shifted from defense to offense for the Senate trial and the preordained ending to the impeachment saga. A slew of Fox regulars jumped from the studio to the Senate chamber to take up Trump's cause. Ken Starr, whose work as an independent counsel eventually led to the impeachment of Bill Clinton and who became a paid Fox News contributor in 2019 when management anticipated another impeachment drama, took a leave from the network to join Trump's defense team. Frequent Fox guests Alan Dershowitz, Pam Bondi, Jay Sekulow, and Robert Ray all joined as well. When Ray got the gig, he thanked Maria Bartiromo for putting him on TV. "If not for you," he said, "I don't know that I would have come to the president's attention." And he was right.

Fox's defense team put on a show for Fox's airwaves. Hannity picked up where they left off in the evening, accompanied by graphics like "DEMS VS. THE CONSTITUTION," and he pressured wayward Republican senators to stay in line. He addressed perceived swing voters Susan Collins and Mitt Romney directly through the camera, threatening that their voters would not tolerate any dissent. "It is not your Republican senators' job to bolster what are pathetically weak articles of impeachment from the House," Hannity lectured. "It is not your senators' duty to call witnesses that the House didn't even subpoena." Everyone got the message: No new witnesses. No new evidence. Let Trump get back to work. Maureen Dowd summed up the strategy perfectly: "The Democrats are relying on facts, but the Republicans are relying on Fox."

On February 5, 2020, Republicans in the Senate acquitted the president on both the abuse of power and obstruction counts. Democratic senator Sherrod Brown told me he saw fear in the eyes of his Republican counterparts. "It's fear of Fox," he said. "It's fear of talk radio." And most of all it was fear of the president, who took his cues from those sources. The sole GOP dissenter, Romney, was excommunicated by Trump and the entire Fox prime time lineup. Anticipating this, Romney gave a single TV interview, to Chris Wallace, to explain his thought process to Fox viewers. "You realize this is war," Wallace said. "Donald Trump will never forgive you for this."

"There is a hymn that is sung in my church," Romney responded, "it's an old Protestant hymn which is 'Do what is right and let the consequence follow.' I know in my heart that I'm doing what's right. I understand there's going to be enormous consequence. And I don't have a choice in that regard."

Trump also gave a single interview as impeachment ended—to Hannity. It was really just a televised exchange of "hoax" talking points. Hannity's sit-down was the much-ballyhooed Super Bowl Sunday interview that went to Bill O'Reilly when the game was on Fox three years earlier. Other networks selected journalists when it was their turn to air the game, but Trump wanted the comfort of Hannity's safe space. So, instead of asking a real question about impeachment, Hannity simply said, "Your reaction to all of it?"

Some Fox staffers mocked the fact that Hannity landed yet another presidential interview but came away with no news to show from it. They missed the point: The purpose wasn't news, it was propaganda. Propaganda was more effective when it masqueraded as news. Anyone who was in denial about this clearly wasn't watching.

"Democracy at risk"

"My name is Sean Graf and I am a news researcher at Fox News," the email began.

I didn't take Graf seriously at first. He was a brand-new source out of the blue and he seemed too good to be true. If he was a trap, and I fell for it, Fox could use it against me and try to discredit all of my reporting. It wouldn't be the first time Fox PR had tried such a thing.

But Graf checked out. He was a lifelong liberal who joined Fox in 2016 after interning at CNN and striking out on job interviews with other networks. "I wanted to better understand how the most powerful name in conservative media, if not all of the news, operates," he said. So Graf went inside the beast. And he found the same thing I did in reporting for this book: "Fox's editorial voice, and disregard for the facts, is rejected by many of those within the organization." Graf wrote the email because he wanted me to know that the internal resistance was real.

Graf said he wasn't claiming that the network's producer and writer ranks were filled with liberal doves, but he said there were more McCain/Romney Republicans than Trump/Pence Trumplicans, and many were unhappy about the network's devolution. "In the same way that the Republican Party has abandoned their core principles, so too has Fox," he wrote. "President Trump represents the antithesis of what Republicans and Fox stood for only a few

years ago. What happened to supporting free trade, fiscal conservatism, defending our allies and promoting the rule of law?"

Graf asked good questions. It reminded me of the way that Fox's
well-versed researchers were so often ignored by the talent. *The
Daily Beast* obtained a 162-page document from the Fox research
team, titled "Ukraine, Disinformation, & the Trump Administration," debunking much of what the Sean Hannity Cinematic
Universe claimed on air every day for months. John Solomon was
singled out for criticism: The document said he played "an indispensable role in the collection and domestic publication of elements
of this disinformation campaign." Yet he was paid by Fox and he
was a regular on *Hannity.*

Inside Fox, Graf told me, there was a divergence "between what
Fox is peddling and what many employees know to be true . . . a
constant frustration and disappointment that Fox personalities continue to promote the Trump Administration with its thoroughly
documented dishonesty."

Widespread disappointment, yes, but Graf was describing the
business model. Fox's profits depended on the wingmen, not on his
carefully researched work. As a former anchor put it to me, "The
Murdochs are mercenaries"—even more than Ailes, "they protect
the bottom line." The GOP had become Trump's party, so Fox
had become Trump's network. The alternative would have been a
whole lot less profitable.

But at what price? "Fox's allegiance to President Trump is putting our Democracy at risk," Graf continued. "Even if the Republican Party refuses to stand up to Trump, Fox must."

I sympathized with his point of view. But that version of Fox no
longer existed. The audience had been radicalized, and the anchors
did whatever they could to keep up with their viewers' demands for
simpering propaganda.

Martha MacCallum had no idea what she was in for when she put on a white dress for 2020's State of the Union coverage. The House chamber filled up with Democratic women who wore white to honor suffragettes and the one hundredth anniversary of the Nineteenth Amendment. On social media, crazed viewers accused her of harboring a pro-Democratic bias. It was actually just one of the last clean dresses she had in the closet.

Similarly, Baier's viewers punished him for running a clip of Chris Wallace's interview with Romney. "Your hatred for our POTUS is so obvious," a Twitterer screamed at him. "You are not fair and balanced! You disgust me!" These viewers didn't know what fairness was anymore. I wondered if they knew what *news* was anymore. They expected propaganda, and when they didn't get it, they demanded it.

"I have no problem with Fox being a conservative news network," Graf wrote as we corresponded back and forth. "What I have a problem with is Fox allowing a president who is not a conservative to masquerade as such—and defending him when they *know* most everything he says is not true. What is happening at Fox seems to mirror what is happening with Senate Republicans and anyone who has been a Republican for over ten years."

Graf was absolutely right. Shamelessness was everywhere. The people willing to admit it were denigrated as "Never Trumpers." There was almost no room for them on air at Fox.

Graf and I agreed that reality-based news coverage from a conservative perspective would have helped both the Trump White House and the country. But it seemed that Trumpism had so severely corrupted the conservative movement that there was no room for right-leaning talk shows that stayed tethered to the truth. It was "fake news" and Lou Dobbs all the way down.

Graf found a way out of Fox in January 2020: a short-lived stint as a researcher on Michael Bloomberg's campaign. Yes, the primaries were underway. Fox continued to offer town hall events to Democratic candidates, using a shiny new brand name that was meant to appeal to marketers, "Democracy 2020." *Pay no attention to our role enabling creeping authoritarianism*, the marketing campaign suggested, *we're the home for democracy*.

A few candidates, like Bloomberg, said yes to Fox's entreaties, but other Democrats ran against Trump *and* against the pro-Trump alternative reality that Fox represented and the destruction of truth that Fox enabled. Biden declined the town hall offer but did say yes to one sit-down interview, with Chris Wallace, following his decisive win in South Carolina. In prime time, Hannity and Carlson workshopped anti-Biden attack lines like comedians testing out new material in front of a live audience. Night after night they suggested that Biden was not mentally fit to hold office, while sidestepping all the concerns about Trump's fitness.

"A few months from now, he'll be reciting Allen Ginsberg poems to strangers at bus stops. He's going fast," Carlson said one night in February.

"Biden is weak and he's getting weaker," he said the following month, calling the candidate—now the front-runner in the Democratic race—"noticeably more confused now than he was even last spring when he entered the race."

Biden's blunders concerned some reporters on his campaign, but Fox stars like Carlson gave up the pretense of concern by mocking and insulting Biden. Trump, as always, imitated his favorite hosts with offensive and conspiratorial remarks. ("They are going to put him in a home and other people are going to be running the country.") A *Politico* reporter dubbed it "the Dementia Campaign" because Trump went viral with his own stumbles, stammerings, and typos on a near daily basis. Everyone thought the election was going to be the biggest story of 2020, but unfortunately it was not.

"Costing the lives of Americans"

When Covid-19 began to attack the lungs of patients in Wuhan, China, a clock started ticking in the United States. The virus was coming; it was only a matter of time. In the words of epidemiologist Dr. Larry Brilliant, "the warnings were everywhere." But most laypeople didn't hear the ticking or see the warning signs until March. And even then Trump failed to muster a forceful government response. The result was a 9/11-level failure of the federal government.

In audiotaped conversations with the author Bob Woodward, Trump made excuses for his lack of leadership. He said he "wanted to always play it down" because he didn't want people to panic about the virus.

He deliberately played down the crisis—and Fox was there to help him.

On January 22, 2020, Trump was asked about the coronavirus for the first time, in an interview with Maria Bartiromo on the sidelines of the World Economic Forum in Davos, Switzerland. She asked how worried Americans should be about the virus, and the president said, "We're in great shape."

At the time, China had only reported seventeen deaths from the virus, and most Americans hadn't even heard of it yet. Trump was preoccupied by the impeachment trial and domestic political concerns. When Health and Human Services secretary Alex Azar had tried to focus the president's attention on the virus on January 18, Trump lit into him about flavored e-cigarettes instead. At the end of the month, on January 30, after the Chinese government quarantined Wuhan and the U.S. began to evacuate Americans from the city, Trump again criticized Azar and told him to stop panicking about the virus.

Trump maintained this position until March, in the face of all available evidence. So did some of Fox's biggest stars. In March scores of Americans wrote to the FCC (even though the broadcast-focused agency had no regulatory power over cable) and argued that the network had blood on its hands. Hannity "has misled his elderly viewers on the risk of pandemic virus. They are most at risk," one Kansas City resident wrote. "My mother, who is 94 years old, believes that the virus threat is very overstated because Fox News and Sean Hannity say so," a Bluffton, South Carolina, resident wrote. "Fox News is now costing the lives of Americans," a Russellville, Alabama, resident wrote.

I heard it from insiders as well. "Some of our programming was outlandish," a top exec at Fox Corp admitted. The Covid-era criticism of Fox News was the most scathing I'd ever seen in my sixteen years covering the network. But it was not evenly distributed. Some people at Fox were almost exempt, like Tucker Carlson, who covered the virus earlier than almost anyone on American television.

The Covid-19 narrative fit neatly into Carlson's long-established ideas about China. Carlson criticized Chinese culture—calling it "repulsive" that people eat snakes, bats, and koalas—and called out America's dependence on Chinese manufacturing lines. On January 27, he raised the notion of a China "travel ban" with Fox medical analyst Dr. Marc Siegel, who endorsed the idea and said the situation in Wuhan was terrifying. Later in the week Siegel came back and did a Coronavirus 101 tutorial for the audience. A Carlson colleague observed that *Tucker Carlson Tonight* was filling in as the President's Daily Brief, since the president famously ignored the actual daily briefs put together by the CIA. The show's banners practically gave Trump instructions: One read, "TIME TO STOP FLIGHTS FROM CHINA," four days before Trump did just that.

Once the restrictions were in place, Trump boasted to Hannity that "we pretty much shut it down," and tuned out the warnings about new outbreaks erupting in Italy and elsewhere. Inside the White House, Dr. Anthony Fauci, deputy national security advisor Matthew Pottinger, and other experts were ignored when they pushed for restrictions on flights from Europe. Infectious disease specialists were ignored when they warned about shortages of ventilators and personal protective equipment. Even Carlson's televised alerts fell on deaf presidential ears. Trump engaged in wishful thinking instead: On February 10 he told Trish Regan, the 8 p.m. host on Fox Business, that he believed China would "have it under control fairly soon. You know in April, supposedly, it dies with the hotter weather. And that's a beautiful date to look forward to."

In the pantheon of infamous presidential falsehoods, "in April, supposedly, it dies with the hotter weather" may be the saddest in history. If the virus had actually faded away in April, hundreds of thousands of people around the world might still be alive today.

Trump repeated his fantasy in a phone call to Geraldo Rivera on February 13. "We think and we hope, based on all signs, that the problem goes away in April," he said, because "heat kills this virus. We think." Trump also revealed his epidemiological ignorance to Rivera by saying, "It's a problem in China" but "has not been spreading very much." His friends at Fox indulged this, and to the extent they covered the coronavirus at all, they opined instead of reported. ABC, CBS, NBC, and CNN all had bureaus in Beijing, but Fox didn't have a bureau in China or anywhere else in Asia. Its only foreign bureaus were in London, Rome, and Jerusalem. So there was no Fox news-gathering operation where the virus originated. Instead, the scrutiny of China's actions was left to anti-China firebrands like Steve Bannon, who sat in comfortable studios back in the States. "This is a biological Chernobyl," Bannon told Jesse Watters, accusing China of a vast cover-up. Bannon had a point; Fox guests and hosts were right to call out China's mendacity. But they also veered into rash speculation that the virus was man-made, despite all evidence to the contrary. Worst of all, they kept looking backward at the fire's faraway origins when America's own house was on fire. At least one woman in California had already died after being infected with the disease. But no one knew that yet because officials were flying blind without tests. Trump talked like the threat had passed when he had merely closed the side door of the house while leaving all the other doors and windows wide open.

Why? Perhaps because he was busy with his post-impeachment purge. He put Richard Grenell, the former Fox commentator turned ambassador to Germany, in charge of the government's spy agencies. And he welcomed back his surrogate daughter Hope Hicks, who was bored of her job running PR at Fox Corp and missed her family on the East Coast. She made a 360-degree spin through the revolving door, going from Trump to Fox and back to Trump. All of this occurred in mid and late February—when different strains of the virus were spreading fast in Washington State, California, and New York. Hundreds of Americans were sick and didn't even know it yet because U.S. agencies were only testing a few dozen people a day. The president and most of the hosts on his favorite channel were telling them not to worry.

"Don't rock the boat"

February 2020, the final normal month in America before social distancing and masks and triage tents and Zoom funerals, was the highest-rated month in Fox News history. Tune-in was fueled by Trump's acquittal in the Senate and the Democratic primaries. Late in the month, I sat across the dinner table from a Fox anchor and compared notes about the cable news wars. "We're just a monopoly," the anchor observed. "We're benefiting from our monopoly status."

I asked if the anchor kept a watchful eye on Newsmax, One America News (OAN for short), or any of the other start-ups that wanted to take on Fox. The answer came in the form of a cackling laugh. The hosts were junior varsity, the production values were high school TV quality, the talk shows were parodies of Fox prime time circa 2005—Why, the anchor asked me, would anyone watch a Fox rip-off when they could watch the real thing?! I heard very similar assessments from other sources at Fox. OAN and Newsmax still were not rated by Nielsen, and the channels were still hard to find on some cable and satellite systems. They lacked Fox's gloss, Fox's edge, Fox's multimillion-dollar studios. But Chris Ruddy, Newsmax's CEO and a longtime friend of Trump's, said he was chipping away at the Fox monopoly. "We are almost complete on distribution," he said in an email message. "The audience is zooming." Charles Herring, the president of OAN, also kept in touch by sending out his own press releases about special programming—a bootstrapped approach that Murdoch circa 1996 might have respected. One of his emails thanked Rudy Giuliani for a shout-out in the press, which reflected OAN's willingness to dive even deeper into conspiracy rabbit holes than Fox would. OAN aired anti-impeachment specials with titles like *The Ukraine Hoax*, and Trump increasingly rewarded the network with tweets. Newsmax staked out a center-right position and hired former Fox talent like Michelle Malkin, who had guest-hosted for Bill O'Reilly, and Greg Kelly, who had covered the White House for Fox in the Bush years. This gave Fox execs another reason to scoff—Newsmax was wearing hand-me-downs—but the dismissiveness would ultimately prove to be a big blunder.

Back at Fox, Suzanne Scott's changes to the daytime schedule pleased the audience and, in the view of her internal critics, further weakened the news product. With Bill Hemmer at the helm at 3 p.m., Shep Smith's former time slot no longer pissed off the White House with Trump-critiquing fact-checks.

"Bill is doing factual but don't-rock-the-boat news," a former colleague said. "Shepard would have rocked the boat all hour long because that is what was called for."

Fact-checking barely existed at Fox. It increasingly fell to liberal guests like Marie Harf and Jessica Tarlov to do the fact-checking that anchors and reporters were supposed to do. Sure, Fox execs *said* they wanted their anchors to challenge Trumpian talking points and hold the administration accountable—but the anchors who wanted to lift the fog of lies felt hemmed in by their own viewers. They cited 3 p.m. to prove the point. Hemmer's ratings were way up from Shep's lows. Trump, who used to mock Shep's ratings, now picked on 4 p.m. anchor Neil Cavuto's ratings instead. On February 20, he bashed Cavuto and guest A. B. Stoddard for some random remark about his 2016 debate performance and claimed that Fox Corp board member Paul Ryan was meddling in Cavuto's show and turning the network anti-Trump.

Anti-Trump?! This was as ridiculous as it was conspiratorial. But Ryan let it slide, just as he had done on countless other occasions when he still had actual power as the House Speaker—and Fox let it slide too.

Cavuto told colleagues he didn't want Fox to issue a statement in his defense. "Let it blow over," he told friends. Trump was like a summer thunderstorm—one minute the sun was shining, the next minute the sky was black, but a few minutes later the sun was back. The only difference was that everyone was soaked. Ryan basically felt the same way. When Trump attacks, "I sort of shrug my shoulders, move on," he said. His disdain for Trump was no secret, but the truth was that Ryan had no voice in Fox's coverage. No one there would have listened to him if he'd tried. Ryan's interest was in learning the media business, and from what he could tell, Fox Corp was a gold mine that might be depleted in the not-too-distant future. Fox's power was in its legacy cable deals, and it would retain that power as long as cable remained bundled up and bulletproof. So: For how long? Most homes were still hooked on, or felt they were stuck with, the basic bundle, but more and more were disconnecting every month. When the execs looked ten years into the future, it was hard to say with any confidence that the next ten years would be as profitable as the last ten. Fox News as a political machine was more influential than ever, but as a business, was it peaking? If the cable bundle unraveled, would the Murdoch kids be stuck managing the decline of their father's news network?

These questions led some people around Lachlan to believe that he was willing to sell Fox News. Not immediately, and certainly not while Rupert was still alive—but when the time and the price were right. At least one private equity firm, undeterred by the $25 to $30 billion hypothesized price tag, knocked on Lachlan's door in the latter months of 2019, I was told. But Lachlan wanted to be a buyer, not a seller. He wanted to acquire start-ups and make Fox Corp bigger, not sell it for parts. Besides, as one of his advisers put it, he didn't need the money. He closed on Chartwell, the Bel-Air mansion seen in *The Beverly Hillbillies*, at a cost of $150 million and began renovations on the ten-acre property. He planned to run Fox Corp from L.A. for years to come.

Lachlan's physical distance from Fox News HQ was matched by his hands-off approach to the content. Brian Kilmeade said on a podcast, "I've had more interaction with him than I had with Roger Ailes in twenty years"—but "I've never felt more autonomy than I do right now." That's what TV hosts typically want and expect—*you run the company, we'll run the shows*—but Lachlan went well beyond deference, all the way to indifference. He didn't watch Fox News religiously. He didn't worry much about Trump's war on truth. He was a soccer dad at heart, which was fine, except for the fact that he was also responsible for the most popular cable channel in the country, and that channel—*his* channel—was grossly misleading people about the worst pandemic in living memory.

On February 23, White House trade adviser Peter Navarro went on Fox with Maria Bartiromo and deployed a new catchphrase. He said that face masks, protective gear, and diagnostics were all being procured in "Trump time." A vaccine is possible in "half the time it usually takes," he said. Bartiromo welcomed his Trump hagiography and gently surveyed him about the economic stakes. "The American economy is extremely strong," Navarro declared, "and not particularly vulnerable to what happens in China."

In public Navarro was cheerleading; in private he was screaming. On the same day as his Bartiromo hit, Navarro wrote an internal memo for White House colleagues that sounded like it came from an entirely different person. "There is an increasing probability of a full-blown COVID-19 pandemic that could infect as many as 100 million Americans, with a loss of life of as many as 1–2 million souls," he wrote.

This was actually Navarro's second memo warning of mass death and economic calamity. The first time, he was pushing Trump to enact the China travel ban. This time, he was making the case for billions in immediate spending on treatments and vaccines. Trump was pissed that Navarro put his warnings in writing.

The three workweeks that followed, from February 24 to March 13, were three weeks of tragic missed opportunities. The stock markets set the tone: The Dow dropped more than a thousand points on the 24th. Trump tried to calm the markets by tweeting, "The Coronavirus is very much under control in the USA" and "Stock Market starting to look very good to me!" Health experts had ample reason to believe he was wrong about containment, but Trump's tweet set a narrative that Fox and other right-wing sources supported. For wannabe stars like Regan, who played a femme fatale version of Hannity, the incentives were clear: Trump worshiper Lou Dobbs was Regan's lead-in, and he had by far the highest ratings of anyone on Fox Business, so she said whatever she had to say to keep Dobbs's fans, like Trump, watching. On February 25, she teed up Trump 2020 spokeswoman Kayleigh McEnany to hail Trump for protecting the country. McEnany had taken a circuitous path onto Fox's airwaves: She started out as a booker for Mike Huckabee's weekend talk show and sought a promotion, but Fox said no. "She was dying to get on air," an exec said. So she left Fox during the 2016 campaign and joined CNN as a professional pundit, then leapt to the GOP, then she was back on Fox as a regular guest, rehearsing for her future role as White House press secretary. Trump must have concluded that she had an ability to lie just as well as he did.

On Regan's show, McEnany said Trump "will always protect American citizens. We will not see diseases like the coronavirus come here." It was a humiliating thing to say since the virus was already spreading from person to person, town to town. Yet "Trish didn't challenge her," a Fox staffer said. "She just sat there." But that was the job as Regan understood it: Don't rock the Trump boat. Keep it afloat.

"The flu is so much worse"

Fox's stars should have stopped and smelled the Clorox.

On February 26, Fox News HQ instituted what it called "extensive commercial grade cleaning procedures" to protect from the coronavirus. But Trump bootlickers were on the air, in freshly cleaned studios, invoking the common flu as a way of downplaying the new threat. "No one's talking about the flu," Fox Business host Kennedy Montgomery moaned. "The flu is so much worse." She meant that tens of thousands of Americans die each year due to the flu, even with therapeutics and vaccines. But there were no therapeutics or vaccines for the coronavirus, so it was even *more* dangerous; that's why she should have been raising the alarm, not trying to silence it.

As the number of cases ballooned and the CDC warned that "disruption to everyday life might be severe" and the bottom fell out of the stock market, Democrats said Trump wasn't taking the threat seriously enough. Trump rebuffed them and claimed the virus was "very well under control in our country." He was lulled into complacency, at least in part, by Fox's downplaying of the disease.

Fox's overarching story line was set: The damn Democrats were unfairly using the virus as a cudgel against Trump. One night Laura Ingraham's show screamed "LEFT WEAPONIZING CORONA-VIRUS FEARS." The next night: "LEFT TRYING TO PANIC AMERICANS." This "coronavirus is being weaponized" message whipped all around right-wing media, from Rush Limbaugh's radio show to Donald Trump Jr.'s Twitter feed and back to *Fox & Friends* and *Hannity*. Some Trump allies accused news outlets of covering the coronavirus just to wound Trump. "They think this is going to be what brings down the president. That's what this is all about," acting chief of staff Mick Mulvaney said to the audience of the Conservative Political Action Conference 2020 (CPAC) on February 28. That night, at a rally in North Charleston, South Carolina, Trump ripped into the Democrats and said, "This is their new hoax," triggering one of those exhausting multiday debates about what-he-said and what-he-meant. The liberal outcast on *The Five*, Juan Williams, argued against the rest of the cast and said Trump's talk was dangerous. No, Williams said, Trump wasn't literally saying the virus was a hoax, but he was inflaming partisan tensions and giving his fans permission to dismiss the danger. The takeaway was "you don't have anything to worry about," Williams warned.

This shit went on for weeks. One producer told me about being chastised for booking an infectious disease expert who dramatically foretold the danger from the virus. The producer recalled being told by his show's anchor, "Book a doctor that's not going to panic our viewers and won't slam Trump."

Of course, Fox News was far from alone in minimizing the threat. Limbaugh spread false statements on the radio every weekday, saying irresponsible things like "the coronavirus is the common cold, folks." Mainstream news sources aired mixed messages about the severity of Covid-19 versus the seasonal flu. Many prominent Democrats were late to perceive the threat just as many Republicans were. Educating the public was a widely shared responsibility, with mayors and governors and hospitals and media outlets all playing a part. So when the death toll spiked, the blame was widely shared as well. But Fox's commentary was uniquely impactful because it influenced the president the most. Trump had the loudest voice in the country and Hannity had the highest perch in cable news. The greater the power, the greater the responsibility, and they blew it in late February and early March. Urging people to stay calm is one thing, but they did something more—they gave their audience license to ignore accurate information about the threat. Ingraham ridiculed "panic pushers." Hannity said the news coverage was "beyond despicable." The president, in turn, was three or five steps behind the curve the entire time. He called in to Hannity on March 4, talked about the virus in the past tense, accidentally called it "corona flu," and praised himself for stopping "tremendous numbers of people coming in from China," even though the virus was now rapidly spreading within the U.S. Hannity asked a single semi-difficult question that foreshadowed where the country would end up: "For those Americans that might be fearful tonight, to those that might be talking about, well, potential, down the road, we will close down schools, and maybe there'll be more telecommuting kind of working situations, what do you say to them?"

"Well," Trump said, "I just say that it's, you know, a very, very small number in this country. And we're going to try and keep it that way as much as possible."

That was it. In the forty-minute phone call, Trump did nothing to prepare Americans for the inevitable shutdowns that were already being implemented in Washington State and contemplated by other states.

Hannity was actually a little bit baffled by his friend—because he knew that Fox was making plans to hunker down. Suzanne Scott had set up an executive task force at the end of February to make contingency plans for the looming pandemic. The execs consulted with doctors, dramatically increased the amount of cleaning in the building, and talked about how to keep the network on the air if the city shut down. On March 2, Scott decided to cancel the annual advertiser showcase that Fox was going to hold at the end of the month. On March 6, she and Jay Wallace held a company-wide conference call to talk about safety protocols. On March 9, staffers tested their telecommuting options to work out the kinks in case it became required.

A hand sanitizer station was added outside every door at Fox. In-person meetings were cut back. Some TV guests were asked to join via Skype instead of coming into the studio. But Hannity and other Fox stars still talked out of both sides of their mouths. One minute Hannity was saying the virus was "serious"; the next minute he was accusing other media outlets of "sowing fear." Many segments were framed to support Trump and mock anyone who was taking the virus more seriously than the president. Pete Hegseth said, "The more I learn about this, the less there is to worry about." Jeanine Pirro said, "If you listen to the mainstream media, it's time to buy the family cemetery plot." A month later, Pirro was broadcasting her show from the back of a truck in order to maintain social distance. She was calling the White House and leaning on aides to get more masks to a New York hospital she favored. But in early March her mission was to stay on the Trump script. Trump was modeling worst behaviors instead of best practices: His CDC said older Americans should limit travel, yet he flew to Mar-a-Lago the weekend of March 6 and vowed to continue holding rallies despite the obvious dangers. His aides said they could not get through to him about the severity of the threat. That's why Tucker Carlson was called in.

On Saturday, March 7, Carlson answered a call from a White House aide. He drove two-plus hours across Florida, from his winter home near Naples to Palm Beach, and tried to talk some sense into Trump.

Carlson kept secret the name of the aide who'd asked him to come. He told only his wife and his executive producer ahead of time about the trip. "I felt I had a moral obligation to be useful in whatever small way I could," he told *Vanity Fair*. "I don't have any actual authority. I'm just a talk show host. But I felt—and my wife strongly felt—that I had a moral obligation to try and be helpful in whatever way possible."

Other Fox stars were regulars at Mar-a-Lago, but Carlson was a first-timer. He asked the Secret Service to help him get in and out discreetly . . . but wound up smack-dab in the middle of a fifty-first birthday bash for Trump Jr.'s girlfriend, Kimberly Guilfoyle. The party, bankrolled by Trump pals and businessmen who wanted to visit the resort, featured disco balls and a "Trump Train" dance set to Gloria Estefan's "Rhythm Is Gonna Get You."

"So, Kimberly, how old are you?" the president joked when it was time to cut the cake. "No, I'm not going to ask you that." He then talked about how young and beautiful Guilfoyle looked, and how she'd done "an incredible job" for his reelection campaign. After the crowd sang "Happy Birthday," Guilfoyle grabbed the mic and chanted "four more years!" The ballroom looked like a *Fox & Friends* booker's dream: Eric Trump, Rudy Giuliani, Matt Gaetz, Lindsey Graham, Charlie Kirk, Richard Grenell. But this was not Carlson's normal scene. He'd never been to Mar-a-Lago in his life. When Carlson had one-on-one time with the president that night, "I said exactly what I've said on TV, which is this could be really bad. My view is that we may have missed the point where we can control it."

Carlson was right about that. In a later commentary, he decried "government incompetence" and described the "devastating bottle-neck" in testing that "may have killed people." He knew about the testing problems firsthand, because it turned out that Guilfoyle's birthday party was a petri dish for the virus. Several people who were at Mar-a-Lago on the 7th were sick by Friday the 13th. Fox management tried to obtain a test for Carlson but couldn't get ahold of one. The Trump administration failed everyone, even Trump's favorite network.

Even Carlson's in-person plea didn't affect Trump right away. On Monday, March 9, the president tweeted, "So last year 37,000 Americans died from the common Flu. It averages between 27,000 and 70,000 per year. Nothing is shut down, life & the economy go on. At this moment there are 546 confirmed cases of CoronaVirus, with 22 deaths. Think about that!" Carlson criticized Trump that night, though not by name, when he said, "People you trust, people you probably voted for, have spent weeks minimizing what is clearly a very serious problem." A related problem was that many of Carlson's A-list colleagues were complicit in the "minimizing." Hannity denounced media "hysteria" one hour later, saying, "This scaring the living hell out of people—I see it, again, as like, let's bludgeon Trump with this new hoax." On Tuesday, March 10, he compared coronavirus deaths to gun violence deaths in Chicago without noting that shootings are not contagious. On Wednesday, March 11, he compared the virus to the 2009 H1N1 swine flu outbreak without explaining that Covid-19 was more novel and more transmissible. He was grasping at hopefully sterile straws—and his friends said it was Trump's fault.

"Sean didn't want to get ahead of the president," a Fox source said.

Another staffer likened Hannity to a presidential parrot. He could say whatever he wanted, as a Trump supporter; do whatever he wanted, as a Trump adviser; with virtually zero oversight.

To Hannity, this autonomy was a point of pride. When a reporter from *Newsweek* asked him, "Have any of your bosses at Fox

News told you to change the tone of your reporting and opinion regarding coronavirus?" Hannity said, "Absolutely not."

I wondered: What if they had? What if Hannity had been prodded to scrap his ridiculous flu rhetoric and prepare people for the looming shutdown? What if Trump and Hannity had introduced the public to concepts like social distancing and flattening the curve two weeks earlier? Or just one week earlier? Every day could have made a difference in the ultimate death toll.

But no one had the backbone or the stomach to manage prime time. When outsiders pointed to Scott as the source of the problem, her allies pointed over to executive vice president Meade Cooper, who was in charge of the opinion shows. Cooper held Bill Shine's old job, but she was "not respected" like Shine, a well-placed source said. Some of Cooper's colleagues said she was effective at mediating intramural disputes, say, between Juan Williams and Jesse Watters, but was rolled over by Hannity and Ingraham. Others said blaming an EVP was a cop-out and that Scott and the Murdochs were responsible. But Lachlan was hardly plugged in to Fox's programming problems in early March; he was far away in L.A. and finishing a deal to buy a streaming service called Tubi. And Rupert was trying not to get sick himself. He and his family canceled their plans for an eighty-ninth birthday party in his honor.

"Hazardous to our viewers"

On the same night that Sean Hannity condemned the Democrats' "new hoax," Trish Regan said coronavirus warnings from Democrats were "yet another attempt to impeach the president."

Trump acolytes like Regan were still in denial about the looming danger, and the result was enormous turmoil inside Fox.

"The attempt to deflect and blame the media and Democrats from Trish Regan, Sean Hannity, Laura Ingraham, Lou Dobbs, Jesse Watters, and Greg Gutfeld—instead of addressing the coronavirus—is really irresponsible and hazardous to our viewers," a Fox producer wrote to me. "It's also ironic they're accusing the media of fear-mongering given our infamous coverage of the migrant caravan back in 2018."

During Regan's reckless segment, a graphic over her shoulder said "CORONAVIRUS IMPEACHMENT SCAM." Regan played clips from other networks, including a clip of me saying "The president should lead, or else he should get out of the way." I thought that was a pretty mild assessment, but to Regan it was scandalous. She exclaimed, "This is impeachment all over again."

Regan was singing from the same song sheet as Hannity. But when Regan's idiocy went viral, Fox bosses cringed—and she wasn't nearly as popular or powerful as Hannity, or even Dobbs for that matter, so by the cold, hard math of TV, she was in trouble. Whether true or not, word spread around HQ that Regan had been told ahead of time to tone down her "scam" monologue, but went ahead with it anyway. Management saw an opening to cut her loose and send a message to everyone on staff: no more Covid-19 denialism.

The following few days were a blur. The NBA suspended its season. Broadway theaters went dark. Disney World closed. "This is the biggest story since 9/11," *New York Times* executive editor Dean Baquet said to his staff. At Fox, Scott and Wallace sent out a memo that attempted to set a similar tone. "Please keep in mind that viewers rely on us to stay informed during a crisis of this magnitude and we are providing an important public service to our audience by functioning as a resource for all Americans," they wrote on Thursday the 12th.

Fox & Friends didn't get the message right away. On the morning of the 13th, Ainsley Earhardt said it's "the safest time to fly," in spite of Fox's in-house prohibition on all nonessential business travel. Geraldo Rivera spread a debunked way to test for the virus—"if you can hold your breath for ten seconds, then you don't have this disease"—without any objections from Earhardt or the other hosts. Jerry Falwell Jr. suggested that Covid-19 was a bioweapon created by North Korea and China. As media blogs filled up with video clips of the wacky segments, Scott scolded the producers. "You will have a doctor on set every day," she told them, and Falwell will not be booked again.

In retrospect, Friday the 13th was the clear turning point for Fox—and, not coincidentally, also for the president. Just as the virus was a threat to Fox's audience, virus denialism was a threat to Fox's business. By the end of the day Regan's show was put on hiatus, ostensibly so that Fox Business could shift resources to stock market hours, but everyone got the intended message. Scott was telling them all to cut the crap.

"It's hard not to be cynical," a Fox producer said of Regan's removal, "when we've seen even more inflammatory and dangerous rhetoric from some of the other prime time hosts with no push back." Two weeks later, when Regan was hoisted overboard, Trump rushed to her defense and retweeted her fans, including one who asked, "How is that any different than what Hannity has said? Neither said anything wrong." Regan felt she was scapegoated, but agreed to have her contract paid out in exchange for her silence. By the end of the year she was a regular on Newsmax.

As New York City shut down and affluent New Yorkers fled to their Hamptons homes and Jersey Shore beach houses, Fox HQ emptied out. About two hundred staffers still needed to come in to operate control rooms and keep the network on the air; for their service, they received an extra $75 per day, Fox's version of hazard pay. Scott knew it was only a matter of time before a staffer tested positive for Covid-19. (At least six, including *Fox & Friends Weekend* host Jedediah Bila, fell ill in the first couple of weeks.) Scott directed the installation of dozens of home studios for anchors, and the network operated remotely for months.

Former *Fox & Friends* host Gretchen Carlson laughed out loud when she saw the show enforcing social distancing all of a sudden. "Just 2 days ago we were all nuts & overreacting," she quipped on Twitter. Now the hosts were placed in different corners of the studio. Internally this was called "going to boxes" because each person was in a different box on-screen. Fox's other big studio show, *The Five*, went to boxes too, and Watters expressed regret about previously dismissing the pandemic. Media critics said there was a U-turn underway, but that gave Fox too much credit—the shows were still full up with propaganda, it was just framed differently. "America has had the best response to coronavirus in the world," Congressman Matt Gaetz of Florida, a Trump loyalist, said on Sunday, March 15. Trump campaign aide Jenna Ellis appeared on the same show and said the crisis was going to be Trump's "shining moment."

There were fewer Democrats on the air than usual, but there were no shortages of Republican commentators. The biggest change was the sudden number of new doctors on the air, mostly of the Trump-friendly variety. Dr. Mehmet Oz, a member of Trump's Council on Sports, Fitness and Nutrition, began to appear multiple times a day. It was a fancy bit of corporate synergy, as Fox's local stations were partners on Oz's syndicated daytime talk show. Unbeknownst to most, Fox and the administration shared docs: Medical contributor Dr. Janette Nesheiwat advised the White House, and at least two other contributors were in regular touch with Trump administration officials. Trump posted praise for Dr. Nicole Saphier, who used his tweet to promote her book *Make America Healthy Again.*

While the home studios were being set up, early morning anchor Heather Childers unnerved staffers when she showed up to work on the 18th "sweating, visibly sick," according to a staffer. She coughed and sneezed on the air but went to see a doctor after the show and insisted she was fine. Colleagues were scared and execs were pissed, so Childers was told to stay home and remained off the air. In a classically Fox move, Childers tweeted to the president when she tested negative for Covid-19, and she encouraged fans to lobby Fox to let her return to work. None of her weird Twitter pleas worked. She never appeared on Fox again, and she quietly reemerged months later as an anchor on Newsmax.

By the week of March 23, the *Fox & Friends* hosts were all in remote studios. Almost everyone who wanted a home setup had one; there were other options too, like trucks that drove to the homes of Juan Williams and Jeanine Pirro. Williams climbed in the back of a truck each weekday to cohost *The Five.* At Martha MacCallum's home in New Jersey, there was a new rule: No streaming video during the 7 p.m. hour, because it could slow down her connection to the control room. "Every night at some point in the show I hear the dog barking and running over my head upstairs," she said. The hosts admitted they were lucky to have these problems; at many other media companies, people were losing their jobs. But there was no risk of that at Fox. The ratings in March surpassed February's record-high. All the cable newsers were up, but Fox was still the total-viewer champion.

Fox employed the same trick Roger Ailes had used after Hurricane Katrina: an immediate shift toward optimistic "getting America back on its feet" stories. States were still in the beginning stages of shutting down when Sunday night host Steve Hilton said, on March 22, "You know that famous phrase, 'the cure is worse than the disease'? That is exactly the territory we're hurtling towards." Trump watched Hilton on his Genie DVR a couple hours later, then tweeted in all caps, "WE CANNOT LET THE CURE BE WORSE THAN THE PROBLEM ITSELF."

This was the Trump-Fox feedback loop at its loopiest. On March 23 the confirmed U.S. death toll was under one thousand, and models showed it on a path to surpass a hundred thousand, which meant the shutdown would need to continue for months, but commentary on Fox triggered days of confusing, contradictory get-back-to-work chatter weeks before it was rational. "I would love to have the country opened up and just raring to go by Easter," Trump said on March 24. He backtracked a few days later—which meant those days were wasted. A better focus would have been on supply shortages, problems with the Paycheck Protection Program, outbreaks at veterans homes and aircraft carriers—anything else, really. But those issues were depressing and damaging to Trump's political standing. "Reopen America" was uplifting and easy to sell as an us-versus-them story. In other words, the perfect Fox story.

Reality intruded as hospitals in New York City ran out of places to store dead bodies. Every six minutes another American died from the disease, and everyone knew the true number was even higher, since many died at home without having been tested. The suffering was most pronounced in Trump's home borough, Queens, at Elmhurst Hospital Center, where sick residents lined up in the cold and prayed for a chance to see a doctor. Elmhurst was already out of beds, and would soon be out of ventilators too. The hallways were jammed with patients who could barely stand or say their own names. The scene was far worse than any of the vague, hopeful pablum issued by the White House would have led you to believe.

Trump called in to Hannity at 9 p.m. on March 26 to try to spin his way out of it. Hannity started the show with his usual sermon about Democrats endangering the country. On this night, he ripped into New York governor Andrew Cuomo and New York City mayor Bill de Blasio. Hannity accused the two Democrats of "politicizing this national emergency" by criticizing Trump and said "both of you need to stop." Then he politicized the national emergency himself with the help of his caller, Donald from Queens.

"Is he there?" Hannity asked his producers. He heard nothing, and momentarily freaked out. He waited for the control room to tell him what to do.

Then came a Voice of God, just the savior this host needed: "I am, I'm right here. Hi, Sean."

"Mr. President!" Hannity exclaimed. "Thank you . . ."

And they were off. Trump began by flattering his facilitator: He claimed that he had postponed a critical phone call with Chinese president Xi Jinping in order to talk with Hannity. This interview, if you could even call it that, was a love-in and a lie-fest. But there was a little bit of truth embedded in Trump's first comment. He really did keep the Chinese president waiting. "I am talking to him at ten-thirty, right after this call," Trump told Hannity.

Beijing noticed Trump's televised stunt and kept him waiting for a while after 10:30, according to a White House source. Trump tweeted at 1:19 in the morning, Eastern time, that he "just finished a very good conversation with President Xi."

Unfortunately it was his forty-minute chat with Hannity that was more consequential to the body politic. Trump's remarks proved that he still didn't fundamentally grasp the urgency of the pandemic. He professed doubt about the computer models that showed a catastrophe ahead. His default setting was disbelief. It was where he was most comfortable.

The next day, the president called the host with a question: "How'd we do?"

Hannity knew the real meaning of the question was "How did we rate?"

The two men still spoke by phone almost every day, but the purpose of this particular call was disgraceful. In the midst of a crippling pandemic, on a day when another 393 Americans would die gasping for air without their loved ones by their side, the president needed to know about his ratings.

For the record, and I can't believe I'm even getting into this, the ratings for *Hannity* the night before were higher than usual, but it wasn't primarily due to Trump's presence, it was due to the pandemic. On the night Trump called in, Tucker Carlson ended his 8 p.m. hour with 5 million viewers, and Hannity started with 5.6 million, which means about one in ten viewers tuned in specifically to see Hannity and the president. The rest would have been watching anyway. Once POTUS was on the phone, viewership ticked up to 5.7 million, and by the time he hung up, it had ticked down to 5.4 million, the same way some Trump rallygoers always left before the end of the show. The truth was, the president was not a huge ratings magnet anymore. Almost no one flipped from CNN or MSNBC to see him speak on Fox. Trump had a base, the base was hooked on Fox, and the base wasn't growing. The ratings data was a warning sign for Trump's reelection bid—and Trump's obsession with his ratings in the midst of a pandemic was a warning sign for the country.

True to form, Trump finally came to grips with the deadly reality when he saw it on TV. "I've been watching them bring in trailer trucks—freezer trucks, they're freezer trucks, because they can't handle the bodies, there are so many of them," he said on March 29. "This is essentially in my community, in Queens, Queens, New York." The next day, he raised the goalposts for the U.S. response, claiming that a total of one hundred to two hundred thousand deaths would be "a very good job" by his administration.

Two hundred thousand deaths, a very good job.

On Trump's final day in office, the U.S. death toll surpassed four hundred thousand souls.

"No reason to go backwards"

Coronavirus was, the anti-Fox group Media Matters said, a "low point in the network's shameful history."

Other progressive activists all but accused the Murdochs of being accomplices to murder. One advocacy group tried and failed to sue Fox. Among the critics was an estranged member of the family, Laura Ingraham's older brother Curtis, who called Fox "the killing channel."

As hospitals in New York City filled up with acutely sick patients, a new conspiracy theory was hatched on social media. Lunatics claimed that the hospitals were actually empty, and they stalked the entrances and parking lots with their cell phone cameras to come up with "proof." Look, they said, there aren't many cars in the parking lot! A nurse at Elmhurst, Dr. Ashley Bray, heard this shit secondhand. "They think the hospital is empty," she said, positively stunned, and she wondered, *Where are they getting this stuff?* The answer, in part, was Fox. The network often mainstreamed ideas from the far right fringe, and that's exactly what Fox News contributor Sara Carter did on March 29, during a segment on a Sunday night talk show. "You can see it on Twitter," she said. "People are saying, 'Film your hospital,' people are driving by their hospitals and they're not seeing—in the ones that I'm seeing—they're not seeing anybody in the parking lots. They're not seeing anybody drive up. So, people are wondering what's going inside the hospital."

Bray's reaction: She *wished* her hospital was empty. "This is worse than war," she said.

Anyone who thought Fox would run out of ways to downplay the emergency didn't appreciate the network's capacity for self-deception and diversion. When the death toll in the U.S. surpassed Italy, on April 11, it was Jeanine Pirro's turn to interview Trump. She didn't ask about the awful milestone, or his impossible Easter goal, or his asinine gaslighting of the public. Instead she brought up his "relationship with God" (nonexistent, according to multiple biographers) and asked about "reopening the country" when companies were still figuring out how to shut down.

The ugly truth was that it was in the shared interest of both Fox and the White House not to look backward. Press secretary Stephanie Grisham literally said so: "There's no reason to go backwards and figure out tick-tocks of what happened when."

When media critics did revisit Fox's thoughtless coverage, Hannity lashed out. He said, "This program has always taken the coronavirus seriously and we've never called the virus a hoax." He retained one of the president's outside lawyers and threatened to sue *The New York Times* over its scrutiny of his Covid-19 commentary. Hannity's PR people argued that other media outlets had soft-pedaled coronavirus around the same time Fox had—but most of the links they provided were to news stories from January and early February, before the virus was spreading rapidly in major U.S. metro areas. Hannity's most damaging remarks, like "new hoax," were made in March.

"The Trump party line swaps new lies for old," David Frum wrote in *The Atlantic*. "Whereas once the ideological enforcers called concern over the virus a hoax, now they say that it's a hoax to remember they said it was a hoax."

Poll after poll showed that Fox viewers were less concerned about the virus than avid consumers of other news sources, strongly suggesting a linkage between the network's commentary and the audience's beliefs. The Knight Foundation and Gallup found that 57 percent of respondents with a "conservative news diet" believed that the new virus was "less deadly than or as deadly as the flu." The Pew Research Center asked people to identify their main source for political news, then they asked a series of questions about the virus. Compared with all U.S. adults and CNN and MSNBC fans, Fox fans were less likely to say the outbreak was a major threat to their personal health; more likely to say the threat was exaggerated; and more confident that local hospitals would be able to withstand the surge. Fox fans were also more likely to express confidence that a vaccine would be available in the next few months, contrary to the expectations of virtually every expert. And they were far more likely to say that they treated Trump's televised Covid-19 briefings as a source of news. Baier's ratings-challenged hour was suddenly No. 1 on all of cable because the briefings often filled up his 6 p.m. slot. And Fox didn't care if they cut away from the show. One day, knowing Trump was going to swallow up his entire hour again, Baier sat in Fox's designated seat in the briefing room, and Trump was thrilled.

"It's an honor to have Bret Baier here," he said.

"It's the only way I could get on, Mr. President," Baier quipped.

The exchange reflected the fact that the briefings had emerged as a rally replacement for Trump's ego, a new stage for his narcissistic show. Trump touted his ratings ("so high," "record ratings," "through the roof") at least seven different times during the height of the pandemic. It was grotesque. He watched *Fox & Friends* in the morning; hosted his own TV show in the briefing room in the afternoon; watched the reviews of his show at night; and examined the ratings the next day. This was never healthy, and it was especially hurtful amid a public health emergency. In Fox corporate, numerous execs wished Trump would watch less TV. They thought the president was a moron (one of the many foul words they used), and they continued to question his mental health. But they wouldn't dare say so publicly. I couldn't get anyone to truly look backward and reflect on how we had gotten here.

"I've been watching you"

"Laura," Dr. Stephen Smith said on Laura Ingraham's show April 2, "I think this is the beginning of the end of the pandemic. I'm very serious."

Smith ran a center for infectious diseases in New Jersey. He said he had treated dozens of Covid-19 patients with a regimen of hydroxychloroquine and azithromycin and none of them had to be intubated. He spoke with the confidence of a man who had found a silver bullet. "Well Dr. Smith," Ingraham said, "all the naysayers and the people dismissing this, just wait, okay? The good news is coming."

Ingraham's promotion of hydroxychloroquine, or HCQ for short, ordinarily used to treat malaria, rheumatoid arthritis, and lupus, began in mid-March, three days after a blockchain investor and an attorney published an official-looking paper on Google Docs pitching HCQ as a Covid-19 treatment. Ingraham had the lawyer, Gregory Rigano, on her show March 16; Carlson booked him on March 18; and Trump mentioned the drug for the first time on March 19. "It's been around for a long time," said Trump, so if it doesn't help Covid-19 patients, at least "it's not going to kill anybody."

There was, in fact, a very real risk of death from careless uses of the drug. But Fox glommed onto HCQ carelessly, talking about the drug in dozens of segments, even though evidence of its effectiveness was limited and flawed. The original Google Doc was taken down by Google, for example, for violating its terms of service. A small French study of the drug, cited by Trump, was criticized by the very same professional society that published the study. Ingraham touted whatever anecdote came along each day—on March 19 her show booked Dr. William Grace, whom she called an "oncologist with Lenox Hill Hospital in New York City," and Grace said, "We have not had a death in our hospital" while seeming to credit HCQ. While his drug endorsement whipped around right-wing media, an eagle-eyed viewer pointed out that Grace wasn't employed by Lenox Hill; "he is a private physician who has admitting privileges," the hospital said. Fox News ran a correction on the web, and Twitter forced Ingraham to remove the misinformation from her Twitter feed, but the misrepresentation was never addressed on TV. It went on and on like this. Fox's rah-rah segments gave false hope to the president and millions of viewers. The segments also shifted attention from the government's failures to protect the public. As *The New York Times* put it, Trump's media supporters have "appeared more interested in discussing miracle cures than testing delays or ventilator shortages."

By March 31, the drug had been mentioned more than five hundred times on Fox's airwaves. Some guests rightly urged caution, like Dr. William Haseltine, who told daytime host Dana Perino that "it's sad to me that people are promoting that drug." Hyping the anecdotal evidence was "irresponsible," he said. Ingraham played that sound bite for her much bigger audience and called it "completely disgusting." Privately, some people at Fox News thought the word "disgusting" applied to Ingraham's drug-pushing, but no one intervened. Ingraham's executive producer was on paternity leave. On-lookers disagreed about whether Meade Cooper or Suzanne Scott or someone else was at fault.

The morning after Smith said that HCQ represented "the beginning of the end of the pandemic," he walked into the White House, spread-sheets in hand, for a meeting with the president.

"I've been watching you," Trump told him in the Oval Office.

Laura Ingraham was there too. She set up the visit for Smith and cardiologist Ramin Oskoui, two members of what she playfully called her "medicine cabinet." This meeting was deadly serious, though. Ingraham and the docs pitched Trump on the dreamy pos-sibilities of HCQ. Trump told FDA commissioner Stephen Hahn to attend too, because Trump was pressuring Hahn to be more pub-licly supportive of the drug. "Hydroxychloroquine—I don't know, it's looking like it's having some good results," Trump said at his press briefing later in the day.

The Washington Post reported, "Some senior Republicans who heard about the meeting cringed about a television host's special access to offer medical advice to the president." But those "very senior Republicans" never spoke out. Meanwhile, the Oval Office door remained wide open to Ingraham, who was back on April 14 for another advisory meeting. HCQ trials continued, but most Fox shows stopped hyping the drug after the FDA, the NIH, and the De-partment of Veterans Affairs all issued cautions. The FDA explicitly cautioned against its use "outside of the hospital setting or a clinical trial due to risk of heart rhythm problems." Ingraham, undeterred, continued to highlight anecdotal success stories and urged the FDA to yank the "unnecessary warning." And on May 18 the president said he was personally taking HCQ as a preventative drug, since he might have been exposed to Covid-19 through one of his personal valets at the White House. His evidence of HCQ's benefits? "I get a lot of positive calls about it." Including from Ingraham.

No one outside the Fox bubble knew whether to believe that he was really taking the drug. He was able and willing to lie about everything. Most Americans recognized that by 2020; even half of Republicans told pollsters that they lacked trust in what the president said about the pandemic. But his base, his "Fox News Republicans," still insisted that he told the truth. These supporters were so alienated from the rest of American society, so distrustful of institutions, so disdainful of the non-Fox news media, that they watched Fox and trusted Trump almost exclusively. But it was to their own detriment. They watched shows that mocked liberal "safe spaces" but from their own safe space, which distorted their understanding of a rapidly changing country.

"He Wants Trump TV"

In the weeks before he died in 2017, Roger Ailes told one of his mentees that Trump's win proved that the cable TV model also applied to politics. When there were only a few broadcast networks, all sharing the same more or less genteel sensibility, politics had to be broad—candidates had to appeal to the whole of the country. Provocation and extremism were turn-offs. But those same techniques were turn-ons in the cable model. Cable channels weren't for everyone, they were for specific demographics. The winners knew how to rabidly excite their base and blow off everyone else. Turn the levers just right and you ended up with the monstrosity at work at the end of the decade: an untouchable politician protected by his untouchable media apparatus.

Fox's cable power extended to the internet, where microtargeting on social networks meant that candidates didn't have to cultivate just a single base, they could tell different stories to different audiences simultaneously. Lachlan and Rupert still had to figure out Fox's position in that world. But the network's website increasingly functioned as a propaganda workhorse. The trashier FoxNews.com became, the more popular it became.

In accordance with Newton's third law, Fox's extremism provoked a reaction from the left. James, the odd son out in the Murdoch family, looked at Fox News with ever-growing horror. To him, Fox and Trump both kept proving that there was no bottom, validating his decision to break off ties with the company. For the time being he remained on the board of the family's publishing business News Corp, though, which made for some awkward directors' meetings. James was "testing the proposition of making change from the inside," a friend said, justifying the board seat.

People in James's orbit floated a scenario that could put him back in charge of Fox News sometime down the road. Lachlan, James, Elisabeth, and Prudence all held power through their shares in the Murdoch Family Trust. In the event of Rupert's death, these people suggested, James could partner with his sisters to wrest control of Fox Corp from Lachlan. Sources said that Elisabeth would surely side with James, and Prudence likely would as well—three votes against one. Was this a serious possibility, or just a liberal fantasy? "Time will tell," a source said. Meantime, every step James took in the outside world burnished his reputation with an eye toward a shareholder fight in the future. He and his wife stepped up their donations to Biden's campaign and bided their time.

Was there any other threat on the horizon? Anything that could derail the Fox-Trump train? When I met a confidant of Rupert and Lachlan's for breakfast in early 2020, the person said that the most immediate risk to Fox, far more concerning than shareholder fight fantasies or existential threats to the cable TV industry, was the Fox News addict in the Oval Office.

"Trump wants control," the insider said. "He wants Trump TV." If Trump didn't win reelection, the theory went, multiple billionaires stood ready to bankroll a media empire of Donald's own with both television and internet components. He wouldn't need Fox anymore; he would be in business against Fox. This possibility was clearly on the mind of the men running Fox Corp.

I told the insider that I'd always figured Rupert and Lachlan would give Trump a prime time show for his post–White House years. "Think bigger," the insider said. With an entire network, Ivanka could have a show, and Don Jr. could have a show, and the Trump brand could span politics and culture and entertainment. The Trump 2020 campaign was already testing this premise with webcasts. What would America prefer to watch—people on Fox talking about the Trumps, or the real thing, straight from Mar-a-Lago?

I was still quite skeptical. Trump's webcasts were getting minuscule audiences. And streaming services were very hard to get off the ground. Fox was learning that firsthand with Fox Nation, a $5.99-a-month bundle for super-fans that was struggling to make it past the 250,000 subscriber mark. Netflix, Fox Nation was most certainly not.

But maybe Trump could pull it off. Maybe he could outfox the Murdochs. "Trump is like Fox's Frankenstein," one of Fox's stars told me. "They helped make him and he's out of control. And no one knows how they will do once he's gone."

THE COLLAPSE

"Looking for a new outlet"

"Suzanne, the president is trying to reach you."

No matter how friendly Fox was, Trump always wanted more. That's why, as the pandemic raged, he called Suzanne Scott multiple times. Sources said he bitched and moaned about "mean" anchors and "nasty" commentators. Simultaneously, however, with the Fox hosts he deemed "fair" he collaborated to change the subject— to shift attention from the gutting death toll to the origins of the Russia probe.

Trump dubbed it "Obamagate," and accused the former president of vague, unspecified crimes. He called in to *Fox & Friends* on a Friday morning, and the hosts let him ramble on about "Obamagate" for twenty minutes before they asked a single question about the worst economic collapse since the Great Depression. When I called out this misconduct, Trump attacked me—"@brianstelter is just a poor man's lapdog for AT&T!" he wrote on Twitter—and his MAGA trolls unleashed hours of vile attacks. Hannity kept it going the next night, accusing me of being complicit in "one hoax after another." This machine was the modern-day version of "*Lügenpresse*," the

Nazi slur for "lying press" that was used to destroy truth and cover up crimes in and around Germany in the 1930s. Media bashing held the base together. And it stopped unpleasant truths about Trump from getting to the people who needed to know.

Knight and Gallup polling in April found that 94 percent of Americans who only cited Fox and other conservative outlets as their top sources thought Trump was doing a good job handling the crisis. Among Americans with a mixed news diet, only 36 percent said the same thing. Conservative-news junkies were also far more likely to say the media was giving the virus too much attention. Incredibly, this continued to be a talking point on Fox well into April, even after the U.S. had more confirmed deaths than any other country in the world. "We're going to have fewer fatalities from this than from the flu," Fox News contributor Bill Bennett, a former U.S. secretary of education, said on *Fox & Friends* April 13. By May 13, more than seventy-six thousand Americans were dead from the virus, and the total would have been unknowably higher if social distancing rules had been relaxed sooner, like Bennett wanted.

For all of Fox's service journalism and viewer Q&A segments and social distancing PSAs and added hours of live coverage, it was stuff like that—anti-journalistic arguments and crusades for miracle cures—that defined Fox's brand. When guests like Bennett embarrassed the network, Fox PR people hid behind the opinion excuse: *"It's just their opinion." "That's an opinion show."* But Fox viewers strongly preferred the "opinion shows" over the news. Hannity and Ingraham were trusted, while Fox newsmen were viewed skeptically, even scornfully, by the audience. "We are trying to hold the line," an exhausted Fox journalist said in mid-May. But covering Trump accurately at Fox meant going up against the viewers and the crazy things many of them believed. When 4 p.m. anchor Neil

Cavuto warned that the president could be harmed by taking HCQ, Fox fans virtually screamed at him, and Trump retweeted messages like "CAVUTO IS AN IDIOT."

"@FoxNews is no longer the same," Trump wrote that night, because Cavuto had dared cross him. "You have more anti-Trump people, by far, than ever before. Looking for a new outlet!"

Most of Trump's threats were hollow, just like his promises, but he actually made good on this one. Continually perturbed by some of the lowest-rated shows on the Fox schedule, the weekend afternoon newscasts, he tweeted one Sunday, "@FoxNews weekend afternoons is the worst! Getting into @CNN and MSDNC territory. Watch @OANN & @newsmax instead. Much better!"

This was Trump playing *TV Guide* editor, attempting to steer his fans in new directions. He name-dropped One America News more often in 2020 than all his past years combined, to the delight of Charles Herring, the OAN boss. Behind the scenes, Herring fielded offers from prominent Trump donors to buy OAN, but Herring wouldn't part with his family's business.

Trump also began to promote Newsmax more often—perhaps owing to his calls and chats with Ruddy. But both Ruddy and Herring were in the cable TV business with a hand tied behind their backs since their channels lacked the distribution and name recognition of Fox. Trump's plugs didn't make a dent in Fox's ratings—yet.

"You have to dominate"

When protests over the murder of George Floyd erupted in Minneapolis in late May, Fox's programming was uneven. The country felt like a powder keg, with disproportionate illness and fatalities from Covid-19 among black, brown, and poor people plus massive unemployment plus viral videos of police brutality adding up to an unprecedented nationwide protest effort. Support for the Black Lives Matter movement was at record highs. Fox's "law and order" programming felt out of step amid a national dialogue about how law enforcement was failing so many Americans. But it made more sense when viewed through the frame proposed by *Vox* writer Emily VanDerWerff: "It's structured like a soap opera."

VanDerWerff wrote that Fox, particularly in prime time, "molds reality into a serialized TV drama," attacking "everything from trans rights to campus speech to Black Lives Matter to antifa, constantly shifting targets to find new boogeymen."

Trump was almost always the hero in these episodes. "What will Trump do?" was often the question. When vandals set fire to buildings in Minneapolis and violence spread to other cities, in what became the worst period of civil unrest since the 1960s, VanDerWerff's frame was readily apparent all over Fox: "Define a threat, elaborate on the threat, then propose a solution to said threat that will require viewers to keep tuning in to see how the proposed solution plays out."

Trump sounded just like the Fox pundit class when he said his solution was the use of force. "When the looting starts, the shooting starts," he tweeted, echoing the 1967 words of a notorious Miami police chief. "You have to dominate or you'll look like a bunch of jerks," he told governors. Fox viewers tuned in to see the "domination" and to hear excuses when people were caught in the crossfire. Trump's use of force at Lafayette Park (to clear a path for a presidential photo op) horrified the public, so Fox engaged in tear-gaslighting by casting doubt on the use of tear gas, even though protesters felt it in their eyes and reporters found canisters on the streets afterward. Government officials later admitted that a variety of irritants were used to disperse the crowd, but by then Fox had moved on.

Shows like *Fox & Friends* and *Tucker Carlson Tonight* kept showing old video of fires and looters, even weeks later, with insufficiently small labels on screen. I called it "riot porn." The shows pretended that the rioting was still a present-tense threat, something that could reignite at any time, even though a few nights of lawlessness had been overpowered by weeks of peaceful, powerful, sustained protest all across the country. The broken windows and graffiti on my block in midtown Manhattan had already been cleaned up—but Fox's banners claimed there was "GROWING LAWLESSNESS IN MAJOR CITIES" and hosts like Tucker Carlson said "they're destroying our cities." This too became a big narrative for the pundit in chief. Activists in Seattle occupied six city blocks in the Capitol Hill neighborhood in early June and renamed it the Capitol Hill Autonomous Zone, or CHAZ for short, in a typically lefty protest that harked back to the days of Occupy Wall Street. The local news called it an experiment in alternative community; faraway guests on Fox called it "Communist cosplay in the streets" and likened it to Mogadishu and worse. *The Seattle Times* caught FoxNews.com running fake photos—one story about Seattle was headlined "CRAZY TOWN" and illustrated with burning buildings, but the fires were from Saint Paul, Minnesota, not Seattle. Fox apologized, but the network had a nasty habit of these screwups.

Trump watched Fox's warped coverage of Seattle and claimed that "Domestic Terrorists have taken over" the city. Well-known activists had taken over six blocks, but Fox repeated Trump's lies verbatim. In the midst of all this, Fox's ad sales department had to work overtime to keep additional advertisers from bailing. A twenty-five-minute-long Carlson monologue about the "Black Lives Matter riots," declaring that the BLM movement was "definitely not about black lives," spurred yet another ad boycott. "Bye-bye Tucker Carlson!" the CEO of T-Mobile tweeted. A few weeks later CNN's Oliver Darcy broke the news that Carlson's top writer, Blake Neff, had a years-long history of posting racist and sexist remarks on an online forum, under a pseudonym. When Darcy contacted Neff for comment, he notified Fox about the incoming story, and by the time it came out, he had resigned. Fox management condemned the "horrific racist, misogynistic and homophobic behavior" and took the line that no one at Fox knew about his conduct. Carlson said the same thing when he finally commented three days later: Neff's hateful words "have no connection to the show," Carlson said. But Neff was responsible for Carlson's scripts for years. Fox braced for further advertiser defections.

Tucker's time slot was propped up by one big advertiser: My-Pillow, whose founder, infomercial star Mike Lindell, had become a cult icon at Trump rallies. Every time sponsors yanked their spots, MyPillow took their place. Hypnotized by the ads, I ordered a couple, and chalked it up to research for this book. The pillows were lumpy.

Dozens of segments about "Black Lives Matter riots" that were meant to demean the movement. Hundreds of TV segments about Antifa that fearmongered about the left. And countless segments about statues being vandalized. *This* was VanDerWerff's "serialized TV drama" in action. "If you're a Republican," columnist Paul Waldman wrote, "there's an entire cable network devoted to filling your evenings with terror." And it all distorted the president's sense of what was happening in his country. Trump didn't express concern about protesters being injured or reporters being assaulted, but he called federal authorities "to ensure damaged statues are fixed quickly" after he saw the damage on Fox, as *The Washington Post* reported. He didn't evaluate any police reform proposals, but he obsessed over the anti-police slogan "pigs in a blanket, fry 'em like bacon."

That repulsive chant was only uttered on one occasion, back in 2015, at a march by a local group in Minnesota. It did not spread nationally. But the video clip was still a staple of Hannity's show five years later. Carlson's show re-ran it in 2020 too. Trump invoked the "bacon" chant in interviews and in tweets as if it was still being screamed, all the time, and everybody knew it. This was "Fox News brain," as one of his aides said.

As a percentage of his overall TV viewing, Fox News and Fox Business actually managed to gain market share at the tail end of Trump's term, because he spent less and less time DVR-surfing to CNN and other networks. He was in a cave of his own making, and on the outside, he was told, there were threats in every direction, so it's no wonder why his speeches were so dark and scary. He marked the Fourth of July by flying to Mount Rushmore to read an anti-leftist address that included passages like this: "Our nation is witnessing a merciless campaign to wipe out our history, defame our heroes, erase our values and indoctrinate our children."

That's what America looked like, from inside his Fox cave.

"Rotten to the core"

Every morning, while the other major networks covered the summertime surge in Covid-19 cases, *Fox & Friends* began with local crime news and cultural war noise. When CHAZ was dismantled in Seattle, attention turned to Portland, where fires set by radical leftists were met by a massive federal response. It was a show of force for the Fox cameras—and a welcome distraction for a White House and an audience base that was tired of hearing about the coronavirus.

Trump was prone to talking about the virus in the past tense, when he talked about it at all. He refused to wear a mask in public, in defiance of his own government's recommendations. In a June 17 phone call with Hannity, Trump said the virus was "fading away," even as U.S. cases surged and the death toll climbed well above one hundred thousand. Eight days later, appearing again with Hannity, this time in front of MAGA-hatted supporters at a Green Bay, Wisconsin, airplane hangar, he bragged about the U.S. mortality rate and suggested the U.S. case count was overstated: "If we didn't do testing, we'd have no cases."

Deep down inside, Fox management knew the deadly truth about the virus, and their actions proved it. The company's plans for a fuller return to work were again and again postponed due to safety concerns. Staffers who weren't able to work from home were reminded, in late June, to don a mask whenever they were in shared office spaces. At the Wisconsin event with the president, audience members were required to wear masks and to have their temperatures checked. *They knew.* The Fox anchors and hosts knew. Yet they rarely challenged on the air Trump's irresponsible and ignorant conduct. "We acted like it was business as usual," one producer said with regret.

In early July, I ran the data and found that the word "coronavirus" was uttered on CNN more than twice as often as on Fox. I could almost hear Ailes's voice echoing off the walls of the editorial meetings, telling his staff that no one wanted to watch coverage of a war America was losing. Invent a war to win instead. That's what Fox did—one of Lou Dobbs's go-to banners was "LEFT'S WAR ON AMERICA"—and that's what Trump did too: He tweeted about "the radical left" and about Fox more often than the virus. In a particularly odd post one summer night, Trump bitched about Donna Brazile's presence on Fox and asked, "Where are you Roger

Ailes?" After thirty-four straight minutes of mockery (One guy tweeted to him: "Oh buddy. Sit down for a second. Oh man. I hate to be the one to tell you but . . .") Trump followed up: "I know better than anyone that my friend Roger Ailes died 3 years ago, just look at what happened to @FoxNews. We all miss Roger!!!"

That was the president—alone in the White House residence, muttering into his phone, tweeting about his dead friend.

"We all miss Roger!" was a view still shared by some of the talent, but certainly not among Fox's battalion of lawyers, who were still haunted by Ailes's abuse and the rotten culture he allowed. Several lawsuits in 2019 and 2020 alleged that a sexualized climate lingered long after Ailes was ousted. "The culture has not changed," attorney Lisa Bloom said when she filed a lawsuit on behalf of commentator Britt McHenry, alleging misconduct and retaliation. "They give lip service to the idea that they have improved but they have not," Bloom said. "This is my fifth client I'm representing against Fox News. Nothing has changed."

McHenry continued to work at Fox, and so did the cohost she accused of harassment, Tyrus, who denied the allegations.

In another instance, Fox immediately fired a news anchor who was accused of misconduct: Ed Henry. Rumors about Henry's behavior with women had been batted away for years—*The Daily Beast* interviewed Fox staffers who said Henry's conduct was "long an open secret"—but on the last Thursday in June the network received a complaint that it could not ignore. Jennifer Eckhart, who had recently been let go by Fox Business, in a complaint filed in federal court in Manhattan in July 2020, alleged that Henry had raped her and described a years-long ordeal that began in 2014, when Ailes still ran the network. She alleged that Henry forced her to perform oral sex in a guest office at Fox's midtown Manhattan HQ in 2015. She also alleged that he handcuffed, raped, and hit her in a hotel room in 2017.

Fox handed the complaint to an outside law firm and removed Henry from his morning show while awaiting the firm's findings. It didn't take long. Henry was fired the following Wednesday. Some observers viewed the head-spinning firing as proof that Fox's corporate culture truly had been cleaned up; others viewed it as further evidence of just how rancid the place was. Eckhart's attorneys made the latter argument: "Today's Fox News is the same old Fox News," they said. "Some of the names in leadership may have changed since Roger Ailes' regime, but Fox News' institutional apathy towards sexual misconduct has not."

Eckhart sued Henry personally, and his lawyers fought back by calling her accounts "fictional," then by releasing text messages and even some intimate photos of Eckhart in an attempt to prove that she and Henry had a consensual relationship. Eckhart remained unemployed and determined to receive justice. Others reckoned with what it all meant. Alisyn Camerota, the longtime Fox host who now helmed CNN's morning show, told me that she had been thinking about a question I asked her in 2017, in the immediate aftermath of Bill O'Reilly's downfall: "Roger Ailes, now Bill O'Reilly, is Fox just rotten at its core?"

"Well, no, Fox isn't rotten at its core," Camerota said in 2017. "I mean, Roger was the king and, obviously, everything trickled down from him. So, when he said grossly inappropriate things about women's bodies, there was a feeling there then that's more appropriate and you're not going to get in trouble for that. So, on that level, he certainly had an impact in terms of the culture and the feelings there. However, there are tons of good people there. There are real journalists. They're trying to do their jobs."

Camerota flashed back to that conversation when she heard about Eckhart's rape allegation against Henry. "I'd like to amend my answer now if I may," she told me on the air in July 2020. "Because given everything that has come out since then, I guess it *is* rotten to the core. I guess that even though there are really good people there who are trying to do their jobs, it's not enough, because unless you get rid of and stamp out the predators, then of course the culture is still going to be rotten."

All across the cable dial, election coverage gobbled up every hour. "Our country's future hangs on this election, and it won't be easy," Barack Obama said as he endorsed Biden for president. "The other side has a massive war chest. The other side has a propaganda network with little regard for the truth."

Obama viewed Fox as rotten from a political perspective. Both Trump and Fox, he believed, were the culmination of decades of Republican Party trend lines, and were buttressed by a universe of disinformation. Altogether, he said, the information war was "the single biggest threat to our democracy."

On Fox, the single greatest threat was Democrats like Obama. Biden's pick for VP, Kamala Harris, was demonized as an un-American, un-electable radical. Certain Dems were so thoroughly demonized by the network that viewers fled en masse when they appeared on screen. On July 30 Fox showed the entire funeral service for the civil rights hero John Lewis, just like every other network, but the celebration of the African American congressman's life was a total turnoff for the Fox base. Fox viewership *collapsed*, from 1.9 million viewers before the funeral to a meager 540,000 when Obama was eulogizing Lewis. The audience slowly came back afterward. These Democratic valleys were matched by Republican peaks: Trump's first rally in the age of Covid-19 sent Fox's ratings soaring from 2.1 million to 8.2 million viewers.

Fox was holding the GOP's shrinking coalition together. But polls in the summer of 2020 showed that it probably wouldn't be enough to win Trump a second term. Hannity tried out different anti-Biden talking points every night, and said America would be "unrecognizable" if Trump lost, but the host seemed tired of his own hyperbole. The elderly white male candidate simply wasn't as appealing a villain as Obama or Hillary Clinton.

That was one of the reasons why Fox ignored long stretches of the Democratic National Convention and ran Hannity's show instead. Trump's base was sheltered from the patriotic speeches and videos that CNN and MSNBC viewers saw. As for the DNC speeches that were shown in the 10 p.m. hour, they were sandwiched in between nonstop Biden bashing before and afterward. From a ratings standpoint, this was the right programming call: One night, Hannity averaged 3.9 million viewers, and nearly half of those viewers retreated the following hour, when Fox showed Michelle Obama's keynote speech. Only 2.1 million stayed tuned. It was another Democratic valley. Off Fox, however, the Democratic convention was more of a ratings magnet than the Republican convention one week later. Cranks like Dobbs could shout all they wanted about the "LEFT'S WAR ON AMERICA," but the pandemic was out of control, the Trump White House was failing to persuade anyone, and most of America was leaning toward a leftward change.

"Unforced errors"

By the middle of September, six weeks before Election Day, Rupert Murdoch was telling his pals to expect a President Biden. He believed that Trump was going down, possibly in a landslide.

Rupert didn't make these predictions with any particular pleasure or remorse. He said it more matter-of-factly, like a man with a stack of chips on the table who knew the casino would eventually win. He believed his corporate marriage of convenience was almost over. And he always had people around him who would leak what he was saying, making the mogul look prescient and world-weary in all the right ways. How convenient.

I confirmed with sources on both sides of the relationship that Rupert's telephone relationship with Trump fizzled out in 2020. And Rupert was quite all right with that. To ride out the pandemic the elder Murdoch flew from his vineyard in California to his mansion in Henley-on-Thames, forty miles from London. He'd acquired the property, known as Holmwood, for $15 million just a few months before Covid-19 froze life as we knew it. Again, how convenient.

Back stateside, Rupert's election forecast was *not* reflected in Fox's commentary. Jeanine Pirro was on the air making absurd insinuations about Biden's health. "I have a sense that something is going to happen before the election and he's not even going to be on the ticket," she said. Weeks later, she "interviewed" Trump at the White House, and he charged Biden with using performance-enhancing drugs. "I think there's probably, possibly drugs involved. That's what I hear," he said, and she sat quietly, never batting a fake eyelash. Her business model hinged on wearing earmuffs to block out all of Trump's bullshit. Shamelessly, she titled her next book *Don't Lie to Me* and dedicated it "to one person": President Trump.

Trump claimed not to trust Fox's "phony polls," but Rupert did. He paid for the polling unit, after all. He blamed Trump's sorry standing in the polls on the president's own failings—"unforced errors," he said, during the first few months of the shutdown. *The Washington Post* said he believed that Trump's bruises "could have been avoided if he had followed Murdoch's advice about how to weather the coronavirus pandemic." When I read this, my blood boiled. Followed Murdoch's advice?! Trump watched Murdoch's networks for hours every day and heeded what he heard. Fox hosts condemned Covid-19 restrictions and questioned mask mandates; guests claimed Covid-19 death statistics were inflated and said other countries were much worse off. Trump reflected all of this when he called in to *Fox & Friends* and said "this thing's going away." Experts who knew better, experts like Dr. Anthony Fauci, who were lauded by the reality-based news media, were trashed on Fox. Fauci told me in a September interview that some of Fox's prime time talk about the pandemic was "outlandish."

Fox had some reporters "that are really, really good that I totally respect," he cautioned. "But there are others that just, you know, anything that I would say they'll distort a bit. And I'm not sure there's anything I can do about that."

Murdoch could do something about that, but didn't. So his gripes about Trump rejecting his advice were dumbfounding. Murdoch wanted Trump to adopt a wartime president stance, but Murdoch's network barely acknowledged the war.

With Rupert quarantining in the UK, Fox News staffers rarely heard anything about him, save for secondhand talk about whatever he told Suzanne Scott in their phone calls. The rank and file, largely working from home offices and living room couches, were abuzz about a younger Murdoch instead.

Some Fox staffers read the first edition of this book in the fall of 2020 and asked each other: Are we going to be working for James

Murdoch someday? My description of a potential liberal takeover of Fox Corp landed with some force. "A Potential Murdoch Family Civil War Looms Over Fox News," *The Daily Beast* exclaimed in a headline about the book. James's decision to quit the News Corporation board in the heat of the summer further dramatized his estrangement from Rupert and Lachlan. "My resignation is due to disagreements over certain editorial content published by the Company's news outlets and certain other strategic decisions," James said. His PR person, the DC power player Juleanna Glover, was mum about what the "other strategic decisions" were, but it sounded like a criticism of News Corp's languishing stock.

James was now finally, totally free of any corporate responsibilities tied to his last name. No board meetings. No grip-and-grins. But he was still a beneficiary of the family trust, which meant he could vanquish his older brother someday. He didn't want people to think that his investments in film festivals and comic book companies were just a pit stop on the way back to Fox Corp, but, well, that's what some thought.

Glover set up a lunch for James at Maureen Dowd's townhouse in Georgetown. The end product was a long profile in *The New York Times*, the archrival of Daddy's *Wall Street Journal*, that let James and wife Kathryn go on the record for the first time since he quit the board. "I decided that I could be much more effective outside," he said, in between elliptical references to "disinformation" and "agendas" and his family empire's toxicity.

Dowd placed the news about James's takeover possibility twenty-nine paragraphs into the profile, but everyone found it right away. She went one important step further than I did in the first edition of this book, crediting vague "Murdoch watchers across media" with the knowledge that yes, in fact, Prudence would side with James and Elisabeth in a succession battle. "When Rupert, 89, finally leaves the stage and his elder children take over, that could make three votes in the family trust against one," Dowd wrote.

Kathryn alluded to the looming battle in a Zoom call with Dowd "from their farm in Connecticut, where they live with their three teenagers, chickens and sheep." She smiled as she spoke about James being "free of that tension" at News Corporation, but added: "When a family is very involved in the business, it's a big decision to leave that. I don't know if it's ever ending. It's always, you know, ongoing."

One or two or ten years into the future, could James and his sisters effect regime change and tame Fox News? If they could, would stars like Sean Hannity still fit in? Would viewers still pledge allegiance to the channel, or would they run into the open arms of Newsmax and One America News? Fox was about to be tested like never before.

"Shit show"

Trump and Biden's first time meeting onstage, on September 29, 2020, was a testament to Fox's centrality in American politics. For the first debate of the season, typically the highest-rated of the four, the debate commission had tapped Fox's Chris Wallace to moderate.

It was a crowning achievement of Wallace's career.

Or at least it should have been.

Trump signaled ahead of time that he would revert to media-bashing. He called in to Brian Kilmeade's Fox News Radio show and predicted that "it'll be unfair, I have no doubt about it." Trump, who could have taught an entire class about working the refs, said Wallace will "be controlled by the radical left. That's what—they control him."

Trump kept yammering away, insulting Wallace, and Kilmeade

eventually spoke up to defend his colleague: "I will tell you for sure he is not controlled by anyone, Chris Wallace."

"Let's see," Trump said.

Fox execs stayed out of Wallace's way. When I said to one of Wallace's friends, Is this a "Fox debate"? they said "It's a Chris Wallace debate, and his esteemed masterful moderating record speaks for itself." Wallace intended to blend into the background. "If I've done my job right," he said, "at the end of the night, people will say, 'That was a great debate, who was the moderator?' "

Unfortunately for Wallace, everyone remembered that he was the moderator.

Trump bulldozed Wallace from the very beginning. The dialogue was incoherent. Trump basically became the moderator, and Biden used his opponent's pugilism to argue against another four years of it. Afterward, Wallace said he "never dreamt that it would go off the tracks the way it did." This struck me as a massive failure of imagination, given Trump's inability to ever stay on a track.

Forty-five minutes in, according to his own recollection of the debate, Wallace realized it was a runaway disaster. A "disservice" to the country, he said in retrospect.

Sixty-five minutes in, he tried to assert himself. "If you want to switch seats," he told Trump, "we can do that."

His quip was supposed to disarm Trump and re-exert his control. But the truth was, Wallace lost control of the debate in the first five minutes. Biden came up to him afterward and whispered, "I bet you didn't think you were signing up for a boxing match." Trump merely nodded in the moderator's general direction. Trump's flouting of the rules and Wallace's failure to corral the candidates became the most memorable part of the debate, more than any single talking point or gesture. CNN's Dana Bash called it a "shit show" on the air.

Wallace ducked into a town car and rode to the private jet terminal where Lachlan Murdoch and Suzanne Scott were waiting to toast him before the charter flight home to Washington. No amount of champagne could help, though. "I didn't feel much like celebrating," Wallace told *The New York Times.*

More than 73 million people watched that disgrace of a debate, nearly a record high. What none of the viewers knew was that Trump was ill with the coronavirus while he was shouting on stage. Three days later, Wallace was back in his Covid-era studio, in the guest apartment above his garage in Annapolis, Maryland, covering the president's health crisis.

While Trump was rushed to Walter Reed Medical Center, and other hosts tiptoed around the obvious and ominous, Wallace put it bluntly: "The president is being hospitalized for the coronavirus. We all hope and pray for a quick and dramatic recovery, but this is not good news."

Trump had teed up the news of his coronavirus diagnosis in a televised call with Hannity the night before. Hannity brought up Bloomberg's report about Hope Hicks testing positive and Trump confirmed it was true. Then he said, "I just went for a test, and we will see what happens. I mean, who knows." Trump implied that Hicks's illness was the result of her interactions with members of the military and law enforcement: "They come over to you and they want to hug you and kiss you because we really have done a good job for them. You get close, and things happen."

The White House refused to reveal Trump's Covid-19 testing history, so it was unclear when he last tested negative or first tested positive for the disease. Both Biden and Wallace were tested, since they had shared the debate stage with Trump, and thankfully they tested negative.

Pumped up on a drug cocktail that was inaccessible to the patients intubated in hospitals all across the country, Trump flew home to the White House and embarked on a Fox-produced comeback tour. He went on three different Fox shows—coughing and clearing his throat during one—and said he was ready to battle Biden again. "Let's get a fair anchor," Trump said. "Somebody like the great Sean Hannity. We'll get Rush. We'll get Mark. We'll get Laura. We'll get Judge Jeanine." He kept rattling off Fox friends, by their first names only, disregarding the fact that the debate commission would never pick a right-wing propagandist for a job that presupposes neutrality.

In any event the October 15 rematch was canceled since Trump refused to debate virtually despite his recent Covid-19 illness. Biden and Trump participated in dueling town halls on ABC and NBC instead, and Trump brought some Fox with him.

On the subject of masks to protect against coronavirus, Trump peddled BS from *Tucker Carlson Tonight*, proclaiming that "just the other day, they came out with a statement that 85 percent of the people that wear masks catch it."

"They" had done no such thing. Trump was lying about a Carlson segment that distorted the meaning of a minor study about masks.

NBC town hall moderator Savannah Guthrie was prepared for this lie. "They didn't say that. I know that study," she said.

"Well, that's what I heard," Trump said, "and that's what I saw."

Trump invoked the 85 percent figure again later, and Guthrie shut him down again, and commentators said it was unusual to see Trump challenged live on TV, since almost every host on Fox would have just played along with the propaganda. Guthrie interjected too when Trump tried to minimize America's failure to slow the spread of the disease. Trump pulled out a piece of paper that was titled "MORE DAILY CASES THAN THE U.S." It was a graphic from Laura Ingraham's show the night before, printed from YouTube, with months-old data about European infections that only made an ounce of sense in the reality distortion field of Fox News. Transported onto NBC, it was gobbledygook.

A believer in karma might say that the coronavirus stalked Fox all year long precisely because of the network's coverage. Unlike most other major networks, Fox dispatched its lead anchors and commentators to the debate locales; while the October 15 face-off was scrapped, the final scheduled debate of the season still took place on October 22, in Nashville, and Bret Baier and Martha MacCallum were both there. An employee on the overnight charter flight back east later tested positive, which meant the anchors and Jay Wallace all had to quarantine in the week leading up to Election Night. They didn't get sick, but other cases cropped up in other cities; Fox kept a careful lid on the news, citing privacy rights. Sources told me that one of Fox's loudest voices against Covid-19 lockdowns, Pete Hegseth, had his own bout with the virus, which helped explain why he cohosted *Fox & Friends Weekend* from his home studio for weeks at a time. Hegseth could have done some good by educating viewers about the virus, the way his cohost Jedediah Bila did after she recovered, but he never talked about it. (A spokesperson for Hegseth declined to comment on my reporting.)

Hegseth was the quintessential Fox viewer—defensive of Trump, dismissive of the virus, and determined to reopen businesses even at the risk of worsening the infections. The Pew Research Center found that Republicans were largely convinced that the U.S. could not have controlled the outbreak any better, in spite of all the evidence to the contrary. A whopping 90 percent of Republicans who listed only Fox or talk radio as major sources of news agreed with that assessment, versus only 46 percent of Republicans who listed other sources of news, and only 11 percent of Democrats. Most Fox loyalists also said the outbreak was overblown. The Fox echo chamber worked really, dangerously well: The U.S. government's management of public health was a shit show, but on Fox it looked like a success.

On October 26, Scott and Wallace wrote to the staff and reported a "few" new positive Covid-19 cases around the company. The execs needed to protect election coverage at all costs. So, they said, "we will be further reducing some of the workforce in our buildings and operating virtually whenever possible" to reduce the chances of Fox stars and producers being sickened and sidelined on Election Night.

There were similar concerns over at CNN. Some hair and makeup employees had recently returned to work with masks and face shields, but in the run-up to Election Night, they stayed home and anchors reverted to doing their own faces, all to limit interactions and preserve the election cast and crews. The election was everything. It was a series finale four years in the making, and it was shaping up to be Fox's biggest show ever.

"We're in charge"

Jon Decker wanted the answer to a simple question: "Where is the river?"

Decker covered the White House for Fox's radio division, and when I say "covered," I mean he actually reported, actually hustled,

actually cared about holding the administration accountable. He
was one of Fox's rare exceptions to the right-wing rule, which is
why it wasn't surprising when he left the network at the beginning
of 2021, but in the run-up to the election, he was working for Fox
and he was getting hounded by Fox fans about Trump's nightmarish
voter fraud tales.

Trump and his wingmen sowed doubt about the integrity of
the election almost every single day for months. A typical hour of
Hannity was full of terrifying talk about "rampant fraud surrounding mail-in ballots" that was being "ignored by the media mob."
For the most part the claims were paper-thin—and Decker proved
this by using a rare White House press briefing to ask Kayleigh
McEnany about Trump's claim that ballots that were cast for Trump
"are being dumped in rivers."

Decker asked: "The other day, he said, 'They found a lot of ballots in a river.' Who is 'they'?"

McEnany couldn't answer because "they" didn't find anything
in any body of water. There *were* some local news stories about mail
being found in a ditch in Wisconsin, but there was never any proof
of ballots being found there. So McEnany deflected and insulted
Decker instead.

Decker kept asking: "Where is this river, anywhere in this country?"

"It was a ditch in Wisconsin," McEnany said.

So Trump misspoke?

McEnany deflected: "You're missing the forest for the trees
here."

No, Decker said, "when the president says, 'They found a lot of
ballots in a river,' I simply want to know where the river is."

"Where is the river?" went viral, but it won Decker few fans
inside his company. Most of the Fox machine was committed to

Trump's Big Lie about the election. Trump continued to talk about this nonexistent river for months—he even brought it up to Maria Bartiromo live on TV on November 29—and no one corrected him.

This deference to Trump explained the profound fears, in the run-up to Election Night, about what Fox would do. As *Slate* put it in a headline, "The Fox News Decision Desk Controls the Fate of American Democracy."

The network's decision desk was managed by Arnon Mishkin, a registered Democrat, and staffed with eight statistical and political pros, a purposeful mix of Republicans and Democrats. They were guided by the numbers, not by personal preferences, and they knew their reputations were on the line with every race call. No one who knew Mishkin thought that his team would bend their projections just to please Trump. But how would the projections be reported on the air? Would the news anchors win out, or the propagandists?

"We're in charge," Baier told people who inquired.

He meant that the news division was in charge of Election Night coverage. Hannity was out of the picture.

Thus the evening of November 3 was, for Fox addicts, an unwelcome ice bath—a numbing shock to the system. Until Baier and MacCallum's special report began at 6 p.m. Eastern, the Fox narrative was so pro-Trump that viewers were fooled into thinking that the race was a toss-up. On-screen banners celebrated "MASSIVE ENTHUSIASM FOR TRUMP" and promised that he was "CLOSING THE GAP IN KEY BATTLEGROUND STATES." Hour after hour talked of a tightening race when, in fact, the polls had been fairly consistent all year long, and more than 100 million votes had been cast before Election Day. These distortions frustrated Mishkin to no end; he recognized that Fox viewers were being misled about the most likely outcome of the election. Biden's advantages were innumerable. But experts like Mishkin weren't invited on the air to point that out. Even Fox's own polls were downplayed. Fox's hosts depicted Biden as a corrupt swamp monster (yet also sleepy and dim) and Harris as a far left extremist. How could these radicals possibly be elected? The only obvious explanation could be fraud, right? That was the undercurrent of the coverage, all the way up until Trump's phone call with *Fox & Friends* at 7 a.m. on Election Day.

The call mostly sounded like a repeat of 2016. Trump pointed to his crowd sizes as proof that he would prevail, never mind the fact that Biden consciously limited his events due to Covid-19; Fox viewers didn't want to hear about any of that. He bragged about the stock market's performance, even though the gains in Obama's first four years outpaced Trump's first four years; again, Fox viewers didn't want that fact-check.

There were moments, I thought, when it sounded like Trump was contemplating losing. Why else would he be setting the stage for his Big Lie ("Philadelphia will be a disaster," he said, previewing his blame-big-diverse-cities plan) and demanding to know the winner of the election by midnight?

The Fox hosts sounded wistful. Brian Kilmeade wrapped the interview by harking all the way back to "Monday Mornings with Trump" phoners from 2011: "Mr. President, we thank you for opening up with us before you ran for president; while you were running for president; and when you won the presidency. Best of luck to getting four more years."

While the rest of America voted, Lachlan Murdoch pressed unmute on his speakerphone and pronounced Fox to be the ultimate winner of the election.

"This very moment, as we speak," Lachlan told investors on an 8:30 a.m. quarterly earnings conference call, "our viewers are starting their Election Day turning on their TV sets to where they left them last night, the Fox News Channel, or opening their web browsers to FoxNews.com, or checking the Fox News app for the latest report."

Lachlan did his best impression of Rupert on these calls, sparing no adjective to describe to Wall Street Fox's supremacy.

"Fox News has been the most watched network in all of television, from Memorial Day through Election Day," even bigger than the Fox broadcast network, Lachlan said.

Total day ratings were up 31 percent in the demo. Prime time ratings were up 54 percent. "Last Tuesday," he bragged, "*Tucker Carlson Tonight* on the Fox News Channel had more total viewers than the season premiere of NBC's *This Is Us.*"

Lest anyone say Fox had brainwashed only conservatives, Lachlan highlighted Fox's performance in swing states and its appeal among independents. He claimed that this was a testament to "the quality of our journalism and the balance of our reporting." Left unmentioned was the fact that Fox News had just laid off sixty to seventy people, largely from the reporting ranks, including the so-called Brain Room of researchers who tried to keep the network's coverage somewhat straight. The Brain Room department was "always a reliable and unbiased source for us," a disappointed staffer said. "Seeing the company cut down on their staff only further reinforces the idea that the likes of Sean Hannity and Tucker Carlson are running the asylum."

For the entirety of the Trump years, the story was the same: Opinion won, news lost. But the suits had to keep up appearances, had to justify the word "News" in the network's name, so they crowed about quality journalism while firing journalists.

The name Trump never came up on the Election Day earnings call, but Michael Morris of Guggenheim Securities lobbed a question about the president "perhaps starting a news network."

Lachlan very much enjoyed the chance to swat away the notion of MAGA TV. "We love competition," he said. "We have always thrived with competition, and we have strong competition now."

He didn't regard Newsmax or One America News as a legit part of Fox's competitive set. They were mere flies on the back of the elephant. Fox and CNN were now getting daily Nielsen data for Newsmax, so there was finally some visibility into Ruddy's television reach. "Puny" was a fair characterization. Newsmax averaged fifty to one hundred thousand viewers in the evening hours when Fox averaged 3 to 5 million. The highest-rated hour, *Greg Kelly Reports*, at 7 p.m., was one-fortieth the size of *The Story* on Fox at the same time. Trump went on Kelly's show in late October but barely made a ratings dent—Kelly and Trump together only averaged 112,000 viewers. So Lachlan's confidence in Fox's dominance was backed up by data. But Election Day was the last day that was true.

"Bad dream"

On Sunday, November 1, Jonathan Swan of Axios telegraphed exactly what would happen on Election Night. "President Trump has told confidants he'll declare victory on Tuesday night if it looks like he's 'ahead,' " Swan reported, citing three sources.

The Big Lie, in other words, was premeditated. Trump planned to exploit the so-called "red mirage," an illusion that was created when rural Republican strongholds counted all their votes before big Democratic cities. But Mishkin's decision desk torpedoed the plan by bathing Arizona in blue.

At great expense, Fox broke away from the other major networks and their National Election Pool after the 2016 election. Fox partnered with the Associated Press on an election surveying system. The AP called it VoteCast, and Fox called it the Fox News Voter Analysis, a mouthful of a name that described a massive survey of the American electorate in all fifty states. The AP and Fox believed that their system was superior to the in-person exit polls that had led the networks astray in past election cycles. It had worked well during the 2018 midterms, and this was its first presidential test.

Mishkin's team modeled all the swing states, studied the survey data, and compared the actual raw vote counts to what they expected would happen. Execs at other networks said the Fox decision desk was aggressive—meaning they tended to make key race calls more quickly than rivals—but impressive. So when Fox put Arizona's eleven electoral votes in Biden's column at 11:20 p.m. Eastern, everyone noticed. Without Arizona, Trump's paths to the presidency were narrowed dramatically, and his ploys to lie his way into a second term were weakened considerably.

Trump erupted. "Call Rupert," he told Jared Kushner. "CALL RUPERT."

Fox's Arizona call was the pivot point of the night, signaling that Biden was on the way to winning the White House. It was a breaking point for MAGA heads who turned off Fox in disgust. In the weeks and months after November 3, the projection was disputed and dissected beyond any reasonable standard. There were ratings declines and shouting matches and layoffs and retirements at Fox, and all of it, to some degree, was related to the Arizona call.

So let's make one thing clear: Rupert had nothing to do with it. Neither did Lachlan. Nor did anyone in the management ranks. Mishkin made the call. Fox's DC managing editor Bill Sammon verified the call. Digital politics editor Chris Stirewalt went on air to defend the call. And they were ultimately right: Biden *did* win the state of Arizona. But the other networks didn't project a winner in the state for nine days.

Was Mishkin right at 11:20 p.m. on Election Night? Was it a responsible projection to make only two hours and twenty minutes after the state's polls closed? Was it delivered on air the right way?

Regarding that last question, the answer is an unequivocal no. Networks rehearse every call and block every camera angle ahead of time, but Fox botched the critical moment when Arizona turned blue, and it haunted the network. The control room should have cued Baier to announce the projection, but instead it was revealed by accident when anchor Bill Hemmer was running through various "what if . . ." scenarios that showed how Biden and Trump could both reach the 270 electoral vote mark.

"What is this happening here?" Hemmer said, pointing his index finger at Arizona, awash in blue on the oversized TV monitor to his right. "Why is Arizona blue?" he asked, hoping for an answer from Baier or the control room. "Did we just call it? Did we make a call in Arizona?" He toggled between maps on his monitor, zooming into the state and showing the requisite check mark next to Biden's beaming face.

Hemmer looked at the camera, absolutely lost, and said, "There's a check mark, did our decision desk make it?" It was just a fluke of timing—Sammon had just checked the box in the computer system, turning Arizona blue on Hemmer's map, and Hemmer noticed before Sammon had time to notify the control room. This was exactly what the networks tried mightily to avoid on Election Nights: uncertainty, confusion, chaos.

"Yes," MacCallum said off-camera, "we can conf—" and she didn't finish saying the word "confirm." "I believe we have a yes."

The director took a split screen with the anchors on the left and Hemmer on the right. Baier was still wearing his glasses.

"If you lose Arizona, where do you win now?" Hemmer said, clearly referring to the Trump team's hopes.

"Okay, time-out," Baier said, "this is a big development. The Fox News decision desk is calling Arizona for Joe Biden. That is a big get for the Biden campaign."

The anchors tried to retake command, but the damage was done, in more ways than one. The Arizona call was a punch in the belly of the Fox base, but no one on the air explained it right away. "The math was right. The messaging was wrong," a Fox insider said to me later. Another source argued that Fox wasn't "respectful" enough to the Trump operatives who called and complained. I stifled a laugh when I heard that.

Shortly after midnight, Baier alluded to the calls that were pouring in. "My phone is lighting up with Republicans," he said. Tucker Carlson indicated that he was hearing the same protests, and then he went off on a tangent about media mistakes, which left viewers thinking that he didn't believe the Fox decision desk.

Arizona was the first state to flip from red to blue versus the 2016 election results. But Mishkin's team didn't think it was a decisive moment in the presidential race. They viewed it as an electoral college dogfight and thought Trump was still very much in it. The Trump campaign's furious reaction, however, showed that Arizona was pivotal to their math. On the third floor of the White House residence, Trump demanded that someone do . . . something. "They've got to change it," one source recalled him saying. Axios reported that Trump dispatched Kushner to call the Murdochs, and senior adviser Jason Miller to call Hemmer, and chief of staff Mark Meadows to call Bill Sammon.

Campaign aides couldn't magically talk TV networks into reversing projections, and the aides should have known that, but they called in vain anyway. Rupert never commented on his conversation with Kushner, but he told *The Washington Post* in an email message that the president never called directly to complain.

"If he had, I would not have interfered or changed our call," Murdoch wrote.

Sammon was the main decision-maker who defended the projection. He oversaw the decision desk, and he made clear to Trumpworld that the call wasn't going to be withdrawn. Reality was crashing up against the floodwall of Fox's pro-Trump fantasies, and 14 million viewers were watching it happen live.

At 12:25 a.m. Baier and MacCallum turned to Karl Rove, who looked glum. "There are more votes out there" in Arizona, he said halfheartedly, suggesting that Mishkin's decision was maybe "a little premature." As soon as he finished speaking, Baier called the state of Minnesota for Biden—yet another blow to Trump's chances. Up next was another conservative commentator, Katie Pavlich, a native Arizonan who said she was in touch with "a number of people in Arizona who cast their votes who don't believe that Arizona is at least this far gone this early." The coverage was bordering on pathetic at this point. Rove and Pavlich didn't have access to Mishkin's models or data sets. Finally, at 12:33, Baier brought Mishkin on for an interview, and assumed a detective stance.

"Arnon, we're getting a lot of incoming here, and we need you to answer some questions," he said. "Arizona: Are you 100 percent sure of that call, and when you made it, and why did you make it?"

Mishkin began: "Absolutely. We made it after basically a half hour of debating 'is it time yet?' because it's been clear for a while." He even said "I'm sorry," to no one in particular, as he reaffirmed his ruling: "The president is not going to be able to take over and win enough votes to eliminate that seven-point lead that the former vice president has."

Mishkin was tapping into survey data that only Fox and the AP had; the other networks were using an entirely different set of data. "What do they know that we don't know?" was the prevailing question. As the hours went by and the AP didn't make an identical call, surprise turned to suspicion: "Did Fox get it wrong?"

But Mishkin and Sammon did not waver. At 2:50 a.m. the AP joined Fox in turning Arizona blue. Trump had just exited the East Room, where he stood before a bank of live TV cameras and lied. "We have won Georgia," he said. He went on to lose Georgia. "We're winning Pennsylvania," he said. He went on to lose Pennsylvania. "We are winning Michigan," he said. He went on to lose Michigan. "Frankly, we did win this election," he said.

Fox was once again torn between Trump and the truth. Initially the truth won: Chris Wallace said, "This is an extremely flammable situation" and "the president just threw a match into it. He hasn't won these states." When the sun came up Wednesday morning, Mishkin was booked on *Fox & Friends* to explain why states like Pennsylvania weren't called yet. But a few minutes later Trump adviser David Bossie was on the morning show mocking "your so-called expert." Fox leaned hard on its "Breakfast with Friends" trick, interviewing legions of Trump supporters at diners to lift viewers' spirits. But reality—as determined by the decision desk—kept intruding. By Wednesday afternoon Fox and the AP showed Biden on the cusp of winning the presidency, with 264 electoral votes, and several states still in play. The world was watching American democracy in action. Or as Sean Hannity called it, a "bad dream."

· · ·

On Election Night 2020, during the prime time 8 to 11 p.m. hours, when it looked like Trump very well could win a second term, Fox News averaged 13.6 million viewers, which was even higher than its 2016 election average of 12.1 million. CNN came in second place with 9.1 million. Near midnight, something interesting happened, something that no one noticed in the next day's ratings reports. After Fox called Arizona for Biden, Fox's audience started to shrink and Newsmax's audience started to grow.

The shift was minor, all things considered, since Fox still had 12 million viewers at midnight and Newsmax had a measly five hundred thousand. But the Newsmax base held steady until two in the morning, while half of the Fox base went to bed. When I revisited the Nielsen numbers months afterward, I realized that this was the very first sign of an exodus. A sliver of the Fox audience was so invested in Trump, and so infuriated by Fox's reporting, that they went off in search of a safer space. And they landed on Newsmax, where there was no decision desk, where Arizona wasn't blue, where Trump wasn't on the verge of losing. The Fox-turned-Newsmax audience was audible outside an election office in Maricopa County, Arizona, on Wednesday afternoon. Pro-Trump protesters alternated between two slogans: "Count the votes" and "Fox News sucks."

"Arrogant fucks"

"What separates the winners from the losers is how a person reacts to each new twist of fate."

That's what Donald Trump said on Twitter in 2014.

During Election Week in 2020, he acted like a loser. His flailing campaign pressed every available button to transform him into a winner. They even blasted out an email attacking Mishkin's personal voting record.

But Fox's decision desk did not waver. "We are not pulling back that call," Mishkin told MacCallum on Fox Wednesday night.

MacCallum knew all of the Trump campaign's talking points, and she recited some of them to Mishkin, pointedly taking the side of the president and his followers. "They are saying that the outstanding vote is over six hundred thousand, and that the president is on schedule of what they see to be over 60 something percent," she said. "If that were the case, would that state move?"

"If a frog had wings," Mishkin answered. He was running out of patience. Trump was closing the gap with Biden in Maricopa County, but it wasn't going to be enough to flip the state back to red. So Trump and his brainwashers needed to make an emotional rather than mathematical argument. By Wednesday night, that's exactly what his shows were doing. Hannity asked leading questions: "Is the fix already in?" "Do you believe these election results are accurate?" Laura Ingraham blamed "the propagandistic media." Fox contributor Mollie Hemingway said, "There are many ways that the media can rig an election." The decision desk's truth was buried by this garbage and innuendo. Fox's biggest stars and highest-rated shows asserted that they knew the destination—the election was rigged against Trump—and they tried out ways to get there. They were being egged on by the White House: "Arizona is going the other way," Kellyanne Conway insisted on *Fox & Friends* Thursday morning. Brian Kilmeade awkwardly said, "We stand by the Arizona decision, but that's done by the decision desk," basically trying to shift the blame to Mishkin. Fox's shows acted like Trump's toothless lawsuits actually had merit. They acted like a massive conspiracy was at work. Lou Dobbs said the Justice Department should "move in" to ferret out the mass voter fraud that, of course, didn't exist. Hannity declared that "Americans will never be able to believe in the integrity and legitimacy of these results."

These words did enormous damage. These words inflamed the president and an incalculable number of his fans. No one should have been surprised when polls in early 2021 showed that only one in four Republicans believed Biden won fair and square; the Trump-Fox narrative was overwhelming. Even Baier and MacCallum, supposedly Fox's truth-tellers, contributed to the disinformation. When Trump walked into the White House briefing room on Thursday evening and accused his opponents of "trying to steal an election," the Fox anchors pretended it was normal. In reality, it was so abnormal that most other networks cut away and refused to air Trump's remarks live. On CNN afterward, Jake Tapper said Trump was attacking democracy. Anderson Cooper called it "pathetic" and "dangerous." Dana Bash texted Republican lawmakers, asking when they planned to intervene. But not a single host or guest on Fox denounced Trump's undemocratic conduct. Not a single one.

When I asked why, I heard excuses and evasions that always led to the real answer: The pressure from the audience was debilitating. Because of the decision desk, Fox had lost the trust of the audience. Thus the rage against the decision desk was intense, even inside Fox HQ. "They are arrogant fucks," one senior staffer told me. "They are rubbing it in our viewers' faces."

Rubbing what?

"Biden. They're rubbing Biden in our faces."

I cringed at the visual but sort of saw where this person was coming from. Fox had wrongly prepared viewers for a second Trump term. Now that was falling apart and no one knew what to do. Things were getting really heated—GOP senator Kevin Cramer of North Dakota said the "knuckleheads" who called Arizona for Biden should be fired. "Fox News owes the American people an apology," he said, in an accurate summary of the Trump base's feelings by Friday on Election Week.

Rather than help Trump fans process their losing feelings, hosts like Hannity stoked their rage in explicit collaboration with Trump and his party. NPR obtained an internal memo about chairwoman Ronna McDaniel's planned appearance on *Hannity*, which "set out in great specificity the intended flow of the show's lengthy opening segment—including its guests, articles and subjects—and the primary points Hannity would make." It was scripted like World Wrestling Entertainment, but with American democracy at stake.

By Friday, November 6, Biden was closing in on the presidency, and all eyes were on Pennsylvania's count. Biden pulled ahead in the state, as expected, and the major networks prepared for the inevitable moment when Biden would cross the 270 electoral vote threshold. CNN's prime time team signed off at midnight and resumed anchoring at 7 a.m.—a crystal-clear sign of an imminent projection. But *Fox & Friends* kept acting like Trump's lies were legit. In at least two different divisions of Fox, staffers were told to keep up the act even after Biden reached 270. Two different memos obtained by CNN told staffers not to call Biden "president-elect" once Biden was the projected winner. The memos cited Trump's bogus legal challenges. "Former Vice President Biden does not become 'President-elect' until the votes are certified," one of the memos stated. "Please stick to something along that phrasing."

Keep Trump's hopes alive! That's what these middle-level managers were telling the rank and file. I don't know if the leakers intended to get the guidance revoked, but that was the practical effect. After I went on television and reported on the existence of the memos, Fox's PR shop tried to tamp down the controversy by saying that no company-wide guidance had gone out yet. Baier said on the air that Biden would, of course, be dubbed "president-elect" after hitting the magic 270 mark. Baier pressed McDaniel for tangible evidence of the fraud she was imagining: "There's all kinds of stuff flying on the internet. But when we look into it, it doesn't pan out," he said.

Friday came and went without a projection. This time it wasn't the Trump campaign calling Fox to complain—an official with the Biden campaign called me to unload about the excessively cautious decision desks. "Every one of the networks knows that they're going to call this race for Biden," the official said, so the delay was just allowing Trump to sow doubt and spread disinformation. I agreed that the president was exploiting the situation, but the decision desks were guided by mathematical models, nothing more, nothing less. We hung up on each other. Everyone was exhausted. Everyone wanted the election to be over. Fox's savvier hosts, like Laura Ingraham, shifted into the past tense. She said losing was "awful," but "President Trump's legacy will only become more significant if he focuses on moving the country forward."

Did she really believe he was capable of such patriotic, selfless leadership? No, no, a friend of Ingraham's said, she was just venturing to give him some free advice. The words "arrogant fucks" came to mind again.

"Whoa, whoa, whoa"

At 11:24 a.m. on Saturday, November 7, CNN became the first network to project Biden would win Pennsylvania and thus win the presidency. NBC followed forty-five seconds later, then CBS thirty seconds after that, and ABC and the AP, all within a frenetic two-and-a-half-minute window. Street parties broke out in New York, Philadelphia, Washington, Atlanta, Los Angeles, and smaller blue precincts across the country. Anyone who flipped over to Fox News wanting confirmation or contradictory coverage or conservative tears saw . . . ads for MyPillow instead. Neil Cavuto kept anchoring normal news coverage for a full fifteen minutes, at times alluding to the projections of other networks but noting, at one point, "We at Fox have not yet made that call."

Where was the Fox decision desk?! Jon Favreau of *Pod Save America* fame joked on Twitter that Mishkin was "still tied up in a Fox News basement somewhere." But the delay was not his fault—sources blamed the holdup on the special events producers who failed to have Baier and MacCallum ready for the climactic moment. On CNN Wolf Blitzer and company were on marathon duty for this very reason, but Fox had stuck with regular programming instead, and that's why Saturday morning was such a mess. At 11:40, Baier belatedly broke in with the projection. "Keep in mind," MacCallum said, "the Trump campaign is in the midst of waging legal challenges in several states, but the path is clear for the new president-elect."

With those words, those accurate but agonizing words, hundreds of thousands of Fox fans went running to Newsmax.

Picture Fox News as a dormant volcano that erupted on November 7, spewing hot magma and harmful gases in every direction. The next day the region was covered in rocks and ash and pumice. Most of the volcanic mountain was still intact, and was the dominant sight on the skyline, but the landscape was changed. New hills and valleys were formed by the lava flows. Boulders were strewn about, creating new hazards. It was hard to tell what was what.

For the first time since launch day in 1996, Fox was facing true competition from the right. It was visible on TV, at Newsmax and One America News, and on the web, at streaming sites like Right Side Broadcasting. The most devoted members of the Trump cult refused to believe that Biden was president-elect. They swore off Fox and lumped it in with—gasp!—CNN and NBC.

Charles Herring, the One America News boss, felt the eruption in the form of viewer feedback emails and messages. "A massive wave of former Fox News viewers have abandoned Fox and have found a home at OAN," he told me. His channel still wasn't rated by Nielsen, but he looked at proprietary data from a major cable provider and saw that OAN was suddenly in the top ten. He scrolled through the emails from new viewers and said that disillusioned former Fox watchers "believe new pro-left voices have infiltrated the network." If that had happened, I would have known. It would have been the entire story line of this book. Alas, the opposite had occurred—right-wing voices had prevailed and suffocated the dissent at Fox. But the MAGAsphere felt betrayed by Fox nonetheless.

Chris Ruddy at Newsmax sensed the same opening as Herring. "Newsmax has not called the election for Joe Biden," he proudly proclaimed during a live interview with me on CNN on Sunday the 8th.

That was Ruddy's new pitch to viewers: We haven't accepted reality like Fox has. We won't offend you with the truth.

Ruddy and Trump had gabbed on the phone earlier in the week, and Trump vented about Fox—especially Wallace, Baier, and Mac-Callum. "He's very disappointed in Fox News," Ruddy told me. "Chris Wallace's moderating was terrible. It really hurt, I think, the president. And then, you know, they call the election." He brought up Arizona and suggested a nefarious scheme was at work: "What was going on at Fox News that they didn't want to give the president the sense that he was winning or had the potential shot of winning?"

This is how Fox was punished by Republicans for reporting the news accurately. Fox was—I can't believe I'm writing these words!—depicted as insufficiently loyal to the GOP. When Fox aired news coverage of Biden's prime time victory speech in place of Jeanine Pirro's show, that too was seen as a betrayal. Newsmax threw up a breaking news banner: "JEANINE PIRRO SUSPENDED FROM FOX NEWS." No she was not; she was rightly preempted for the president-elect's speech. "Let's give each other a chance," Biden said that night in Wilmington. "It's time to put away the harsh rhetoric, lower the temperature, see each other again, listen to each other again."

Suffice it to say, none of that happened. All of the hateful noise on TV and social media cemented anti-Fox attitudes among a conspiracy-minded segment of Fox's former audience. On Monday evening Greg Kelly's 7 p.m. show on Newsmax topped eight hundred thousand viewers, a 1,000 percent increase from his pre-election average. The 6 p.m. lead-in, cohosted by Sean Spicer, also grew by 1,000 percent. A ten-times increase in one week—I had never seen anything like this in sixteen years covering television.

It was obvious where these viewers were coming from. Fox's afternoon and evening hours were off by 20, 25, 30 percent, even though we were in the midst of an epic news cycle. This was much more precipitous than an ordinary post-election slump. "Our audience hates this," one exec said. "They're pissed," said a second source. "Seething," said another. Fox's problem was that the audience suddenly had somewhere else to go. On Newsmax, Biden wasn't president-elect and Trump wasn't a loser. Kelly kept saying that he believed Trump could stay in office for four more years. "IT ISN'T OVER YET," Newsmax's banners proclaimed. Fox only dabbled in election denialism at first, while Newsmax went all-in. Veteran political analyst Jeff Greenfield quipped: "Fox is losing viewers to Newsmax and OAN for the same reason *Playboy* lost readers to *Penthouse* and *Hustler*—who boldly went where no publication had gone before."

And that's why the Newsmax insurgency posed an existential threat to Fox's profits.

A television CEO explained it this way: When Fox had a right-wing TV monopoly, it had the ability to say "fuck you." Distributors who wanted to appeal to "the rest of America," as the CEO put it, had no choice but to cough up carriage fees and pay for Fox News. They had no alternative to offer Trump-loving customers. Newsmax's emergence changed the power dynamic. Now the distributors could say "go fuck yourself" to Fox, drop the channel, and offer the much-less-costly Newsmax instead. The end result would likely be a decline in Fox's carriage fee in exchange for continued distribution. "The first readjustment with one cable operator will be catastrophic for Fox News," the CEO told me, because contracts with providers like Comcast specify that if one big distributor starts to pay less, the others can start to pay less too.

That was the theory, anyway. It wasn't bulletproof. Fox News was still one of the highest-rated channels in the United States and was beloved by millions of people, some of whom, it must be said, did accept Biden's election. But it must also be said that an astonishing number of Republicans rejected the result. If Trump was "the only middle finger available" to voters in 2020, as *National Review* editor Rich Lowry wrote, then denying that Trump lost was a middle finger to American democracy. It was the new birtherism. Ailes kept the birther lie in check at Fox, but this time there was no one in charge to hold back the Big Lie. Fox reacted to Newsmax's ratings gains by wading deeper into the voter fraud depths. "We don't know how many votes were stolen," Carlson said on his first show after Biden declared victory. "We don't know anything about the software that many say was rigged. We don't know. We ought to find out." Even Baier, the man who'd announced Biden was president-elect, went there: He told viewers that "we are not going to stop digging and following up on leads." The language of journalism was being exploited to lend cover to a coup attempt.

As always, some Fox journalists resisted. On Monday the 9th Cavuto cut away from a Trump campaign press conference when Kayleigh McEnany leveled crazy charges at the Democrats.

"Whoa, whoa, whoa," Cavuto said as he interrupted. "I just think we have to be very clear: She's charging the other side as welcoming fraud and welcoming illegal voting; unless she has more details to back that up, I can't in good countenance continue to show you this."

Cavuto couldn't, but Hannity could. He booked McEnany practically every night.

Different Fox hosts took different approaches to election denialism. Some let guests do the heavy "Stop the Steal" lifting while they sat back and nodded along. Others, like Mark Levin and Lou Dobbs, went full constitutional-crisis mode. "The fate of the republic hangs in the balance here!" Dobbs bellowed. Pete Hegseth insisted that "there is no president-elect, yet." Maria Bartiromo blasted viewers in the face with a fire hose of lies about voting tech providers like Dominion and Smartmatic. The overall tone of the programming was one of thievery and mystery. Fox accurately reported the news about Biden's election, then spent weeks undermining its own reporting. On Friday the 13th, the marketing department debuted a promo that was tailored to win back viewers. "FOX NEWS," the announcer boomed, "THE VOICES AMERICA TRUSTS," teeing off a series of sound bites:

> Ingraham: "These legal efforts are critical."
> Carlson: "There are apparent irregularities."
> Hannity: "The media mob and the Democrats, they lie."

The announcer jumped in and said they're "SPEAKING UP FOR YOU," and it continued:

Steve Doocy: *"They thought there would be a blue wave. Not the case."*

Greg Gutfeld: *"You're going to see something even bigger than Trump in 2022 and 2024."*

Ingraham: *"The truth does need to come out."*

Carlson: *"Can we speak freely again? Can we have America back?"*

Hannity: *"We the people deserve better."*

The viewers deserved better than this election denialism—but they *wanted* it. One of Fox's only bright spots, ratings-wise, was Bartiromo's Sunday morning show, which featured fraud fabulists like Rudy Giuliani without any pushback. The BS claims on Bartiromo's show made reporters at Fox cringe, but the base needed to hear it. They tuned in just for her and tuned out right afterward.

Wherever there was demand to be lied to, there was plenty of supply. "One thing I can't comprehend," said Al Schmidt, the Republican city commissioner of Philadelphia, "is how hungry people are to consume lies and to consume information that is not true." It only made sense through the prism of radicalization. If you watched enough Fox, Trump *was* the truth. So the network's biggest stars enabled Trump's Last Stand. They cheered for his pitiful legal crusade and dreamed that he'd make it all the way to the Supreme Court. They instilled false hope in millions of people. Then they turned around and justified their immoral coverage by saying that their viewers *felt* robbed. "A lot of Americans believe this election was rigged," Carlson said on November 19. "They aren't saying that because they are crazy. They're not just saying it because they're mad. They *mean* it, and that is a potentially fatal problem for this country."

It would, indeed, turn fatal, on January 6.

"Bleeding eyeballs"

"It's really emotionally taxing," a dissident Fox contributor said as the Covid-19 case count exploded and Trump's legal challenges imploded. "We denied the pandemic and now we're denying the election outcome."

At the end of 2020 the news was unrelenting and grim. The only big events on the horizon were the Senate runoff races in Georgia, which would determine control of the Senate, and then Biden's inauguration a couple of weeks later. On Fox the runoffs were spun into a life-or-death matter—which was discouraging since the vast majority of the viewers weren't able to vote.

"Life as we know it hangs in the balance," Jesse Watters insisted. "If the Dems take these seats and control the Senate, it'll be 'bye bye America.' " With Democrats in control, "we're probably not even going to have a national anthem," he said, insanely, and no one even batted an eyelash, because insanity was Fox's rhetorical baseline. Viewers could react to the panicked commentary in one of two ways: freak out, or tune out. Rupert Murdoch wanted them to stay freaked.

"Rupert is not happy" was the prevailing impression in the Fox ranks in December. Lachlan's "we love competition" muscle flex from Election Day was looking worse and worse by the day. Both Murdochs were pressuring Suzanne Scott and the management team to lure the Fox audience back home.

Fox's post-election ratings problems were multifaceted. Everything I wrote at the beginning of this book about Fox's two decades of dominance? Now there was a huge asterisk. Rather than waking up every day on third base, Fox was slugging it out, hoping to steal second, while CNN was knocking balls out of the park. CNN was beating Fox every single day in the twenty-five-to-fifty-four-year-old demographic. Fox was sometimes coming in third behind MSNBC.

"We're bleeding eyeballs," a Fox producer colorfully said. "And we're scared."

The data suggested that some viewers were sampling Newsmax while others were gravitating to CNN and many others were turning off the news altogether. "We're losing people to Netflix. We're losing people to Hallmark," the producer said.

For people whose value and self-worth were measured in fifteen-minute increments of ratings, this was disorienting, and for some downright terrifying. So was the best way to stem the bleeding through news or through opinion? Margaret Sullivan of *The Washington Post* penned a column proposing a newsier Fox News. "Keep appealing to a right-leaning audience," she wrote, "but commit to doing it within the realm of the truth."

But the truth realm really didn't rate.

The predicament reminded me of a drunken night out with an empty pint glass in hand. Do you settle your tab, call an Uber home, and sober up? That's what the responsible voice in your head tells you to do. But the booze beckons you to order another round. Fox heeded the alcohol's advice. Fox ordered shots for the entire bar.

"We turned so far right we went crazy," said one commentator, sounding hung over.

There were hints of this approach in mid-November when Fox began a new marketing campaign, "Standing Up For What's

Right," to promote the prime time entertainers. *Fox & Friends* and the daytime shows were instructed to make liberal use of clips from Carlson's show in particular. Entire segments were framed around what Carlson had said sixteen or eighteen hours earlier.

The next instruction to show producers was specifically about Newsmax. Keep a close eye on Newsmax's bookings, management said, and figure out which guests are appearing on both channels. The intent was to pressure conservative guests to stop saying yes to Newsmax—and to "pause" booking those who didn't abide. Fox used to be on the receiving end of this tactic: When CNBC felt threatened by Fox Business, it insisted on getting CEOs first and froze out companies that went on Fox. Now Fox was doing it to remind guests who was boss.

Rupert envisioned much bigger changes. He wanted Scott to overhaul the underperforming parts of the lineup, including MacCallum's 7 p.m. hour, *The Story*, which he deemed a failure. Newsmax was strongest at 7 thanks to Greg Kelly—and he wanted to cut Newsmax off at the knees.

I could see why. On Monday, December 7, Newsmax beat Fox in the ratings for the first time. It was for a single hour, 7 p.m., but it was a landmark moment for both channels. I called Ruddy's cell phone to hear his reaction, and I ended up breaking the news to him. Evidently I had received the overnight ratings in my inbox before he did. "We're here to stay," Ruddy said. "The ratings are showing that."

The next day Mike Allen of Axios called it "America's new news war." Fox PR called Axios and complained and tried to get the piece watered down, but the gist was correct: Fox was fighting "a two-front war." And a third front was about to open up.

. . .

Fox's election-denying commentary in late 2020 included at least one hundred mentions of Smartmatic, a provider of voting machines and software. Every mention came back to haunt the network when Smartmatic threatened to sue.

"Fox News has engaged in a concerted disinformation campaign against Smartmatic," lawyers for the firm charged in a twenty-page letter to the general counsel for Fox News on December 10. "Fox News told its millions of viewers and readers that Smartmatic was founded by Hugo Chávez, that its software was designed to fix elections, and that Smartmatic conspired with others to defraud the American people and fix the 2020 U.S. election by changing, inflating, and deleting votes." All of this was bunk—and Fox would have known it, the Smartmatic lawyers said, by "performing even a modicum of investigation."

Newsmax and OAN received similar letters. Smartmatic demanded fulsome retractions and signaled that it might sue regardless. One of Smartmatic's rivals, Dominion, which was mentioned on Fox at least seven hundred times, followed up with a similar flurry of legal letters. Hosts like Bartiromo and Dobbs were named and shamed for smearing the firms with easily disproved claims.

What happened next was described by *New York Times* media columnist Ben Smith as "one of the strangest three-minute segments I've ever seen on television." Lou Dobbs said, "There are lots of opinions about the integrity of the election," so "we reached out to one of the leading authorities on open source software for elections, Eddie Perez, for his insight and views." Then Dobbs tossed to a pretaped interview with Perez, conducted by some off-screen producer, refuting many of the previous claims made about Smartmatic on Dobbs's show. It looked like what TV producers call a "bites" interview—when an expert is interviewed to obtain sound bites for a story. Perez told CNN that he had no idea his answers would be used as a sort of shield against Smartmatic's legal threats. But he was glad it aired on Fox, he said, because the network's hosts had been making "harmful" allegations.

The corrective segment was shown on Pirro and Bartiromo's shows the weekend of December 19. Fox's lawyers waited to see if the companies would file suit in the New Year. Meanwhile, crusaders like Bartiromo were hardly chastened by the prospect of crippling defamation suits. Bartiromo kept the words "Smartmatic" and "Dominion" out of her mouth, but on December 14, several days *after* the first legal letter arrived, she continued to conjure up a vast conspiracy to defraud the United States. There's "an intel source telling me that President Trump did in fact win the election," Bartiromo said on her Fox Business morning show. No, her "source" wasn't vetted by Fox's newsroom. No, her startling claim wasn't approved for air. She just said it and moved on, and it only became a scandal when media blogs asked Fox for comment, knowing the network would never say a word. What could they possibly say—Bartiromo violated our best practices? We don't enforce our editorial standards? We don't have standards at all? We just want people to stay tuned?

My question was more specific: Where were Rupert and Lachlan? Weren't they concerned about the destabilizing nature of the Big Lie?

"People are missing the reason why Fox prime time hosts continue to peddle the horseshit of voter fraud: Rupert has always been afraid to dictate to them," an old Murdoch family friend told me.

Rupert was much more comfortable gossiping with his newspaper editors. He spoke their language. *The Wall Street Journal* and the *New York Post*'s editorial boards repeatedly advised Trump to man up, take the loss, and move on. But this positioning rarely made it onto TV. Rupert didn't force it. On the day the *Post* ran a front-page cover imploring Trump to "STOP THE INSANITY," the hosts of *Fox & Friends* ignored it. Never mentioned it at all. As for Lachlan, well, "he's focused on securing the next NFL contract for Fox Sports," an insider said.

On paper there were generations of owners and layers of managers and more than enough levels of oversight to stop Fox from blindly following Trump's antidemocratic lead. But in practice there were just a bunch of fiefdoms controlled by hosts and producers who wanted to get back to No. 1 in the ratings. I used a drinking analogy earlier, but allusions to harder drugs were probably more accurate.

"What you're seeing today," the former Fox contributor Julie Roginsky told me, "is a combination of journalists at Fox who are trying to report the news, the Chris Wallaces of the world, competing with the much higher-rated opinion hosts who . . . are absolutely giving Trump and their viewers the crack that they want."

"Wait," I said, "did you just say crack?"

"Well, I hate to say it, but it *is* a drug," she said. She was still in touch with dozens of friends in and around the Fox orbit. "They are literally giving a drug to the viewers. The viewers are determining what they want to hear, and in order to get ratings, some of these 'journalists,' which they're really not, are giving their viewers what the journalists themselves know is fallacy. They know full well that this is absolutely untrue, but yet because their social media demands it, because their ratings demand it, because their superiors apparently demand it, they allow this to go on. It's absolutely as toxic for the viewers as drugs would be."

Later, I asked one of Roginsky's former on-air sparring partners about this, and he just nodded. He still worked at Fox, and I think he didn't want to agree with the drug abuse parallel out loud. But after five or six seconds of silence he said one word: heroin.

If Smartmatic and Dominion sued, the addiction could cost billions.

"What have we done?"

By 2021, the notion of a tug-of-war between a news side and an opinion side was obsolete. Fox News was really now Fox Opinion with a strange news appendage that caused discomfort from time to time. The network's narrative was entirely about feelings over facts. And still it wasn't enough for Trump. It was never, ever enough. On New Year's Day he tweeted that Fox's weekend daytime lineup was unwatchable: "Switching over to @OANN!" But he never switched for long. Historian Nicole Hemmer said, "President Trump is furious at Fox News—and addicted to it."

The *Fox & Friends* gang had gotten him into office. But they couldn't keep him there. "People who are staunch conservatives in our country just feel so—just so defeated because of this election," Ainsley Earhardt said January 4. "They do feel like it was rigged." It was the beginning of a wicked week. January 5 was the Senate runoff in Georgia, followed by the certification of Biden's victory on January 6. Weekend opinionators Will Cain and Pete Hegseth were dispatched to Atlanta for in-person coverage of the runoff, for no logical reason, since they just sat behind an anchor desk in a dark parking lot. Cain proceeded to offer absolution to the Americans who bought Trump's Big Lie. "I think Americans, I think Republicans, conservatives, can be forgiven for their skepticism," he said. "Because whether or not an election was rigged, it certainly feels like society is rigged right now." What Cain should have said next, but didn't, was "Because Fox has been lying to you for a really long time."

Hegseth flew to DC for Wednesday's congressional action. He

stood along the National Mall and wore an American flag ball cap and promoted the "March to Save America" rally like he was a participant. "We believe the president will take the stage at eleven . . . and then the big show continues on Capitol Hill with the fight over the electoral college," he told viewers.

There was no legitimate "fight" to have, but hosts across the right-wing TV trifecta—Fox, Newsmax, and OAN—had been promising a fight for weeks. Thus the storming of the Capitol shouldn't have been a complete surprise. Pirro spoke of the Revolutionary War and wondered if anyone in Congress was "willing to battle for the America that those soldiers fought for, the one that you and I believe in." Mark Levin said that "any Republican who doesn't stand up" and object to the results will be "shredding the Constitution" right along with the Democrats. They wanted a coup. They *needed* a coup.

Hegseth called the moment "a constitutional tinderbox" during his pre-show coverage on Wednesday. Once the fire started, Fox's news appendage took charge for a few hours, and covered the riot more or less like the other networks did, but once night fell, the network returned to normal. The banner on Carlson's show benignly described "CHAOS ON CAPITOL HILL" instead of attributing the chaos to "PRO-TRUMP RIOTERS" or "DOMESTIC TERRORISTS."

"We got to this sad chaotic day for a reason," Carlson said. "It is not your fault; it is *their* fault." He blamed elected officials for not listening to, and addressing the concerns of, the protesters who felt compelled to break in to the Capitol. Later in the evening Hannity resumed his lies about the election, and Ingraham praised the peaceful "patriots" in DC who were maligned by a "small contingent of loons" who ruined the day. Ingraham and her guests floated bogus theories about Antifa instead, implying that left-wing radicals were actually responsible for the riot. Federal authorities compiled a mountain of evidence to the contrary, including many testimonials from rioters who said they were acting on what they believed were Trump's orders. But on Fox there was always a presumption of innocence, solely for the populist base, solely for the Republicans who stayed in line.

Fox's Capitol Hill producer Jason Donner knew better. He tweeted during the riot, "What's happening at the Capitol today is disgusting and Republicans will have a lot to answer for." Donner said the press corps "will hold them accountable because that's what we do in a democracy in the greatest nation in the world." That *is* what we do, but that's not what Fox did.

January 6 lives in infamy as an act of domestic terrorism against the United States. "This would never have happened," the conservative author Max Boot wrote, "if Fox 'News,' OAN, Newsmax, Mark Levin, *Daily Wire*, and all the rest had not been spreading poisonous lies about the election. This would never have happened if 100+ House members and 13 senators had not endorsed those lies." A writer for *Vox*, Sean Illing, called it the fantasy-industrial complex: "This is America's brain on misinformation," he wrote on January 8 as a sprawling federal investigation started to identify suspects. In theory a terror investigation would have been catnip to Fox's programmers. But because it was right-wing terrorism inspired by Trump, they stuffed it down the memory hole as forcefully as possible.

The veteran staffer who texted me full of guilt—"what have we done?"—was in the definite minority. I picked up on precious little introspection. Some staffers dismissed the riots as Newsmax viewers, not Fox fans. (I did notice a huge One America News flag among the marchers.) From a PR perspective, Fox's goal was to distance itself from the insurrectionists and move on. The network needed to woo its audience back; in-depth coverage of the crimes at the Capitol wasn't going to accomplish that. But Rupert had a plan.

"We are lost"

Fox's tagline that had sounded like a boast in 2020, "AMERICA is Watching," registered more like a plea, "America IS Watching," in 2021. It sounded like the announcer needed to convince viewers that they weren't alone.

As CNN extended its ratings gains in the wake of the Capitol attack, Fox announced what it trumpeted as a "new daytime lineup." But the biggest change was at night: MacCallum was booted from the 7 p.m. hour because the suits decided that her show, while sharply right of center, was not far *enough* right to satisfy the base. In MacCallum's place, they said, would be a new talk show led by opinion talent To Be Determined. Brian Kilmeade and Maria Bartiromo were the first two hosts to try out in the time slot.

MacCallum was moved to the much lower-rated 3 p.m. time slot. She played along with the shift in public, but she was disappointed that she wasn't given more time at 7 to prove herself. A source threw up their hands when I asked about the 7 p.m. revamp: "The viewers want opinion. That's their opinion."

Every change was about having less news and more opinions-about-the-news. It was like serving dessert without dinner, when the dessert consisted of screaming about how awful the dinner was, and warning that the meal might be a socialist plot, and hey, while we're at it, why are chefs so corrupt?

The man in charge of this menu, so to speak, was Rupert Murdoch. "These were all Murdoch's calls," a Fox anchor said on the day of the big announcement. Because MacCallum moved to 3, Bill Hemmer had to move back to a morning co-anchor shift, only a year after he was finally given his own newscast. He was paired with Dana Perino, who also lost her own solo hour. Harris Faulkner's 1 p.m. show moved to 11 a.m., leading into *Outnumbered*, which was prodded even further rightward by booking liberal panelists less and less often. At 1 p.m., White House correspondent John Roberts was paired with Sandra Smith. A rival TV exec emailed me a *Titanic* reference: "This is the biggest rearranging of the deck chairs ever." An insider put it even more pithily: "We are lost."

"Fox is a really different place than it was pre-election," a commentator said in mid-January. The shows spun off radical ideas like it was a game of bingo. Producers fought with each other to book the subset of conservative guests that viewers loved—media bashers like Mollie Hemingway and shouters like Dan Bongino—while ignoring more rational Fox contributors like Jonah Goldberg and Stephen Hayes. The chosen guests fed from the network's trough of resentment and then vomited it right back up.

Segments about the fallout from the riot were minimized while segments about "BIG TECH CENSORSHIP" were scheduled twice an hour. Management even ordered special "CENSORSHIP" graphics packages. Facebook, Twitter, and other tech platforms were trying to clean house by banning QAnon content and removing "Stop the Steal" lies. But they were cleaning up a months-old garbage heap while fresh garbage was being created elsewhere. Big Tech's belated actions, especially the suspension of the president's accounts, were met by ritualized whippings on Fox.

"Fox News whipped people into a frenzy for years," NBC's Ben Collins observed. "When it became clear the monster they created attacked the Capitol and they couldn't blame Antifa after arrest reports rolled in, they refused to reflect. They instead shifted to attacking platforms for banning insurrectionists."

Savvy viewers saw the Big Tech bashing as a skirmish in Murdoch's never-ending campaign for better financial deals with Facebook and Google. Mostly left unspoken in Fox's condemnations of content moderation was this salient fact: Twitter and Facebook and YouTube were tackling the supply problem, but the much bigger problem was the demand. There was extraordinary demand for "Trump won" content, even after Biden's win was certified. And where there was demand, there were always Fox pundits willing to supply it. On January 14 Maria Bartiromo hosted White House trade adviser Peter Navarro, who insisted that Trump was "legally elected on November 3."

"We know that there were irregularities in this election," Bartiromo said, undeterred.

There were other Trump dead-enders too, like Hannity, but Tucker Carlson, always the more savvy operator, moved on: His monologues sounded like warm-ups for presidential stump speeches. Several of his colleagues told me they could see Carlson on the primary ballot in 2024.

Next came the purge. Some of the people most closely associated with the Arizona call were suddenly out of work. Bill Sammon retired, and the next day Chris Stirewalt was fired along with more than a dozen other journalists in the digital operation. Scholar Jay Rosen interpreted the moves this way: "Fox said Biden would win Arizona. Biden did win Arizona. Which created a crisis at Fox. Now, heads have rolled. This would never happen at a reality-based newsroom."

Some members of Foxworld spoke up on Stirewalt's behalf, including Goldberg, who tweeted, "I think it was an abjectly terrible decision for Fox to let him go. And if saying so is a problem with some folks, so be it."

Stirewalt declined to speak about what went wrong at Fox, but he penned an op-ed that generalized about America's "nation of news consumers" being both "overfed and malnourished."

"The rebellion on the populist right against the results of the 2020 election was partly a cynical, knowing effort by political operators and their hype men in the media to steal an election or at least get rich trying," he wrote on January 28. "But it was also the tragic consequence of the informational malnourishment so badly afflicting the nation. When I defended the call for Biden in the Arizona election, I became a target of murderous rage from consumers who were furious at not having their views confirmed."

Murderous rage—for telling the truth.

Without a Twitter account, Trump couldn't thank Fox's propagandists or shit on its news anchors anymore. On January 13, he wrote a Twitter-like statement and gave it to Fox exclusively instead. "In light of reports of more demonstrations, I urge that there must be NO violence, NO lawbreaking and NO vandalism of any kind," he said, acceding to pressure from Republican leaders to man up for a minute.

The House of Representatives impeached Trump, for a second time, later that day. The major networks produced special coverage, but Fox covered the process with its usual daytime anchors—yet another appeasement to the base. At night, Ingraham said impeachment was actually an attempt to "impeach the Americans who support his policies," which was nonsense. Her guest Lara Logan imagined a new "war on terror" targeting Trump supporters. Then her next guest, Mike Huckabee, said, "This was a lynching of Donald Trump." On-air comments that would have prompted days of outrage five years ago now came and went with nary a tweet. I feared for what new forms of extremism would emerge in the years ahead. And I was far from alone.

Re-enter Shep Smith, who had begun to anchor a nightly newscast on CNBC in September 2020. Throughout all of the interviews promoting his new show, he assiduously sidestepped questions about Fox, saying bland things like "I felt it was the right time for me to leave." Why? He didn't say. He said he read the first edition of this book, thought it was "an interesting read," and didn't want to comment further. But that changed in mid-January, after the Big Lie, after the insurrection. Smith spoke with CNN's Christiane Amanpour and said the Fox machine's falsehoods were "injurious to society."

"I don't know how some people sleep at night," he said, seemingly trying to wake up his former colleagues. "I know that there are a lot of people who have propagated the lies and who have pushed them forward over and over again who are smart enough and educated enough to know better.

"Those of us who are so honored and grateful to have a platform of public influence," he said, "have to use it for the public good."

The next day, inauguration day, Trump slunk away to Mar-a-Lago. He boarded Air Force One for the final time and watched his plane take off via a TV monitor tuned to Fox News. During the flight, his skeleton staff announced one literally last-hour addition to the long list of pardons Trump had granted the night before. The surprise name was Albert J. Pirro Jr., aka Judge Jeanine's ex-husband, who had been convicted on conspiracy and tax evasion charges in 2000. Pirro had been so loyal to Trump for so long. She had broadcast Trump infomercials for four straight years. So she was pissed when Albert's name wasn't on the list. She lobbied Trump early on inauguration morning, and by the time Trump touched down in West Palm Beach, Pirro Jr. was a pardoned man.

"The Biden team has no idea"

Back in July, during one of Tucker Carlson's typically obnoxious essays about liberals attacking free speech, he said, "What do you think they plan to do to Fox News if they take power?" His implication, ridiculous as usual, was that the Biden White House would wipe poor little Fox off the map.

The actual answer to his question was evident in December when incoming White House press secretary Jen Psaki granted her first TV interview to . . . *Fox News Sunday* moderator Chris Wallace.

I messaged Psaki, since I had been lobbying for an interview with her, and asked if it was intentional that Fox was her first stop. Yes, it was. Psaki was reflecting Biden's commitment to work "for all Americans," including those who would never vote for him. Every word Biden and Psaki uttered was in contrast to Trump. More than at any point in history, "part of the job of the White House press secretary is to rebuild trust with the American people," Psaki said at the end of December.

So the liberals who wanted Fox News banned from the briefing room were not going to get their wish. Fox promoted Steve Doocy's son Peter, who'd covered the Biden campaign, to White House correspondent.

In yet another contrast to Trump, Biden went out of his way to take questions from the younger Doocy, and disarmed him with Bidenisms.

After Biden took office and held his first phone call with the Russian president, Doocy called out at an unrelated event, "Mr. President, what did you talk to Vladimir Putin about?"

Biden turned and said, "You! He sends his best."

Some right-wingers pretended to be offended, but Doocy wasn't. Neither were his bosses. They liked the rapport that was developing between Doocy and the president. "I know he always asks me tough questions," Biden said of Doocy the next day, "and he always has an edge to them, but I like him anyway."

Peace in our time? More like a show for the cameras. Behind the scenes there was nonstop consternation about Fox's unique power to pollute the political discourse. Some days Fox went 24/7 on Hunter Biden innuendo; other days were devoted to tearing down Biden's so-called "far left" agenda and denigrating VP Kamala Harris. In some Democratic quarters, there were doubts that the new White House was equipped to fight the information wars. "The Biden team has no idea what they are up against," a liberal voice inside Fox told me.

When talk radio king Rush Limbaugh died on February 17, 2021, Fox turned into a virtual memorial service, with the kind of coverage usually reserved for the passing of a president. Trump called in to the network for the first time in months and paid his respects before repeating his Big Lie about the election. The anchors didn't challenge him one bit. Absolute deference to the Trumpified audience was now the rule. Fox News was the Trump administration in exile. Kayleigh McEnany held job talks with the network while still technically serving as press secretary. Larry Kudlow came aboard to host an afternoon show on Fox Business. Other aides desperately chased Fox airtime because they knew the likes of NBC would never offer them a contract.

The Murdochs renewed Suzanne Scott's contract despite all of the turbulence. The CEO positioned herself as an expansionist, leading Fox into new lines of businesses like lifestyle (they produced a Christmas movie!) and livestreaming weather coverage. But these experiments belied the fact that Fox was more dependent than ever on its propaganda players.

Lachlan Murdoch sometimes sounded like he didn't know what he owned. "We believe where we're targeted, to the center-right, is exactly where we should be targeted," he told investors on February 9. "We don't need to go further right. We don't believe America is further right, and we're obviously not going to pivot left. All of our significant competitors are to the far left." His dismissive attitude toward Newsmax and OAN was mixed with denialism about what Fox had become. Every move was further to the right: fewer news reports. Fewer Democratic guests on talk shows. More Tucker Carlson all day long. Shannon Bream saw her 11 p.m. hour bumped to midnight in favor of Greg Gutfeld, the comedian who ranted about the "Russia hoax" and occasionally knocked his own news-side colleagues. Fox would now have its own late-night comedy show because, Scott said, "people need a reason to laugh."

Inside Fox, staffers bit their nails and braced for further changes. The legal fallout from the Big Lie terrified some. On February 9, Smartmatic dropped a bombshell $2.7 billion lawsuit on the heads of Fox, Rudy Giuliani, and Sidney Powell; the suit named three Fox hosts: Lou Dobbs, Maria Bartiromo, and Jeanine Pirro. Fox called the lawsuit meritless and said "we are proud of our 2020 election coverage," which deserved a little chuckle.

One day later, Fox benched Dobbs and canceled his show, but sources insisted that the plan predated the lawsuit; he had pissed off management one too many times, and his show struggled to turn a profit, so he wasn't worth the headache. (One America News offered to hire him.) Dobbs's dismissal left other talent feeling vulnerable, but, in reality, the only people who were really exposed were liberals like Juan Williams, who were increasingly fighting not just their fellow panelists but Fox's entire editorial bubble. As Fox downplayed the Trump impeachment trial, Williams lost his cool, shouting on *The Five* that "you don't want to deal with the news!"

That's because the base didn't want to deal. Nielsen rated Fox No. 1 the first time Trump was acquitted; Fox ranked No. 3, well behind MSNBC and CNN, the second time around.

But some viewers started to come home, just as the Murdochs expected. Trump privately mocked Fox's ratings declines, boasting that they deserved it because they weren't loyal enough to him. He was still mad that Fox hadn't cut him a discount on ad time during his campaign. But when Limbaugh's death was announced, he called Fox first. He came home.

That night, after weeks of uncharacteristic silence, Trump tried something he had never done before: a right-wing TV trifecta. He taped interviews with One America News and Newsmax as well as *Hannity*, bestriding the entire landscape, that parallel reality he had brought to life. These channels now competed for his and his base's affection. He could play them off one another. He could have "Trump TV" for free.

"I have a funny feeling we're going to hear a lot more from Donald Trump," Hannity said at the end of their phone call.

"Well, there's a lot to talk about," Trump said. "And our country is a great place. And we're going to make it even greater."

EPILOGUE

Having a Fox News president left the rest of the country without a properly functioning chief executive from 2017 to 2020. In 2021 the Biden administration began to repair the damage and reverse Trump's Fox-inspired actions. But the Trump years unleashed something that was out of control.

It didn't have to happen. At the beginning of 2017 Trump, hot off his first election win ever, needed *help*. He needed vetted information. He needed to hear hard truths from people he respected. And he needed to be held accountable.

But his Fox wingmen didn't do any of that. Instead, they fed his worst impulses and helped him deceive the people who voted for him. They encouraged him to perform like a cable news bomb-thrower: to pick fights instead of finding common ground. To govern for TV ratings instead of tangible results. To supply endless content for talk shows. And, in 2020, to stoke denialism about the pandemic and the election.

Profits over principle—that was the priority of the Trump years. Rupert and Lachlan Murdoch are much richer for it. But the rest of us are poorer.

Throughout the Trump presidency, there were straight lines from Fox's misguided segments to Trump's mistakes. Those who tried to correct him, like Shep Smith and Neil Cavuto and Chris Wallace, were vilified. Those who *excused* his misconduct were idolized.

That's why the Trump age was really the "hoax" age. Fox viewers came away with the impression that nothing was truly knowable. Everything was relative. There were distortions and deceptions in every direction. Up could be down and left could be right and real news could be fake. Many people, exhausted by the uncertainty, gave up on knowing for sure whether Russia had helped Trump win the 2016 election, or if the administration was doing all it could to end the pandemic. This sorry state of affairs reminded me of Peter Pomerantsev's book *Nothing Is True and Everything Is Possible*, about the influence of propaganda media in Vladimir Putin's Russia. Pomerantsev said Fox's rejection of balance and indulgence of conspiracy reminded him of Putin.

"For anyone who knows Russia, Trump's aim in the use of the word 'hoax' is uncannily familiar," he told me. "In Russia the regime dismisses any criticism as 'information war,' thus making any kind of evidence-based debate impossible: All information is just a weapon, a form of manipulation, there is no rational ground on which to have a debate, you are either 'with us' or 'against us.'"

"Likewise," said Pomerantsev, "Trump dismisses all criticism as just part of an info op against him, a 'hoax' where the content of the criticism is just a cover for manipulation by some vast, murky conspiracy." He said the end point of Putin's Kremlin and Trump's White House was the same: "to undermine the epistemic ground on which evidence-based debate and deliberative democracy can be practiced."

The word "hoax" was uttered more than one thousand five hundred times on Fox News in 2020. Every time Trump tweeted it, or Hannity shouted it, a little bit more truth was chipped away from America's foundation—precisely at a time when the country was beset by multiple crises and needed honesty and accuracy, compassion and sound science. Having no truth to tell the public, ever, Trump set the people against each other, stirring up strife. He told the public not to believe their own eyes and ears, and he thought he could get away with it because, on Fox—arguably his only reality— he always did. *Don't believe what you read. Journalists are enemies of the people. "What you're seeing and what you're reading is not what's happening." Just trust in the Fox News president.*

That was the biggest hoax of all.

ACKNOWLEDGMENTS

This book would not have been possible without my wife, Jamie, who supported me even though this project coincided with the birth of our son, Story. She was my sounding board and stress-tester. Our older child, Sunny, was a constant source of inspiration. When Fox was on the living room TV, she would see Trump's face and ask, "Is he your friend?" Seeing the world through the eyes of a three-year-old is the best gift in the world.

Thank you to my book agent, Pilar Queen, and the team at UTA; to Nell Scovell, who broke my bad writing habits and challenged me to tell the truth; to Scott Nover, who flexed his research muscles; and to Ewa Beaujon, who fact-checked key sections.

Most of all, thank you to my editor Julia Cheiffetz, who knew what I was trying to say before I knew how to say it. Thank you for motivating me and molding lumpy raw material into a readable story. Thanks as well to the indispensable assistant editor Nicholas Ciani; to indefatigable production editor Mark LaFlaur; and to Libby McGuire, Jonathan Karp, Adam Rothberg, Joanna Pinsker, and Amara Balan for championing the book even when I blew through deadlines.

Thank you to CNN publicist extraordinaire Emily Kuhn; *Reliable Sources* team leader Jonathan Auerbach and producers Katie Pellico, Diane Kaye, and Marina di Marzo; editors Alex Koppelman, An Phung, and Robert McLean; and other colleagues who tolerated my chapter-writing binges. A special thanks to Oliver Darcy.

Thank you to the reporters and scholars who documented the Trump-Fox merger in real time, especially Mark Knoller and Martha Kumar, who tracked all of the president's interviews. Essential databases and resources included Factba.se, the Trump Twitter Archives, TVEyes, and the Internet Archive.

Finally, thank you to my mother, Donna, for instilling in me the confidence to call total strangers and convince them to talk. Thank you to my in-laws Helen and Neil for cheering me on. My late mentor David Carr used to ask sources, "What do you think the story is that I should tell?" That was my approach with *Hoax*, before the book even had a publisher or a title. I am grateful to every source who answered my questions, especially those who don't want to be named here, and to the people who are valiantly trying to keep the News in Fox News.

NOTES

PROLOGUE

1 *Kevin McCarthy sheltered in place:* Michael Ruiz, "Lawmakers, Aides and Others Sheltering Inside Capitol Describe Chaos; at Least 1 Dead." Fox News, FOX News Network, January 6, 2021, https://www.foxnews.com/us/lawmakers -aides-and-others-sheltering-inside-capitol-describe-chaos.

1 *"People are getting hurt":* Kevin McCarthy, *Bill Hemmer Reports,* Fox News, January 6, 2021.

2 *"stay peaceful":* Donald Trump, Twitter post, January 6, 2021, 2:38 p.m.

3 *"His initial reaction was not horror":* Maggie Haberman, CNN, January 10, 2021.

3 *"I am asking for everyone at the U.S. Capitol":* Donald Trump, Twitter post, January 6, 2021, 3:13 p.m.

4 *"Why is it that in these major states":* Donald Trump, *Ingraham Angle,* Fox News, August 31, 2020.

4 *"Trump was probably watching the interview":* Steve Benen, *The Rachel Maddow Show,* MSNBC, January 7, 2020.

6 *"The thing that's going to end this is the warmer weather":* Greg Gutfeld, *The Five,* Fox News, February 24, 2020.

6 *"It's going to disappear":* "Remarks by President Trump in Meeting with African American Leaders," 2020, the White House, the United States Government, February 28, 2020, https://www.whitehouse.gov/briefings-statements /remarks-president-trump-meeting-african-american-leaders/.

6 *"coronavirus hysteria":* Acyn Torabi, Twitter post, March 17, 2020, 9:14 p.m., https://twitter.com/pablo_honey1/status/1240084563159744512.

6 *"panDEMic party":* Laura Ingraham, *Ingraham Angle,* Fox News, February 26, 2020.

7 *"at worst, at worst":* Marc Siegel, M.D., *Hannity,* Fox News, March 6, 2020.

7 *"actually the safest time to fly"*: Ainsley Earhardt, *Fox & Friends*, Fox News, March 13, 2020.

7 *Four out of five Fox viewers were over the age of fifty-five:* Nielsen Media Research, March 2020 audience report.

7 *"minimize harm"*: SPJ Code of Ethics, Society of Professional Journalists, September 6, 2014, https://www.spj.org/ethicscode.asp.

8 *"Coronavirus. They're politicizing it"*: Donald Trump, February 28, 2020, https://www.rev.com/blog/transcripts/donald-trump-charleston-south-carolina-rally-transcript-february-28-2020.

8 *"a total, and very expensive, hoax!"*: Donald Trump, Twitter post, December 6, 2013, 10:13 a.m., https://twitter.com/realdonaldtrump/status/4089776169 26830592.

9 *when the Covid-19 death toll surpassed two hundred thousand souls:* "Covid: US Death Toll Passes 200,000," *BBC News*, BBC, September 23, 2020, https://www.bbc.com/news/world-us-canada-54244515#:~:text=The%20US%20coronavirus%20death%20toll,including%20North%20Dakota%20and%20Utah.

10 *When he came down with the virus himself:* Donald Trump, Twitter post, October 1, 2020, 9:54 p.m.

10 *"The Democrats know it's a hoax"*: "President Trump Campaigns in New Hampshire," C-SPAN, October 25, 2020, https://www.c-span.org/video/?477323-1%2Fpresident-trump-campaigns-hampshire.

10 *"You don't want the ballot hoax"*: "President Trump Campaign Event in Lititz, Pennsylvania," C-SPAN, October 26, 2020, https://www.c-span.org/video/?477338-1/president-trump-campaign-event-lititz-pennsylvania.

10 *"the whole ballot hoax"*: "President Trump Campaign Rally in Omaha, Nebraska," C-SPAN, October 27, 2020, *https://www.c-span.org/video/?477342-1/president-trump-campaign-rally-omaha-nebraska.*

10 *"You know, they throw away ballots"*: "President Trump Campaign Event in Lititz, Pennsylvania," C-SPAN, October 26, 2020, https://www.c-span.org/video/?477338-1/president-trump-campaign-event-lititz-pennsylvania.

10 *"It's a big tech hoax"*: "President Trump Holds Rally in Rome, Georgia," C-SPAN, November 1, 2020, https://www.c-span.org/video/?477676-1/president-trump-holds-rally-rome-georgia.

10 *"Mail-in ballot hoax"*: Donald Trump, *Life, Liberty & Levin*, Fox News, November 8, 2020.

10 *"Rigged election hoax"*: Donald Trump, Twitter post, November 15, 2020, 7:04 a.m.

10 *"Election Hoax"*: Donald Trump, Twitter post, November 20, 2020, 6:10 a.m.

11 *On November 27, Fox announced:* Maane Khatchatourian, "Trump Sets First Live Interview Since Election Loss on Fox News Channel," *Variety*, November 27, 2020, https://variety.com/2020/tv/news/trump-first-interview-since-election-fox-business-1234841248/.

11 *"This election was a fraud"*: Donald Trump, *Sunday Morning Futures*, Fox News, November 27, 2020.

12 *Republicans were pushing two stories*: Marie Harf, *Outnumbered*, Fox News, November 20, 2020.

15 *covering up the truth about AIDS*: Marc Fisher, "The Making of Sean Hannity: How a Long Island Kid Learned to Channel Red-State Rage," *Washington Post*, October 10, 2017, https://www.washingtonpost.com/lifestyle/style /the-making-of-sean-hannity-how-a-long-island-kid-learned-to-channel -red-state-rage/2017/10/09/540cfc38-8821-11e7-961d-2f373b3977ee_story .html.

15 *"He saw something that I didn't even think I knew I had"*: Brian Stelter, "Victory Lap for Fox and Hannity," *New York Times*, October 10, 2011, New York edition, sec. B.

17 *Hannity sent suggestions to the campaign apparatus*: Greg Sargent, "Opinion: The Final Implosion of Trump's Fox News Propagandists," *Washington Post*, November 5, 2020, https://www.washingtonpost.com/opinions/2020/11/05 /final-implosion-trumps-fox-news-propagandists/.

17 *"It's a bad example. We don't need it"*: Josh Feldman, "Geraldo Asks Hannity to Tell Trump: 'For the Good of the Nation, Stop Shaking Hands,'" Mediaite, March 11, 2020, https://www.mediaite.com/tv/geraldo-asks-hannity-to-tell -trump-for-the-good-of-the-nation-stop-shaking-hands/.

18 *Hannity kept inviting Kayleigh McEnany*: Kayleigh McEnany, *Hannity*, Fox News, November 11, 2020.

20 *It kept the hedges trimmed*: James McClain, "Rupert Murdoch's Son Lachlan Buys $150 Million Bel Air Estate, Setting California Record," *Variety*, December 17, 2019, https://variety.com/2019/dirt/moguls/rupert-murdochs -son-buys-150-million-bel-air-estate-setting-california-record-1203434081/.

21 *$23 million-a-year deal*: Cheyenne Roundtree, "NBC's '$69 million mistake,'" *Daily Mail*, October 5, 2017, https://www.dailymail.co.uk/news/article -4948276/Floundering-Megyn-Kelly-makes-23m-year-NBC.html.

23 *at least 657 instances*: Matt Gertz, "Trump Sent 657 Live Tweets of Fox Programming in 2019," Media Matters for America, January 19, 2020, https:// www.mediamatters.org/fox-news/study-trump-sent-657-live-tweets-fox -programming-2019.

27 *"the most powerful person in television news"*: Tucker Carlson, *Tucker*, MSNBC, July 14, 2006.

29 *Tea Party supporters in Louisiana*: Arlie Russell Hochschild, *Strangers in Their Own Land: Anger and Mourning on the American Right* (New York: The New Press, 2018).

30 *"Fox News Republicans"*: "Fractured Nation: Widening Partisan Polarization and Key Issues in 2020 Presidential Elections," PRRI, October 20, 2019, https://www.prri.org/research/fractured-nation-widening-partisan -polarization-and-key-issues-in-2020-presidential-elections/.

THE CREATION

31 *"squish Rupert like a bug"*: Bill Carter, "ABC and NBC Look Ahead To Rival All-News Channels," *New York Times*, December 6, 1995, https://www.nytimes.com/1995/12/06/business/abc-and-nbc-look-ahead-to-rival-all-news-channels.html.

33 *"He says rude, obnoxious things"*: Scott D. Pierce, "Fox News Chief Ailes Is Certainly Arrogant," *Salt Lake City Deseret News*, July 31, 1996.

33 *"with the art of the return phone call"*: Jimmy Breslin, "Jimmy Breslin's columns on Donald Trump," *Newsday*, March 19, 2017, https://www.newsday.com/opinion/jimmy-breslin-s-columns-on-donald-trump-1.13288319.

34 *Donald Trump posing as a flack for Donald Trump*: John Cassidy, "Trump's History of Lying, from John Barron to @realDonaldTrump," *New Yorker*, April 24, 2018, https://www.newyorker.com/news/our-columnists/trumps-history-of-lying-from-john-barron-to-realdonaldtrump.

36 *Louis Aguirre cohosted the first show*: WSVN-TV News Team, "Biography of Louis Aguirre," WSVN-TV, April 13, 2010.

36 *the very first in-studio guest*: Fox & Friends, Fox News, February 1, 1998.

36 *"I don't even want to use the word—fear"*: Bob Woodward, *Fear: Trump in the White House* (New York: Simon & Schuster, 2018).

39 *War on Christmas*: Liam Stack, "How the 'War on Christmas' Controversy Was Created," *New York Times*, December 19, 2016, https://www.nytimes.com/2016/12/19/us/war-on-christmas-controversy.html.

41 *"55 to dead"*: Roger Ailes, quoted by Joan Walsh, "My Only Meeting with Roger Ailes," *The Nation*, May 18, 2017, https://www.thenation.com/article/archive/my-only-meeting-with-roger-ailes/.

41 *"If you torture the data enough"*: Ronald H. Coase, *Essays on Economics and Economists* (Chicago: University of Chicago Press, 1994).

42 *"I said, 'Wait a minute, Donald' "*: Billy Bush, *Real Time with Bill Maher*, HBO, March 16, 2018.

42 *"Do you think it's any coincidence?"*: Brian Stelter, "Victory Lap for Fox and Hannity," *New York Times*, October 9, 2011, https://www.nytimes.com/2011/10/10/business/media/fox-news-and-hannity-at-the-top-after-15-years.html.

43 *In 2009 I had the unenviable*: Brian Stelter, "A Dispute Over Obama's Birth Lives on in the Media," *New York Times*, July 24, 2009.

44 *"social movement orchestrator"*: Vanessa Williamson and Theda Skocpol, *Tea Party and the Remaking of Republican Conservatism* (New York: Oxford University Press, 2012).

44 *"We don't promote the Tea Party"*: Rupert Murdoch, interview with Patricia Sellers, *Fortune*, 2014.

45 *"home team"*: Brian Stelter, Paul Rittenberg, "Fox's Volley with Obama Intensifying," *New York Times*, October 11, 2009, https://www.nytimes.com/2009/10/12/business/media/12fox.html.

46 *Jon Stewart once called cable TV:* Jon Stewart, "Closing Speech at the Rally to Restore Sanity and/or Fear," October 30, 2010, http://faculty.washington.edu /jwhelan/Documents/Speeches/Stewart%20Sanity%20Rally.pdf.

49 *On March 28:* "Fox Goes Birther: Trump Tells Unquestioning Co-Hosts, 'I'm Starting to Wonder . . . Whether or Not [Obama] Was Born in This Country,'?" Media Matters for America, March 28, 2011, https://www .mediamatters.org/fox-friends/fox-goes-birther-trump-tells-unquestioning -co-hosts-im-starting-wonderwhether-or-not.

49 *"Monday Mornings with Trump":* Frances Martel, "You Saw This Coming: Fox News Announces 'Mondays with Trump' on *Fox & Friends,*" Mediaite, April 1, 2011, https://www.mediaite.com/tv/you-saw-this-coming-fox-news -announces-mondays-with-trump-on-fox-friends/.

50 *"I'm not sure that I ever would have been":* Michael Barnes, *Man in the Arena,* documentary, 2020.

50 *"The fact that Fox likes Trump":* Dave Trumble, Twitter post, May 7, 2014, 7:30 a.m., https://twitter.com/dktrumble/status/464004386012676096.

53 *"TRUMP CUTS AID":* Brian Stelter, "Fox News Apologizes for '3 Mexican Countries' Headline," CNN.com, March 31, 2019, https://www .cnn.com/2019/03/31/media/fox-news-mexican-countries-stelter/index .html.

56 *"It was like The LEGO Movie":* Kimberly Guilfoyle, *The Five,* Fox News, June 16, 2015, https://www.foxnews.com/transcript/is-donald-trump-a -serious-candidate-for-president.

57 *"He did ISIS, Obamacare":* Greg Gutfeld, *The Five,* Fox News, June 16, 2015, https://www.foxnews.com/transcript/is-donald-trump-a-serious-candidate -for-president.

57 *Trump tweeted out a thank-you:* Donald Trump, Twitter post, June 22, 2015, 6:39 a.m., https://twitter.com/realDonaldTrump/status/612932881623711744.

58 *"When is Donald Trump going to stop embarrassing his friends":* Rupert Murdoch (@RupertMurdoch), Twitter, July 18, 2015, 8:06 p.m., https://twitter.com /rupertmurdoch/status/622558129742573568.

59 *"What did you do to piss off Trump?":* Megyn Kelly, *Settle for More* (New York: HarperCollins, 2016).

60 *Kelly confronted a* Daily Beast *reporter:* Josh Feldman, "Megyn Kelly Confronts *Daily Beast* Reporter over Trump Piece: Why Is This Relevant?" Mediaite, July 29, 2015, https://www.mediaite.com/tv/megyn-kelly-confronts-daily -beast-reporter-over-trump-piece-why-is-this-relevant/.

60 *"O'Reilly didn't put it on his show":* Kelly, *Settle for More.*

60 *"You've called women you don't like":* Megyn Kelly, "Fox News August Presidential Debate," Fox News, August 6, 2015, https://video.foxnews.com /v/4406746003001#sp=show-clips.

61 *Trump's campaign-within-the-campaign:* Kelly, *Settle for More.*

61 *"Wow, @megynkelly really bombed tonight":* Donald Trump, Twitter post,

August 7, 2015, 3:40 a.m., https://twitter.com/realdonaldtrump/status/6295 57762427604992.

61 *His lawyer Michael Cohen:* Ben Schreckinger, "Top Trump Deputy Retweets 'Gut Her' Attack on Megyn Kelly," *Politico*, August 7, 2015, https://www .politico.com/story/2015/08/donald-trump-deputy-megyn-kelly-gut-her -retweet-121160.

61 *Twenty-four hours after the debate:* Donald Trump, Don Lemon, *CNN Tonight with Don Lemon*, CNN, https://www.cnn.com/videos/us/2015/08/08/donald -trump-megyn-kelly-blood-lemon-intv-ctn.cnn.

62 *Her family had to bring an armed bodyguard:* Kelly, *Settle for More.*

62 *Fox News PR boss Irena Briganti:* Brian Stelter, "Fox News Knocks Trump over Megyn Kelly 'Conspiracy Theories,' " *CNNMoney*, CNN, August 14, 2014, https://money.cnn.com/2015/08/14/media/donald-trump-roger-ailes-dispute /index.html.

62 *"Donald Trump's vitriolic attacks":* Alex Weprin, "Fox News: Trump's Megyn Kelly Tweets 'Beneath the Dignity' of Presidential Candidate," *Politico*, https:// www.politico.com/blogs/on-media/2016/03/donald-trump-megyn-kelly -tweets-fox-220987.

THE CANDIDATE

65 *"friend Donald has to learn":* Rupert Murdoch, Twitter post, August 8, 2015, 3:27 a.m., https://twitter.com/rupertmurdoch/status/629916805306281984.

68 *"Gretchen will be a big success!":* Donald Trump, Twitter post, October 1, 2013, 2:47 p.m., https://twitter.com/realDonaldTrump/status/385113809922191360.

69 *her contract expired, June 23:* Gabriel Sherman, "The Revenge of Roger's Angels," *New York*, September 5, 2016, https://nymag.com/intelligencer /2016/09/how-fox-news-women-took-down-roger-ailes.html.nd.

69 *wouldn't be allowed back on the air to say goodbye:* Ibid.

69 *a couple of months before women spoke out en masse:* Ibid.

71 *Guilfoyle told colleagues:* Megyn Kelly, *Settle for More* (New York: HarperCollins, 2016).

71 *Guilfoyle's cheerleading for Ailes: Julie Roginsky v. Fox News Network LLC, Roger Ailes, and Bill Shine,* filed in the Supreme Court of the State of New York, April 3, 2017. See also Gabriel Sherman, "Fox News' Julie Roginsky Files Sexual-Harassment Lawsuit," *New York*, April 3, 2017, https://nymag.com/intelligencer/2017/04/fox -news-julie-roginsky-files-sexual-harassment-lawsuit.html.

72 *Three days after Carlson sued:* Gabriel Sherman, "The Revenge of Roger's Angels," *New York*, September 5, 2016, https://nymag.com/intelligencer /2016/09/how-fox-news-women-took-down-roger-ailes.html.

73 *He was able to keep pretending until noon:* Gabriel Sherman, "Sources: Megyn Kelly Told Murdoch Investigators That Roger Ailes Sexually Harassed Her," *New York*, July 19, 2016, https://nymag.com/intelligencer/2016/07/sources -kelly-said-ailes-sexually-harassed-her.html.

73 *"Don't believe the crap":* Geraldo Rivera, Twitter post, July 19, 2016, 1:32 p.m., https://twitter.com/GeraldoRivera/status/755455245946347520.

73 *she silently entered and exited the arena:* Kelly, *Settle for More.*

74 *"There will be no lies":* Donald Trump, 2016 RNC Speech, Republican National Convention, July 7, 2016, retrieved from https://www.politico.com /story/2016/07/full-transcript-donald-trump-nomination-acceptance-speech -at-rnc-225974.

75 *James wanted to hire a new Fox News head:* Jonathan Mahler and Jim Rutenberg, "How Rupert Murdoch's Empire of Influence Remade the World," *New York Times,* April 3, 2019, https://www.nytimes.com/interactive/2019/04/03 /magazine/rupert-murdoch-fox-news-trump.html.

82 *"we've got a couple of surprises left":* Rudy Giuliani, *Fox & Friends,* October 25, 2016, video via RealClearPolitics, https://www.realclearpolitics.com/video /2016/10/25/giuliani_we_got_a_couple_of_surprises_left.html.

83 *"the Red Bull of TV news anchors":* Jon Friedman, "Fox's Shep Smith Takes The Work Seriously—But Not Himself," CBS News, August 24, 2007, https:// www.cbsnews.com/news/foxs-shep-smith-takes-the-work-seriously-but-not -himself/.

86 *"you had to think Clinton was going to win":* Interview with Chris Wallace, "In Their Own Words: The Story of Covering Election Night 2016," CNN.com, January 5, 2017, https://money.cnn.com/2017/01/05/media/election-night -news-coverage-oral-history/index.html.

87 *shared the early exit poll results:* Doug Wead, *Inside Trump's White House: The Real Story of His Presidency* (New York: Center Street, 2019).

89 *"I was wrong":* Bret Baier, Ben Schreckinger, "Inside Donald Trump's Election Night War Room," *GQ,* November 7, 2017, https://www.gq.com/story /inside-donald-trumps-election-night-war-room.

90 *Scared or concerned:* 2016 exit poll data published by CNN, https://www.cnn .com/election/2016/results/exit-polls.

THE COMMANDER

95 *conservatives reacted more strongly to the images than liberals:* Michael Dodd, Amanda Balzer, Carly M. Jacobs, Michael W. Gruszczynski, Kevin B. Smith, and John R. Hibbing, "The Political Left Rolls with the Good and the Political Right Confronts the Bad: Connecting Physiology and Cognition to Preferences," *Philosophical Transactions of the Royal Society B: Biological Sciences* 367, no. 1589 (May 2012): 640–49, https://doi.org/10.1098/rstb.2011.0268.

96 *"The conservative entertainment news complex":* Jason Sattler, "The Mystery of the Wrong-Track Majority," *USA Today,* October 27, 2016, https://www.usatoday .com/story/opinion/2016/10/27/obamas-right-track-kills-poll-question-jason -sattler/92791354/.

97 *"unpersuaded by conventional understanding of facts, evidence, and science":* Norman Ornstein and Thomas E. Mann, *It's Even Worse Than It Looks: How the*

American Constitutional System Collided with the New Politics of Extremism (New York: Basic Books, 2012).

97 *"Like someone dying of thirst":* Bruce Bartlett, "How Fox News Changed American Media and Political Dynamics," Social Studies Resource Network, June 3, 2015, https://papers.ssrn.com/sol3/papers.cfm?abstract_id=2604679.

110 *"wedding-cake figurine come to life":* Molly Langmuir, "America's (President's) Sweetheart," *Elle*, August 2018.

121 *"The secret sauce for Fox":* Chris Hayes, Twitter post, November 6, 2020, https://twitter.com/chrislhayes/status/1324914302701219843.

128 *"I'm not a journalist, jackass":* Steven P. Grossman, "Hannity Right—He's No Journalist," Associated Press, April 20, 2018. Hannity later deleted the tweet. https://apnews.com/7c9f36d3cc904e74bc452e1f64fb64a7000.

143 *"has angered many":* Gabriel Sherman, "Is a Management Shake-up Looming at Fox News?," *New York*, April 27, 2017, https://nymag.com/intelligencer /2017/04/is-a-management-shake-up-looming-at-fox-news.html.

149 *"He toyed with the idea":* Michael Barnes, *Man in the Arena*, documentary, 2020.

157 *the deal was done on October 12, 2020:* Ben Smith, "Fox Settled a Lawsuit Over Its Lies. But It Insisted on One Unusual Condition," *New York Times*, January 18, 2021, https://www.nytimes.com/2021/01/17/business/media/fox -news-seth-rich-settlement.html.

160 *"Russia and its government's support for Mr. Trump":* Matt Apuzzo, Jo Becker, Adam Goldman, Maggie Haberman, "Trump Jr. Was Told in Email of Russian Effort to Aid Campaign," *New York Times*, July 10, 2017, https://www.nytimes .com/2017/07/10/us/politics/donald-trump-jr-russia-email-candidacy.html.

THE CULT

185 *"but at some point I won't":* Donald Trump, Twitter post, January 10, 2019, 8:41 a.m., https://twitter.com/realDonaldTrump/status/1083358150214979585.

186 *"Give me a nice one":* Gretchen Carlson, Steve Doocy, Brian Kilmeade, *Fox & Friends*, Fox News, October 11, 2018, https://www.youtube.com/watch?v= _CI6dPvi2bY.

201 *Fox posted a job wanted ad:* Jen Kirby, "The Most Influential Job in America Is Open: Head Writer at *Fox & Friends*," *Vox*, February 8, 2018, https://www .vox.com/2018/2/8/16992278/fox-and-friends-head-writer-trump-job -opening.

204 *"We are careening":* Matt Welch, "Op-Ed: Americans don't trust their government, its institutions, or each other. This is not a good place to be," *Los Angeles Times*, November 22, 2018, https://www.latimes.com/opinion/op-ed /la-oe-welch-low-trust-20181122-story.html.

221 *"I see them, I'm going to shoot them, bye":* Brian Stelter, *Reliable Sources*, CNN, August 5, 2018, https://www.cnn.com/videos/cnnmoney/2018/08/05/brian -stelter-journalists-receiving-death-threats-vpx.cnn.

222 *"his morning workout":* Tess Owen, "The MAGA Bomber Planned His Morning

Routine Around 'Fox & Friends,' " *Vice*, July 23, 2019, https://www.vice
.com/en_us/article/wjvvzw/the-maga-bomber-planned-his-morning-routine
-around-fox-and-friends.

226 *Instagrammed a photo of him:* Chloe Murdoch (chloemurdoch), Instagram post,
December 1, 2020, https://www.instagram.com/chloemurdoch/?hl=en.

230 *"Would you describe it as a crisis?":* Peter Hegseth, Steve Doocy, et al., *Fox &
Friends*, Fox News, January 10, 2019, retrieved from https://www.mediaite
.com/tv/trump-promises-fox-friends-host-steve-doocy-he-wont-cave-on-the
-wall/.

230 *Trump heard him and tweeted straight to Doocy:* Donald Trump, Twitter post,
January 10, 2019, 8:41 a.m., https://twitter.com/realDonaldTrump/status
/1083358150214979585.

230 *"just whipped the president of the United States":* Andrew Blake, "Donald
Trump's Conservative Media Boosters Diverge on Shutdown Deal," *AP News*,
Associated Press, January 26, 2019, https://apnews.com/8c0aff15c219ef1217
9c8461449ca7c9.

231 *"causing real harm to our country right now":* *Reliable Sources*, CNN, August 19,
2018, http://transcripts.cnn.com/TRANSCRIPTS/1808/19/rs.01.html.

232 *"I was affected by that":* Brian Stelter, "Former News Corp Exec Explains How
He Was Affected by Fox's 'Anti-Immigrant Rhetoric,' " CNN, April 8, 2019,
https://www.cnn.com/2019/04/07/media/joseph-azam-news-corporation
-rupert-murdoch-reliable-sources/index.html.

233 *"garbage and waste that degrade the soil and kill wildlife":* Mae Anderson, "Some
Advertisers Leave Carlson Show After Immigrant Comments," *AP News*,
Associated Press, December 18, 2018, https://apnews.com/df70891e69414
cd5805b2113c7427e54.

235 *When NBC and Murdoch's* Wall Street Journal *asked if the president had been
"honest and truthful":* NBC News/Wall Street Journal Survey, October 4–6,
2019, https://s.wsj.net/public/resources/documents/19401NBCWSJEarly
OctoberPoll.pdf.

THE CONTROL FREAK

238 *Mayer dropped a bomb in* The New Yorker: Jane Mayer, "The Making of the Fox
News White House," *New Yorker*, March 11, 2019.

239 *"left, right, and Trump":* Coppins McKay, "Q&A with Bret Baier, the News
Guy at Fox News," *Atlantic*, October 6, 2017, https://www.theatlantic.com
/politics/archive/2017/10/bret-baier/542010/.

239 *"President Trump, his administration and Fox News":* Jessica Taylor, "DNC Bars
Fox News from Hosting 2020 Primary Debates," NPR, March 6, 2019,
https://www.npr.org/2019/03/06/700807729/dnc-bars-fox-news-from
-hosting-2020-primary-debates.

239 *"hate-for-profit racket":* Michael M. Grynbaum and Matt Stevens, "Warren Calls
Fox News a 'Hate-for-Profit Racket' and Refuses an Appearance," *New York*

Times, May 14, 2019, https://www.nytimes.com/2019/05/14/us/politics /elizabeth-warren-fox-news.html.

240 *"actually not a real problem in America"*: "Tucker Carlson: White Supremacy Is 'Actually Not a Real Problem in America,' " Media Matters for America, August 6, 2019, https://www.mediamatters.org/fox-news/tucker-carlson -white-supremacy-actually-not-real-problem-america.

241 *"an iceberg problem"*: Paul Begala, CNN, Twitter post, March 8, 2019, 4:35 p.m., https://twitter.com/cnn/status/1104133689229877248.

242 *"I think your people are actually going to kill me if I don't stop now"*: Tim Hains, "Trump Interview: Immigration Reform, China Trade, Iran, Terror, Tax Cuts, 2020," *RealClearPolitics*, May 20, 2019, https://www.realclearpolitics .com/video/2019/05/20/trump_interview_immigration_reform_china _trade_iran_terror_tax_cuts_2020.html.

242 *one chat on Fox every two weeks*: *Six Presidents and Their Interchanges with Reporters at 30 Months: 892 Days into an Administration*, 2021st ed., Vol. 47, The White House Transition Project, 2021.

243 *Trump found a plum job for her*: "President Donald J. Trump Announces Intent to Nominate and Appoint Individuals to Key Administration Posts," The White House, The United States Government, March 29, 2019, https://www .whitehouse.gov/presidential-actions/president-donald-j-trump-announces -intent-nominate-appoint-individuals-key-administration-posts-11/.

243 *The revolving door continued to turn*: Scott McDonald, "Former Fox News Contributor Morgan Ortagus Replaces Another Former Fox Personality as State Department Spokesperson," *Newsweek*, April 4, 2019, https://www .newsweek.com/fox-news-contributor-morgan-ortagus-replaces-another -former-fox-personality-1385670.

244 *"Islamic religious beliefs stand in opposition to the US Constitution"*: Jeanine Pirro, Twitter post, March 9, 2019, 9:14 p.m., https://twitter.com/JudgeJeanine /status/1104566165995704321.

244 *"You have Muslims working at the same network you do, including myself"*: Hufsa Kamal, Twitter post, March 10, 2019, 12:06 p.m., https://twitter.com/hufkat /status/1104775656934686720.

244 *"We strongly condemn Jeanine Pirro's comments"*: Jeremy Barr, "Fox News 'Strongly' Condemns Host Jeanine Pirro's Comments About Muslim Congresswoman," *Hollywood Reporter*, March 11, 2019, https://www .hollywoodreporter.com/news/fox-news-condemns-host-jeanine-pirros -comments-ilhan-omar-1193660.

245 *"America is Watching"*: Brian Steinberg, "Fox News Shakes Up Ad Pitch to Madison Avenue (EXCLUSIVE)," *Variety*, February 11, 2019, https://variety .com/2019/tv/news/fox-news-tv-advertising-upfront-america -watching-1203135697/.

245 *misogynistic, racist, and homophobic comments*: Madeline Peltz, "In Unearthed Audio, Tucker Carlson Makes Numerous Misogynistic and Perverted

Comments," Media Matters for America, March 10, 2019, https://www
.mediamatters.org/tucker-carlson/unearthed-audio-tucker-carlson-makes
-numerous-misogynistic-and-perverted-comments.

247 *"Ratings don't trump values, and I know you know that":* Joe Lockhart, Twitter
post, March 11, 2019, 9:34 p.m., https://twitter.com/joelockhart/status
/1105280777711833088.

247 *Pirro herself copped to it later:* Jeremy Barr, "Jeanine Pirro Opens Up About
Fox News Suspension and Trump on Her Book Tour," *Hollywood Reporter,*
September 13, 2019, https://www.hollywoodreporter.com/news/jeanine
-pirro-opens-up-fox-news-suspension-trump-her-book-tour-1238980.

247 *Trump related to the victimhood script:* Donald Trump, Twitter post, March 17,
2019, 9:18 p.m., https://twitter.com/realDonaldTrump/status/1107269978
678611969.

249 *Shep's speech was one massive subtweet of the prime time lineup:* "Leonard
Zeidenberg First Amendment Award 2019," RTDNF First Amendment
Awards, January 3, 2020, https://www.firstamendmentawards.org/leonard
-zeidenberg-first-amendment-award-2019/.

250 *former DNC interim chair Donna Brazile:* David Bauder, "Fox News Hires Donna
Brazile as Political Contributor," *AP News,* Associated Press, March 18, 2019,
https://apnews.com/bfc04ffbeb3c4a1482ff5ab810925542.

251 *Paul Ryan, a longtime pal of Rupert and Lachlan's:* "SEC Filing," Fox, March 14,
2019, https://investor.foxcorporation.com/node/7251/html.

252 *About $12 billion in proceeds from the sale were divided equally among the six:*
Anouska Sakoui. Bloomberg.com. Bloomberg, February 21, 2019, https://
www.bloomberg.com/news/articles/2019-02-22/murdochs-are-said-to
-divvy-up-disney-payday-limiting-influence.

252 *Fox mainstreamed the Ukraine conspiracy theory that got Trump impeached:* Sean
Hannity, March 20, 2020, *Hannity,* Fox News, March 20, 2020.

252 *Lutsenko made all sorts of sordid allegations:* "Top Ukrainian Justice Official Says
US Ambassador Gave Him a Do Not Prosecute List," *The Hill,* February 19,
2020, https://thehill.com/hilltv/rising/434875-top-ukrainian-justice-official
-says-us-ambassador-gave-him-a-do-not-prosecute.

253 *DiGenova brought up Yovanovitch twice:* Ryan Saavedra, Twitter post, March 23,
2019, 4:05 p.m., https://twitter.com/RealSaavedra/status/110954662967
2009728.

254 *"Only the president knows the details of their work":* Josh Feldman, "Chris Wallace
Reports Details of Rudy Giuliani Ukraine Work," Mediaite, September 29,
2019, https://www.mediaite.com/tv/chris-wallace-reports-details-of-who
-rudy-giuliani-was-working-with-on-ukraine-off-the-books/.

254 *"behind-the-bars justice":* Tamar Auber, "Jeanine Pirro Returns to Fox News,
Calls for Trump's Accusers to Face 'Behind the Bars Justice,' " Mediaite,
March 31, 2019, https://www.mediaite.com/tv/jeanine-pirro-returns-to-fox
-news-calls-for-trumps-accusers-to-face-behind-the-bars-justice/.

255 *"a special evening tonight":* Donald Trump, Twitter post, April 18, 2019, 3:29 p.m., https://web.archive.org/web/20190418234732/, https://twitter.com/realDonaldTrump/status/1119004969191890944.

255 *Chris Wallace called out Barr's role:* Aaron Rupar, "Even Fox News's Chris Wallace Questioned William Barr's Defense of Trump," *Vox,* April 18, 2019, https://www.vox.com/policy-and-politics/2019/4/18/18484911/chris-wallace-william-barr-mueller-report-trump.

256 *In a Washington Post/ABC News poll:* Emily Guskin, "How Americans View Mueller and Impeachment, in Five Charts," *Washington Post,* July 23, 2019, https://www.washingtonpost.com/politics/2019/07/23/how-americans-view-mueller-impeachment-five-charts/.

256 *"I hadn't heard that before":* NBC News, Twitter post, May 30, 2019, 3:23 p.m., https://twitter.com/nbcnews/status/1134178456835678208.

258 *Mueller's report contained evidence of obstruction:* Andrew Napolitano, "Judge Andrew Napolitano: Did President Trump Obstruct Justice?" Fox News, April 25, 2019, https://www.foxnews.com/opinion/judge-andrew-napolitano-did-president-trump-obstruct-justice.

259 *"Also asked for pardon for his friend":* Donald Trump, Twitter post, April 27, 2019, 10:57 p.m., https://twitter.com/realdonaldtrump/status/1122334000519868416.

259 *45-minute chat with Hannity:* "President Trump Has Made More than 10,000 False or Misleading Claims," *Washington Post,* August 2, 2019, https://www.washingtonpost.com/video/politics/fact-checker/president-trump-has-made-more-than-10000-false-or-misleading-claims—the-fact-checker/2019/07/26/080f8376-225a-49cc-9c66-9b685abc3d5e_video.html.

261 *credited with stopping Trump from bombing Iran:* Eliana Johnson, "The Fox News General Who 'Spooked' Trump out of Attacking Iran," *Politico,* July 2, 2019, https://www.politico.com/story/2019/07/02/keane-fox-news-iran-trump-1394148.

261 *"cocked and loaded":* Donald Trump, Twitter post, June 21, 2019, 9:03 a.m., https://twitter.com/realDonaldTrump/status/1142055375186907136.

261 *Trump was "spooked" when he heard Keane tell that story:* Ibid.

262 *"Lyin' Brian Williams":* Donald Trump, Twitter post, July 7, 2019, 7:50 p.m., https://twitter.com/realdonaldtrump/status/1148016422783803392.

263 *"no human being would want to live there":* Donald Trump, Twitter post, July 27, 2019, 7:24 a.m., https://twitter.com/realdonaldtrump/status/1155076476930338816.

263 *"The President saw my work. This just made my day":* Donald Trump, Twitter post, July 27, 2019, 7:34 a.m., https://twitter.com/kimkbaltimore/status/1155078925124538368.

264 *"I don't take responsibility at all":* "User Clip: 'No I Don't Take Responsibility at All,' " C-SPAN, March 13, 2020, https://www.c-span.org/video/?c4861158/user-clip-no-dont-responsibility-all.

264 *former Obama senior adviser David Plouffe:* Bobby Lewis, "Brian Kilmeade Gets Mad at the Idea That Fox News Is on Trump's Side," Media Matters for America, March 5, 2020, https://www.mediamatters.org/brian-kilmeade /brian-kilmeade-gets-mad-idea-fox-news-trumps-side.

265 *Shep Smith had diagnosed the problem:* Daniel D'Addario, "Shepard Smith Has the Hardest Job on Fox News," *Time*, March 15, 2018, https://time.com/longform /shepard-smith-fox-news/.

266 *Trump-loving pastor Robert Jeffress:* "Robert Jeffress," GLAAD, December 3, 2018, https://www.glaad.org/tap/robert-jeffress.

266 *a paid contributor on the network:* "Dr. Robert Jeffress," Fox News, https://www .foxnews.com/person/j/robert-jeffress, accessed May 6, 2020.

267 *"So weird to watch Crazy Bernie on @FoxNews":* Donald Trump, Twitter post, April 16, 2019, 10:11 a.m., https://twitter.com/realdonaldtrump/status/11181 55023849017345.

268 *"You are going to be called on, Sean":* "Democrats and Republicans Battle over 'Hearsay' During Impeachment Hearings," Fox News, November 15, 2019, https://www.foxnews.com/transcript/democrats-and-republicans-battle-over -hearsay-during-impeachment-hearings.

268 *His Trump allegiance "has cost me schisms in the family":* Peter Baker, Michael M. Grynbaum, Maggie Haberman, Annie Karni, and Russ Buttner, "Trump Employs an Old Tactic: Using Race for Gain," *New York Times*, July 20, 2019, https://www.nytimes.com/2019/07/20/us/politics/trump-race-record.html.

268 *Geraldo attacked the Ukraine whistleblower:* Connor Mannion, "Geraldo Rivera Says He'd Like to Beat Up 'Rotten Snitch' Whistleblower for Trump," Mediaite, September 27, 2019, https://www.mediaite.com/tv/geraldo-rivera -says-hed-like-to-beat-up-rotten-snitch-whistleblower-for-trump/.

268 *"the most serious charge against the president":* Josh Feldman, "Andrew Napolitano: Ukraine Call 'Most Serious' Trump Charge," Mediaite, September 23, 2019, https://www.mediaite.com/trump/foxs-judge-napolitano-potential-ukraine -call-most-serious-charge-against-trump/.

269 *Steve Doocy, of all people, agreed:* Justin Baragona, " 'Fox & Friends' Host: 'Off-the-Rails Wrong' If Trump Sought Quid Pro Quo from Ukraine," *Daily Beast*, September 24, 2019, https://www.thedailybeast.com/fox-and-friends-host -steve-doocy-off-the-rails-wrong-if-trump-sought-quid-pro-quo-from -ukraine-on-biden.

269 *Dan Bongino declared. "I have no doubt":* "Deciphering the Latest Fake Scandal (Ep 1075): The Dan Bongino Show Transcripts," Podgist, September 26, 2019, https://www.podgist.com/the-dan-bongino-show/deciphering-the-latest -fake-scandal-ep-1075/index.html.

269 *Trump committed a crime on the July 25 call:* Sam Dorman, "Judge Napolitano: Trump Has Admitted Committing Crime in Talks with Ukraine," Fox News, September 24, 2019, https://www.foxnews.com/media/judge-napolitano -trump-admitted-crime.

270 *"Unlike maybe some dayside hosts, I'm not very partisan"*: Lindsey Ellefson, "Fox News' Tucker Carlson Slaps Back at 'Partisan' Shepard Smith's Rebuke of His Guest (Video)," *The Wrap*, September 26, 2019, https://www.thewrap.com /fox-news-feud-tucker-carlson-shepard-smith-partisan/.

271 *"stop attacking Carlson"*: https://www.vanityfair.com/news/2019/09/madness -at-fox-news-as-trump-faces-impeachment-lachlan-murdoch.

273 *"There's plenty of stuff on Fox News that I disagree with"*: Dominic Patten. "James Murdoch Admits He Doesn't Watch Fox News; Was 'Disappointed' Shep Smith Left—Vanity Fair Summit," Deadline, October 23, 2019, https:// deadline.com/2019/10/james-murdoch-fox-news-critic-pete-buttigieg -shepard-smith-rupert-murdoch-disney-succession-1202767011/.

273 *"I'm Shepard Smith, Fox News, New York"*: Shepard Smith, *Shepard Smith Reporting*, Fox News, October 11, 2019, https://www.foxnews.com/transcript /is-donald-trump-a-serious-candidate-for-president.

275 *"Shep had power that almost none of us had"*: Brian Stelter and Oliver Darcy, "Bill Hemmer to Succeed Shep Smith as Fox's Afternoon News Anchor," CNN, December 9, 2019, https://www.cnn.com/2019/12/09/media/bill-hemmer -shep-smith-fox-news/index.html.

276 *"did you or your administration pressure Fox News to get rid of Shepard Smith?"*: "President Trump on Shepard Smith Leaving Fox News," C-SPAN, October 11, 2019, https://www.c-span.org/video/?c4822175/president-trump -shepard-smith-leaving-fox-news.

276 *"WHY IS WILLIAM BARR MEETING WITH RUPERT MURDOCH?"*: Eric Lutz, "Why Is William Barr Meeting with Rupert Murdoch?" *Vanity Fair*, October 11, 2019, https://www.vanityfair.com/news/2019/10/why-is-william -barr-meeting-with-rupert-murdoch.

THE CRISIS

279 *In her testimony:* U.S. Congress, Senate, Permanent Select Committee on Intelligence, *Deposition of: Fiona Hill*, 116th Cong., 1st sess., October 14, 2019.

280 *"Schiff show charade"*: Donald Trump, Twitter post, November 21, 2019, 10:39 p.m., https://twitter.com/realDonaldTrump/status/1197721298245 443584.

280 *50 percent of Americans wanted Trump impeached and removed:* Dana Blanton, "Fox News Poll: Trump Job Approval Ticks Up, Views on Impeachment Steady," Fox News, December 15, 2019, https://www.foxnews.com/politics/fox-news -poll-trump-job-approval-ticks-up-views-on-impeachment-steady.

280 *"MEDIA DECLARES TRUMP SHOULD BE IMPEACHED"*: Brian Stelter, "Editorial Boards of *Los Angeles Times* and *Boston Globe* Call for Trump's Impeachment," CNN, December 8, 2019, https://edition.cnn .com/2019/12/08/media/newspaper-editorials-trump-impeachment/index .html.

280 *versus people who predominantly watched other channels:* "How News Outlets Are Influencing Public Opinion on Impeachment," Ipsos, December 11, 2019, https://www.ipsos.com/en-us/news-outlet-influence-on-impeachment-opinions.

281 *"baseless conspiracy theories told by known liars on Fox News":* "Schumer Floor Remarks on the Need for Republicans to Stop Spreading Debunked Conspiracy Theories, The Inclusion of Paid Parental Leave for Federal Employees in the NDAA, and Senate Dems' Effort to Save Net Neutrality," Senate Democratic Leadership, December 10, 2019, https://www.democrats.senate.gov/newsroom/speeches/schumer-floor-remarks-on-the-need-for-republicans-to-stop-spreading-debunked-conspiracy-theories-the-inclusion-of-paid-parental-leave-for-federal-employees-in-the-ndaa-and-senate-dems-effort-to-save-net-neutrality.

282 *"After this day":* Bret Baier, *Special Report with Bret Baier,* Fox News, December 18, 2020.

282 *"we will never talk about the 45th president of the United States the same way again":* Adrian Horton, "Debates and Democratic 'Rage': the Impeachment View from Fox News," *The Guardian,* December 19, 2019, https://www.theguardian.com/media/2019/dec/18/trump-impeachment-fox-news-response.

282 *Hannity's show was on tape:* Sean Hannity, *Hannity,* Fox News, December 18, 2020.

284 *threatening that their voters would not tolerate any dissent:* Josh Feldman, "Hannity Says GOP Senators Shouldn't Help 'Bolster' Articles of Impeachment with Witnesses: 'No Do-Overs,'" Mediaite, January 21, 2020, https://www.mediaite.com/tv/hannity-says-gop-senators-shouldnt-help-bolster-articles-of-impeachment-with-witnesses-no-do-overs/.

285 *"The Democrats are relying on facts, but the Republicans are relying on Fox":* Maureen Dowd, "Notorious D.J.T. on Trial," *New York Times,* January 25, 2020, https://www.nytimes.com/2020/01/25/opinion/sunday/trump-senate-impeachment-trial.html.

285 *Romney gave a single TV interview, to Chris Wallace:* Fox News, "Mitt Romney Defends Vote to Convict Trump on Abuse of Power," *YouTube* video, 15:00, February 5, 2020.

287 *Sean Hannity Cinematic Universe claimed on air every day for months:* Maxwell Tani, and Will Sommer, "Fox Internal Documents: Hannity Regulars Spread 'Disinformation,'" *Daily Beast,* February 6, 2020, https://www.thedailybeast.com/fox-news-internal-document-bashes-john-solomon-joe-digenova-and-rudy-giuliani-for-spreading-disinformation.

288 *one hundredth anniversary of the Nineteenth Amendment:* Karen Zraick, "Why Democratic Women Wore White at State of the Union," *New York Times,* February 5, 2020, https://www.nytimes.com/2020/02/04/us/politics/women-in-white-state-of-the-union.html.

291 *Trump lit into him about flavored e-cigarettes:* "The U.S. was beset by denial and dysfunction as the coronavirus raged," *Washington Post*, April 4, 2020.

291 *Trump again criticized Azar:* "He Could Have Seen What Was Coming: Behind Trump's Failure on the Virus," *New York Times*, April 11, 2020.

291 *Carlson criticized Chinese culture: Tucker Carlson Tonight*, January 27, 2020, obtained via the Internet Archive, https://archive.org/details/FOX NEWSW_20200128_050000_Tucker_Carlson_Tonight/start/869/end /929?q=virus.

293 *Its only foreign bureaus:* Fox News Corporation Information, accessed June 9, 2020, http://press.foxnews.com/.

293 *"This is a biological Chernobyl":* Steve Bannon, *Watters' World*, Fox News, February 8, 2020, obtained via the Internet Archive, https://archive.org /details/FOXNEWSW_20200209_010000_Watters_World/start/720/ end/780.

293 *At least one woman in California:* "California says a person who died February 6 had COVID-19, suggesting the first US coronavirus death happened at least 3 weeks earlier than previously thought," *Business Insider*, April 22, 2020.

293 *He put Richard Grenell:* "Trump names staunch loyalist and current US Ambassador to Germany Richard Grenell as acting intelligence chief," CNN, February 20, 2020.

293 *he welcomed back his surrogate daughter Hope Hicks:* "Hope Hicks to Return to the White House After a Nearly Two-Year Absence," *New York Times*, February 13, 2020.

295 *Hemmer's ratings were way up from Shep's lows:* "Fox's Bill Hemmer sees sizable viewer increase for debut in Shep Smith's former time slot," *The Hill*, January 21, 2020, https://thehill.com/homenews/media/479227-foxs-bill -hemmer-sees-sizable-viewer-increase-for-debut-in-shep-smiths-former.

295 *He bashed Cavuto:* @realDonaldTrump, February 20, 2020, 4:53 p.m., https:// twitter.com/realdonaldtrump/status/1230611451431153666.

296 *"I sort of shrug my shoulders":* Paul Ryan, quoted by the *Milwaukee Journal Sentinel*, February 21, 2020.

296 *at a cost of $150 million:* " 'Beverly Hillbillies' estate sells to media heir Lachlan Murdoch for about $150 million," *Los Angeles Times*, December 12, 2019.

297 *Brian Kilmeade said:* Interview on the *Whiskey Politics* podcast, May 15, 2020, transcribed by *The Hollywood Reporter*.

297 *Navarro wrote an internal memo:* "Navarro memos warning of mass coronavirus death circulated in January," Axios, April 7, 2020.

298 *"We will not see diseases like the coronavirus come here":* Kayleigh McEnany, *Trish Regan Primetime*, February 25, 2020, video clip accessed via Twitter, https:// twitter.com/KFILE/status/1246454626905468931.

299 *"extensive commercial grade cleaning procedures":* Internal memo from Suzanne Scott and Jay Wallace to Fox News employees, February 26, 2020.

299 *"No one's talking about the flu"*: Kennedy Montgomery, *Kennedy*, Fox Business, February 25, 2020, obtained via the Internet Archive, https://archive.org /details/FBC_20200226_050000_Kennedy/start/2040/end/2100.

299 *"very well under control in our country"*: President Trump, press conference in New Delhi, India, February 25, 2020, https://www.whitehouse.gov/briefings -statements/remarks-president-trump-press-conference-4/.

300 *"They think this is going to be what brings down the president"*: Kevin Breuninger, "Media's coronavirus stories trying to hurt Trump, Mick Mulvaney says as he urges public to turn off TV," CNBC online, February 28, 2020, https://www .cnbc.com/2020/02/28/trump-chief-of-staff-mulvaney-suggests-people -ignore-coronavirus-news-to-calm-markets.html.

300 *"the coronavirus is the common cold, folks"*: Rush Limbaugh, *The Rush Limbaugh Show*, February 24, 2020.

301 *"beyond despicable"*: Sean Hannity, *Hannity*, March 9, 2020.

301 *"For those Americans that might be fearful tonight"*: Interview: Sean Hannity Interviews Donald Trump Via Telephone, March 4, 2020, Factba.se, https:// factba.se/transcript/donald-trump-interview-sean-hannity-fox-telephone -march-4-2020.

302 *Scott decided to cancel:* "Fox News Is First to Cancel an Upfront over Coronavirus," MediaPost, March 4, 2020, https://www.mediapost.com /publications/article/347967/fox-news-is-first-to-cancel-an-upfront-over -corona.html.

302 *On March 6:* Internal memo from Suzanne Scott and Jay Wallace to Fox News employees.

302 *"The more I learn about this"*: Pete Hegseth, *Fox & Friends*, March 8, 2020.

302 *"it's time to buy the family cemetery plot"*: Jeanine Pirro, *Justice with Judge Jeanine*, Fox News, March 8, 2020.

303 *"I felt I had a moral obligation"*: Tucker Carlson, interview with Joe Hagan, *Vanity Fair*, March 17, 2020.

303 *"I said exactly what I've said on TV"*: Ibid.

304 *"let's bludgeon Trump with this new hoax"*: Sean Hannity, *Hannity*, Fox News, March 9, 2020.

305 *Hannity said, "Absolutely not"*: Interview with Paul Bond, "Sean Hannity defends Fox News after journalism professors publish critical letter about coronavirus coverage," *Newsweek*, April 2, 2020.

305 *buy a streaming service called Tubi:* "Fox Looks to Buy Streaming Service Tubi," *Wall Street Journal*, February 21, 2020.

308 *they received an extra $75 per day:* March 18 internal memo to Fox News employees.

308 *"Just 2 days ago"*: Gretchen Carlson, Twitter, March 17, 2020, https://twitter .com/gretchencarlson/status/1239915122765824001.

308 *Watters expressed regret:* "Fox News Personalities Shift to Urgency of

Coronavirus Crisis after Some Decried Media Overreaction," *Deadline*, March 17, 2020, https://deadline.com/2020/03/fox-news-coronavirus-shift -jesse-watters-sean-hannity-1202885636/.

308 *"America has had the best response":* Matt Gaetz, *The Next Revolution*, Fox News, March 15, 2020, via YouTube, https://www.youtube.com/watch?v=J7zZ3k xvobk&feature=emb_title.

309 *Childers tweeted to the president:* Heather Childers, @HeatherChilders, Twitter, April 9, 2020, https://twitter.com/HeatherChilders/status/12482678972 28668928.

309 *"Every night at some point":* Martha MacCallum, interviewed by Cindy Schweich Handler, NorthJersey.com, May 13, 2020.

309 *Fox was still the total-viewer champion:* "Fox News has highest-rated quarter in network's history," *Forbes*, March 31, 2020.

310 *"raring to go by Easter":* President Donald Trump, Fox News, March 24, 2020, https://www.whitehouse.gov/briefings-statements/remarks-president-trump -vice-president-pence-members-coronavirus-task-force-fox-news-virtual -town-hall/.

311 *"just finished a very good conversation with President Xi":* Donald Trump, Twitter post, March 27, 2020, 1:19 a.m., https://twitter.com/realdonaldtrump/status /1243407157321560071?lang=en, https://www.nytimes.com/2020/03/25 /business/media/trump-coronavirus-briefings-ratings.html.

313 *"low point in the network's shameful history":* Matt Gertz, Media Matters for America, March 18, 2020.

313 *"the killing channel":* Curtis Ingraham, @CurtisIngraham1, Twitter, March 21, 2020, https://twitter.com/CurtisIngraham1/status/1241346085819256838.

313 *"You can see it on Twitter":* Sara Carter, Zachary Petrizzo, "Fox News Contributor Deletes Nuts Tweet Questioning Whether Hospitals Are Actually Overrun By Coronavirus," *Mediaite*, March 30, 2020, https://www.mediaite .com/tv/fox-news-contributor-deletes-nuts-tweet-questioning-whether -hospitals-are-actually-overrun-by-coronavirus/.

314 *"There's no reason to go backwards":* Stephanie Grisham, quoted by The Associated Press, March 23, 2020, https://apnews.com/5dd6b30e03542 b435e2716e3e3a483e4.

314 *"we've never called the virus a hoax":* "Hannity, With a Straight Face, Claims He Has 'Always Taken the Coronavirus Seriously,' " *Daily Beast*, March 19, 2020.

314 *threatened to sue The New York Times:* "New York Times waves off Hannity threat," *Daily Beast*, April 28, 2020.

314 *"The Trump party line swaps new lies for old":* "No Empathy, Only Anger," David Frum, *The Atlantic*, March 19, 2020.

315 *"conservative news diet":* Knight Foundation/Gallup, poll conducted March 17–29, 2020, published April 9, 2020, https://news.gallup.com/opinion /gallup/307934/amid-pandemic-news-attention-spikes-media-favorability-flat .aspx.

315 *more likely to say the threat was exaggerated:* "Cable TV and COVID-19: How Americans perceive the outbreak and view media coverage differ by main news source," Pew Research Center, April 1, 2020, https://www.journalism.org/2020/04/01/cable-tv-and-covid-19-how-americans-perceive-the-outbreak-and-view-media-coverage-differ-by-main-news-source/.

316 *Ingraham had the lawyer:* "Why Did Fox News's Laura Ingraham Relentlessly Push Hydroxychloroquine?," *GQ*, April 24, 2020.

316 *"it's not going to kill anybody":* President Donald Trump, press briefing, March 19, 2020, https://www.whitehouse.gov/briefings-statements/remarks-president-trump-vice-president-pence-members-coronavirus-task-force-press-briefing-6/.

317 *Fox News ran a correction on the web:* Nancy Levine, "How I Got Fox News to Correct Laura Ingraham and Twitter to Remove Her Tweet," RanttMedia, March 31, 2020, https://rantt.com/fox-news-laura-ingraham-coronavirus-tweet.

317 *"more interested in discussing miracle cures than testing delays":* "Touting Virus Cure, 'Simple Country Doctor' Becomes a Right-Wing Star," *New York Times*, April 2, 2020.

317 *more than five hundred times on Fox's airwaves:* "The rise and fall of Trump's obsession with hydroxychloroquine," *Washington Post*, April 24, 2020.

318 *"Some senior Republicans":* "34 days of pandemic: Inside Trump's desperate attempts to reopen America," *Washington Post*, May 2, 2020.

318 *FDA explicitly cautioned against its use:* "FDA cautions against use of hydroxychloroquine or chloroquine for COVID-19 outside of the hospital setting or a clinical trial due to risk of heart rhythm problems," U.S. Food and Drug Administration, April 30, 2020, https://www.fda.gov/drugs/drug-safety-and-availability/fda-cautions-against-use-hydroxychloroquine-or-chloroquine-covid-19-outside-hospital-setting-or.

319 *"I get a lot of positive calls about it":* Remarks by President Trump, May 18, 2020, https://www.whitehouse.gov/briefings-statements/remarks-president-trump-roundtable-restaurant-executives-industry-leaders/.

319 *even half of Republicans:* "AP-NORC poll: Few Americans trust Trump's info on pandemic," Associated Press, April 23, 2020, https://apnews.com/87f1545cea4b5e8c96e6e902a8d9e9bd.

321 *Fox Nation:* Brian Stelter, "Why Fox News Is Launching the 'Fox Nation' Streaming Service," CNN, November 27, 2018, https://www.cnn.com/2018/11/27/media/reliable-sources-11-26-18/index.html.

THE COLLAPSE

324 *"We're going to have fewer fatalities":* "Fox News Contributor Compares Coronavirus to the Flu, Claims It's 'Not a Pandemic,'" *Daily Beast*, April 13, 2020.

325 *"@FoxNews is no longer the same":* @realDonaldTrump, May 18, 2020, https://twitter.com/realdonaldtrump/status/1262563582086184970.

325 *protests over the murder of George Floyd:* Derrick Bryson Taylor, "George Floyd Protests: A Timeline," *New York Times*, May 30, 2020, https://www.nytimes .com/article/george-floyd-protests-timeline.html.

326 *"It's structured like a soap opera":* Emily VanDerWerff, "How Fox News Molds Reality into a Serialized TV Drama," *Vox*, October 8, 2020, https://www.vox .com/culture/21503196/fox-news-tv-drama-serialized-lost.

326 *"When the looting starts, the shooting starts":* Donald Trump, Twitter post, May 29, 2020, 12:53 a.m.

326 *"You have to dominate":* Kevin Liptak, Ryan Nobles, and Sarah Westwood, "An Agitated Trump Encourages Governors to Use Aggressive Tactics on Protesters," CNN, June 1, 2020, https://www.cnn.com/2020/06/01/politics /donald-trump-race-police/index.html.

326 *Trump's use of force at Lafayette Park:* Tom Gjelten, "Peaceful Protesters Tear-Gassed to Clear Way for Trump Church Photo-Op," NPR, June 2, 2020, https://www.npr.org/2020/06/01/867532070/trumps-unannounced-church -visit-angers-church-officials.

327 *"GROWING LAWLESSNESS IN MAJOR CITIES":* Jake Lahut, "Protests This Past Week Have Been Largely Peaceful, but Fox News Continues to Show Old Footage to Rile up Viewers," *Business Insider*, June 11, 2020, https:// www.businessinsider.com/fox-news-replays-violent-old-protest-footage -actual-protests-calm-2020-6.

327 *"they're destroying our cities":* Tucker Carlson, *Tucker Carlson Tonight*, Fox News, June 12, 2020.

327 *Capitol Hill Autonomous Zone:* Daniella Silva and Matteo Moschella, "Seattle Protesters Set Up 'Autonomous Zone' After Police Evacuate Precinct," NBCNews.com, June 12, 2020, https://www.nbcnews.com/news/us-news /seattle-protesters-set-autonomous-zone-after-police-evacuate-precinct -n1230151.

327 *"Communist cosplay in the streets":* Guy Benson, *Guy Benson Show*, Fox Nation, June 11, 2020.

327 The Seattle Times *caught FoxNews.com:* Jim Brunner, "Fox News Runs Digitally Altered Images in Coverage of Seattle's Protests, Capitol Hill Autonomous Zone," *Seattle Times*, June 14, 2020, https://www.seattletimes .com/seattle-news/politics/fox-news-runs-digitally-altered-images-in -coverage-of-seattles-protests-capitol-hill-autonomous-zone/.

327 *"Domestic Terrorists have taken over":* Donald Trump, Twitter post, June 10, 2020, 11:38 p.m.

327 *"definitely not about black lives":* Tucker Carlson, *Tucker Carlson Tonight*, Fox News, June 15, 2020.

327 *"Bye-bye Tucker Carlson!":* Mike Sievert, Twitter post, June 9, 2020, 11:02 p.m., https://twitter.com/MikeSievert/status/1270551871183155200.

328 *Blake Neff, had a years-long history:* Oliver Darcy, "Tucker Carlson's Top Writer Resigns After Secretly Posting Racist and Sexist Remarks in Online Forum,"

CNN, July 11, 2020, https://www.cnn.com/2020/07/10/media/tucker
-carlson-writer-blake-neff/index.html.

328 *"horrific racist, misogynistic, and homophobic behavior"*: Brian Flood, "FOX News
Media Condemns 'Racist, Sexist and Homophobic' Behavior After Staffer
Resigns over Offensive Posts." Fox News, July 12, 2020, https://www
.foxnews.com/media/fox-news-media.

328 *"have no connection to the show"*: Tucker Carlson, *Tucker Carlson Tonight*, Fox
News, June 13, 2020.

328 *MyPillow:* "MyPillow®: Official My Pillow Site," MyPillow, https://www
.mypillow.com/.

328 *"serialized TV drama"*: Emily VanDerWerff, "How Fox News Molds Reality
into a Serialized TV Drama." *Vox*, October 8, 2020.

328 *"If you're a Republican"*: Paul Waldman, "Opinion: Why Republicans Are More
Afraid of Change Than Ever," *Washington Post*, July 24, 2020, https://www
.washingtonpost.com/opinions/2020/07/24/why-republicans-are-more-afraid
-change-than-ever/.

328 *"to ensure damaged statues are fixed quickly"*: Josh Dawsey, "Trump's Twitter Feed
Reads Like a Local Crime Blotter as He Stokes a Culture War," *Washington
Post*, July 1, 2020, https://www.washingtonpost.com/politics/trumps
-twitter-feed-reads-like-a-local-crime-blotter-as-he-stokes-a-culture-war
/2020/06/30/2e1a48c6-baed-11ea-86d5-3b9b3863273b_story.html.

329 *"pigs in a blanket, fry 'em like bacon"*: CBS News, " 'Pigs in a Blanket' Chant at
Minnesota Fair Riles Police," CBS Interactive, August 31, 2015, https://www
.cbsnews.com/news/pigs-in-a-blanket-chant-at-minnesota-fair-riles-police/.

329 *back in 2015:* Ibid.

329 *a staple of Hannity's show:* Hannity, various 2020 episodes.

329 *Carlson's show re-ran it in 2020:* Tucker Carlson, *Tucker Carlson Tonight*, Fox
News, June 15, 2020.

329 *"Our nation is witnessing a merciless campaign"*: "President Trump Departure
Remarks," C-SPAN, July 3, 2020.

330 *the virus was "fading away"*: Donald Trump, *Hannity*, Fox News, June 17, 2020.

330 *"If we didn't do testing, we'd have no cases"*: Staff, "President Trump Visits Green
Bay for Town Hall," "President Trump Arrives at Green Bay Austin Straubel
International Airport," *Green Bay Press-Gazette*, June 25, 2020, https://www
.greenbaypressgazette.com/picture-gallery/news/2020/06/25/president
-trump-arrives-green-bay-austin-straubel-international-airport/3256965001/.

330 *audience members were required to wear masks:* Ibid.

330 *"LEFT'S WAR ON AMERICA"*: Lou Dobbs Tonight, Fox News, August 24,
2020.

330 *"Where are you Roger Ailes?"*: Donald Trump, Twitter post, June 30, 2020,
9:54 p.m.

331 *"I know better than anyone"*: Donald Trump, Twitter post, June 30, 2020,
10:28 p.m.

331 *"The culture has not changed":* Maria Puente, "Why Is Fox News Being Sued Again over Alleged Sexual Harassment?" *USA Today*, December 12, 2019, https://www.usatoday.com/story/entertainment/celebrities/2019/12/11/why-fox-news-being-sued-again-over-alleged-sexual-harassment/4398373002/.

331 *"long an open secret":* Diana Falzone, "Ed Henry's Accusers Say His Behavior Was an Open Secret at Fox News," *Daily Beast*, August 31, 2020, https://www.thedailybeast.com/ed-henrys-accusers-say-his-behavior-was-an-open-secret-at-fox-news.

331 *a complaint that it could not ignore:* CBS News, "Former Fox News Employee Who Accused Ed Henry of Rape 'Was Paralyzed by Fear' Working at the Network," CBS CBS Interactive, July 21, 2020, https://www.cbsnews.com/news/jennifer-eckhart-fox-news-ed-henry-lawsuit/.

332 *"Today's Fox News is the same old Fox News":* Brian Stelter, "How Fox News Has Changed in the Four Years since Roger Ailes Was Ousted," CNN, July 22, 2020, https://www.cnn.com/2020/07/22/media/fox-news-trump-roger-ailes-four-years-later/index.html.

333 *"I'd like to amend my answer now":* Alysin Camerota, *Reliable Sources,* CNN, July 21, 2020.

333 *"Our country's future hangs on this election":* "Barack Obama's endorsement of Joe Biden, annotated," *Washington Post*, April 14, 2020.

333 *Fox viewership* collapsed: David Bauder, "Fox News Channel Viewers Tune Out for John Lewis' Funeral," Associated Press, August 4, 2020, https://apnews.com/article/entertainment-george-w-bush-bill-clinton-u-s-news-tv-a7f2d9f88e22f35dbc85fcfd2f54f386.

334 *Fox ignored long stretches of the Democratic National Convention:* David Bauder, "A Different View of the Democrats on Fox News Prime Time," Associated Press, August 19, 2020, https://apnews.com/article/election-2020-entertainment-c9b851f612939bce41b0dffa832fdeac.

335 *his mansion in Henley-on-Thames:* Charlotte Griffiths for *The Mail on Sunday*, "Jerry Hall Snaps Up a Little Place in the Oxfordshire Countryside for £11million," *Daily Mail Online*, Associated Newspapers, November 10, 2019, https://www.dailymail.co.uk/tvshowbiz/article-7668737/Jerry-Hall-snaps-little-place-Oxfordshire-countryside-11million.html.

335 *"I have a sense that something is going to happen":* Jeanine Pirro, *The Five*, Fox News, August 12, 2020.

335 *"I think there's probably, possibly drugs involved":* Donald Trump, *Justice with Judge Jeanine*, Fox News, September 10, 2020.

335 *Don't Lie to Me:* Jeanine Pirro, *Don't Lie To Me: and Stop Trying to Steal Our Freedom* (New York: Center Street, 2021).

335 *"unforced errors":* Sarah Ellison, Jeremy Barr, "What Happens to Fox News If Trump Loses? Rupert Murdoch Is Prepared," *Washington Post*, October 29, 2020, https://www.washingtonpost.com/lifestyle/media/rupert-murdoch

-thinks-trump-is-going-to-lose—and-thats-not-a-bad-thing-for-fox
-news/2020/10/28/9547fbdc-1192-11eb-bc10-40b25382f1be_story.html.

336 *"could have been avoided"*: Ibid.

336 *"this thing's going away"*: Donald Trump, *Fox & Friends*, Fox News, August 5, 2020.

336 *Fauci told me in a September interview*: Anthony Fauci, *Reliable Sources*, CNN, September 28, 2020.

337 *"A Potential Murdoch Family Civil War"*: Maxwell Tani, "Murdoch Family Civil War Looms over Fox News, Says New Book," *Daily Beast*, August 24, 2020, https://www.thedailybeast.com/a-potential-murdoch-family-civil-war-looms-over-fox-news-insiders-tell-brian-stelter.

337 *"My resignation is due to disagreements"*: Ibid.

337 *"I decided that I could be much more"*: Maureen Dowd, "James Murdoch, Rebellious Scion," *New York Times*, October 10, 2020, https://www.nytimes.com/2020/10/10/style/james-murdoch-maureen-dowd.html.

338 *"it'll be unfair, I have no doubt about it"*: Donald Trump, *The Brian Kilmeade Show*, Fox News Radio, September 29, 2020.

339 *"never dreamt that it would go off the tracks"*: Michael M. Grynbaum, "Chris Wallace Calls Debate 'a Terrible Missed Opportunity.'" *New York Times*, September 30, 2020, https://www.nytimes.com/2020/09/30/business/media/chris-wallace-debate-moderator.html.

339 *"If you want to switch seats"*: "Trump-Biden First Debate," C-SPAN, September 29, 2020, https://www.c-span.org/video/?475793-1/trump-biden-debate.

339 *"shit show"*: Dana Bash, *The Lead*, CNN, September 29, 2020.

340 *"I didn't feel much like celebrating"*: Michael M. Grynbaum, "Chris Wallace Calls Debate 'a Terrible Missed Opportunity.'"

340 *"The president is being hospitalized for the coronavirus"*: Chris Wallace, *Fox News Live*, Fox News, October 2, 2020.

340 *"I just went for a test"*: Donald Trump, *Hannity*, Fox News, October 1, 2020.

341 *"Let's get a fair anchor"*: Donald Trump, *Hannity*, Fox News, October 8, 2020.

341 *"just the other day, they came out with a statement"*: Donald Trump, *NBC News Trump Town Hall*, NBC News, October 15, 2020.

341 *"They didn't say that"*: Savannah Guthrie, *NBC News Trump Town Hall*, NBC News, October 15, 2020.

343 *"Where is the river?"*: Aaron Blake, "Analysis: Kayleigh McEnany's First Post-Debate Briefing Goes Off the Rails," *Washington Post*, October 1, 2020, https://www.washingtonpost.com/politics/2020/10/01/kayleigh-mcenanys-first-post-debate-briefing-goes-off-rails/.

344 *he left the network at the beginning of 2021*: Marisa Sarnoff, "White House Reporter Jon Decker Leaves Fox News Radio for Gray TV," Mediaite, January 5, 2021, https://www.mediaite.com/premium/white-house-reporter-jon-decker-leaves-fox-news-radio-for-gray-tv/.

345 *"The Fox News Decision Desk Controls the Fate"*: Ben Mathis-Lilley, "The Fox News Decision Desk Controls the Fate of American Democracy," *Slate*, September 24, 2020, https://slate.com/news-and-politics/2020/09/can-trump -supreme-court-decide-election.html.

345 *"MASSIVE ENTHUSIASUM FOR TRUMP"*: Various programs, Fox News, November 3, 2020.

345 *"CLOSING THE GAP IN KEY BATTLEGROUND STATES"*: Ibid.

346 *Trump's phone call with* Fox & Friends: Donald Trump, *Fox & Friends*, Fox News, November 3, 2020.

347 *Total day ratings were up 31 percent:* Fox Corporation quarterly earnings call, November 3, 2020, transcribed by Seeking Alpha, https://seekingalpha.com /article/4384495-fox-corporation-fox-ceo-lachlan-murdoch-on-q1-2021 -results-earnings-call-transcript.

347 *"Tucker Carlson Tonight on the Fox News Channel":* Ibid.

348 *"President Trump has told confidants":* Jonathan Swan, Axios, November 1, 2020.

349 *Fox put Arizona's eleven electoral votes in Biden's column:* DDHQ 2020 Election Forecast, Fox, November 3, 2020, https://forecast.decisiondeskhq.com /president/P2020AZ.

349 *"Call Rupert":* Annie Karni and Maggie Haberman, "Fox's Arizona Call for Biden Flipped the Mood at Trump Headquarters," *New York Times*, November 4, 2020, https://www.nytimes.com/2020/11/04/us/politics/trump -fox-news-arizona.html.

350 *"What is this happening here?":* Bill Hemmer, *NewsNOW*, Fox News, November 3, 2020.

352 *"If he had, I would not have interfered":* Jeremy Barr, Sarah Ellison, "Arnon Mishkin, the Fox News Analyst Who Called Arizona for Biden, Is Under Attack from the Trump Campaign," *Washington Post*, November 5, 2020, https://www.washingtonpost.com/media/2020/11/05/arnon-mishkin-fox -news-arizona-trump/.

352 *"There are more votes out there":* Karl Rove, *NewsNOW*, Fox News, November 4, 2020.

352 *"Arnon, we're getting a lot of incoming here":* Bret Baier, *NewsNOW*, Fox News, November 4, 2020.

353 *the AP joined Fox in turning Arizona Blue:* "Election 2020," AP NEWS, November 4, 2021, https://apnews.com/hub/election-2020.

353 *"We have won Georgia":* "Election Night 2020," C-SPAN, November 3, 2020, https://www.c-span.org/video/?477417-1/election-night-2020&fbclid=Iw AR0pIK7GpjagApbpAB8cZlUr-IM1Ruplsi5pHXadqB4qj8UhxRrWvIFL QlM.

353 *"This is an extremely flammable situation":* Chris Wallace, *Fox News*, Fox News, November 4, 2020.

353 *Mishkin was booked on* Fox & Friends: *Fox & Friends*, Fox News, November 4, 2020.

353 *"your so-called expert"*: David Bossie, *Fox & Friends*, Fox News, November 4, 2020.

353 *"bad dream"*: Sean Hannity, *Hannity,* Fox News, November 4, 2020.

354 *Fox's audience started to shrink:* Brian Stelter and Oliver Darcy, CNN, https://view.newsletters.cnn.com/messages/16051551460435dab42de3791 /raw?utm_term=16051551460435dab42de3791&utm_source=Reliable %2BSources%2B-%2BNovember%2B11%2C%2B2020&utm_medium =email&utm_campaign=257694_1605155146044&bt_ee=on 8707Dsm7cEmK5AdYfqzKTL2TCVPUXbv3XzNgrHqyfi02VGyPJb P3TJT1AU22JB&bt_ts=1605155146044.

354 *Newsmax's audience started to grow:* Ibid.

354 *outside an election office in Maricopa County:* Simon Romero, "With Arizona Too Close to Call, Trump Supporters Gather at a Vote-Counting Site in Phoenix," *New York Times*, November 5, 2020, https://www.nytimes.com/2020/11/04 /us/politics/trump-supporters-protest-arizona.html.

354 *"What separates the winners from the losers"*: Donald Trump, Twitter post, December 30, 2014, 1:50 p.m.

355 *"We are not pulling back that call"*: Arnon Mishkin, *Fox News*, Fox News, November 4, 2020.

355 *"They are saying that the outstanding vote is over six hundred thousand"*: Martha MacCallum, *Fox News*, Fox News, November 4, 2020.

355 *"Is the fix already in?"*: Sean Hannity, *Hannity*, Fox News, November 4, 2020.

355 *"the propagandistic media"*: Laura Ingraham, *The Ingraham Angle*, Fox News, November 4, 2020.

355 *"There are many ways that the media"*: Mollie Hemingway, *The Ingraham Angle*, Fox News, November 4, 2020.

355 *"Arizona is going the other way"*: Kellyanne Conway, *Fox & Friends*, Fox News, November 5, 2020.

355 *"We stand by the Arizona decision"*: Brian Kilmeade, *Fox & Friends*, Fox News, November 5, 2020.

356 *"trying to steal an election"*: "President Trump Remarks on Election Results," C-SPAN, November 5, 2020, https://www.c-span.org/video/?477858-1 /president-trump-challenges-latest-election-results-claims-voter-fraud.

356 *Jake Tapper said Trump was attacking democracy:* Jake Tapper, CNN, November 5, 2020.

356 *"pathetic" and "dangerous"*: Anderson Cooper, CNN, November 5, 2020.

356 *Dana Bash texted Republican lawmakers:* Dana Bash, CNN, November 5, 2020.

356 *"Fox News owes the American people an apology"*: Kevin Cramer, "What's on Your Mind Hour 2—Talk Radio with Senator Kevin Cramer," Am 1100 the Flag, November 6, 2020.

357 *"set out in great specificity the intended flow"*: David Folkenflik, "With Trump's Loss, Murdoch's Fox News Faces Wrath and Tough Choices," NPR, November 7, 2020, https://www.npr.org/2020/11/07/932203022/as-trumps -chances-fade-murdoch-s-fox-news-faces-wrath-and-tough-choices.

357 *Biden pulled ahead in the state:* "Pennsylvania Polls," FiveThirtyEight, February 1, 2021, https://projects.fivethirtyeight.com/polls/pennsylvania/.

357 *"Former Vice-President Biden does not become 'President-elect' "*: "Fox News Tells Anchors Not to Call Biden 'President-Elect,' Then Seems to Change Its Tune," Oliver Darcy and Brian Stelter, CNN Business, November 6, 2020, https://www .cnn.com/2020/11/06/media/fox-news-election-projection-plan/index.html.

358 *"There's all kinds of stuff flying on the internet"*: Brett Baier, *Special Report with Brett Baier,* Fox News, November 6, 2020.

358 *"President Trump's legacy"*: Laura Ingraham, *The Ingraham Angle,* Fox News, November 6, 2020.

358 *CNN became the first network to project Biden:* *CNN News,* CNN, November 7, 2020.

358 *NBC followed forty-five seconds later: NBC News,* NBC, November 7, 2020.

358 *CBS thirty seconds after that: CBS News*, CBS, November 7, 2020.

358 *and ABC: ABC News*, ABC, November 7, 2020.

358 *and the AP:* "Election 2020," AP NEWS, November 4, 2021, https://apnews .com/hub/election-2020.

358 *Street parties broke out:* Minyvonne Burke and Natalia Abrahams, "Biden's Win Sparks Street Celebrations Around the Country," NBCNews.com, November 8, 2020, https://www.nbcnews.com/politics/2020-election/biden -s-win-sparks-street-celebrations-around-country-n1246922.

359 *"We at Fox have not yet made that call":* Neil Cavuto, *Cavuto Live,* Fox News, November 7, 2020.

359 *"still tied up in a Fox News basement somewhere":* Jon Favreau, Twitter post, November 7, 2020, 11:33 a.m., https://twitter.com/jonfavs/status/13251141 37085583360.

359 *"Keep in mind":* Martha MacCallum, *Fox News,* Fox News, November 7, 2020.

360 *"Newsmax has not called the election for Joe Biden":* Chris Ruddy, *Reliable Sources,* CNN, November 8, 2020.

361 *"Let's give each other a chance":* "Transcript of President-Elect Joe Biden's Victory Speech," Associated Press, November 8, 2020, https://apnews.com /article/election-2020-joe-biden-religion-technology-race-and-ethnicity-2b96 1c70bc72c2516046bffd378e95de.

361 *A ten-times increase in one week:* "Trump Voters Are Flocking to a TV Channel That Claims Biden Is Not President-Elect," Brian Stelter, CNN Business, November 12, 2020, https://www.cnn.com/2020/11/12/media/fox-news -newsmax-reliable-sources/index.html.

361 *"IT ISN'T OVER YET":* Jeremy Barr, "Newsmax Hopes Conservative

Anger at Fox News and a Few Trump Tweets Can Boost the Much Smaller Network," *Washington Post*, November 11, 2020, https://www.washingtonpost.com/media/2020/11/10/newsmax-fox-news-trump-tweets/.

361 *"Fox is losing viewers to Newsmax and OAN"*: Jeff Greenfield, Twitter post, January 19, 2021, 10:45 a.m., https://twitter.com/greenfield64/status/1351556464758849542.

362 *"the only middle finger available"*: Rich Lowry, "The Only Middle Finger Available," *National Review*, October 26, 2020, https://www.nationalreview.com/2020/10/the-only-middle-finger-available/.

362 *"We don't know how many votes were stolen"*: Tucker Carlson, *Tucker Carlson Tonight*, Fox News, November 9, 2020.

363 *"Whoa, whoa, whoa"*: Neil Cavuto, *Cavuto Live*, Fox News, November 9, 2020.

363 *"the fate of the republic hangs"*: Lou Dobbs, *Fox Business*, Fox News, November 14, 2020.

363 *"there is no president-elect, yet"*: Pete Hegseth, *Fox News*, Fox News, November 18, 2020.

363 *the marketing department debuted a promo:* " 'Can We Have America Back?' Fox News Video Echoes Trump Election Claims," *Guardian*, November 14, 2020, https://www.theguardian.com/media/2020/nov/14/fox-news-criticized-for-echoing-baseless-trump-claims-about-election.

364 *"One thing I can't comprehend"*: Al Schmidt, CNN, November 11, 2020.

364 *"A lot of Americans believe this election was rigged"*: Tucker Carlson, *Tucker Carlson Tonight*, Fox News, November 19, 2020.

365 *"Life as we know it"*: Jesse Waters, *The Five*, Fox News, November 11, 2020.

366 *"Keep appealing to a right-leaning audience"*: Margaret Sullivan, "Perspective: Fox News Needs to Reinvent Itself for the Post-Trump Era. Here's One Radical Idea," *Washington Post*, December 1, 2020, https://www.washingtonpost.com/lifestyle/media/fox-news-reinvent-post-trump/2020/11/30/1915059e-3313-11eb-8d38-6aea1adb3839_story.html.

366 *"Standing Up For What's Right"*: Mia Jankowicz, "Fox News Launched Its New Marketing Campaign, 'Standing Up For What's Right,' Soon after Trump Stepped Up His Criticism of the Network," *Business Insider*, November 17, 2020, https://www.businessinsider.com/fox-news-new-slogan-looks-like-dig-trump-network-feud-2020-11.

367 *When CNBC felt threatened by Fox Business:* Dylan Byers, "At CNBC, a Strict Guest Policy," *Politico*, February 15, 2013, https://www.politico.com/blogs/media/2013/02/at-cnbc-a-strict-guest-policy-157149.

367 *Newsmax beat Fox in the ratings for the first time:* Brian Stelter, "Newsmax TV Scores a Ratings Win over Fox News for the First Time Ever," CNN, December 8, 2020, https://www.cnn.com/2020/12/08/media/newsmax-fox-news-ratings/index.html.

368 *"Fox News has engaged in a concerted disinformation"*: Mary Papenfuss, "Lou

Dobbs' Vote Fraud Lies Debunked on His Program After Legal Threat by Vote Tech Firm," *HuffPost*, December 20, 2020, https://www.huffpost.com /entry/fox-news-lou-dobbs-smartmatic-lawsuit-threat_n_5fdec28cc5b60f828 856e401.

368 *"one of the strangest three-minute segments"*: Ben Smith, "The 'Red Slime' Lawsuit That Could Sink Right-Wing Media," *New York Times*, December 21, 2020, https://www.nytimes.com/2020/12/20/business/media/smartmatic-lawsuit -fox-news-newsmax-oan.html.

368 *"There are lots of opinions"*: Lou Dobbs, *Fox Business*, Fox News, December 18, 2020.

369 *"an intel source telling me"*: Maria Bartiromo, *Fox Business,* Fox News, December 18, 2020.

369 *"STOP THE INSANITY"*: Post Editorial Board, "The Post Says: Give It Up, Mr. President—for Your Sake and the Nation's," *New York Post*, December 29, 2020, https://nypost.com/2020/12/27/give-it-up-mr-president-for-your-sake -and-the-nations/.

371 *"Switching over to @OANN!"*: Donald Trump, Twitter post, January 1, 2021, 12:36 p.m.

371 *"President Trump is furious at Fox News"*: Nicole Hemmer, "Perspective: Trump Ruled Conservative Media as President. Will He Find His Next Job There?," *Washington Post*, November 12, 2020, https://www.washingtonpost.com /outlook/2020/11/12/trump-tv-fox-news-media/.

371 *"People who are staunch conservatives"*: Ainsley Earhardt, *Fox & Friends*, Fox News, January 4, 2021.

371 *"I think Americans, I think Republicans"*: Will Cain, *Fox News,* Fox News, January 5, 2021.

372 *"We believe the president will take the stage at eleven"*: Peter Hegseth, *Fox News,* Fox News, January 6, 2021.

372 *"willing to battle for the America"*: Jeanine Pirro, *Fox News,* Fox News, January 2, 2021.

372 *"any Republican who doesn't stand up"*: Mark Levin, *Life, Liberty and Levin*, Fox News, January 3, 2021.

372 *"a constitutional tinderbox"*: Peter Hegseth, *Fox News,* Fox News, January 6, 2021.

372 *"We got to this sad chaotic day for a reason"*: Tucker Carlson, *Tucker Carlson Tonight*, Fox News, January 6, 2021.

373 *"What's happening at the Capitol today"*: Jason Donner, Twitter post, January 6, 2021, 3:09 p.m., https://mobile.twitter.com/jason_donner/status/1346911 811166203904.

373 *"this would never have happened"*: Max Boot, "Opinion: Trump Is Guilty of Sedition. Impeach Him Again," *Washington Post*, January 11, 2021, https:// www.washingtonpost.com/opinions/2021/01/06/trump-is-guilty-sedition -impeach-him-again/.

373 *"This is America's brain on misinformation"*: Sean Illing, "The Fantasy-Industrial

Complex Gave Us the Capitol Hill Insurrection," *Vox*, January 8, 2021, https://www.vox.com/policy-and-politics/22217822/us-capitol-attack-trump -right-wing-media-misinformation.

374 *"new daytime lineup"*: "FOX NEWS CHANNEL TO LAUNCH NEW DAYTIME PROGRAMMING LINEUP," Fox News, January 11, 2021, http://press.foxnews.com/2021/01/fox-news-channel-to-launch-new-day time-programming-lineup/.

375 *"Fox news whipped people into a frenzy"*: Ben Collins, Twitter post, January 9, 2021, 1:00 p.m., https://twitter.com/oneunderscore__/status/134796637 5877345280.

376 *"legally elected on November 3"*: Peter Navarro, *Fox Business*, Fox News, January 14, 2020.

376 *"We know that there were irregularities"*: Maria Bartiromo, *Fox Business*, Fox News, January 14, 2020.

376 *Bill Sammon retired:* Jordan Williams, "Fox News's DC Managing Editor Bill Sammon to Retire," *The Hill*, January 19, 2021, https://thehill.com/home news/media/534720-fox-dc-managing-editor-to-retire.

376 *Chris Stirewalt was fired:* "Fox News Political Editor Chris Stirewalt Out in Company Restructuring," *Los Angeles Times*, January 19, 2021, https:// www.latimes.com/entertainment-arts/business/story/2021-01-19/fox-news -political-editor-chris-stirewalt-out-in-company-restructuring.

376 *"Fox said Biden would win Arizona"*: Jay Rosen, Twitter post, January 19, 2021, 6:33 p.m., https://twitter.com/jayrosen_nyu/status/1351674256770392065.

376 *"I think it was an abjectly terrible decision"*: Jonah Goldberg, Twitter post, January 19, 2021, 7:21 p.m., https://twitter.com/JonahDispatch/status/135 1686216152965121.

377 *"nation of news consumers"*: Chris Stirewalt, "Op-Ed: I Called Arizona for Biden on Fox News. Here's What I Learned," *Los Angeles Times*, January 28, 2021, https://www.latimes.com/opinion/story/2021-01-28/fox-news-chris -stirewalt-firing-arizona.

377 *"In light of reports of more demonstrations"*: fox8webcentral and Associated Press, "President Trump Urges 'No Violence' in Light of Reports of More Demonstrations," fox8.com, January 13, 2021, https://fox8.com/news /president-trump-urges-no-violence-in-light-of-reports-of-more -demonstrations/.

377 *The House of Representatives impeached Trump:* Nicholas Fandos, "Trump Impeached for Inciting Insurrection," *New York Times*, January 13, 2021, https://www.nytimes.com/2021/01/13/us/politics/trump-impeached.html.

377 *"impeach the Americans who support his policies"*: Laura Ingraham, *The Ingraham Angle*, Fox News, January 13, 2021.

377 *"war on terror"*: Lara Logan, *The Ingraham Angle*, Fox News, January 13, 2021.

377 *"this was a lynching of Donald Trump"*: Mike Huckabee, *The Ingraham Angle*, Fox News, January 13, 2021.

378 *"injurious to society":* Shep Smith, *CNN with Christiane Amanpour,* CNN, January 19, 2021.

378 *one literally last-hour addition:* Dan Mangan, "Trump Issues Last-Second Pardon to Fox News Host Jeanine Pirro's Tax Cheat Ex-Husband Al," CNBC, January 20, 2021, https://www.cnbc.com/2021/01/20/trump-pardons-judge -jeanines-ex-husband-al-pirro.html.

379 *"What do you think they plan to do":* Tucker Carlson, "Tucker Carlson: The Left Doesn't Want Biden to Debate Trump," Fox News, July 9, 2020, https://www .foxnews.com/opinion/tucker-carlson-left-biden-debate-trump.

379 *"part of the job of the White House press secretary":* Steve Inskeep, "Biden's Incoming Press Secretary: Briefings Won't Be a Platform for Right-Wing Spin," NPR, December 31, 2020, https://www.npr.org/sections/biden -transition-updates/2020/12/31/951452717/bidens-incoming-press-secretary -briefings-wont-be-a-platform-for-right-wing-spin.

379 *"what did you talk to Vladimir Putin about?":* "President Biden Remarks on Combating the Coronavirus Pandemic," C-SPAN, January 26, 2021, https:// www.c-span.org/video/?508352-1/president-biden-announces-purchase -additional-200-million-vaccines.

380 *"I know he always asks me tough questions":* Lindsey Ellefson, "Biden Sasses Fox News' Peter Doocy over Question About Putin," *TheWrap,* January 26, 2021, https://www.thewrap.com/biden-doocy-putin-joke/.

380 *Trump called in to the network:* Donald Trump, *Hannity,* Fox News, January 17, 2021.

380 *The Murdochs renewed Suzanne Scott's contract:* "Suzanne Scott, the Chief Executive of Fox News, Will Extend Her Tenure at the Network," *New York Times,* February 9, 2021, https://www.nytimes.com/2021/02/09/business /suzanne-scott-fox-news-ceo.html.

381 *"We believe where we're targeted":* Helen Coster and Eva Mathews, "Fox Corp CEO Endorses 'Center Right' Strategy; Company Beats Revenue Expectations," Reuters, February 9, 2021, https://www.reuters.com/article /us-fox-results/fox-corp-ceo-endorses-center-right-strategy-company-beats -revenue-expectations-idUSKBN2A91PZ.

381 *Smartmatic dropped a bombshell $2.7 billion lawsuit:* Jonah E. Bromwich and Ben Smith, "Fox News Is Sued by Election Technology Company for Over $2.7 Billion," *New York Times,* February 4, 2021, https://www.nytimes .com/2021/02/04/business/media/smartmatic-fox-news-lawsuit.html.

381 *Fox benched Dobbs:* Michael M. Grynbaum, "Lou Dobbs's Show Is Canceled by Fox Business." *New York Times,* February 5, 2021, https://www.nytimes .com/2021/02/05/business/media/lou-dobbs-fox.html.

381 *"you don't want to deal with the news!":* Juan Williams, *The Five,* Fox News, February 10, 2021.

382 *"I have a funny feeling":* Sean Hannity, *Hannity,* Fox News, January 17, 2021.

382 *"Well, there's a lot to talk about":* Donald Trump, *Hannity*, Fox News, January 17, 2021.

EPILOGUE

385 *"What you're seeing and what you're reading is not what's happening":* President Trump's remarks to Veterans of Foreign Wars national convention, Kansas City, Missouri, July 24, 2018. See Mahita Gajanan, " 'What You're Seeing . . . Is Not What's Happening.' People Are Comparing This Trump Quote to George Orwell," *Time* online, July 24, 2018, https://time.com/5347737 /trump-quote-george-orwell-vfw-speech/.

INDEX

ABOUT THE AUTHOR

Brian Stelter is the chief media correspondent for CNN World-wide and anchor of *Reliable Sources*, which examines the world's top media stories every Sunday. Before joining CNN in 2013, Stelter was a media reporter at *The New York Times*. His first book, *New York Times* bestseller *Top of the Morning*, inspired the Apple TV+ drama *The Morning Show*. Stelter is a consulting producer on the series. He is also the executive producer of the HBO documentary *After Truth: Disinformation and the Cost of Fake News*. He lives in New York with his wife and two children.